EUCHARISTIC SACRAMENTALITY IN AN ECUMENICAL CONTEXT

This book explores the *epiclesis* or invocation of the Holy Spirit in the Eucharistic Prayer, using the Anglican tradition as an historical model of a communion of churches in conscious theological and liturgical dialogue with Christian antiquity.

Incorporating major studies of England, North America and the Indian sub-Continent, the author includes an exposition of Inter-Church ecumenical dialogue and the historic divisions between western and eastern Eucharistic traditions and twentieth-century ecumenical endeavour.

This unique study of the relationship between theology and liturgical text, commends a theology and spirituality which celebrates the presence of the Holy Spirit in the Eucharist as present and eschatological gift. It thus sets historic, contemporary and ecumenical divisions in a new theological context.

ASHGATE NEW CRITICAL THINKING IN RELIGION, THEOLOGY AND BIBLICAL STUDIES

The *Ashgate New Critical Thinking in Religion, Theology and Biblical Studies* series brings high quality research monograph publishing back into focus for authors, international libraries, and student, academic and research readers. Headed by an international editorial advisory board of acclaimed scholars spanning the breadth of religious studies, theology and biblical studies, this open-ended monograph series presents cutting-edge research from both established and new authors in the field. With specialist focus yet clear contextual presentation of contemporary research, books in the series take research into important new directions and open the field to new critical debate within the discipline, in areas of related study, and in key areas for contemporary society.

Other Titles in the Series:

Evagrius Ponticus
The Making of a Gnostic
Julia Konstantinovsky

Exodus Church and Civil Society
Public Theology and Social Theory in the Work of Jürgen Moltmann
Scott R. Paeth

Anamnesis and the Eucharist
Contemporary Anglican Approaches
Julie Gittoes

Pseudo-Dionysius as Polemicist
The Development and Purpose of the Angelic Hierarchy in Sixth Century Syria
Rosemary A. Arthur

Wolfhart Pannenberg on Human Destiny
Kam Ming Wong

Postmodernism and the Ethics of Theological Knowledge
Justin Thacker

Revelation, Scripture and Church
Theological Hermeneutic Thought of James Barr, Paul Ricoeur and Hans Frei
Richard R. Topping

Eucharistic Sacramentality in an Ecumenical Context
The Anglican *Epiclesis*

DAVID J. KENNEDY
Durham Cathedral, UK

ASHGATE

Published by
Ashgate Publishing Limited
Gower House
Croft Road
Aldershot
Hampshire GU11 3HR
England

Ashgate Publishing Company
Suite 420
101 Cherry Street
Burlington, VT 05401-4405
USA

www.ashgate.com

British Library Cataloguing in Publication Data
Kennedy, David J.
Eucharistic sacramentality in an ecumenical context : the Anglican epiclesis. –
(Ashgate new critical thinking in religion, theology and biblical studies)
1. Church of England – Liturgy 2. Epiclesis
I. Title
264'.03036

Library of Congress Cataloging-in-Publication Data
Kennedy, David, 1957–
Eucharistic sacramentality in an ecumenical context : the Anglican epiclesis / David J. Kennedy.
p. cm.—(Ashgate new critical thinking in religion, theology, and biblical studies)
Includes bibliographical references (p.) and index.
ISBN 978-0-7546-6376-8 (hardback : alk. paper)
1. Epiclesis. 2. Eucharistic prayers—Anglican Communion. I. Title.

BV825.54.K46 2008
264'.03036—dc22

2008006975

ISBN 978-0-7546-6376-8

Printed and bound in Great Britain by
MPG Books Ltd, Bodmin, Cornwall.

In memory of my father,
John Kennedy
1927-1989

Contents

Acknowledgements

The origins of this study lie in doctoral research submitted to the University of Birmingham when I was on the staff of The Queen's College (now The Queen's Foundation), Birmingham. I would like to express my gratitude to my erstwhile colleagues, both in the College and in the Department of Theology in the University of Birmingham, for their encouragement and assistance in that original research. Particular thanks are due to the members of staff of the Church of England Records Centre in South Bermondsey, London, the Archives of the Episcopal Church (USA) in Austin, Texas and the Archives of the Anglican Church of Canada in Toronto. I am also indebted to members of the International Anglican Liturgical Consultation in Toronto (1991) and Dublin (1995), who answered many questions and assisted me in the collection of texts. The archive of Anglican liturgies assembled by the Revd Paul Gibson, the ACC Co-ordinator for Liturgy, has also been most helpful.

Ten years on, I was granted sabbatical leave by my colleagues on the Chapter of Durham Cathedral, which provided the necessary space and time to return to my original research and prepare it for publication. I would like to express my profound gratitude to my colleagues at the Cathedral for their support, and also to my secretary, Mrs Jill Chipchase, who assisted me in many practical ways. I also received most valuable assistance from members of staff of the Chapter Library, the University Library, and St John's College Library, in Durham, and from the Revd Terrie Robinson of the Anglican Communion Office in South London. I am also grateful the Revd Dr Stephen Burns, Mr Jamie McMahon and the Revd Tomas Maddela, who assisted me in tracking down articles and books.

Throughout this whole project, I have been indebted to many people, but among them I owe particular thanks to the Rt Revd Dr Colin Buchanan, who supervised my original research, and to the Rt Revd Dr Kenneth Stevenson and the Revd Dr Phillip Tovey for their encouragement. I am also grateful to Sarah Lloyd of Ashgate Publishing for her helpfulness in bringing this book to birth. Finally, to my wife Janet, and children Rachel, Christopher and Claire, I owe an incalculable debt of gratitude, for all their love, understanding and patience.

David Kennedy

Introduction

This book is a study of the *epiclesis*, or invocation of the Holy Spirit, in the eucharistic prayer.

It explores the Anglican tradition as an example of how one Christian communion, itself claiming to be both 'catholic' and 'reformed', is in dialogue with Christian history and contemporary ecumenical scholarship. The study is undertaken in the light of historic divides concerning the role of the *epiclesis* between the Christian East and West, and the insights gained from shared and vigorous academic endeavour arising from the twentieth-century 'liturgical movement'. It also takes account of the resurgence of interest in pneumatology in biblical studies and systematic theology, the latter often in the context of enquiry into the doctrine of the Trinity. Contemporary eucharistic prayers in many historic Christian traditions attempt to give more overt expression to the Trinitarian nature of the Christian Faith, and this has meant the recovery of a pneumatological emphasis often through the medium of the *epiclesis*.[1] Such a recovery has been quickened, not only by theological enquiry but also through scholarly and ecumenical study into Christian origins, and the development of eucharistic traditions of prayer in the first five centuries.

This study aims to complement other books in similar or related themes. The most prominent contemporary study of the *epiclesis* from a theological standpoint is by the Roman Catholic scholar John McKenna in his book *Eucharist and Holy Spirit* (1975). McKenna's work is an enquiry into twentieth-century writing, against the background of the historic debate about the 'moment' of eucharistic consecration, so central to Scholastic thought.[2] Richard Buxton's work, *Eucharist and Institution Narrative* (1976), is a comprehensive study of eucharistic consecration in the Roman and Anglican traditions with special emphasis on the role of the institution narrative. Sections of this present study cover the same ground but from the point of view of pneumatology.[3] As the liturgical linkage between *anamnesis* and *epiclesis* is often fundamental, Kenneth Stevenson's *Eucharist and Offering* (1986) is a seminal historical and ecumenical study of eucharistic oblation, often embracing the invocation of the Spirit in this context.[4] Major twentieth-century treatments of the *epiclesis* in the Anglican tradition, namely H.R. Gummey's *The Consecration of the Eucharist* (1908),[5] and E.G.C.F. Atchley's *On the Epiclesis of the Eucharistic Liturgy and in the Consecration of the Font* (1935),[6] are concerned to set developments in

1 As evidenced by the modern texts collected in Max Thurian and Geoffrey Wainwright (eds), *Baptism and Eucharist: Ecumenical Convergence in Celebration* (Geneva, 1983).

2 John H. McKenna, *Eucharist and Holy Spirit* (Great Wakering, 1975).

3 Richard F. Buxton, *Eucharist and Institution Narrative* (Great Wakering, 1976).

4 Kenneth W. Stevenson, *Eucharist and Offering* (New York, 1986).

5 Henry Riley Gummey, *The Consecration of the Eucharist* (Philadelphia, 1908).

6 E.G. Cuthbert F. Atchley, *On the Epiclesis of the Eucharistic Liturgy and in the Consecration of the Font* (Oxford and London, 1935).

the Anglican tradition in the context of Patristic, western and Roman prehistory; indeed, Atchley's account of the Anglican divines is brief, the case for the *epiclesis*, in his view, being confirmed by the testimony of antiquity. The present study does not include an up-dated account of either the Patristic background,[7] or western pre-Reformation developments;[8] rather, it seeks to chart out and examine both Anglican theological enquiry as to the role of the Spirit in the eucharistic action and the liturgical data relating to the *epiclesis*, and so how theology and liturgy relate to each other. So the question of the *epiclesis* is set in the context of a whole series of learned publications by Anglican writers, often within a broader framework of thought about eucharistic sacramental theology and in conscious dialogue with the breadth of Christian tradition.

A major motivation for undertaking this subject is that the *epiclesis* has been, and in some respects still is, a divisive issue within Anglicanism. The question is how Christians discern the activity of the Spirit. One disputed question is whether on biblical and theological grounds the Spirit can rightly be invoked on *material* objects; some Anglicans, mainly from a conservative evangelical perspective, would contend that there are few, if any grounds, for making such an assertion. Another related issue is the meaning of eucharistic consecration, a concept that is approached from different standpoints. What is the relationship between the 'outward and visible' and 'inward and spiritual' aspects of sacramental theology? If the eucharistic gift is essentially inward and spiritual, is the role of the Spirit in effecting the sacramental union between Christ and the believer not better understood as related wholly to the worshippers? Or, does this lead to an unacceptable dualism between the material and the spiritual? Where more emphasis is placed on the elements, must a so-called consecratory *epiclesis* always precede the institution narrative to safeguard the primary role traditionally assigned to the words of Christ in effecting consecration? Or can different forms and positions for the *epiclesis* stand together in creative tension? Or can certain aspects of the eucharistic prayer be interpreted in such a way as not to prejudice the role and spirituality of the entire prayer? Or where consecration by thanksgiving is stressed, is there any need for an explicit *epiclesis* at all? The contention of this study is that for too long discussion of the *epiclesis* has been restricted to narrow issues concerning theories of eucharistic consecration. Rather, there are rich biblical and theological themes associated with the work of the Spirit which enable us to see the importance of the *epiclesis* not only for theology but also spirituality and Christian discipleship. Perhaps one of the most pressing needs of the Church is to recover a dynamic eucharistic spirituality, embracing not only the spiritual benefits bestowed on the communicant, but also the eucharist as a pledge and promise of eschatological hope embracing humanity and all creation, the ecumenical sign of the bringing together of all things in Christ, and the means

7 See McKenna, *Eucharist and Holy Spirit*, pp. 15-71; also, Palle Dinesen, 'Die Epiklese im Rahmen altkirchlicher Liturgien', *Studia Theologica*, 16 (1962): 42-107. For a summary of recent research into the origins of the *epiclesis*, see Paul F. Bradshaw, *Eucharistic Origins* (London, 2004), pp. 93-94, 124-128.

8 See McKenna, *Eucharist and Holy Spirit*, pp. 71-90; Buxton, *Eucharist and Institution Narrative*, pp. 41-51.

of empowerment for Christian discipleship and mission, until the kingdom of God comes.

A second, but by no means lesser motivation is in the realm of pan-Anglican studies. The Anglican Communion is a family of national and regional autonomous Churches, bound together by common roots, the Scriptures and Creeds, the historic episcopate, a shared ethos of worship and church organization, and bonds of friendship. Early Lambeth Conferences were exercised on the question as to what extent the 1662 Prayer Book should be the liturgical norm for the Communion, recognizing that Scotland and the USA already had their own recensions of the communion rite, and not least of the prayer of consecration. Lambeth 1958 proved to be the watershed, asserting the principle of local autonomy in matters liturgical. Since 1958, there has been an avalanche of revised Anglican eucharistic rites, most of them, up to 1984, catalogued by Bernard Wigan and Colin Buchanan.[9] So this study examines in depth the often controversial place of the *epiclesis* in the revised rites of the Church of England, along with case studies from the wider Anglican Communion in North America and in the Indian subcontinent.

One fundamental prior question is the definition of *epiclesis*. W. Jardine Grisbrooke defined its use as principally a petition for the consecration of bread and cup; thus it is 'usually restricted to that form of it which asks the Father to send the Holy Spirit upon them [the elements] to change them into the body and blood of Christ'.[10] The developed form in the east by the middle of the fourth century, included three aspects: the petition for the operation of the Spirit; the description of the effects of this operation as the change of the bread and cup into the body and blood of Christ; the statement of the ends for which this is sought, the fruits of communion.[11] John McKenna also expresses the 'developed' *epiclesis* in three equivalent movements: an appeal for the Holy Spirit; to transform or sanctify the bread and wine; so that they may benefit those who partake of them worthily.[12] However, such a narrow use, while accurate in relation to, for example, eastern fourth-century developments, is unnecessarily restrictive. Indeed, as McKenna and others demonstrate, in terms of early development, the term '*epiclesis*' can equally be applied to any invocation, whether of God generally or particular divine names, or particular Persons of the Trinity, and be applied to the community as well as, or instead of, the elements.[13] So, in 1980, in view of this wide range of forms of expression both in antiquity and

9 Bernard Wigan (ed.), *The Liturgy in English*, 2nd ed. (London, 1962); Colin O. Buchanan (ed.), *Modern Anglican Liturgies 1958-1968* (London, 1968), henceforth *MAL*; *Further Anglican Liturgies 1968-1975* (Bramcote, 1975), henceforth *FAL*; *Latest Anglican Liturgies 1976-1984* (London and Bramcote, 1985), henceforth *LAL*.

10 W. Jardine Grisbrooke, 'Anaphora', in J.G. Davies (ed.), *A New Dictionary of Liturgy and Worship* (London, 1986), p. 18.

11 Ibid., p. 19.

12 John H. McKenna, 'The Epiclesis Revisited', in Frank C. Senn (ed.), *New Eucharistic Prayers* (New York, 1987), p. 169.

13 See McKenna, *Eucharist and Holy Spirit*, pp. 16-28; William R. Crockett, *Eucharist: Symbol of Transformation* (New York, 1989), pp. 54-63; Bryan D. Spinks, 'The Consecratory Epiklesis in the Anaphora of St. James', *Studia Liturgica*, 11 (1976): 25-29. See also Robert Taft, 'From Logos to Spirit: On the Early History of the Epiclesis' (printed paper, 1991).

in Anglican history, the Liturgical Commission of the Church of England outlined four aspects:

a) an invocation of the Spirit upon the elements in the Eastern position following the anamnesis
b) an invocation of the Spirit upon the elements regardless of position
c) an invocation (whether of the Spirit or not) to the Father to effect consecration
d) an invocation of any sort, as, for instance, either to effect consecration or to effect fruitful reception.[14]

However, in the period since 1980, the scope of epicletic texts has developed yet further; for example, and again reflecting some precedent in antiquity, some texts invoke the Holy Spirit upon the whole eucharistic action, while others, and especially those following the 'eastern' pattern, extend the scope of invocation to embrace more developed supplication, invoking the Spirit on the wider life of the world. Such forms of expression go far beyond 'in church' concerns about 'consecration' or 'fruitful reception' by the communicants.

For that reason, and because of the variety of forms of expression found in the eucharistic prayers of the Anglican Communion, I have categorized the forms of the *epiclesis* into six types:

1. a single *epiclesis* after the institution narrative, invoking the Holy Spirit on the eucharistic elements and, in some cases, also on the worshippers
2. a single *epiclesis* after the institution narrative, invoking the Holy Spirit upon the worshippers only
3. a preliminary *epiclesis* (before the institution narrative) invoking the Holy Spirit on the elements, and in some cases, a 'congregational'[15] *epiclesis* or reference to the work of the Spirit after the institution narrative
4. a preliminary petition for consecration, with or without reference to the Spirit, and in some cases, a 'congregational' *epiclesis* or reference to the work of the Spirit after the institution narrative
5. a preliminary petition for consecration after the manner of 1662, and an invocation of the Spirit, or reference to the work of the Spirit, or prayer for fruitful communion, after the institution narrative

14 *The Alternative Service Book 1980: A Commentary by the Liturgical Commission* (London, 1980), p. 83, fn 53. In relation to the *ASB* rites, the commentary places inverted commas around the word *epiclesis* to show that the form of the petition has been carefully worded to allow some liberty of interpretation as to whether the Spirit is actually invoked on the elements.

15 This is sometimes referred to as a 'communion' *epiclesis*, but authors use terms differently. For example, Bridget Nichols and Alistair MacGregor use 'communion epiclesis' to designate 'a request for the descent of the Holy Spirit to sanctify the eucharistic *elements* of bread and wine' and 'congregational epiclesis' to designate invocations on the worshippers. I have followed this designation for the latter, but not for the former. See Bridget Nichols and Alistair MacGregor, *The Eucharistic Epiclesis* (Durham, 2001), p. xiii.

6. a single *epiclesis* after the institution narrative, invocating the Holy Spirit upon the whole eucharistic action.

Within these six basic categories, there are many *different* forms of expression in, for example, the use of different verbs and imagery, or, in prayers with an extended supplication, the scope of the petitions.

In this study, 'invocation' is used interchangeably with *epiclesis*, partly because of style, but also because before the middle of the twentieth century it was often the preferred term. 'Petition for consecration' is used especially in reference to the petition in 1662 and related rites ('Hear us, O merciful Father, we most humbly beseech thee, and grant ... may be partakers of his most blessed Body and Blood'), and carefully nuanced texts where there is a degree of studied ambiguity. 'Prayer for fruitful reception' is sometimes used in places where there is a reference to the gift of the Holy Spirit as one of the fruits of communion in the post-*anamnesis*, but where there can hardly be said to be an explicit invocation.

Chapters1 to 3 give an historical survey of aspects of Anglican thinking about the *epiclesis* from the Reformation to the end of the nineteenth century. The natural starting point is the communion rite of 1549, notable for the inclusion of a preliminary *epiclesis* in the canon. While the rite was short-lived, it continued to exercise a notable influence in aspects of Anglican thinking into the twentieth century. This section reviews successive revisions and attempted revisions of the *Book of Common Prayer* from across the spectrum of theological and devotional emphases in the Elizabethan and Caroline periods, revisions in Scotland and the United States, the influence of the Non-jurors, John and Charles Wesley, the rise of the Oxford Movement, and evangelical responses to the Oxford Movement. It seeks to chart the thinking of influential Anglican theologians, with special emphasis on how they interpreted the eucharistic rites in relation to activity of the Holy Spirit and the understanding of the dynamics of consecration.

Chapters 4 and 5 act as a backcloth to twentieth-century liturgical renewal with an examination of various 'pan-Anglican' statements about the eucharist and the engagement of representatives of the Anglican Communion in ecumenical dialogue with other Christian traditions. One methodological consideration was the placing of this part of the study, the contents of which belong overwhelmingly to the second half of the twentieth century, before chapter 6, which charts Church of England developments from 1900 to 1950, dominated by the 1928 Prayer Book *débâcle* and its aftermath. However, the position accorded to chapters 4 and 5 is mainly symbolic, to make the point that the Church of England is, no more, no less, a member Church of the Anglican Communion, whatever 'primacy of honour' may or may not be attached to it by its sister churches, especially in these challenging and difficult days for the Communion itself.

Chapters 6 and 7 are concerned with the Church of England. They give a survey of English scholarly enquiry into the role and purpose of the *epiclesis*, and the story of the various rounds of liturgical revision, namely those leading to the abortive attempts at Prayer Book revision in 1927 and 1928 and the successive series of 'Alternative Services' revision from the 1960s to the advent of *Common Worship* in 2000. Between these two principal rounds of revision, the eclipse of the *epiclesis* is evident in the light of the then current research into the origins of the eucharistic rite and prayer; this period is dominated by scholars of the calibre of Gregory Dix, Edward Ratcliff and Arthur Couratin.

Chapters 8 and 9 are two case studies of the development of the *epiclesis* in two very different contexts, the Americas and the Indian subcontinent. The former embraces the Episcopal Church and the Anglican Church of Canada. The latter embraces two Anglican Churches, the Church of Ceylon and the Church of the Province of Myanmar; one ancient, autonomous Church in communion with the See of Canterbury, the Mar Thoma Syrian Church; and four ecumenical Churches, the Church of South India, the Church of North India, the Church of Pakistan, and the Church of Bangladesh, which are member Churches of the Anglican Communion and whose bishops are invited to the Lambeth Conference.

Chapter 10 seeks to bring the study together, looking at the Anglican inheritance regarding the *epiclesis*, in relation to the historic east–west divide, the insights of contemporary scholarship, particularly with regard to creation, re-creation and eschatology, an examination of the concepts of 'blessing' and 'consecration' with their biblical roots, and the emerging understanding of the spirituality of the eucharistic prayer, in the hope that the role of the Spirit in the eucharist might be regarded as something to celebrate, and not the cause of division.

Biblical quotations are from the Revised Standard Version. Transliterated forms of Greek and Hebrew terminology are generally used, except in book quotations or bibliographical references where the Greek and Hebrew alphabets are employed.

Durham
Feast of Pentecost, 2007

Chapter 1

The Reformation Heritage

The liturgical revisions of the English Reformation are chiefly associated with Thomas Cranmer, Archbishop of Canterbury from 1533 to 1556. Cranmer was the main architect of three eucharistic liturgical rites: the 1548 Order for the Communion, and the communion services from the 1549 and 1552 editions of the *Book of Common Prayer*.[1]

The 1548 Order was a vernacular eucharistic devotion, encouraging general reception in both kinds, to be inserted in the Sarum mass after the priest's communion; it thus left the Sarum canon intact.[2] It made provision for supplementary consecration of the wine, if required, using the eucharistic words of Jesus concerning the cup from the Sarum rite.[3] The notion of consecration here was perfectly in line with medieval western eucharistic theology[4] save that the prohibition on elevating the chalice for the supplementary consecration heralded the first liturgical sign of a move away from the understanding that there is an objective presence of Christ in the elements. The 1549 canon included a preliminary *epiclesis* before the narrative of institution:

> Heare us (o merciful father) we beseche thee; and with thy holy spirite and worde, vouchsafe to bl+esse and sanc+tifie these thy giftes, and creatures of bread and wyne, that thei maie bee unto us the body and bloud of thy moste derely beloued sonne Jesus Christe.[5]

The rendering of the institution narrative in the 1549 canon included the statement 'and when he had blessed, and geuen thankes' in the bread saying, but only 'geuen thankes' in the cup saying.[6] The 1552 rite, while retaining a petitionary prayer to God which led into the institution narrative, deleted reference to the blessing and sanctification of the elements by the Holy Spirit and word so that the petition related directly to the worshippers:

> Heare us O mercifull father, we beseche the, and graunt that we receiuyng these thy creatures of breade and wine, according to thy sonne oure sauiour Jesu Christes holy

1 The case for primary authorship being ascribed to Cranmer is sufficiently made by Buxton, *Eucharist and Institution Narrative*, pp. 52-57. See also, Diarmaid MacCulloch, *Thomas Cranmer: A Life* (New Haven and London, 1996), pp. 384-386, 410-417, 504-506.

2 Texts from Colin Buchanan (ed.), *Eucharistic Liturgies of Edward VI: A Text for Students* (Bramcote, 1983), p. 4.

3 Ibid., p. 6.

4 E.C. Ratcliff, 'The English Usage of Eucharistic Consecration 1548-1662 – I', *Theology*, 60 (1957): 230-232; Buxton, *Eucharist and Institution Narrative*, pp. 63-64.

5 Buchanan, *Eucharistic Liturgies of Edward VI*, p. 14.

6 Ibid., pp. 14, 15.

> institution, in remembraunce of his death and passion, may be partakers of hys most blessed body and bloude, who in the same ...[7]

The reference to the blessing of the bread was also deleted from the narrative of institution.

In addition to Cranmer's liturgical writing, his major theological explanations of his position were published in his *A Defence of the True and Catholic Doctrine of the Sacrament of the Body and Blood of our Saviour Christ*[8] in 1550 and his *An Answer unto a Crafty and Sophistical Cavillation devised by Stephen Gardiner*[9] written in 1551, and incorporating the *Defence*. Both works were written with 1549 in view, although it may be regarded as probable that Cranmer already had his 1552 revision in mind or even on paper.[10] A proper starting place therefore is to enquire what light Cranmer's writings shed on the meaning of the 1549 *epiclesis*.

Cranmer's clearest definition of consecration is in book 3 of his *Defence*: 'Consecration is the separation of any thing from a profane and worldly use unto a spiritual and godly use.'[11] In relation to baptism, Cranmer argues that when water is separated from ordinary usage for the administration of the sacrament, such water may be called consecrated water, or water put to a holy use. He continues:

> Even so when common bread and wine be taken and severed from other bread and wine, to the use of the holy communion, that portion of bread and wine, although it be of the same substance that the other is from the which it is severed, yet it is now called consecrated or holy bread and holy wine.[12]

Cranmer is clear that the eucharistic bread and wine have no holiness in themselves but because of their use and the fact that they represent Christ's body and blood they may rightly be called holy. So in his *Answer* he writes:

> And yet do I not utterly deprive the outward sacraments of the name of holy things, because of the holy use whereunto they serve, and not because of any holiness that lieth hid in the insensible creature. Which although they have no holiness in them, yet they be signs and tokens of the marvellous works and holy effects, which God worketh in us by his omnipotent power.[13]

---

7 Ibid., p. 30.

8 Text from *The Work of Thomas Cranmer* (ed. G.E. Duffield, Appleford, 1964), henceforth, *Defence*.

9 From *Writings and Disputations of Thomas Cranmer, Archbishop of Canterbury, Martyr, 1556* (ed. John Edmund Cox, Cambridge, 1844), henceforth, *Answer*.

10 Colin Buchanan, *What Did Cranmer Think He Was Doing?* 2nd ed. (Bramcote, 1982), pp. 7-10; A.H. Couratin, *The Service of Holy Communion 1549-1662* (London, 1963), p. 4.

11 *Defence*, p. 181.

12 Ibid. The prayer over the baptismal water in 1549 (placed in the private baptism service) also refers to 'word' and 'Spirit'. It is significant that this prayer is essentially for the worshippers.

13 *Answer*, p. 11.

This is verified in the *anamnesis* of 1549 rite where the elements are indeed designated 'holy':

> WHerfore O Lorde and heauenly father, accordyng to the Institucion of thy derely beloued sonne, our sauior Jesu Christ, we thy humble seruantes do celebrate, and make here before thy diuine Maiestie, with these thy holy giftes, the memoriall whiche thy soone hath willed us to make ...[14]

For Cranmer, the heart of the communion service is the reception of the elements by the worthy communicant; the body and blood of Christ are not received physically through the medium of transubstantiation or Luther's variant on it, but spiritually through reception of the elements in remembrance of Christ's death, so that 'by the exercise of our faith our souls may receive the more heavenly food'.[15] It is in this context that the elements can be called 'holy'. Colin Buchanan has rightly observed that Cranmer is not opposed to 'realist' language *'so long as it is concerned with what is received by* the *faithful*'.[16] Therefore, Cranmer's view of consecration is specific and limited, and it is in this sense that the verbs 'bless' and 'sanctify' are to be interpreted. However, in relation to the means of consecration, in his *Defence* Cranmer assigns a special role to the eucharistic words of Jesus: 'But specially they may be called holy and consecrated, when they be separated to that holy use by Christ's own words, which he spake for that purpose, saying of the bread, *This is my body*; and of the wine, *This is my blood.*'[17]

Citing ancient authors, Cranmer is explicit that it is 'after those words be pronounced over them' that the elements are taken as consecrated or holy bread and wine. Earlier in his *Defence* he refers to the eucharistic words of Jesus as 'words of consecration',[18] but he rejects any notion of transubstantiation. The role of the narrative is again asserted thus:

> And lest we should forget the same, he ordained not a yearly memory, (as the Paschal lamb was eaten but once every year,) but a daily remembrance he ordained thereof in bread and wine, sanctified and dedicated to that purpose, saying, *This is my body; this cup is my blood, which is shed for the remission of sins. Do this in the remembrance of me.*[19]

Again, in his discussion of 1 Corinthians 11, Cranmer, albeit answering Gardiner, nevertheless repeatedly refers to the narrative of institution in that chapter as 'the sanctification', concluding: 'Wherefore, gentle reader, weigh St. Paul's words, whether he call it bread after the sanctification, or only before ...'.[20] However, the spiritual effect of the sacrament is entirely in the worthy communicant.

Stephen Gardiner, in his work *An Explication and Assertion of the True Catholic Faith, Touching the Most Blessed Sacrament of the Altar, with Confutation of a Book*

---

14 *Buchanan, Eucharistic Liturgies of Edward VI*, p. 15.
15 *Answer*, p. 181.
16 Buchanan, *What Did Cranmer Think He Was Doing?* p. 6, emphasis his.
17 *Defence*, p. 181.
18 Ibid., pp. 82–83.
19 *Defence*, p. 166.
20 *Answer*, p. 250.

Written Against the Same,[21] written in response to the *Defence* and which provoked Cranmer's *Answer* makes explicit reference to the 1549 *epiclesis* as suggesting conversion of the substance of the elements into Christ's body and blood. Cranmer's response is clear:

> And the bread and wine be made unto us the body and blood of Christ, (as it is in the book of common prayer,) but not by changing the substance of bread and wine into the substance of Christ's natural body and blood, but that in the godly using of them they may be unto the receivers Christ's body and blood … And therefore, in the book of the holy communion, we do not pray absolutely that the bread and wine may be made the body and blood of Christ, but that unto us in that holy mystery they may be so; that is to say, that we may so worthily receive the same, that we may be partakers of Christ's body and blood, and that therewith in spirit and in truth we may be spiritually nourished.[22]

It could be argued that Cranmer's petition of 1552 gives much clearer expression to his theology than 1549. Or can we perceive a change in his theology between the two prayer books, a change anticipated by his *Answer* and *Defence* so that in both we see an exposition of 1549 through 1552 spectacles? Three observations are important. The first is that 1549 bears all the marks of a well thought-out piece of liturgical writing and Cranmer in his later theological works betrays no sense of a change of theological emphasis – indeed, in his *Defence* he concludes by stating that the 1549 order for communion 'is agreeable with the institution of Christ, with St. Paul and the old primitive and apostolic Church'.[23] Second, the 1549 invocation includes a significant change from Sarum in the effect desired upon the elements:

> *Sarum* ... ut nobis cor+pus et san+guis fiat dilectissimi Filii tui Domini nostri Jesu Christi.
>
> 1549 ... that thei maie bee unto us the body and bloude ...

The use of the verb 'be' as opposed to 'become' or 'be made' suggests a more open theological context. As his response to Gardiner above shows, in Cranmer's thought the stress of the 1549 petition falls on 'may be unto us'.[24] The comment of Geoffrey Cuming is apposite: 'he is able to keep the phrase "that they may be unto us the body ..." by placing great stress on the words "to us", which he expounds in the *Defence* as meaning "to those who receive worthily"'.[25] While it is true that the Latin petition includes *nobis* and that Cranmer's phrase could be accepted as a straight translation of *Quam oblationem*,[26] in his new theological framework, Cranmer interprets the phrase in the context of what he regarded as the primitive and true catholic understanding of the sacrament. The third is that in his response to Gardiner's comments on the 1549

21 The text of which Cranmer reproduces in his *Answer*.

22 *Answer*, p. 79.

23 Ibid., p. 231.

24 See also *Answer*, p. 271.

25 Geoffrey Cuming, *The Godly Order* (London, 1983), p. 94; contra Ratcliff, 'The English Usage of Eucharistic Consecration 1548-1662 – I', p. 232.

26 Buxton, *Eucharist and Institution Narrative*, p. 71.

epiclesis Cranmer does not comment on what he meant by 'and with thy holy Spirit and word vouchsafe to bless and sanctify these thy gifts and creatures'.

So what role did Cranmer here ascribe to the Spirit and word in the eucharistic action? In Cranmer's theological writings there are a number of places where word and Spirit occur in close proximity. In book 1 of his *Defence*, Cranmer speaks of the faith necessary to believe that Christ gave his body and shed his blood on the cross for us. He continues: 'And this faith God worketh inwardly in our hearts by his Holy Spirit, and confirmeth the same outwardly to our ears by hearing of his word, and to our other senses by eating and drinking of the sacramental bread and wine in his holy Supper.'[27] The most natural interpretation of 'word' in this passage is the institution narrative because of the use of the verb 'confirmeth'; the repetition of the eucharistic words confirm Christ's promise, given once in time, at each celebration. The reception of Christ by faith comes through the inspiration of the Spirit, in conjunction with the hearing of Christ's promise, and the physical eating and drinking of the elements. In his discussion of a sermon by Cyprian,[28] the most natural interpretation is that God's word here relates to the institution narrative and that reception of the elements by the worshippers includes a gift of the Spirit:

> And yet the bread is changed, not in shape, nor substance, but in nature, as Cyprian truly saith, not meaning that the natural substance of bread is clean gone, but that by God's word there is added thereto another higher property, nature, and condition, far passing the nature and condition of common bread, that is to say, that the bread and wine doth show unto us, as the same Cyprian saith, that we be partakers of the Spirit of God, and most purely joined unto Christ, and spiritually fed with his flesh and blood; so that now the said mystical bread is both a corporal food for the body, and a spiritual food for the soul.[29]

This is one of the rare occasions where Cranmer's use of the adjective 'spiritual' is in close proximity to a reference to the Holy Spirit. In book 3 he argues:

> And as Almighty God by his most mighty word and his Holy Spirit and infinite power brought forth all creatures in the beginning, and ever sithence hath preserved them; even so by the same word and power he worketh in us from time to time this marvellous spiritual generation and wonderful spiritual nourishment and feeding, which is wrought only by God, and is comprehended and received of us by faith.[30]

Here the word of God is set in a broader context; while the Spirit is not related explicitly to the communion, by analogy with creation, the power of the Spirit in the eucharist would seem to be understood. The gift of Christ, received by faith, is accomplished in the believer by God's Spirit and power and word. There is a further reference to the word alone in book 1 of the *Defence*: 'For as the word of God preached putteth Christ into our ears; so likewise these elements of water, bread, and wine, joined to God's word, do after a sacramental manner put Christ into our

27 Ibid., p. 74.
28 Now held to be spurious.
29 Ibid., p. 108.
30 Ibid., p. 190.

eyes, mouths, hands, and all our senses.'[31] In this passage Cranmer is referring to the word both in a general sense, the preaching of Scripture, and also in a more specific sense – the elements joined to God's word – where again the institution narrative would appear to be the natural reference. We have already noted above that Cranmer assigned a special significance to the eucharistic words of Jesus in his understanding of consecration. While 'word' can carry a more general sense, in the context of his eucharistic writing again the primary reference appears to be the institution narrative – that particular 'word' added to the eucharistic elements.

There are also further references to the Holy Spirit. Cranmer's treatment of the Holy Spirit is interesting. His biblicism is apparent in his frequent comparisons between baptism and holy communion. Because there are a number of New Testament passages explicitly relating the Spirit to baptism, Cranmer naturally refers to the gift of the Spirit through the sacrament. There are no equivalent scriptural passages relating the work of the Spirit to communion and so Cranmer, in concert with western eucharistic theology generally, adopts an essentially Christocentric approach. However, the Spirit is not entirely absent. Indeed, perhaps his clearest theological statement comes in the 1551 preface to his *Answer*:

> And sometime by this word 'sacrament' I mean the whole ministration and receiving of the sacraments, either of baptism, or of the Lord's supper: and so the old writers many times do say, that Christ and the Holy Ghost be present in the sacraments; not meaning by that manner of speech, that Christ and the Holy Ghost be present in the water, bread, or wine, (which be only the outward visible sacraments,) but that in the due ministration of the sacraments according to Christ's ordinance and institution, Christ and his holy Spirit be truly and indeed present by their mighty and sanctifying power, virtue, and grace, in all them that worthily receive the same.[32]

Again we have a clear reference to Christ's 'ordinance and institution' and the work of the Spirit in the communicant when the elements are administered. In his writings Cranmer cites a number of examples of such 'old writers' where he explicitly refers to the Spirit. Expounding St Ambrose's *De Sacramentis*, he writes:

> For he saith not that the substance of bread and wine is gone, but he saith that their nature is changed; that is to say, that in the holy communion we ought not to receive the bread and wine as other common meats and drinks, but as things clean changed into a higher estate, nature, and condition, to be taken as holy meats and drinks, whereby we receive spiritual feeding and supernatural nourishment from heaven, of the very true body and blood of our Saviour Christ, through the omnipotent power of God and the wonderful working of the Holy Ghost.[33]

The Spirit is here related to the spiritual nourishment received by the communicant through reception. This is echoed by a further reference to John Chrysostom:

31 Ibid., p. 70.

32 Ibid., p. 3.

33 *Defence*, pp. 117–118.

And where St. Chrysostome and other authors do speak of the wonderful operation of God in his sacraments, passing all man's wit, senses, and reason, they mean not of the working of God in the water, bread, and wine, but of the marvellous working of God in the hearts of them that receive the sacraments, secretly, inwardly, and spiritually transforming them, renewing, feeding, comforting, and nourishing them with his flesh and blood, through his most Holy Spirit, the same flesh and blood still remaining in heaven.[34]

Here once again, the Spirit brings spiritual nourishment in the heart of the believer. Expounding his understanding of John Damascene, Cranmer stresses union with the whole Christ through the sacrament, by the Spirit:

... but to such as by unfeigned faith worthily receive the bread and wine, to such the bread and wine are called by Damascene the body and blood of Christ, because that such persons through the working of the Holy Ghost be so knit and united spiritually to Christ's flesh and blood, and to his Divinity also, that they be fed with them unto everlasting life.[35]

Stressing St Paul's exhortation that communicants should not eat and drink unworthily, Cranmer states:

... yet should we come to this mystical bread and wine with faith, reverence, purity and fear, as we would do, if we should come and see and receive Christ himself sensibly present. For unto the faithful, Christ is at his own holy table present with his mighty Spirit and grace, and is of them more fruitfully received, than if corporally they should receive him bodily present.[36]

The gift of Christ, whose true flesh and blood is in heaven, is mediated to the worthy communicant through the power and grace of the Spirit. In his *Answer*, in the context of a discussion of Pope Gelasius, Cranmer illustrates how he can use realist language while anchoring the debate in the context of reception:

And therefore when he speaketh of the going of the sacraments into the divine substance, he meaneth not that the substances of the sacraments go into the substance of God ... but that in the action of that mystery, to them that worthily receive the sacraments, to them they be turned into divine substance through the working of the Holy Ghost, who maketh the godly receivers to be the partakers of the divine nature and substance.[37]

The point is that while the elements themselves cannot be changed, to those who receive them, they are received as the body and blood of Christ through the work of the Spirit. The 'to them' in this passage corresponds to the 'may be to us' of the 1549 invocation. A final reference reiterates Cranmer's insistence that the benefits of Christ's passion are received through the Spirit:

And in token hereof he hath prepared bread to be eaten and wine to be drunken of us in his holy supper, to put us in remembrance of his said death, and of the celestial feeding,

34 Ibid., p. 185.
35 Ibid., p. 191; see also, *Answer*, p. 150.
36 *Defence*, p. 205.
37 Ibid., p. 296.

nourishing, increasing, and of all the benefits which we have thereby; which benefits through faith and the Holy Ghost are exhibited and given unto all that worthily receive the said holy supper.[38]

There is a marked consistency in all Cranmer's references to the Spirit. The work of the Spirit is related at every point to the worshippers and not the elements. In the light of Cranmer's theological exposition, the 1549 *epiclesis* is not intended to suggest any objective holiness in the elements themselves; rather the Spirit is related to Christ's spiritual presence in the communicants. In receiving the bread and wine the communicant is nourished with the spiritual food of Christ's body and blood and thus united to Christ through the power of the Spirit.[39] In view of Cranmer's use of 'word' and 'Spirit' in the texts we have been considering it is reasonable to conclude that in the 1549 invocation, the reference to 'word' designates the institution narrative which *de facto* 'blesses' and 'sanctifies' the elements, that is, sets them apart because of Christ's institution. The reference to the Spirit is on this understanding directly related to the petition 'may be to us' – that the faith required for the reception of the sacramental gift is itself inspired by the Spirit and the gift is conveyed by the Spirit. It was to clarify this understanding of the role of the Spirit that Martin Bucer suggested the amendment in his so-called *Censura*:

Hear us O merciful Father, bless us and sanctify us by thy Word and Holy Spirit, that with true faith we may receive in these holy mysteries the body and blood of thy Son to be the food and drink of eternal life.[40]

Bucer's concern was the lack of any reference in the New Testament to a prayer for God's blessing and sanctification of the bread and wine in the eucharist, and that the prayer as it stood 'is twisted by Anti-Christ into a means for maintaining and confirming the infinitely wicked and blasphemous dogma of the transubstantiation of the bread and wine'.[41] Yet Bucer was also at pains to make clear that Christ instituted the sacrament 'so that we may not receive them simply as bread and wine' because of the eucharistic words:

... there would have been no reason for the Lord when he distributed the bread and wine to the disciples, and said 'Take, eat, drink', to have added 'This is my body, This is my blood'. And so in this sacrament we receive not only bread and wine but at the same time

38 Ibid., p. 328.

39 This would concur with Bryan Spinks's judgment that, out of the three models suggested by Brian Gerrish for Reformed understanding of eucharistic presence, namely, symbolic memorialism (Zwingli), symbolic instrumentalism (Calvin, Beza and Vermigli) and symbolic parallelism (mature Bullinger, Bucer), it is into the last category that Cranmer should be placed, with his careful distinction between the outward and the inward, *Two Faces of Elizabethan Anglican Theology* (Lanham and London, 1999), pp. 10-11.

40 E.C. Whitaker, *Martin Bucer and the Book of Common Prayer* (Great Wakering, 1974), pp. 52, 54.

41 Ibid., p. 54. Or, in Bryan Spinks's phrase, in Bucer, 'The physical cannot mediate the spiritual. The two may be parallel, but they are quite different and distinct', *Sacraments, Ceremonies and the Stuart Divines* (Aldershot, 2002), p. 4.

> his body and blood, and indeed not these only but with them the whole Christ, both God and man.[42]

It was in the light of criticism from fellow Reformers and Gardiner's assertion that 1549 was 'not distant from the catholic faith in my judgement',[43] that Cranmer went for utter clarity in his 1552 revision. The invocation of word and Spirit on the eucharistic elements was deleted as was the petition for the hallowing of water in the baptismal rite. The suggestion is that if, as Buchanan maintains, Cranmer's eucharistic theology was consistent during the period 1548-53,[44] then the 1549 *epiclesis* was not intended to suggest any objective change in the elements and that the consecration itself was intimately related to reception. This would underline the conclusion reached by Bryan Spinks in the most recent investigation of the 1549 *epiclesis*.[45] Questioning traditional interpretations of the *epiclesis* as being influenced by Byzantine Basil, Spinks reiterates suggestions by Brightman and Ratcliff that the 1549 petition was dependent on western sources.[46] He suggests further, however, that *Reformed* sources may be the immediate source of Cranmer's petition, citing references to the operation of both word and Spirit in Martin Bucer and more especially, Peter Martyr Vermigli.[47] For example, Spinks cites Martyr's *Disputatio*: 'He is able to make common bread and wine a most effectual sacrament ... such a change in it, in which bread and wine are translated from the natural order, and profane degrees in which they were, to a sacramental state and order, both by the work of the Holy Spirit and by the institution of the Lord.'[48] Spinks conjectures that Martyr may well have been happier with Cranmer's 1549 petition than Bucer, but the importance of his article is in suggesting that Cranmer's 1549 petition is understandable in a Reformed theological framework,[49] as Cranmer's own writings

---

42 Whitaker, *Martin Bucer and the Book of Common Prayer*, p. 64.

43 *Answer*, p. 92.

44 Buchanan, *What Did Cranmer Think He Was Doing?*, pp. 7-8.

45 Bryan D. Spinks, '"And with thy Holy Spirite and Worde": Further Thoughts on the Source of Cranmer's Petition for Sanctification in the 1549 Communion Service', in Margot Johnson (ed.), *Thomas Cranmer* (Durham, 1990), pp. 94-102.

46 Ibid., pp. 95-96, cf. Ratcliff, 'The English Usage of Eucharistic Consecration 1548-1662 – I', p. 232, 233. Cuming, *The Godly Order*, p. 96, also agrees that 1549 invocation is dependent on western sources. Gregory Dix followed Brightman's suggestion that Paschasius Radbert's work *De Corpore et Sanguine Domini* may have influenced Cranmer's combination of word and Spirit, *The Shape of the Liturgy*, 2nd ed. (London, 1986) p. 657, fn. 1. Geoffrey Cuming, in his *A History of Anglican Liturgy*, 2nd ed. (Basingstoke, 1982), p. 56, states that the 1549 invocation was one of the 'usages of the primitive Church' referred to in the Act of Uniformity.

47 Salvatore Corda, *Veritas Sacramenti: A Study of Vermigli's Doctrine of the Lord's Supper* (Zurich, 1975), pp. 107, 108 (fn. 23), 112-114, 119, 120.

48 Spinks, '"And with thy Holy Spirite and Worde"', p. 99.

49 This sets in a new light Ratcliff's contention that to the Edwardine and modern reader, the *Defence* and 1549 were not in theological harmony, 'The English Usage of Eucharistic Consecration 1548-1662 –I', p. 235. Basil Hall is cautious in his treatment of Cranmer's debt to Martyr, arguing that the former had a higher doctrine of the presence, 'Cranmer, the Eucharist and the Foreign Divines in the Reign of Edward VI', in Paul Ayris

demonstrate. It is also noticeable that in the quotations cited, Bucer and Martyr as well as Cranmer, all witness to the utter centrality of the institution narrative, in line with western sacramental theology, but nevertheless understood in the light of the rejection of transubstantiation. The clear role of the institution narrative in Cranmer's writing might also suggest that the contentious issue about whether Cranmer entirely abandoned any notion of consecration in 1552 needs to be more nuanced. For example, Buchanan argues that Cranmer had changed his mind concerning consecration on the evidence of 1552: '... They are not even "separated unto a holy use" any more'.[50] He suggests that the 1549 *epiclesis* designated a clear 'moment' of consecration. The issue is what effects the 'separation'? If the 1549 reference to the Spirit is essentially related to the reception of the elements, Cranmer's intention is not so much a moment but a movement, a process culminating in reception.[51] In the light of this, the 1552 petition becomes simply a more compact and unambiguous statement of Cranmer's convictions. The role of the Spirit there is understood. The fact, however, that in 1552 Cranmer retains the 'word', the narrative within a prayer formula, suggests that Cranmer would still regard the elements as 'separated' but only in so far as the context of communion remained. Only Christ's institution with the response of lively faith through the power of the Spirit (to paraphrase 1549) effected the sacrament. Outside of that, there could be no 'spiritual presence', and so there is nothing remarkable about the Curate taking the remains of the elements home for his own use as the 1552 rubric directed.[52]

---

and David Selwyn (eds), *Thomas Cranmer: Churchman and Scholar* (Woodbridge, 1993), pp. 229-234.

50 Buchanan, *What Did Cranmer Think He Was Doing?*, p. 22.

51 The presence is '*in usu sacramenti*', P.N. Brooks, *Thomas Cranmer's Doctrine of the Eucharist*, 2nd ed. (Basingstoke, 1992), p. 149.

52 Buchanan, *What Did Cranmer Think He Was Doing?*, pp. 22-25, follows Ratcliff, 'The English Usage of Eucharistic Consecration 1548-1662 – I', p. 236, in suggesting that Cranmer banished the concept of consecration in the 1552 rite.

Chapter 2

Scripture and Tradition: Post-Reformation Exploration in the Sixteenth and Seventeenth Centuries

Introduction

The question as to how far the Reformation should go was a vexed issue in sixteenth- and seventeenth-century English church life. The criticisms surrounding the reception of 1549 and the response to them in 1552 are a ready illustration. Cranmer, however, retained elements of traditional liturgy and ceremonial and the threefold ministry. For some this was compromise and meant that Anglican formularies retained 'unscriptural' elements, so that the reform was not as 'pure', as for example, the reform in Geneva. The call for more radical reform and, in relation to worship, a conviction that Scripture prescribed not only the theology of sacramental rites but also their form, that ceremonies should be limited to those explicitly discernible from Scripture, became identified with a diverse movement commonly called 'Puritanism'. Moreover, the terms 'Puritan' and 'Anglican' have often been used in contra-distinction, as if designating two distinct parties. However, the accuracy and usefulness of this terminology has been severely called into question by contemporary scholarship, witnessed by Bryan Spinks's seminal study of sacramental theology and liturgy in both England and Scotland from 1603 to 1662.[1] Spinks questions whether the term 'Anglican' can be usefully employed before the 1662, while many dubbed 'Puritans' before the Restoration were in fact loyal members of the Church of England, some conformist, others contending for a 'Presbyterian' Anglicanism or for further ceremonial and liturgical reform, while others left, whether willingly or unwillingly, to become Independents or Separatists. Spinks, following historians such as Patrick Collinson, prefers the term 'godly'.[2]

Moreover, the rank and file of those loyal to the Elizabethan Settlement were Reformed in their theology in the style of what has been termed 'international Calvinism'. It was only later that a *minority* group, among them Lancelot Andrews and the 'Durham House' group, commonly designated as 'Laudian', espoused an understanding of 'Anglicanism' that differentiated it from other Protestant groups, looked to the Patristic period in particular for an understanding of the Church's

1 Spinks, *Sacraments, Ceremonies and the Stuart Divines*, pp. xii-xiii.

2 See Patrick Collinson, *From Cranmer to Sancroft* (London, 2006), pp. 114-122; also, Spinks, *Two Faces of Elizabethan Anglican Theology*, pp. 1-8, for a discussion of further issues of definition.

catholicity, had a higher regard for 'tradition', and so developed aspects of ceremonial.[3]

The Elizabethan Period 1558-1603

After Elizabeth's accession in 1558, a new Act of Uniformity in April 1559 re-established the 1552 Prayer Book with minor changes. The combination of the 1549 and 1552 words of administration may give some indication of a more objective view of eucharistic presence.[4] Some had wished for the restoration of 1549, but here the *epiclesis* was a sensitive issue, as illustrated by a letter attributed to Edmund Guest to the Queen's secretary, Sir William Cecil. Guest gives two objections to the 1549 invocation:

> The first, because it is taken to be so needful for the consecration, that the consecration is not thought to be without it. Which is not true: for petition is no part of consecration. Because Christ, in ordaining the sacrament, made no petition, but a thanksgiving.
>
> The second cause why the foresaid prayer is to be refused, is for that it prays that the bread and wine may be Christ's body and blood; which makes for the popish transubstantiation: which is a doctrine that hath caused much idolatry: and though the Doctors so speak, yet we must speak otherwise, because we take them otherwise that they meant, or would be taken.[5]

On the other hand, however, Dr Cuthbert Scott, Bishop of Chester, objected in Parliament to the 1559 communion rite on the basis that it had *no* consecration. Drawing attention to the *Quam oblationem* in the Roman canon which has a petition for consecration, he asserted:

> ... but as for this newe booke, there is no such thinge mentyoned in it, that dothe eyther declare any suche intente, eyther make any suche request unto God, but rather to the contrarye; as dothe appeare by the requeste there made in these words, 'That we receavinge these thy creatures of bread and wyne,' &c. which wordes declare that they intende no consecration at all. And then let them glory as muche as they will in their communion, it is to no purpose, seeynge that the body of Christe is not there, which, as I have said, is the thinge that should be communicated.[6]

However, Scott's view did not become the official line as evidenced by the trial of Robert Johnson before the Queen's commissioners for failing to repeat the eucharistic words of Jesus after replenishing the emptied cup. Bryan Spinks comments that

---

3 Spinks, *Sacraments, Ceremonies and the Stuart Divines*, p. 81; see also his article 'What Was Wrong with Mr Cosin's Couzening Devotions? Deconstructing an Episode in Seventeenth Century Anglican "Liturgical Hagiography" ', *Worship*, 74 (2000): 318-320.

4 Christopher J. Cocksworth, *Evangelical Eucharistic Thought in the Church of England* (Cambridge, 1993), p. 34.

5 Edward Cardwell, *A History of Conferences and Other Proceedings Connected with the Revision of The Book of Common Prayer*, 3rd ed. (Oxford, 1849), pp. 52-53.

6 Ibid., p. 113.

Johnson was following the custom of Geneva and the theological understanding of such writers as Fulke and Cartwright.[7] The commissioners however gave judgement that the recital of the narrative effected consecration, and so by implication the prayer 'Hear us ...' was a petition for consecration.[8]

Two major Church of England apologists wrote during Elizabeth's reign. The first, John Jewel, Bishop of Salisbury from 1560 to 1571, was engaged in theological dispute with the Roman Catholic, Thomas Harding. Jewel understood consecration as 'the converting of the natural elements into a godly use',[9] and he clearly assigned a central place to the reading of the words of institution; by these God's word is joined to the elements and they become the sacrament.[10] Jewel, like Calvin and Cranmer, held a *sursum corda* view of the union of the communicant with the ascended Christ. While his discussion with Harding is almost entirely Christologically based, nevertheless at the end of the section on the real presence, having argued that the presence of Christ is a spiritual presence, he can conclude: 'Thus the holy fathers say Christ is present, not corporally, carnally, naturally; but as in a sacrament, by his Spirit, and by his grace.'[11] The role of the Spirit is not developed, although he does cite references to the work of the Spirit in St Paul, St Augustine and St Basil, to illustrate the fact that 'we are in Christ sitting in heaven, and Christ sitting in heaven is here in us, not by a natural, but by a spiritual mode of being'.[12]

The second was Richard Hooker (?1554-1600) and his magisterial work *Of the Laws of Ecclesiastical Polity*. Book five, which included his section on worship and the sacraments, appeared in 1597. Hooker's essential thesis is that through the eucharist the recipient engages in a real participation in Christ. Through receiving the elements the communicant becomes united to Christ in a mystical and personal encounter. Hooker has a clear view of consecration. At the Last Supper, the action of Jesus was to 'bless and consecrate' the elements 'made for ever the instruments of life by virtue of his divine benediction'.[13] Thus he can speak of the eucharistic species as 'this hallowed food' which, 'through concurrence of divine power, is in verity and truth, unto faithful receivers, instrumentally a cause of that mystical

---

7 Bryan D. Spinks, *From the Lord and "The Best Reformed Churches"* (Rome, 1984), p. 95. However, Johnson himself made the defence that he was simply complying with the Prayer Book, which made no provision for supplementary consecration. The 1549 Order for the Communion (1548) made provision for supplementary consecration of wine, but there was no such rubric in 1549, 1552 and 1559.

8 Richard Buxton points out that there is nothing in extant visitation articles or discussion of reform of Canon Law to witness to any legal requirement for supplementary consecration during Elizabeth's reign and it is to be doubted whether the Johnson case was widely reported, *Eucharist and Institution Narrative*, pp. 90-92.

9 *The Works of John Jewel, Vol. 1* (Cambridge, 1845), p. 123.

10 Ibid.

11 Ibid., p. 479.

12 Ibid., p. 477. John Booty develops this reference to the Spirit against the background of the sacramental theology of Vermigli (Jewell's teacher) and Bucer, *John Jewel as Apologist of the Church of England* (London, 1963), pp. 171-175.

13 Richard Hooker, *Of The Laws of Ecclesiastical Polity: The Fifth Book* (London, 1902), p. 375.

participation' whereby Christ gives himself fully to the communicant with all saving grace that his sacrificed body can yield.[14] In his discussion of Tertullian, Irenaeus, Theodoret and Cyprian,[15] he expounds them as teaching that Christ, by his divine power, adds to the elements 'supernatural efficacy, which addition to the nature of those consecrated elements changeth them and maketh them that unto us which otherwise they could not be'. It is through the consecrated elements that the recipient mystically and truly enjoys communion with Christ and a real participation in the fruits of his redemption, so that there is 'a kind of transubstantiation in us, a true change both of soul and body'. [16]

While the elements are 'instrumentally a cause' of participation with Christ, Hooker stops short of affirming any sense of an objective presence of Christ in the elements: 'The real presence of Christ's most blessed body and blood is not therefore to be sought for in the sacrament, but in the worthy receiver of the sacrament.'[17] The eucharist does, however, impart a gift of the Holy Spirit: 'that to whom the person of Christ is thus communicated, to them He giveth by the same sacrament His Holy Spirit to sanctify them as it sanctifieth Him which is their head'.[18]

On the role of the Holy Spirit in the sacrament, the Elizabethan Prayer Book is silent; Hooker, however, sees an explicit role of the Spirit in relation to the communicants and an implied role in relation to the elements in by his use of the word 'instrument' and such language as 'hallowed food, through concurrence of divine power'. As we shall see, those theologians employing the notion that the elements are an instrument, conveying grace, normally develop this with regard to pneumatology, suggesting that they would have had little difficulty with Cranmer's *epiclesis* of 1549 or Bucer's suggested emendation to relate it solely to the worshippers.[19]

Theological Writing before 1662

The first to consider is Lancelot Andrewes (1555-1626), designated by Spinks as among the Avant-Garde Conformists,[20] and so atypical of this period. This is illustrated in his *Preces Privatae*, by his use of material from the Patristic liturgies as devotional aids supplementing the Prayer Book. So, at the offertory, there is a prayer including an invocation:

---

14 Ibid., p. 384.

15 Hooker cites *De coena Domini*, which as John Booty has demonstrated, should be attributed to Arnold, twelfth-century Abbot of Bonneval, 'Hooker's Understanding of the Presence of Christ in the Eucharist', in John E. Booty (ed.), *The Divine Drama in History and Liturgy* (Eugene, 1984), pp. 135, 140; see also John E. Booty, *Reflections on the Theology of Richard Hooker* (Sewanee, 1998), p. 122.

16 Hooker, *Of The Laws of Ecclesiastical Polity: The Fifth Book*, pp. 381-382.

17 Ibid., p. 376.

18 Ibid., p. 378.

19 So Gerrish's definition of 'symbolic instumentalism' is cited by Spinks, *Two Faces of Elizabethan Anglican Theology*, p. 10: 'Here the sacraments cause and communicate what they signify ... the Spirit uses them to confer what they symbolize'.

20 Spinks, *Sacraments, Ceremonies and the Stuart Divines*, p. 45.

Behold, O Lord our God
from heaven thy dwelling place
and from the throne of the glory of thy kingdom,
and come to hallow us.
Thou that sittest on high with the Father,
and art here with us invisibly,
come to hallow the gifts that are set forth,
and them for whom and them by whom and the ends whereunto they are brought.[21]

Andrewes's main source here is the prayer of elevation of the Byzantine Liturgy of St Basil and the Liturgy of St John Chrysostom. However, the petition 'come and hallow the gifts that are set forth' is reminiscent of the *epiclesis* in the Liturgy of St Basil.[22] The prayer continues with a series of petitions drawn from the post-communion prayer of Basil. The petition for the hallowing of the gifts in Basil is clearly pneumatological. However, in Andrewes, it is unclear whether it is pneumatological or Christological as the phrase 'Thou that sittest on high with the Father, and art here with us invisibly' is ambiguous. If anything, the context suggests a Christological reference.[23]

Andrewes however understood participation in the Spirit as one of the fruits of communion,[24] and in his prayer 'After the consecration', a composite prayer based on the *anamnesis* of Basil and a prayer after the *anaphora*, one of the petitions asks that the communicants will become temples of the Spirit. The interesting feature here is that Andrewes constructs a sequence of invocation, prayer of consecration, *anamnesis* with fruits of communion. He does not follow the eastern pattern of an invocation after the *anamnesis*. His scheme is more reminiscent of 1549.

The role ascribed by Andrewes to the Spirit comes out very clearly in his sermons. Partaking of the eucharist imparts the gift of the Spirit. So, in his Christmas Day sermon of 1605, he says:

> It is most kindly to take part with Him in that which He took part in with us, and that, to no other end, but that He might make the receiving of it by us a means whereby He might 'dwell in us, and we in Him;' He taking our flesh, and we receiving His Spirit; by His flesh which He took of us receiving His Spirit which He imparteth to us ...[25]

Andrewes made much of 1 Corinthians 12:13: 'For by one Spirit we were all baptized into one body ... and all were made to drink of one Spirit', and 1 Corinthians 10:1-4, where baptism and spiritual food and drink are typologically applied to the Israelite wilderness wanderings. For Andrewes, both passages established an intimate link between the two sacraments, and the role of the Spirit in the sacraments. Of the latter passage he says in his Whitsun sermon of 1608:

---

21 Lancelot Andrewes, *The Preces Privatae of Lancelot Andrewes* (translation, introduction and notes by F.E. Brightman, London, 1903), pp. 121-122. In the *BCP*, the 'offertory' was solely concerned with money.

22 Brightman ascribes the petition to this source, ibid., p. 339.

23 A Christological interpretation is supported by Atchley, *On the Epiclesis*, p. 194.

24 Andrewes, *The Preces Privatae of Lancelot Andrewes*, p. 122.

25 Lancelot Andrewes, *Ninety-Six Sermons, Vol. 1* (Oxford, 1841), p. 16.

> In which respect He instituted *escam spiritualem*, 'spiritual food', to that end; so called spiritual, not so much for that it is received spiritually, as for that being so received it maketh us, together with it, to receive the Spirit, even *potare Spiritum* – it is the Apostle's own word.[26]

So the sacramental signs are '*vehicula Spiritus*';[27] they 'procreate the Spirit in us as that flesh and blood which was itself conceived and procreate by the Spirit'.[28] Andrewes makes explicit the identity of Christ's flesh and blood with the eucharistic elements:

> ... as the word and the Spirit, so the flesh and the Spirit go together. Not all flesh, but this flesh, the flesh that was conceived by the Holy Ghost; this is never without the Holy Ghost by Whom it was conceived; so that, receive one, and receive both. Ever with this blood there runneth still an artery, with plenty of Spirit in it, which maketh that we eat there *escam spiritualem*, 'a spiritual meat,' and that in that cup we be 'made drink of the Spirit.'[29]

And,

> ... there is no better way of celebrating the feast of the receiving the Holy Ghost than so to do, with receiving the same body that came of It at his birth, and that came from It now at His rising again.
>
> And so receiving it, He That breathed, and He That was breathed, both of Them vouchsafe to breathe into those holy mysteries a Divine power and virtue, and make them to us the bread of life, and the cup of salvation; God the Father also sending His blessing upon them, that they may be His blessed means of this thrice-blessed effect! [30]

This remarkable passage, with its strong verb 'make' and possible allusion to the *anamnesis* of the Roman rite, expounds a Trinitarian understanding of *epiclesis* as the means by which the eucharistic gift is bestowed. This was not to adopt the doctrine of transubstantiation, for as Nicholas Lossky observes, Andrewes rejects its attempt to explain the unfathomable but more importantly because it 'verges on monophysitism and thus destroys the Chalcedonian purity of the Christological dogma'.[31]

Richard Field (1561-1616) published his great work *On the Church* in 1606. He argues that there is diversity of opinion among the ancient authors of how the change in the eucharistic species takes place, but they agree:

26 Lancelot Andrewes, *Ninety-Six Sermons, Vol. 3* (Oxford, 1841), p. 143, 144.

27 Ibid., p. 161.

28 Ibid., p. 179.

29 Ibid., p. 199.

30 Ibid., p. 279.

31 Nicholas Lossky, *Lancelot Andrewes The Preacher (1555-1626)* (Oxford, 1991), p. 342. He also asserts that Andrewes's pneumatological approach distinguishes him from receptionists and virtualists. While this is certainly true of the former, it is not necessarily true of the latter.

> ... that that which before was earthly and common bread, by the words of institution, the invocation of God's name and divine virtue, is made a sacrament of the true body and blood of Christ, visibly sitting at the right hand of God in heaven, and yet after an invisible and incomprehensible manner present in the Church. And that the body and blood of Christ are in the sacrament, and exhibited and given as spiritual meat and drink for the salvation and everlasting life of them that are worthy partakers of the same.[32]

Consecration is thus by the dual means of institution and invocation.

William Forbes (1585-1634), a Scot, and later to become the first Bishop of Edinburgh, wrote his *Considerationes Modestae* probably in the second decade of the seventeenth century.[33] His contention is that the majority of 'sound Protestants' reject a theory of consecration by the eucharistic words only; rather it is 'by the mystical prayer also whereby the descent of the Holy Ghost is implored, that He may sanctify the elements'. Indeed, his view of consecration is wider, embracing 'the whole service in so far as it is performed, both by the minister and the communicants, according to Christ's institution'.[34] It was his conviction that Scripture and the Fathers supported the view that the elements are consecrated by prayer and invocation.

The role of the Spirit in the eucharist is eloquently attested to by James Ussher (1581-1655), Archbishop of Armagh from 1625 to 1655. In a sermon preached to the House of Commons in February 1620 he expounds his view that through the sacrament the communicant is spiritually united to Christ. As Christ is in heaven and the communicant on earth, the means of union is 'the quickening Spirit descending downward from the Head, to be in us a fountain of supernatural life; and a lively faith, wrought by the same Spirit, ascending from us upward, to lay fast hold upon him ...'.[35] Ussher expounds the Christian possession of the Spirit in general terms and poses the question that if Christians have both the Spirit and faith, of what further avail is the sacrament? His answer is that the Spirit is received, as it were, by instalments, so that the communion is a continual source of spiritual nourishment. However, he warns against preoccupation with the outward elements. Of themselves, they are unable to communicate grace; but by God's blessing upon the eating and drinking of them grace is bestowed. Therefore by a supernatural act of God, there is a real reception of the Spirit through communion.[36]

Thomas Morton (1564-1659), published his *Of the Institution of the Sacrament of the Blessed Bodie and Blood of Christ, (by some called) the Masse of Christ* in 1631, when he was Bishop of Coventry and Lichfield, the year before his translation to Durham. Morton understands the eucharistic words of Jesus in a figurative sense,[37] and rejects a corporal presence of Christ in the sacrament. The bread and wine are

---

32 Richard Field, *Of the Church, Vol. IV* (Cambridge, 1852), p. 302.

33 Kenneth Stevenson, *Covenant of Grace Renewed* (London, 1994), p. 80.

34 William Forbes, *Considerationes Modestae et Pacificae, Vol. 2* (Oxford, 1856), p. 531.

35 *The Whole Works of the Most Rev. James Ussher, Vol. 2* (Dublin and London, 1847), pp. 431-432.

36 Ibid., pp. 434-437.

37 Thomas Morton, *Of the Institution of the Sacrament of the Blessed Bodie and Blood of Christ ..., Eight Bookes* (London, 1631), Book 2, chapters 1, 2, pp. 82-101.

not changed into Christ's body and blood, but, citing Isidore, '*The change of visible things, by the Spirit of God, into a Sacrament of Christ's Body*'.[38] The sacrament has an earthly part, the eating and drinking of the elements, and a heavenly, spiritual part:

> Answerable to both these is the double nourishment and *Union* of a Christian; the one Sacramentall, by communicating of the outward Elements of *Bread and Wine*, united to man's body in his *Taking, Eating*, digesting, till at length it be *transubstantiated* into him, by being substantially incorporated in his *flesh*. The other, which is the *Spirituall*, and Soules food is the *Body* and *Blood* of the Lord (therefore called *Spirituall*, because it is the Object of *Faith*) by a *Union* wrought by God's Spirit, and man's faith; which (as hath been professed by Protestants) is most *Reall* and *Ineffable*.[39]

Thus Morton, like Hooker, has an instrumental understanding of the elements, which enable spiritual union through the work of the Holy Spirit.

John Bramhall (1594-1663), succeeded Ussher as Archbishop of Armagh in 1661 after a five-year interregnum. He defended Anglican belief in 'a true Real Presence', but like Field, asserts that Anglicans follow the teaching of the 'Primitive Church', in contradistinction to Rome, by not speculating unduly about the manner of his presence. So theories about presence are to be regarded as opinions of the Schools not as an article of faith.[40] His understanding of consecration is most clearly expounded in *The Consecration and Succession of Protestant Bishops Justified* of 1658:

> They who are ordained Priests, ought to have power to consecrate the Sacrament of the Body and Blood of Christ, that is, to make Them present after such manner as They were present at the first institution; whether it be done by enunciation of the words of Christ, as it is observed in the Western Church, or by prayer, as it is practised in the Eastern Church; or whether these two be both the same thing in effect, that is, that the forms of the Sacraments be mystical prayers, and implicit invocations. Our Church for more abundant caution useth both forms, as well in the consecration of the Sacrament, as in the ordination of Priests.[41]

He was insistent, however, that Christ is the chief consecrator still.[42] Bramhall clearly regarded the 'Hear us...' clause as the equivalent of the eastern *epiclesis*, placing the emphasis more on the role of petition than explicit reference to the Spirit.

Thomas Jackson (1579-1640), President of Corpus Christi College, Oxford, and Dean of Peterborough, also argues that the ancient church, while holding a real communication of Christ's body and blood in the sacrament, refrained from speculation as to the manner of the gift. Jackson understands the Spirit as the means of union between the Christian and Christ's humanity:

---

38 Ibid., Book 3, chapter 4, p. 134.

39 Ibid., Book 5, chapter 1, p. 210.

40 *The Works of John Bramhall* (Oxford, 1842), *Vol. 1*, pp. 8, 22; *Vol. 2*, p. 211.

41 *The Works of John Bramhall, Vol. 3* (Oxford, 1844), p. 165.

42 Ibid.

> For although the Holy Spirit ... doth immediately and by personal propriety work faith and other spiritual graces in our souls, yet doth he not by these spiritual graces unite our souls or spirits immediately unto himself, but unto Christ's human nature ... The spirit of life, whereby our adoption and election is sealed unto us, is the real participation of Christ's body, which was broken, and of Christ's blood, which was shed for us.[43]

Applied to consecration, the action of the Spirit was necessary if communion was to be effectual:

> We may consecrate the elements of bread and wine, and administer them so consecrated as undoubted pledges of his body and blood, by which the new covenant was sealed, and the general pardon purchased; yet, unless, he grant some actual influence of his Spirit, and suffer such virtue to go out from his human nature now placed in his sanctuary ... we do not really receive his body and blood with the elements of bread and wine ... But with whomsoever he is virtually present, that is, to whomsoever he communicates the influence of his body and blood by his Spirit, he is really present with them, though locally absent from them.[44]

For Jackson, therefore, the presence of Christ is truly a spiritual presence, mediated by the Spirit, whereby the communicant receives the virtue of Christ's body and blood.

The writings of Jeremy Taylor (1613-1667) are most significant, not only for the volume of his work on the eucharist but also for the liturgy he produced during the period of the Commonwealth. In his earlier works, references to the Spirit are somewhat sparse, although there are indications of later development. So in *The Great Exemplar* of 1649 we have a clear statement that the Spirit operates through the sacrament, and a special correspondence is drawn between the Spirit and Christ's blood, a theme to which he returns in later writings: 'Whatsoever the Spirit can convey to the body of the church, we may expect from this sacrament; for as the Spirit is the instrument of life and action, so the blood of Christ is the conveyance of His Spirit.'[45] Similarly, in *Holy Living* (1650) the eucharist and sanctification are intimately linked; the elements are not to be regarded as common bread and wine:

> ... but holy in their use, holy in their signification, holy in their change, and holy in their effect: and believe, if thou art a worthy communicant, thou dost as verily receive Christ's body and blood to all effects and purposes of the Spirit as thou dost receive the blessed elements into thy mouth, that thou puttest thy finger to His hand ...[46]

In *Clerus Domini* (1651) Taylor begins to give fuller expression, particularly in his understanding of consecration. The sacrament of the Lord's Supper 'is hallowed and lifted up from the common bread and wine by mystical prayers and solemn invocations of God'.[47] For Taylor, the traditional 'words of consecration', which he prefers to call 'words of institution', are part of a prayer. They are not simply

43 *The Works of Thomas Jackson, Vol. 10* (Oxford, 1844), p. 40.
44 *The Works of Thomas Jackson, Vol. 9*, p. 610.
45 *The Whole Works of the Right Rev. Jeremy Taylor, Vol. 2* (London, 1850), p. 645.
46 Taylor, *Works, Vol. 3*, p. 218.
47 Ibid., *Vol. 1*, p. 45.

a narration, but in the ancient liturgies they are accompanied by a petition 'let this bread be made the body of Christ, etc.'[48] Such liturgies set out the 'signification of the rite, the glory of the change, the operation of the Spirit, the death of Christ, and the memory of the sacrifice: but this great work which all Christians knew to be done by the holy Ghost, the priest did obtain by prayer and solemn invocation'.[49] Taylor is clear that consecration is 'by way of prayer' and that 'the holy Ghost is the consecrator', 'called down by the prayers of the church, presented by the priests'. The Spirit comes by way of prayer, not simply by the force of 'a certain number of syllables'.[50] Taylor argues that the Greek churches have preserved the first and most ancient form of consecration better than the west, where he clearly has the *epiclesis* in view, while the role of the narrative is 'used for argument to move God to hallow the gifts', and as an expression and determination of the desire.[51] Henry McAdoo, in his full treatment of Taylor's eucharistic theology, comments that for Taylor 'sacraments are not forms automatically producing effects' but that 'the essential sacramental principle' is the prayer of the Church in obedience to Christ; what is ritual is joined with what is moral.[52]

Such an understanding of the role of invocation is illustrated by the liturgy Taylor drew up in 1658 for his ministry at the Golden Grove. The service book *A Collection of Offices* included a eucharistic rite and there are a number of interesting features in relation to the work of the Spirit. In the ante-communion, a prayer following the beatitudes and preceding the readings runs:

> ... and hast commanded to us this service in the power of the holy Ghost, and obedience of the Lord Jesus ... so vouchsafe by the hands of us miserable sinners to finish and perfect this oblation, that it may be sanctified by the holy Ghost, and be accepted in the Lord Jesus ...[53]

This is adapted from the prayer in the *proskomide* of the Liturgy of St James, immediately prior to the prayer of the veil.[54] Later in the rite, the confession requests sanctification of the worshippers by the Spirit, and in the second of the two prayers of absolution forgiveness of sins is asked 'by Thy word and by Thy Spirit'.[55] Taylor adapted this from the Greek Orthodox rite for auricular confession.[56] The ante-communion is concluded by the *sursum corda*, preface and *sanctus/benedictus*. Then the communion rite begins with a period of silence, the Lord's Prayer, a 'denunciation' based on the cherubic hymn from St James, and then the following rubric and *epiclesis*:

48 Ibid., pp. 45-46.

49 Ibid., p. 46.

50 Ibid., p. 48.

51 Ibid., p. 49.

52 H.R. McAdoo, *The Eucharistic Theology of Jeremy Taylor* (Norwich, 1988), p. 58.

53 Taylor, *Works, Vol. 8*, p. 618.

54 Harry Boone Porter, *Jeremy Taylor: Liturgist* (London, 1979), p. 73.

55 Taylor, *Works, Vol. 8*, p. 621.

56 Porter, *Jeremy Taylor*, p. 53. The reference to the Spirit is an addition by Taylor.

> *Then shall follow this prayer of consecration, to be said by the minister standing.*
> HAVE mercy upon us, O Heavenly Father, according to Thy glorious mercies and promises, send Thy holy Ghost upon our hearts, and let Him also descend upon these gifts, that by His good, His holy, His glorious presence, He may sanctify and enlighten our hearts, and He may bless and sanctifie these gifts.
> That this bread may become the holy body of Christ. *Amen.*
> And this chalice may become the life-giving blood of Christ. *Amen.*
> That it may become unto all that partake of it this day, a blessed instrument of union with Christ, of pardon and peace, of health and blessing, of holiness and life eternal, through Jesus Christ our Lord. *Amen.*[57]

The eucharistic action continues with a prayer adapted from the post-*sanctus* of St James, the institution narrative with direction for the minister to touch the elements at the 'this is' clauses, a congregational acclamation, and an *anamnesis* and supplication again drawn from St James. Taylor's *epiclesis* is also based on St James. The double reference to 'hearts' is Taylor's own work, while he substitutes the verb 'may become' for the petition in St James that the Spirit may 'make' the gifts Christ's body and blood. Porter has observed that the manual actions in the narrative are similar (though by no means identical) to the Scottish Liturgy.[58] The position of the *epiclesis* also has a certain correspondence to the preliminary position in 1549 and 1637, a very deliberate amendment to the order of St James. It may well be that Taylor wished to give primacy to the *epiclesis* in the light of what he says in *Clerus Domini*. In this sense, there can be no doubt that consecration is in the context of prayer. As for the fruits prayed for at the end of the *epiclesis*, here, after the phrase 'that it may become for all that partake', Taylor parts company with St James. Bryan Spinks has observed that the fruits listed are the ones which Taylor expounds at length in *The Worthy Communicant*,[59] thus freely leaving his source for the sake of his own theological and practical understanding.[60] Taylor's most eloquent expression of the role of the Spirit comes in his latest work dealing with the eucharist, *The Worthy Communicant* of 1660, written shortly before his consecration as Bishop of Down and Connor. His sacramental teaching is in the context of an understanding that all the graces of Christ are bestowed on a Christian through the Holy Spirit. So, in relation to the 'Bread of Life' discourse of John 6, 'this eating and drinking of Christ's flesh and blood can only be done by ministries of life and of the Spirit ...'.[61] Time and again, he stresses the utter centrality of the action of the Spirit in the efficacy of the sacraments:

---

57 Ibid., p. 624.

58 Ibid., p. 77.

59 Spinks, 'Two Seventeenth-Century Examples of *Lex Credendi, Lex Orandi*: The Baptismal and Eucharistic Theologies and Liturgies of Jeremy Taylor and Richard Baxter', *Studia Liturgica*, 21 (1991): 184.

60 While Taylor's provision of an *epiclesis* can be related directly to the rubric in the Westminster *Directory* that the gifts are blessed and sanctified, Robert Sanderson's liturgy for use in the Commonwealth reproduced with a little amendment the 'Hear us' petition of the Prayer Book, William Jacobson (ed.), *Fragmentary Illustrations of the History of the Book of Common Prayer* (London, 1874), pp. 26–27.

61 Taylor, *Works, Vol. 8*, p. 16.

> ... for neither the external act nor the internal grace and morality does effect our pardon and salvation; but the Spirit of God who blesses the symbols, and assists the duty; makes them holy, and this acceptable ... but neither the outward nor the inward part does effect it; neither the sacrament, nor the moral disposition; only the Spirit operates in the sacrament and the communicant receives it by his moral dispositions, by the hand of faith.[62]

McAdoo, following Darwell Stone, points out that Taylor was influenced by the eucharistic teaching of Origen and Clement of Alexandria. This comes out, both in the quotation from *Clerus Domini* above and in passages in *The Worthy Communicant* such as: 'The "flesh" of Christ is His word; the "blood" of Christ is His spirit; and by believing in His word, and being assisted and conducted by His spirit, we are nourished up to life; and so Christ is our food, so He becomes life unto our souls.'[63] Taylor makes much of biblical and Patristic links between 'blood' and 'Spirit'; the analogy suited his purposes in rejecting crude materialism and underlined his insistence the eucharist is an encounter embracing divine gift and human response. The flesh and blood of Christ are truly given; the receiving of them is also the work of God, inspiring 'belief', bestowing the Spirit, and so nourishing the Christian in all spiritual virtues.

Dugmore, in a passing reference to *The Worthy Communicant*, describes Taylor's theology therein as having a 'strongly mystical note'.[64] This is nowhere expressed more strongly than when Taylor writes that the sacraments 'are instruments of grace in the hand of God, and by these His holy spirit changes our hearts and translates us into a divine nature'.[65] And, 'if the word ministered by the Spirit is so mighty, it must be more when the word and the Spirit join with the sacrament, which is their proper significatory'.[66]

The issue of Christian unity was foundational for Herbert Thorndike (1598-1672). It was necessary for him that Anglican formularies should be seen to conform to the manner of consecration held by the Church from the beginning. From his comprehensive study of primitive Christianity, Thorndike asserts that consecration is not effected by a simple rehearsal of the eucharistic words but rather by thanksgiving and invocation. He assigns a special role to the Spirit and his theology and this is well expressed in a passage from his work *Just Weights and Measures*, first published in 1662. Consecration is effected:

> ... by the act of the Church, upon God's word of institution, praying, that the Holy Ghost, coming down upon the present elements, 'may make them the Body and Blood of Christ'. Not by changing them into the nature of flesh and blood; as the bread and wine, that nourished our Lord Christ on earth, became the Flesh and Blood of the Son of God by becoming the Flesh and Blood of his Manhood, hypostatically united to his Godhead; saith St. Gregory Nyssen: but immediately and *ipso facto* by being united to the Spirit of Christ, that is, His Godhead. For the Flesh and Blood of Christ by incarnation, the elements by

62 Ibid., pp. 27-28.

63 Ibid., p. 18.

64 C.W. Dugmore, *Eucharistic Doctrine in England from Hooker to Waterland* (London, 1942), p. 101.

65 Taylor, *Works, Vol. 8*, p. 32.

66 Ibid., p. 48.

> consecration, being united to the Spirit, that is, the Godhead of Christ, become one both sacramentally, by being both one with the Spirit or Godhead of Christ, to the conveying of God's Spirit to a Christian.[67]

In an earlier work, *Of Religious Assemblies, and the Publick Service of God*, published in 1642, Thorndike asserted his attraction to the liturgy of *Apostolic Constitutions 8* as the model of primitive worship.[68] Here he set out his understanding that consecration is effected by three entities: thanksgiving, the rehearsal of the narrative and a prayer of petition 'for the effect to which the elements, when they became this Sacrament, are deputed'.[69] He argues that the third element would have been part of Jesus's prayer and that such a petition was 'always used in the Church, to obtain of God the promise which the institution of Christ supposeth'.[70] This understanding is also expounded in Thorndike's great work, *An Epilogue to the Tragedy of the Church of England*, which appeared in 1659. It included three books, the last of which, 'Of the Laws of the Church' includes his exposition of eucharistic theology. On the basis of his study of the institution narratives, he asserts the identity of 'blessing' and 'giving thanks'. He refers explicitly to 1 Timothy 3:4, 5 – that food must be received with thanksgiving for then it is sanctified by the word of God and prayer. Here the Church is following the Jewish tradition of thanksgiving. But the reference to 'sanctified by prayer' suggests that, as well as thanksgiving, prayer is made to God for a blessing upon the food.[71] Applied to the eucharist, consecration must include thanksgiving and petition. The narrative of institution does not consecrate, but ought to be retained because of church tradition and the promise enshrined in the words of declaration. In the historic liturgies, petition is identified with the invocation, including in many ancient rites request for the illapse of the Spirit. But he is careful to relate the invocation of the Spirit on the elements to the sanctification of the worshippers:

> And yet there is no more said in those liturgies, which pray, that the Spirit of God may make them the Flesh and Blood of Christ to this intent and effect, that those which received them may be filled with the grace of His Spirit. For the expression of this effect and intent limits the common signification of the words to that which is proper to this action of the eucharist.[72]

Time and again he asserts that, through consecration, the gifts become the means of conveying the Holy Spirit; that as Christ was filled with the Spirit, so the 'supernatural conjunction' of the elements with the body and blood means that the elements convey Spirit to those who receive them rightly.[73] Rejecting transubstantiation, Thorndike understands the change in the elements wrought by consecration as 'consisting in

---

67 *The Theological Works of Herbert Thorndike, Vol. 5* (Oxford, 1854), p. 173.

68 Buxton asserts that he may have been the originator of Anglican interest in this rite, *Eucharist and Institution Narrative*, pp. 122-123.

69 Thorndike, *Works, Vol. 1*, part 1 (Oxford, 1844), p. 342.

70 Ibid., p. 346.

71 Thorndike, *Works, Vol. 4*, part 1 (Oxford, 1852), p. 53.

72 Ibid., p. 77.

73 Ibid., pp. 25, 29, 32, 50.

the assistance of the Holy Ghost, Which makes the elements, in which It dwells, the Body and Blood of Christ; it is not necessary, that we acknowledge the bodily substance of them to be any way abolished'.[74] Rather, through the operation of the Spirit, the elements, remaining bread and wine, become Christ's body and blood sacramentally and mystically by the Spirit's indwelling of the elements, received by Christ's promise as his Body and Blood, in the same way in which the Spirit indwelt Christ in his incarnation. In relation to Anglican liturgy, while he regarded the Prayer Book as agreeable to church tradition on the eucharist, it is not surprising in view of his theology that he regarded the form of consecration in 1549 and the Scottish Liturgy to be superior.[75] Kenneth Stevenson rightly asserts that, in relation to his stress on the place of thanksgiving arising from Jewish *berakoth*, he was 'far ahead of his time'.[76]

Finally in this section, reference ought to be made to a significant commentary on the Prayer Book, Hamon L'Estrange's *Alliance of Divine Offices* first published in 1659. He argues that the Anglican liturgy was, in the most, 'extant in the usage of the primitive Church long before the popish mass was ever dreamt of' and that there is 'an admirable harmony, even in external rites, between the Church of England and those ancient fathers'.[77] He makes a distinction between *eucharistia* and *eulogia*, the latter meaning an invocation of God's blessing upon the elements. Consecration of the elements was made with thanksgiving, not by it: '*by blessing* it was performed, *by blessing* joyned with *thanksgiving* in one continued form of prayer, or *by blessing* concomitant with *thanksgiving* in two distinct formes'.[78] He rejects consecration by narrative only, and the Roman view of transubstantiation, continuing: 'Therefore I must adhere in judgement to those learned men, who derive *Consecration* from *the word of God and Prayer*, the very way by which our Saviour himself sanctified those Elements in His first institution.'[79] When Jesus 'blessed' the elements (Matt. 26:26), the intention was to invoke God's blessing on them 'to those ends, for which he meant by his institution to separate and depute them'.[80] While the ancient Fathers included the narrative of institution with words of thanksgiving and blessing they were clear that the elements are not 'sanctified any other way than by Prayer'.[81] In this respect he is following the same argument as Jeremy Taylor. Thus, the words of institution are not sufficient by themselves to effect consecration, and he argues that the taking of the elements, as required in the 1549 rite, ought to be restored, but from the words 'grant that we receiving' to the end of the institution, for 'the words of Invocation of Gods blessing, joyntly with those of Christ's Institution, constitute the *Consecration*'.[82]

74 Ibid., p. 34.

75 Thorndike, *Just Weights and Measures, Works, Vol. 5*, pp. 245-246.

76 Stevenson, *Eucharist and Offering*, p. 145.

77 Hamon L'Estrange, *The Alliance of Divine Offices* (London, 1659), from the preamble.

78 Ibid., p. 212.

79 Ibid., p. 215.

80 Ibid., p. 216.

81 Ibid.

82 Ibid., p. 217.

Liturgical Revision

Scotland

While Calvin's eucharistic writing included a rich theology of the Spirit,[83] this is not reflected in his liturgical work, where he essentially follows Martin Bucer's *The Psalter, With Complete Church Practice* of 1539. Calvin's *La Forme des prières* (1542) was adapted by some of the English exiles at Frankfurt during the reign of Mary Tudor, including John Knox. Knox himself had previously produced a liturgy for his ministry at Berwick-on-Tweed in 1550. Neither of these rites included any invocatory material. While Knox objected to the oblationary references in the 1549 canon, his later objection to kneeling to receive communion for fear that it suggested adoration may also suggest that he would have regarded the 1549 *epiclesis* on the elements as a dangerous inclusion. Knox was eventually driven out of Frankfurt by those who remained loyal to 1552 and went to Geneva where *The Form of Prayers and Ministration of the Sacraments* was published in 1556. The eucharistic rite includes a prayer of thanksgiving after the minister had taken the bread and wine. This was a variant on Calvin where an exhortation occupies the equivalent place in the rite. The prayer includes no reference to consecration or any role of the Spirit in relation to the eucharistic action. Knox introduced *The Form* to Scotland on his return in 1559. Before 1559, the 1552 *Book of Common Prayer* (*BCP*) had been used in Scotland and it continued 'in some, perhaps many, parishes until well into the 1570s'.[84] The first Scottish edition of *The Form* was published in 1562 and it was formally adopted by the General Assembly in 1564.[85] It eventually became known as the *Book of Common Order* (*BCO*). An abortive attempt to modify the *BCO* was made in 1601. The General Assembly rejected proposals for the alteration and deletion of certain prayers, but agreed that some additional prayers should be provided. This, however, did not come to fruition.[86]

The General Assembly of 1616 appointed a committee for the revision of the *BCO*. In 1616, a revised liturgy, known as *Hewat's* (or *Howat's*) *Draft* was drawn up, but it contained nothing on the sacraments.[87] A second draft, probably to be dated

---

83 John Calvin, *Institutes of the Christian Religion*, Book 4, chapter 17. There is significant development of Calvin's thought between the 1536 and 1559 editions.

84 William D. Maxwell, *A History of Worship in the Church of Scotland* (London, 1955), p. 45.

85 George R. Burnet, *The Holy Communion in the Reformed Church of Scotland 1560-1960* (Edinburgh, 1960), p. 9. Gordon Donaldson makes the clarification that the General Assembly of the Church of Scotland prescribed its use for the sacraments in 1562 and for 'common prayers' in 1564, G. Donaldson, 'Reformation to Covenant', in Duncan Forrester and Douglas Murray (eds), *Studies in the History of Worship in Scotland* (Edinburgh, 1984), p. 36.

86 Gordon Donaldson, *The Making of the Scottish Prayer Book of 1637* (Edinburgh, 1954), p. 31.

87 *A Form of Service to be Used in All the Parish Churches of Scotland upon the Sabbath Day*, from G.W. Sprott (ed.), *Scottish Liturgies of James VI* (Edinburgh, 1901), pp. 1-23.

1616-17, was more comprehensive.[88] The eucharistic rite was entitled 'The Ordour to be Observed in Tyme of Holie Communion'. After the minister came from the pulpit to the table the order specified a taking of the bread and cup and the rubric continued 'he shall blesse and give thanks', using the prayer following or one like it. The prayer contained the following invocation:

> He wes offred to thee on the crosse in a sacrifice for satisfaction of thy justice and is geven to us of thy mercie a food for our soule in this sacrament. Lord bless it that it may be unto us ane effectual exhibiting instrument of the Lord Jesus, for we come here to seeke the Phisician of our soules and to celebrat with thanksgeving the remembrance of his death and passion untill his coming againe ...[89]

At the end of the prayer, the minister was to repeat 'the words of consecration', by which was meant the institution narrative, first the words relating to the bread followed by distribution and exhortation to stir up the affection of the hearers, and then the cup-saying, with distribution and further exhortation. In the latter case, a text is given:

> Lift up your harts unto the Lord, lay hold by faith upon Jesus, whom God the Father, by his Spirit, offers to you in this holie sacrament that ye may draw virtue from the Lord, to quicken and conserve your soules and bodies unto eternal lyfe.[90]

This text is of significance because it makes a distinction between the 'blessing' of the elements in the thanksgiving prayer, and the 'words of consecration' which it identifies as the institution narrative. The exhortation, recalling the *sursum corda*, with the reference to the Spirit, gives explicit liturgical expression to Calvin's theology. Indeed, 'effectual exhibiting instrument' echoes Calvin's language where he argues that the Lord 'works in us inwardly by his holy Spirit, in order to give efficacy to his ordinance, which he has appointed for that purpose as an instrument whereby he wills to do his work in us'.[91]

If the second draft looked to the *BCO* for inspiration, the third draft looked to the *BCP*, reflecting James's attempt to bring Scotland and England closer together in liturgical form. Both drafts two and three are ascribed to William Cowper, Bishop of Galloway, and the date of the third draft is 1618/19.[92] After coming down from the pulpit, the minister read the collect for purity, a reading from 1 Corinthians 11, an exhortation (including a ministerial excommunication of those who continued in sin without repentance) from the *BCO*, the invitation to confession, and then a long prayer beginning with the Prayer Book confession and including in the course of it the words:

---

88 G. Donaldson (ed.), 'A Scottish Liturgy of the Reign of James VI', *Scottish Historical Society Miscellany 10* (Edinburgh, 1965).

89 Ibid., p. 109.

90 Ibid., p. 110.

91 Cited by E.C. Ratcliff, 'Puritan Alternatives to the Prayer Book: The *Directory* and Richard Baxter's *Reformed Liturgy*', in *The English Prayer Book 1549-1662* (London, 1963) p. 69, fn. 1.

92 Donaldson, 'A Scottish Liturgy of the Reign of James VI', pp. 90-91; Donaldson, *Studies in the History of Worship in Scotland*, pp. 45-46.

> Mercifull father wee beseech thee that wee receiving these thy creatures of bread and wine, according to thy sonne our Saviour his holy institution, may be partakers of his most blissed body and blood. Send doune o Lord thy blissing upon this Sacrament, that it may be unto us the effectual exhibitive instrument of the Lord Jesus.[93]

At the end of this prayer the Lord's Prayer was said, and then a rubric directed the minister 'to repeat the words of the institution for consecrating the elements', with prescribed manual acts for the taking of the bread and wine. Another hand has, however, added an alternative form of words in the margin: 'Then shall the Minister pray after this manner, and reading the words of the Institution'. The alternative text avoids the idea of 'words of consecration'. Before the administration, the minister then said the '*sursum corda*' exhortation as above, cast in 'us' form.[94]

In his edition of the text, G.W. Sprott cites a reference from Cowper that the sacramental bread 'appointed by God to be a sign and a seal, and an exhibiting instrument of Christ's body'.[95] In notes on the text, he further amplifies the reference:

> The word 'exhibit' was then understood as equivalent to 'apply'; and it was constantly used of the Lord's Supper to set forth the doctrine of the Reformed Church - that the elements are the instruments by which Christ's body and blood are imparted to the faithful. Thus Cowper says - the elements 'are not only signs representing Christ crucified, nor seals confirming our faith in Him, but also effectual instruments of exhibition, whereby the Holy Spirit makes an inward application of Christ crucified to all that are his.'[96]

On the rubrics relating to the institution narrative, Sprott argues that the uncorrected text mirrors Roman and Anglican views on consecration, and was adhered to by the prelatic party in the Church of Scotland. The anti-prelatic party held to the eastern and primitive doctrine that the elements are sanctified by the word of God and prayer.[97] In the end the revision came to nothing. In the light of the stormy passage of the Five Articles, James did not press for liturgical reform.[98]

The lack of any invocatory reference in the *BCO* was clearly felt by some, who inserted an appropriate petition. William D. Maxwell sets out the evidence in full in his edition of the 1556 *Genevan Service Book*. The key verb appears to be 'bless', applied either to the minister or the Lord. The oft-quoted citation from John Row relating to a communion service in St Giles Cathedral in 1622 refers to a blessing of 'the elements or action'.[99] William McMillan cites a quotation from 1640 stating that 'the minister giveth thanks ... and prayeth earnestly to God for His powerful presence and effectual working

---

93 Sprott, *Scottish Liturgies of James VI* , p. 93.

94 Ibid., pp. 93-94.

95 Ibid., p. 93.

96 Ibid., p. 151.

97 Ibid., p. 152.

98 Burnet, *The Holy Communion in the Reformed Church of Scotland 1560-1960*, p. 94; Donaldson, *The Making of the Scottish Prayer Book*, p. 39.

99 William D. Maxwell, *The Liturgical Portions of the Genevan Service Book* (Westminster, 1965), pp. 134-135; Maxwell, *A History of Worship in the Church of Scotland*, pp. 61 (fn. 1), 63.

to accompany His own ordinances'. Another refers to the practice of a 'common blessing of the elements in the beginning of the action', and describing this blessing as the 'Prayer of Consecration'.[100]

Attempts at liturgical reform were revived by Charles I in 1629 when he asked to see Cowper's liturgy of 1619. The wish of the King and Archbishop Laud was that Scotland should adopt the English Prayer Book. John Maxwell, Bishop of Edinburgh, however, pressed for a liturgy written by the Scots themselves. While the first Scottish edition of the English Prayer Book was printed in 1633, Scottish persistence won the day and in 1634, the King gave the Scottish bishops permission to draw up a liturgy so long as it was as close to the English as possible. In 1634, a copy of the English book with additional material, known as the *Haddington Book*, was signed by the King and brought to Scotland. The communion office was practically unchanged, but the bishops regarded it as a basis for revision. The initiative was seized by James Wedderburn who, on his appointment as Bishop of Dunblane in 1636, sent suggestions for revision to William Laud, Archbishop of Canterbury. Wedderburn clearly looked to 1549 as his inspiration, and while not all his suggestions were accepted, Laud wrote up those that were in a book known as the *Christchurch Book* and it was agreed by the King. As well as restoring the 1549 *anamnesis*, the prayer of oblation and the Lord's Prayer after the institution narrative and re-siting the prayer of humble access after the Lord's Prayer, the book restored a 1549-type *epiclesis* before the narrative. The *epiclesis* was retained in the definitive version, eventually published in 1637.[101] The text reads:

> Hear us, O merciful Father, we most humbly beseech thee, and of thy Almighty goodness vouchsafe so to bless and sanctify with thy word and Holy Spirit these thy gifts and creatures of bread and wine, that they may be unto us the body and blood of thy most dearly beloved Son; so that we, receiving them according to thy Son our Saviour Jesus Christ's holy institution, in remembrance of his death and passion, may be partakers of the same his most precious body and blood.[102]

The prayer containing the *epiclesis* is called 'the Prayer of Consecration' in a rubric which continues 'then, during the time of Consecration, he shall stand at such a part of the holy Table, where he may with all the more ease and decency use both his hands'. Moreover, the presbyter is directed by rubric to take the paten and chalice into his hands and to lay his hands upon any chalice or flagon he intends to consecrate during the institution narrative. The form of consecration is therefore *epiclesis* and institution narrative, though the form for supplementary consecration prescribes the repetition of the narrative only.

While derived from 1549, the Scottish text inverts the order of 'Holy Spirit and word' and combines the 1549 'may be unto us' clause with the 'may be partakers' of the English 1552/1604 prayer. The inversion of the order may well have been to give

---

100 William McMillan, *The Worship of the Scottish Reformed Church 1550-1638* (London, 1931), p. 171.

101 The background to the 1637 rite is fully set out in Donaldson, *The Making of the Scottish Prayer Book of 1637*, pp. 41-59.

102 Text from ibid., pp. 198-199.

primary reference to the 'word' or institution narrative, while the somewhat clumsy combination of texts was probably to allay fears of popery. That such fears were not allayed is evidenced from the violent reaction to the book. George Burnet comments that there is nothing in the rite to suggest any safeguard against transubstantiation.[103] The rubric directing the presbyter to stand in such a way as to use both hands and the omission of Cranmer's 1549 rubric forbidding elevation is a case in point. The historian John Row (c. 1598-1672) argues that the form of *epiclesis* makes it quite different from the 'English Book', 'for severall words in the English Booke, quhilk seeme opposite to the corporall presence of the Sacrament, is left out in the Scottish Booke', so that

> It hath the Oblation of the bread and wyne to God befor the consecration. It hath the verie Popish Consecration, that the Lord wold sanctifie, by His Word and Holy Spirit, 'these creatures of bread and wyne, that they may be vnto vs the bodie and blood of his Sonne;' and then repeits the words of Institution to God for that purpose: It hath ane Oblation of it againe, after it is consecrate … It hath taken away the spirituall eating anmd drinking by faith mentioned in the English Liturgie.[104]

However, the forms of invocation in, for example, *Cowper's Draft* and, in time, the Westminster *Directory*, are more related to a blessing of the elements in their use as a means of grace than a petition for a change in the elements. Gordon Donaldson, in commenting upon the tradition of supplementing the *BCO* by adding an invocation,[105] says that *Cowper's Draft* 'represents the thought – though, one hopes, not the language – which was common'.[106] But there appear to be no grounds for asserting that a different language was employed. In these terms, 1637 could be interpreted as importing a form of prayer equivalent to the *Quam oblationem*, to which the addition of the 1604 'receptionist' words was merely a sop. The objection was not to a 'blessing' but the form of this particular blessing. While the chief objection to 1637 was doubtless political – a perceived 'English' book forced upon unwilling Scots – the form of *epiclesis* can be regarded as leaving the door for such criticism wide open.[107]

In discussing the Scottish Liturgy it is convenient at this point to examine the attitude of William Laud (1573-1645) to the *epiclesis*. In his work *The History of the Troubles of William Laud* he cites the criticism of the *epiclesis* by the Scottish Commissioners for teaching that the corporal presence of Christ's body was in the sacrament, implying a change in the elements by a work of God's omnipotency.

---

103 Ibid., p. 97.

104 John Row, *The Historie of the Kirk of Scotland, Part II* (1842), pp. 501-502; see Donaldson, *The Making of the Scottish Prayer Book of 1637*, p. 72.

105 See Spinks, *Sacraments, Ceremonies and the Stuart Divines*, pp. 124, 125. William Maxwell cites David Calderwood, writing in 1620, that it had been the custom in Scotland for sixty years to 'bless' the bread and wine, *An Outline of Christian Worship* (London, 1936), p. 125.

106 Donaldson, *The Making of the Scottish Prayer Book of 1637*, p. 68.

107 Contra Donaldson, *Studies in the History of Worship in Scotland*, p. 48, who suggests that the 1637 *epiclesis* was a concession to existing Scottish practice.

They argued that the petition was derived from the 'Mass-book' and that it was sharply criticized by Bucer. Laud replied:

> Well, and a work of omnipotency it is, whatever the change be. For less than Omnipotence cannot change those elements, either in nature, or use, to so high a service as they are put in that great Sacrament. And therefore the invocating of God's Almighty goodness to effect this by them, is no proof at all of intending the 'corporal presence of Christ in this Sacrament.' 'Tis true, this passage is not in the Prayer of Consecration in the Service-book of England; but I wish with all my heart it were. For though the consecration of the elements may be without it, yet it is much more solemn and full by that invocation.[108]

Laud also responded to the charge that 'may be to us' could be rendered *ut fiant nobis* and so teach the corporal presence by arguing that 'to us' rather contradicted transubstantiation and affirmed 'the real, and yet spiritual use of them'.[109] A further insight into his thought can be seen in his work *A Summarie of Devotions*, in the section entitled 'Eucharistia': 'I quarrel not the words of Thy Son my Saviour's blessed Institution. I know His words are no gross unnatural conceit, but they are spirit and life, and supernatural.'[110] The implication is that 1549/1637 *epiclesis* gives expression to role of the Spirit in effecting Christ's words. The form of the 1637 prayer of consecration continued to influence the thinking of Anglican writers of the so-called 'Laudian' school.

England

Early English Reformed rites were influenced by *The Form of Prayers* supplemented by material from the Netherlands where some of the Reformed party were exiled during the Marian persecution. Such is *The Waldegrave Book* of 1584-85 and *The Middleburg Book*, based on Waldegrave and issued in three known editions in 1586, 1587 and 1602.[111] Like *The Form*, they included no blessing of the elements or expression of the work of the Spirit.[112] Attempts to gain Parliamentary authorization for the use of either or *The Form* or *The Middleburg Book* failed.[113] Queen Elizabeth herself resisted all attempts to modify 'the Elizabethan Settlement'.

The accession of James VI of Scotland to the English throne raised hopes of further reform, as witnessed by the signatories of the Millenary Petition. In the event, such hopes were largely dashed; the King severely limited the agenda of the

108 *The Works of William Laud, Vol. 3* (Oxford, 1853), p. 354.

109 Ibid., p. 355.

110 Ibid., p. 72.

111 Maxwell, *The Liturgical Portions of the Genevan Service Book*, p. 75. For the texts of Waldegrave and Middleburg (1586), see Peter Hall (ed.), *Reliquiae Liturgicae, Vol 1: The Middleburg Prayer Book* (Bath, 1947), pp. 51-61, 135-137.

112 Bryan Spinks has drawn attention to the worship of the Separatists, to be distinguished from those Puritans who remained within the Church because they were striving for a Reformed Church of England; the Separatists rejected the concept of a national church in favour of independent local churches, *Freedom or Order? The Eucharistic Liturgy in English Congregationalism 1645-1980* (Allison Park, 1984), p. 4.

113 Cuming, *A History of Anglican Liturgy*, pp. 100-101.

Hampton Court Conference appointed to review the worship of the Church; there was no discussion of the holy communion service as such and the 1604 Prayer Book was little changed from 1559. A section on the sacraments, attributed to John Overall, was added to the Catechism, but without reference to issues touching 'consecration'. The Canons of 1604 required that any bread and wine newly brought during the course of the administration should be placed on the communion-table and the words of institution rehearsed. There was no mention of the word 'consecration'.

While those pressing for further reform were concerned that the *BCP* needed to be purged of all 'unscriptural' elements, the restoration of a form of invocation is not represented in the literature of the Elizabethan and early Stuart periods.[114] However, the few concessions that were made at the Hampton Court Conference encouraged even more vigorous examination of the Prayer Book text in succeeding years. This was exacerbated after the death of James by the rejection of the 1637 Scottish Book and the events leading to the English Civil War. An indication that the theology of consecration was becoming more central is illustrated by the 1641 *Proceedings of the Lord's Committee of Divines*. In their 'Considerations upon the Book of Common Prayer', article 15 asserts: 'These words in the form of the consecration, "This is my body – This is my blood of the new testament," not to be printed hereafter in great letters.'[115] Presbyterian and Independent ascendancy resulted in the appointment of 'The Assembly of Divines at Westminster, with the assistance of Commissioners from the Church of Scotland', resulting in the suppression of the Prayer Book and the authorization of *A Directory for the Public Worship of God* in 1645.[116] The *Directory* was drawn up by both Presbyterians and Independents, but the Scottish Commissioners had a clear role in the drafting of the communion rite.[117] While the rubrics of the eucharistic action are not entirely clear, the pattern appears to be: narrative of institution, with optional comment upon it; prayer of thanksgiving, or blessing, of the bread and wine; declaration that the elements are now sanctified by the Word and Prayer; taking, fraction and distribution of bread with the eucharistic words of Jesus; taking and distribution of wine with the eucharistic words. The prayer is described both as 'sanctifying and blessing' the elements and as a 'Thanksgiving, or Blessing' of the elements. The language of 'consecration' was avoided, as witnessed by the account of John Lightfoot (1602-1675), a member of the Westminster Assembly:

> [21 June, 1644] Then fell we upon our work again; this clause – 'The other officers attending the service, the minister is to begin the action with sanctification of the elements

114 There is no reference, for example, in W.H. Frere and C.E. Douglas's collection, *Puritan Manifestoes* (London, 1954), or in 'The Millenary Petition' (1603), cited in H. Gee and W.J. Hardy, *Documents Illustrative of English Church History* (London,1921), pp. 508-511.

115 Cardwell, *A History of Conferences and Other Proceedings Connected with the Revision of The Book of Common Prayer*, p. 275.

116 The *Directory* was also authorized by the Scottish Parliament and the General Assembly of the Church of Scotland.

117 Burnet, *The Holy Communion in the Reformed Church of Scotland 1560-1960*, p. 106.

> of bread', … Then was the word 'sanctification' excepted at, as something uncouth; and did I scruple at it, saying it was a Hebraism – and 'consecrating', which was tendered by some, a Romanism; therefore, I should think 'setting apart' to be a medium, which received some debate: the determination was after a very long time, in a vote, that it should be thus expressed, 'He shall begin the action with sanctifying and blessing the elements.'[118]

This retained biblical categories; the Authorized Version employs the verb 'sanctified' in 1 Timothy 4:5, an important proof-text. The *Directory* thus includes the model petition:

> Earnestly to pray to God, the Father of all mercies, and God of all consolation, to vouchsafe his gracious presence, and the effectuall working of his Spirit in us, and so to sanctify these Elements both of Bread and Wine, and to blesse his own Ordinance, that we may receive by faith the Body and Blood of Jesus Christ crucified for us, and so to feed upon him, that he may be one with us, and we with him; that he may live in us, and we in him, and to him, who hath loved us, and given himself for us.[119]

E.C. Ratcliff argued that the invocatory type petition was not to be taken as a form of *epiclesis*,[120] citing Calvin to the effect that the Lord worked inwardly in the communicant by his Spirit. Clearly, Ratcliff regarded a 'proper' *epiclesis* as relating to the elements. Moreover, he suggested that the petition for sanctification was the work of the *Scottish* Commissioners. Bryan Spinks, however, has demonstrated that the language of the *Directory* is echoed in the writings of *English* divines, while he agrees with Ratcliff's contention that this is not an invocation of the eastern type. Rather, it is a petition to the Father to vouchsafe his presence. Thus the Father sanctifies the elements and works in the communicant through the Spirit.[121] The fact is that the reference to the 'The Elements being now sanctified by the Word and Prayer' in the rite is a clear reference to 1 Timothy 3:4, 5, and both Scottish and English traditions give liturgical expression to this biblical principle. The institution narrative supplies the 'word' and the thanksgiving the prayer. Moreover, the Last Supper accounts in Matthew and Mark state that Jesus, as accurately rendered by the Authorized Version, 'blessed' the elements, understood as the equivalent of 'gave thanks' in Luke and Paul. In all references in the *Directory*, the action of the Spirit is related to the communicants. The work of the Assembly is also reflected in the 1647 Westminster *Confession of Faith*, the *Shorter Catechism* and the *Longer Catechism*. The section on the Lord's Supper in the *Confession* includes the statement: 'The Lord Jesus, hath, in this ordinance, appointed his ministers to declare his word of institution to the people, to pray, and bless the elements of bread and wine, and thereby to set them apart from a common to an holy use …'.[122]

---

118 Journal of the Proceedings of the Assembly of Divines from January 1, 1643 to December 31, 1644, *The Whole Works of the Revd John Lightfoot* (London, 1824), p. 288.

119 *The Westminster Directory* (with an Introduction by Ian Breward, Bramcote, 1980), p. 22.

120 Ibid.

121 Spinks, *Freedom or Order?*, pp. 44-45.

122 Text from Philip Schaff, *The Creeds of the Evangelical Protestant Churches* (London, 1877), p. 665. The later Savoy Declaration of Faith and Order, based on the Westminster text,

When Charles II returned to England in 1660 at the invitation of Parliament, the question of worship loomed large. Defenders of the Prayer Book tradition made schedules of suggested amendments, notably Matthew Wren's *Advices* and John Cosin's *Particulars*, but neither included a text of a more explicit *epiclesis*.[123] Cosin (1594-1672) had not made explicit comment on the *epiclesis* in his previous eucharistic writings, most of which were in the context of Anglican *apologia* in relation to Rome.[124] Similarly, his *A Collection of Private Devotions* of 1627, for which he gives prayers 'At the Consecration' contains nothing epicletic, although he does give the text from 1 Corinthians 3:16-17 as a meditation while others are communicated. What Cosin does have is a clear doctrine of consecration;[125] namely, the use of the narrative in the context of petition.[126] This understanding of consecration is underlined in the first series of 'Annotations' on the text of the 1619 printing of the Prayer Book of 1604 (although here he may have reproduced the work of John Overall). Here consecration is understood as being effected by the institution narrative in the context of prayer, while it is asserted that the primitive understanding of the presence of Christ was 'in virtue of the words of consecration and benediction used by the priest'.[127] Cosin later wrote a second and third series of 'Annotations' in the years immediately preceding the restoration of the Monarchy, the third describing in full the 1549 rite along with Bucer's observations.[128] Cosin's respect for the first Prayer Book is evident in his treatment of the text.

The Presbyterians requested a committee to discuss the ordering of worship, the bishops suggested a Royal Commission, and the King in October 1660 to appoint a representative group of 'learned divines'. Cuming suggests it may have been in response to the King's decision that Cosin prepared a schedule of suggested revisions into a folio 1619 edition of the Prayer Book, known as *The Durham Book*.[129] 'The Prayer of Consecration', so styled in the book, included an *epiclesis* inserted into the 'Hear us' clause:

---

omitted the phrase 'to declare his word of institution to the people', Albert Peel, *The Savoy Declaration of Faith and Order* (London, 1939), p. 65.

123 Cuming cites Wren's involvement in the Scottish Liturgy as a reason for expressing caution here, *A History of Anglican Liturgy*, p. 113. For Wren's suggestions on the prayer of consecration see Jacobson, *Fragmentary Illustrations of the History of the Book of Common Prayer*, pp. 81-82; for Cosin's comments see *The Works of John Cosin, Vol. 5* (Oxford, 1855), pp. 516-517.

124 Cosin's work *Historia Transubstantiationis Papalis* of 1656 does not refer to the *epiclesis* though it does on occasions refer to the work of the Spirit, *Works, Vol. 4* (Oxford, 1851), pp. 171, 201.

125 Stanwood and O'Connor suggest that Cosin's phrase 'At the Consecration' may be the origin of the title 'Prayer of Consecration' in the 1637 rite, P.G. Stanwood and Daniel O'Connor (eds), *John Cosin: A Collection of Private Devotions* (Oxford, 1967), p. 352.

126 Buxton, *Eucharist and Institution Narrative*, p. 119, and, contra Gummey, *The Consecration of the Eucharist*, p. 121.

127 Cosin, *Works, Vol. 5*, p. 131.

128 Ibid., pp. 460, 477, 478.

129 G.J. Cuming (ed.), *The Durham Book: Being the First Draft of the Revision of the Book of Common Prayer in 1661* (London, 1961), pp. xvii-xviii.

> Read: and by ye power of thy holy Word and Spirit vouchsafe so to blesse and sanctifie these thy Gifts & Creatures of Bread & Wine, that wee receiving them..[130]

The narrative of institution also included manual acts. Cuming comments that the *epiclesis* may be adapted either from 1549 or the 1637 Scottish Liturgy, suggesting that it is perhaps closer to the latter.[131] Significantly, in relation to the reception of the Scottish rite, the phrase 'that they may be unto us' is omitted.

The promised committee, known as the Savoy Conference, met from May to July, 1661. The King's warrant for the conference invited the participants to compare the Prayer Book 'with the most ancient liturgies which have been used in the church, in the primitive and purest times'.[132] The Presbyterians were invited to draw up a list of 'exceptions' or criticisms of the Prayer Book. This they did by making both general and 'particular' observations. The final general point responded to the invitation to consider the primitive liturgies; the response is salutary:

> ... we have ... made enquiry, but cannot find any records of known credit, concerning any entire forms of liturgy, within the first three hundred years, which are confessed to be as the most primitive, so the purest ages of the church, nor any impositions of liturgies upon any national church for some hundreds of years after.[133]

Of the particular points, relating to the liturgy of the Prayer Book, one concerned consecration: 'We conceive that the manner of the consecrating of the elements is not here explicite and distinct enough, and the minister's breaking of the bread is not so much as mentioned.'[134] The bishops replied: 'That the manner of consecrating the elements be made more explicit and express, and to that purpose those words be put into the rubr., "Then shall he put his hand upon the bread and break it," "then shall he put his hand unto the cup"',[135] and this was reflected in the manual acts prescribed in the prayer of consecration in the 1662 Prayer Book. A more explicit consecration was one of the issues where the bishops and Presbyterians were in agreement.[136]

However, Richard Baxter, upon invitation, drew up an alternative service book entitled *The Reformation of the Liturgy As it was Presented to the Right Reverend Bishops by the Divines*. The communion order begins with an optional exhortation, including the following passages which relate to the work of the Spirit and consecration:

---

130 Ibid., p. 166.

131 Ibid., p. 167.

132 Cardwell, *A History of Conferences and Other Proceedings Connected with the Revision of The Book of Common Prayer*, p. 300.

133 Ibid., p. 312. They go on to say that they have not seen copies of liturgies 'fathered upon' Basil, Chrysostom, and Ambrose, but received evidence to conclude that they were either spurious or so interpolated that no judgment could be made about their primitive authority.

134 Ibid., p. 321.

135 Ibid., p. 363. The reply did not respond to the point about the fraction, but the changes made did.

136 See Colin Buchanan, *The Savoy Conference Revisited* (Cambridge, 2002), pp. 48-49, 78, 80.

> ... undertaking the pardon, justification, and sanctification of all that by unfeigned faith do take him for their Saviour, repenting of their sins, and consenting to be sanctified by his word and Spirit ... he did himself institute this Sacrament of his body and blood ... appointing his ministers, by the preaching of the Gospel, and administration of the sacraments, to be his agents without, and his Spirit within effectually to communicate his grace.
>
> The Lord's Supper, then, is an holy Sacrament, instituted by Christ: wherein bread and wine, being first by consecration made sacramentally, or representatively, the body and blood of Christ, are used by breaking and pouring out to represent and commemorate the sacrifice of Christ's body and blood upon the cross once offered up to God for sin; and are given in the name of Christ unto the Church, to signify and solemnize the renewal of his holy covenant with them, and the giving of himself unto them, to expiate their sins by his sacrifice, and sanctify them further by his Spirit, and confirm their right to everlasting life.[137]

After a second exhortation a prayer of penitence includes the words:

> Let his flesh and blood be to us meat and drink indeed; and his Spirit be in us a well of living water, springing up to everlasting life ...[138]

The elements being ready, the rubric runs, 'let him bless them, praying in these or the like words',[139] followed then by a prayer to the Father, including the words:

> Sanctify these thy creatures of bread and wine, which, according to thy institution and command, we set apart to this holy use, that they may be sacramentally the body and blood of thy Son Jesus Christ. *Amen.*[140]

The institution narrative follows (or is said before the above prayer), and then a declaration that the elements 'being set apart, and consecrated to this holy use by God's appointment, are now no common bread and wine, but sacramentally the body and blood of Christ'.[141] Then a prayer to Christ for fruitful reception includes petition for the gift of 'thy quickening Spirit, without which the flesh will profit us nothing'.[142] After the fraction and pouring out of wine, a third prayer to the Spirit asks:

> Most holy Spirit, proceeding from the Father and the Son: by whom Christ was conceived; by whom the prophets and apostles were inspired, and the ministers of Christ are qualified and called: that dwellest and workest in all the members of Christ, whom thou sanctifiest to the image and for the service of their Head, and comfortest them that they may shew forth his praise: illuminate us, that by faith we may see him that is here represented to us. Soften our hearts, and humble us for our sins. Sanctify and quicken us, that we may relish the spiritual food, and feed on it to our nourishment and growth in grace. Shed abroad the love of God upon our hearts, and draw them out in love to him. Fill us with thankfulness and holy joy, and with love to one another. Comfort us by witnessing that we are the

137 Text from Hall, *Reliquiae Liturgicae, Vol. 4, The Savoy Liturgy*, pp. 56-57.
138 Ibid., p. 67.
139 Ibid., p. 68.
140 Ibid.
141 Ibid., p. 69.
142 Ibid., p. 70.

children of God. Confirm us for new obedience. Be the earnest of our inheritance, and seal us up to everlasting life. *Amen.*[143]

Baxter allowed the minister either to consecrate and administer each element separately, in which case the above sequence was repeated twice, or to consecrate both kinds together for which he provided a single prayer, including the following formula:

> Sanctify these thy creatures of bread and wine, which, according to thy will, we set apart to this holy use, that they may be sacramentally the body and blood of thy Son Jesus Christ ... give us thy quickening Spirit to shew Christ to our believing souls, that is here represented to our senses. Let him soften our hearts, and humble us for our sins, and cause us to feed on Christ by faith. Let him shed abroad thy love upon our hearts, and draw them on in love to thee, and fill us with holy joy and thankfulness, and fervent love to one another. Let him comfort us by witnessing that we are thy children, and confirm us for new obedience, and be earnest of our inheritance, and seal us up to life everlasting ...[144]

Three observations can be made. First, Baxter has a rich theology of the Spirit in the eucharist. While, as in common with other Puritan rites, there is no invocation of the Spirit on the elements, the role of the Spirit is to make effective the fruits of what the eucharist signifies. This comes out clearly in Baxter's *Brief Directions for Families, about the Sacrament of the Body and Blood of Christ.* He distinguished three movements in the sacrament: consecration, commemoration, communication (corresponding to his liturgy above); of the last he says:

> In the communication, though the sacrament have respect to the Father, as the principal Giver, and to the Son, as both the Gift and Giver, yet hath it a special respect to the Holy Ghost, as being that Spirit given in the flesh and blood, which quickeneth souls; without which, the flesh will profit nothing; and whose operations must convey and apply Christ's saving benefits to us.[145]

Second, Baxter's sequence: prayer to the Father with petition for sanctification; narrative, declaration, prayer to Christ; fraction and pouring; prayer to the Spirit, led E.C. Ratcliff to conclude that Baxter's eucharistic and liturgical ideas approached more closely the historic western position than the ideas expressed or implied in the communion service of the contemporary Prayer Book.[146] Third, Richard Buxton argues that Baxter locates the act of consecration fundamentally in the prayer for the sanctification of the elements, because the short combined version of his prayer does not contain the institution narrative.[147] However, Baxter's own writings suggest that he viewed the narrative as essential to the rite, seeing consecration as a movement

143 Ibid., p. 71. Bryan Spinks comments that in addressing each member of the Trinity, Baxter was in fact giving liturgical expression to the *homoousios*, 'Trinitarian Theology and the Eucharistic Prayer', *Studia Liturgica*, 26 (1996): 222.

144 Hall, *Reliquiae Liturgicae, Vol. 4, The Savoy Liturgy*, p. 73.

145 From his work *A Christian Directory, Practical Works of the Rev. Richard Baxter, Vol. IV* (London, 1830) p. 316, also cited by Spinks, 'Two Seventeenth-Century Examples of *Lex Credendi, Lex Orandi*', p. 186.

146 Ratcliff, 'Puritan Alternatives to the Prayer Book', p. 79.

147 Buxton, *Eucharist and Institution Narrative*, p. 140.

embracing reading of the institution, petition for God's acceptance and blessing and declaration that the elements are sacramentally Christ's body and blood. So, he writes: 'God accepted them, and blesseth them to this use; which he signifieth both by the words of his own institution, and by the action of his ministers, and their benediction'.[148] The reading of the shorter conflated prayer does not preclude the use of the narrative before it.

The Savoy Conference failed to produce an agreement, although the bishops made some small concessions to Presbyterian demands. The fact of the situation was that the Presbyterian cause was in decline and the bishops were in the ascendant, the majority of whom desired little change from the 1604 liturgy. *The Durham Book* passed into the care of William Sancroft, on Cosin's departure for Durham. Another proposal for revision by a group of bishops is extant in Sancroft's hand. Once again there is a preliminary *epiclesis*, similar in substance to *The Durham Book*:

> Hear us, O Merciful Father, we most humbly beseech thee; and by the Power of thy holy Word and Spirit vouchsafe to bless and sanctify these thy gifts, and creatures of Bread and Wine, that we receiving them according to thy Son our Saviour Jesus Christ's holy Institution, in remembrance of him, and to shew forth his Death and Passion, may be partakers of his most blessed Body and Blood.[149]

In the end, the committee of bishops appointed by Convocation in 1661 rejected the attempt to introduce a more explicit invocation. What they did agree was a more explicit consecration as requested by both sets of divines, by introducing the title 'prayer of consecration', five manual acts during the narrative, the addition of 'amen' at the end of the prayer, the repetition of the narrative for supplementary consecration and a rubric requiring the consumption of consecrated remains.

Writers after 1662

While the 1662 Prayer Book settled decisively the liturgical form of consecration, how the rite was interpreted continued to exercise minds. A good example of post-1662 writing is that of Simon Patrick (1626-1707). In his work *Mensa Mystica* Patrick sets out to chart a *via media*, not so defiant to 'the "corporeal" presence, as to deny the "real", and not to reduce things into mere "shadows".'[150] Patrick does not examine ancient authors or liturgies; he provides a theological rationale in what is essentially a pastoral and devotional treatise. Holy communion is the means of attaining a deeper union with Christ, the Head. This sacramental union is realized by the Spirit, and there is a real gift of the Spirit given through worthy reception: 'Christ doth not descend locally unto us that we may feed on him; but as the sun toucheth us by his beams without removing out of his sphere, so Christ comes down upon us

148 Baxter, *A Christian Directory*, p. 315.

149 W. Jardine Grisbrooke, *Anglican Liturgies of the Seventeenth and Eighteenth Centuries* (London, 1958), p. 367.

150 *The Works of Simon Patrick, Vol. 1* (ed. Alexander Taylor, Oxford, 1858), p. 94.

by the power of the Holy Ghost, moving by its heavenly virtue in our hearts ...'.[151] The Spirit bestows 'greater strength' and 'heavenly nutriment' in our souls. Patrick concentrates on the graces received in the sacrament, believing this to be the essence of real presence. Therefore, he follows Hooker in asserting that the real presence is to be sought in the receiver of the sacrament. By the power of the Spirit reception of the elements renders the spiritual blessing effectual in the communicant.[152]

Of particular importance, not least for the influence of his writings on the Non-jurors was John Johnson (1662-1725). Johnson published *The Unbloody Sacrifice of the Altar* in two volumes in 1714 and 1718, with a second edition of *Volume 1* in 1724. While the main thrust of his work concerns the eucharistic sacrifice, Johnson also fully discusses the role of the *epiclesis*, not least because his study of the 'ancient Liturgies' led him to an understanding of a unitive sequence of narrative, oblation and invocation.[153] The sequence can be set out as follows:

> *Narrative* : by which the elements become authoritative representations of Christ's Body and Blood;
> *Oblation* : by which is designated not 'the Sacrifice of the Mass, not the substantial Body and Blood of Christ, much less His Divinity; but the Bread and Wine substituted by the Divine Word for His own Body and Blood';
> *Invocation*: whereby the elements are 'fully consecrated into the spiritual Body and Blood of Christ'.[154]

Johnson is clear that both the oblation and the consecration are not completed until the Spirit has been invoked: 'though the solemn oblation begins in all the Liturgies after the words of institution ... yet the sacrificial service is not ended until after the consecration'.[155] And this, he states, is the teaching of the ancient authors:

> It is evident that they believed the Eucharist to be made the Body and Blood, not by faith of the communicant, but by the power of the Holy Ghost, or Divine benediction, imparted to it by means of the invocation: (I mean perfectly and finally imparted by this means, not exclusively of the words of institution and the oblation).[156]

151 Ibid., p. 149.

152 Stevenson is correct to state that Patrick 'shrinks from any receptionism', 'The *Mensa Mystica* of Simon Patrick (1626-1707): A Case Study in Restoration Eucharistic Piety', in Nathan Mitchell and John F. Baldovin (eds), *Rule of Prayer, Rule of Faith* (Collegeville, 1996), p. 174.

153 *The Works of John Johnson, Vol. 1* (Oxford, 1847) p. 330.

154 Ibid., p. 305.

155 Ibid., p. 340.

156 Ibid., pp. 341-342.

Thus he can say that the *epiclesis* has 'perfected the consecration',[157] or consummated the holy mysteries,[158] or that by it the elements are 'finally and completely consecrated'.[159]

Johnson's theology of consecration, which he cites as being according to the primitive church, declares that the elements are the very body and blood of Christ 'not in substance, but in power and effect'[160] or 'in efficacy and virtue, without changing their natural substances'[161] apprehended by the worshipper to be the body and blood by faith, directed and influenced by the Holy Spirit.[162] This 'power and effect' is the operation of the Spirit:

> … that is, that the Holy Ghost, at the prayers of the Priests and people, is in a peculiar manner present, and imparts a secret power to the Sacramental Body and Blood, by which they are made to be in energy and effect, though not in substance, the very Body and Blood Which they represent.[163]

For Johnson, the *epiclesis* constitutes much more than the consecration of the elements to a holy use; this is fulfilled by placing the gifts on the altar.[164] The *epiclesis* is also a sign of the eucharist as a more perfect sacrifice, surpassing the sacrifices of the old covenant; for whereas the Law knew of no higher means of sanctifying an object than by sacrificing it, the *epiclesis* is a yet further hallowing:

> ... the representative Body and Blood of Christ, were, by the primitive Fathers, supposed to be consecrated in a more perfect manner than any sacrifice under the Law could be: for in all the Liturgies, after the oblation of the Bread and Wine as the memorials of the grand Sacrifice, there is a solemn prayer that God would send His Spirit or His Divine benediction for the further consecration of them, after they had first been offered as a Sacrifice to God.[165]

Johnson understood the liturgy of *Apostolic Constitutions 8* to be the oldest extant liturgy. He cites the *anamnesis* and *epiclesis* twice in *Volume 2*, the latter under the section 'Devotions for the Altar'.[166] A prayer for those who are to communicate includes the following petition:

> Let the fire of Thy Holy Spirit always descend on the Christian Sacrifice, and on those who offer it; that their iniquity may be taken away, and their sin purged.[167]

---

157 Ibid., p. 304.
158 Ibid., p. 335.
159 Ibid.
160 Ibid., pp. 251, 266.
161 Johnson, *Works, Vol. 2*, p. 201.
162 Johnson, *Works, Vol.1*, p. 323.
163 Ibid., pp. 267-268.
164 Ibid., p. 271.
165 Ibid., p. 272.
166 Johnson, *Works, Vol. 2*, pp. 116, 282.
167 Ibid., p. 283.

Johnson sets out what he regards as the necessary elements of the eucharistic action, without which texts are 'defective and imperfect'. He outlines eight areas, including the necessity of an oblation of and *epiclesis* upon the elements.[168] This agenda, as we shall see, was highly influential on the Non-jurors, while the stress on *Apostolic Constitutions 8* brought this liturgy into the centre stage of the quest for primitive forms.

A response to the writings of theologians with a 'high' doctrine of the eucharist such as Johnson or a memorialist doctrine such as the work *A Plain Account of the Nature and End of the Sacrament of the Lord's Supper*, attributed to Benjamin Hoadley, Bishop of Winchester, can be seen in the writings of Daniel Waterland (1683-1740). In his major work, *A Review of the Doctrine of the Eucharist* (1737), Waterland's overriding principle was that of fidelity to Scripture. He, too, cited 1 Timothy 4: 'the bread and wine being "sanctified by the word of God and prayer" ... do thereby contract a relative holiness, or sanctification, in some degree or other'.[169] With regard to the Spirit, Waterland is much happier with an understanding of how the Spirit acts upon the communicants, adapting Hooker's famous phrase to assert that the presence of the Spirit is to be found not in the sacrament, but the worthy receiver of the sacrament.[170] Waterland does not reject the notion that the Spirit can relate to material things but asserts that there is no scriptural or rational proof.[171] As well as regarding an *epiclesis* of the Spirit on the elements to be a later development, Waterland argues that the eastern liturgies including such an invocation would have been more exact if they had stated that the Spirit comes upon the worshippers in the use of the elements.[172] Later in his work, following a discussion of Greek and Latin authors, he concludes:

> ... that the true and ancient intent of that part of the service was not to implore any physical change in the elements, no, nor so much as a physical connection of the Spirit with the elements, but a moral change only in the elements, as to relations and uses, and a gracious presence of the Holy Spirit upon the communicants.[173]

Waterland therefore defends the 1662 petition for consecration in that the work of the Spirit is 'understood and implied':

> After all, I see no reason why it may not be justly thought as modest, and as reverent, to beg God the Father the things which we want, understanding that he will grant them by his Holy Spirit, as to make a formal petition to him, to send his Holy Spirit upon the elements or upon the communicants; unless Scripture had particularly ordered some special form, to be made use of in our sacramental solemnities, which it has not done.[174]

---

168 Ibid., pp. 206ff. He was thus critical of what he understood as the Roman and Greek approaches to consecration, see Peter Doll, *After the Primitive Christians* (Cambridge, 1997), p. 18.

169 Daniel Waterland, *A Review of the Doctrine of the Eucharist* (Oxford, 1896), p. 90.

170 Ibid., p. 94.

171 Ibid.

172 Ibid., p. 93.

173 Ibid., p. 297.

174 Ibid., p. 302.

In contrast to Waterland, Thomas Wilson (1663-1755), Bishop of Sodor and Man, had no doubts about relating the Spirit to the elements.[175] In his work *Sacra Privata* he states that by consecration the bread and wine are made the sacramental body and blood of Christ so that 'we have then a Sacrifice to offer'. The power of the Spirit 'accompanys these elements' to make them 'effectual Meanes of Grace and Salvation'. The Spirit thus communicates a 'Supernatural power'.[176] He demonstrates how this can be given liturgical expression in his 'Private devotions at the Altar'. Wilson expressed a desire for the restoration of 1549,[177] but in the present situation, an epicletic emphasis could be restored by the following prayer, drawing on *Apostolic Constitutions 8*:[178]

> *Immediately after the Consecration.* We offer unto Thee, our King and our God, this bread and this cup. We give Thee thanks for these and for all Thy mercies, beseeching Thee to send down Thy Holy Spirit upon this sacrifice, that He may make this bread the Body of Thy Christ, and this cup the Blood of Thy Christ: and that all we, who are partakers thereof, may thereby obtain remission of our sins, and all other benefits of His Passion.[179]

Like Johnson, Wilson viewed the placing of the gifts upon the altar as the action which sanctifies them or sets them apart to a holy use.[180] But this did not constitute the 'consecration' which required a divine act:

> The priest, by doing what Christ did, by *prayer and thanksgiving*, by breaking the bread and pouring out the wine, obtaineth of God, that these creatures by the descent of the Holy Ghost become, after a spiritual manner, the *body and blood of Christ*, by receiving of which our souls shall be strengthened and refreshed, as our bodies are by bread and wine.[181]

The period towards the end of the seventeenth century and the beginning of the eighteenth century saw the publication of a series of influential commentaries on the 1662 Prayer Book. Two examples reveal the different attitudes to consecration.

---

175 His writings in general 'bear a strong pneumatology', Kenneth Stevenson, 'The Eucharistic Theology of Thomas Wilson (1663-1755), Bishop and Pastor', *Studia Liturgica*, 26 (1996): 258.

176 *The Works of Thomas Wilson, Vol. 5* (Oxford, 1860), p. 339.

177 Ibid., p. 73.

178 The Act of Uniformity did not apply to the Isle of Man, R.C.D. Jasper, *The Development of the Anglican Liturgy 1662-1980* (London, 1989), p. 21.

179 Wilson, *Works, Vol. 5*, p. 74. This text, can be compared with another supplementary epicletic text in his work *A Short and Plain Instruction, Works, Vol. 4* (Oxford, 1851), p. 403.

180 Thomas Wilson, *Parochialia or Instructions to the Clergy, Works, Vol. 7* (Oxford, 1863), p. 20.

181 Ibid., pp. 20-21. A further example of enrichment of the *BCP* text is the interpolation by Bishop Barlow of Lincoln (1675-1692): 'Hear us, O merciful Father, we most humbly beseech Thee, (through the operation of the HOLY GHOST sanctify both us and these gifts, and exalting them above their ordinary use, importance and conception) and grant that we receiving them ...', cited in Tract 81, *Tracts for the Times, Vol. 4* (London and Oxford, 1838), p. 165.

Thomas Comber in his *A Companion to the Temple and the Closet* (1675) understands consecration to be effected by the words of institution. The 'Hear us' clause is a petition for a blessing, and while he cites the *Quam oblationem* of the Roman canon and Ambrose, the *epiclesis* of Basil and the oblation of *Apostolic Constitutions* to show that no liturgy lacks a supplication, the narrative is the consecration itself.[182] By contrast, Charles Wheatley, in the 1720 edition of *A Rational Illustration of the Book of Common Prayer* could write: 'there was always inserted in the primitive forms a particular petition for the descent of the Holy Ghost upon the Sacramental Elements, which was also continued in the first Liturgy of king Edward VI ...'.[183] Wheatley argued that while the explicit *epiclesis* was omitted under Bucer's influence in 1552, the former sense is still implied, 'and consequently by these The Elements are now consecrated, and so become the Body and Blood of our Saviour Christ' He was consequently critical of the Prayer Book supplementary consecration rubric.[184]

Experimental Rites

W. Jardine Grisbrooke has edited a series of liturgies written by individuals, all of which look to what they understood to be primitive practice, with special emphasis on *Apostolic Constitutions 8*. This liturgy was at this time mistakenly attributed to Clement of Rome (and hence sometimes referred to as the 'Clementine' liturgy) and so was deemed to stand within the tradition of the Apostles. The Liturgy of St James was also accorded a similarly primitive status. Grisbrooke sets out the liturgies of Edward Stephens, William Whiston and John Henley, all of whom were critical of 1662, and in their experimental texts drew variously on 1549, 1637, *Apostolic Constitutions 8* and St James. However, the importance of Stephens, Whiston and Henley must not be over-exaggerated. All three hardly belonged to the main-line, although the first two did influence others through their publications. Their importance lies in the way they illustrate quest for the primitive usage and the kind of critique to which 1662 was subjected. This is further illustrated by Latitudinarian suggestions for Prayer Book revision, none more influential than the anonymous *Free and Candid Disquisitions*, written by John Jones, whose mentor was the influential thinker Dr Samuel Clarke.[185] The book criticized the lack of an *epiclesis* of the Spirit on the elements in 1662.

Conclusion – 'Sanctified by the word of God and prayer'

Throughout this chapter, eucharistic exploration has been principally conducted under the shadow of Scholastic theology and the wholesale rejection of the doctrine

182 Thomas Comber, *A Companion to the Temple*, 3rd ed. (London, 1688), pp. 120ff.

183 Charles Wheatley, *A Rational Illustration of The Book of Common Prayer* (London, 1842), p. 290.

184 Buxton sets out the change in Wheatley's ideas between his 1710 and 1720 editions, *Eucharist and Institution Narrative*, pp. 161-169.

185 Jasper, *The Development of the Anglican Liturgy*, pp. 14-15.

of transubstantiation. This is the central unitive factor. It is one thing to demolish a theory and quite another to replace it, especially in a way that will command general assent. The lack of a common unitive theological language regarding eucharistic presence is revealed clearly. The chapter has also posed the classical dilemma of the relationship between Scripture and tradition, especially tradition understood as the practice of 'the primitive church'. Most writers of the period would have professed to want to do justice to both, as a church seeking consciously to defend its position as reformed yet also catholic.

While the denial of transubstantiation was a unitive category, can we point to any more? One would be the understanding that consecration is effected in the context of petition. Successive Church of England Prayer Books retained the 'Hear us' clause, and the introduction of a more explicit *epiclesis* was argued for by some on the grounds that it makes the prayer context even more explicit. In addition, where we have seen creative eucharistic theology, that is, not simply arguing with the Schoolmen on their terms, the role of Spirit in the eucharist has often been expressed; indeed, it has enabled problems of eucharistic presence - how the body of Christ given in the sacrament relates to the body of Christ seated at the right hand of the Father - to be set in a different theological context.

Liturgically, however, the role of the Spirit is more ambiguous. Clearly, some authors simply accepted the role of the Spirit in the eucharist to be understood, with apparently little desire for overt expression. Also, in a significant proportion of the texts we have considered, the presence of an invocation appears to be more important than the position, doubtless reflecting the esteem in which 1549 was held by the more 'high church' Carolines, and a certain security that Anglicanism was not bound by an uncritical adoption of 'Greek' forms. Yet there still remains throughout the period the unresolved tension of the lack of overt scriptural warrant for an *epiclesis* and the degree to which the locus of eucharistic presence is inward and spiritual; how such 'spiritual presence' relates to the action of the Holy Spirit, and how this understanding might be expressed liturgically.

Towards the end of the period in view we see the increasing claims made for *Apostolic Constitutions 8* and the Liturgy of St James – mistakenly regarded as 'apostolic' – with the insistence that Anglican texts must conform if Anglicans are to restore a pristine catholicism. The implications of this approach were set out in the liturgical texts of the Non-jurors and, through their influence in Scotland and so to the USA, with the phenomenon that by the end of the eighteenth century there were three different recognized Anglican canons.

Chapter 3

Anglican Diversification

The English Non-jurors

The accession of William and Mary following the flight of James II led to the suspension of eight bishops and four hundred clergy who refused to take the oath of allegiance to the new monarchs.[1] They were later joined by those who would not take the oath to the House of Hanover. These 'Non-jurors' included a significant number who espoused a 'high' doctrine of the Church and sacraments combined with a strong interest in liturgy. In particular, they looked to John Johnson's writings, whose influence among them Grisbrooke describes as 'all-powerful'.[2]

In the first twenty years after their departure from the Church of England some Non-jurors continued to use 1662, others 1549, the Scottish rite of 1637 or their own adaptations. For example, Thomas Brett, later to become a bishop, added to the *BCP* consecration prayer an oblation and *epiclesis* 'very near the same as it is in the "Clementine Liturgy"'.[3] An example of the kind of theology espoused by the early Non-jurors can be seen in George Hickes's *The Christian Priesthood Asserted* of 1707 and the writings of Robert Nelson. Hickes, former Dean of Worcester, was consecrated titular Bishop of Thetford in 1694. While his eucharistic section is principally concerned with sacrifice, Hickes notes the intimate connection between the oblation and the invocation in the Greek liturgies. Attributing *Apostolic Constitutions 8* to Clement, he regards that text as preserving the most primitive order. Of the Spirit, he writes:

> From all which it will appear, that the ancient Church thought the Holy Spirit to be most especially present at the Eucharistical sacrifice, and to be the chief agent in the ministration of it ... The Holy Ghost then is the principal, and the priests but the instrumental ministers in the ministration of the Eucharistical oblation ... co-agents or workers together with the Holy Spirit in the ministration of it.[4]

Robert Nelson, a layman who associated himself with the Non-jurors, set out his eucharistic theology at length in his book *The Great Duty of Frequenting the Christian Sacrifice* of 1707. This was a revision and enlargement of the eucharistic material from the section on vigils in his 1704 work *A Companion for the Festivals and Feasts of the Church of England with Collects and Prayers for Each Solemnity*.

---

1 Jasper, *The Development of the Anglican Liturgy*, p. 28.

2 Ibid., p. 71; Henry Broxap, *The Later Non-Jurors* (Cambridge, 1924), p. 5.

3 Grisbrooke, *Anglican Liturgies of the Seventeenth and Eighteenth Centuries*, p. 89.

4 George Hickes, *Two Treatises on the Christian Priesthood, 4th ed., Vol. 2* (Oxford, 1847), p. 98.

In this earlier work, which enjoyed an immense circulation, he succinctly gives his understanding of the form of consecration of the primitive church:

> The *Priest* that officiated not only rehearsed the Evangelical History of the Institution of this holy Sacrament, and pronounced these Words of our Saviour, *This is my Body, this is my Blood*; but he offered up a Prayer of Consecration to God, beseeching him, *that he would send down his holy Spirit upon the Bread and Wine presented to him on the Altar, and that he would so sanctify them that they might become the Body and Blood of his Son, Jesus Christ*; not according to the gross *Compages* or Substance, but as to the spiritual Energy and Virtue of his holy Flesh and Blood, communicated to the blessed Elements by the Power and Operation of the Holy Ghost descending upon them ...[5]

In 1716, however, the Non-jurors split into two groups, the 'Non-usagers' and the 'Usagers'. The latter, led by Bishop Jeremy Collier and Bishop Thomas Brett, advocated four distinctive primitive 'usages' in the eucharist, none of which were found in the 1662 rite: the mixed chalice, the oblation of the elements, an explicit *epiclesis* of the Spirit upon the elements and the commemoration of the faithful departed. The 'Usagers' first adopted the 1549 rite which they reprinted in 1717, on the basis that the liturgy included an *epiclesis*.[6] The following year they published a book of services,[7] drafted principally by Collier, Brett and Thomas Deacon. The eucharistic rite includes a collect after the offertory with a petition for the Spirit taken from the Byzantine rite of St Basil:

> ... Receive it, O God, as a sweet smelling savour, and send down the grace of thy Holy Spirit upon us.[8]

The institution narrative includes the 1662 manual acts with capitals and black crosses at the words of institution. The *anamnesis*-oblation is principally drawn from *Apostolic Constitutions*,[9] and the *epiclesis* is a straight rendering of the 'Clementine' text. However, two further manual actions of laying the hand upon the bread and every vessel in which there is wine and water are prescribed for the *epiclesis* at the petition '... that he may make this Bread the Body of thy Christ, and this Cup the Blood of thy Christ...'.

Thomas Brett set out the background to the 1718 rite in his (commonly called) *Dissertation on Liturgies*, first published in 1720.[10] With regard to the 'usages', 1549 was the starting point, except that there, the order *epiclesis*–narrative–*anamnesis* did not conform to the more ancient practice. Following Johnson, he sets out the

---

5 Cited from the 33rd edition (London, 1818), p. 476.

6 The text is reproduced in Peter Hall (ed.), *Fragmenta Liturgica*, Vol. 1 (Bath, 1848), pp. 101-148.

7 A.C. Don, *The Scottish Book of Common Prayer 1929* (London, 1949), p. 24.

8 Grisbrooke, *Anglican Liturgies of the Seventeenth and Eighteenth Centuries*, p. 286.

9 With some correspondence with Henley's rite, Stevenson, *Eucharist and Offering*, p. 164.

10 The edition used here is that of 1838, Thomas Brett, *A Collection of the Principal Liturgies* (London, 1838).

relevant texts to demonstrate that as well as the 'Clementine', the Greek and Eastern, Gallican, Gothic and Mozarabic rites also have the invocation following the oblation. This for Brett is the 'most natural Order, the Holy Spirit by his descent completing and perfecting the Consecration'.[11] For,

> ... the primitive Church did understand that the Holy Ghost descended on the sacramental Body and Blood of Christ, to infuse into them this quickening virtue; without which, material Elements could have no quickening virtue. And therefore they supposed not the elements to be fully consecrated and made the body and blood of Christ in power and effect, that flesh and blood, which communicated eternal life to the worthy receivers, till they had prayed that the Holy Ghost might come down upon the elements, and make them the body and blood of Christ ... [12]

He further argues that as 1 Timothy 4 taught that food is sanctified by the word of God and prayer, the Prayer Book text is defective, because the prayer of consecration concludes with the 'word'; there is no prayer added to it.[13] By contrast, the Non-usagers argued that the Prayer Book faithfully followed Christ's institution, through the giving of thanks and the rehearsal of his words of institution, and these elements were the guarantor of its validity.[14]

The Usagers's adoption of the 'Clementine' text was justified because the liturgy was deemed to be 'the oldest written Liturgy which has been transmitted to us' and the fact it was never used liturgically guaranteed that it was free of later corruptions. It stands as the 'fullest Exemplar of that Traditional Liturgy we have now extant' by which he means that it was composed according to the traditional form received from the Apostles.[15] By this Brett clearly understood the sequence of narrative–oblation–invocation to have Apostolic sanction, and the fact that his book set out in English the relevant texts contributed to the point the Non-jurors were trying to make. The 1718 rite was a skilful blend of elements from the Anglican tradition, but supplemented by 'primitive' texts and arranged in the 'natural' and primitive order. It therefore provided a ready model of what, in their view, a catholic and reformed rite might look like.[16]

In 1732, an attempt was made to heal the divisions between the 'Usagers' and 'Non-usagers'. An Instrument of Union was signed, declaring that the 'Hear us' clause from the Prayer Book 'intends to bless, that is to pray to God to bless & sanctify by His Holy Spirit ye Elements before offered'.[17] The holding to the agreement were known as 'Unionists' but the agreement did not hold, and led to the creation of 'Extreme Usager' and 'Extreme Non-usager' parties. The 'Extreme

11 Ibid., p. 225.

12 Ibid., pp. 228-229.

13 Ibid., pp. 264-265.

14 See James David Smith, *The Eucharistic Doctrine of The Later Nonjurors* (Cambridge, 2000), pp. 19-25.

15 Ibid., p. 104.

16 For Brett's response to objections to the *epiclesis* in the 1718 text see, *A Collection of the Principal Liturgies*, pp. 247-251.

17 Grisbrooke, *Anglican Liturgies of the Seventeenth and Eighteenth Centuries*, p. 113.

Usagers' continued to use the 1718 rite. Eventually, in 1748, Thomas Deacon, consecrated bishop in 1733 and by now the leader of the 'Extreme Usagers' decreed that his revision of 1718, published in 1734, should be the liturgy of his group of Non-jurors. Deacon provided a full prayer book, with a eucharistic rite drawing further on *Apostolic Constitutions 8*. The text of the *epiclesis* is very similar to 1718, but there was a significant difference in the ceremonial. In the narrative of institution, Deacon prescribes the five manual acts, but the black crosses are used at the *epiclesis* rather than at the institution, accompanied by a further hand-laying at 'to make this Bread the Bo+dy of thy Christ, and this Cup the Blo+od of thy Christ …'.[18] This change of emphasis underlines the fact that the invocation completes consecration as the proper climax of the sequence. The Lord's Prayer and peace follows the *anaphora*, then a prayer adapted from the 'Clementine' prayer of inclination which also petitioned for the sanctification of the worshippers:

> ... Sanctify us in body and soul; and grant, that we being cleansed from all filthiness of flesh and spirit, may partake of the mystick blessings now lying on thine altar.[19]

Deacon's understanding of the role of the *epiclesis* is set out in the 'Longer Catechism' from *A Full, True, and Comprehensive View of Christianity*, published in 1747:

> ... and in order to make the gifts efficacious instruments of conveying these great advantages, the Priest prays to GOD the Father to sanctify them, by sending his Holy Spirit upon the Bread and Cup offered to him, that he may enliven those Representations of CHRIST's dead Body and effused Blood, and make them his spiritual life-giving Body and Blood, by filling them with the divine vertue and power of his natural Body and Blood, and thereby making his Sacramental the same thing with his Natural Body and Blood in effect though not in substance, so that the receivers thereof may obtain all the blessings of the institution.[20]

While Deacon's liturgy restored all the verbosity of the Clementine Rite, and in this sense made it greatly inferior to 1718, nevertheless, his work was held in high esteem by the bishops responsible for the liturgical developments in Scotland.

The Scottish Liturgy of 1764

While episcopacy was restored in Scotland from 1661 to 1689, there was no attempt to restore the Prayer Book and worship continued broadly according to the pattern of the Westminster *Directory* even if technically the Act Rescissory had laid it aside.[21] It was only in 1707-8 that worship according to the English Prayer Book became

18 Ibid., p. 311.

19 Ibid., p. 313.

20 Text cited in ibid., p. 133.

21 Gordon Donaldson, 'Covenant to Revolution', in Forrester and Murray, *Studies in the History of the Church of Scotland*, p. 56.

more common for Episcopalians.[22] While some clergy and laity doubtless would have preferred the restoration of the 1637 rite, theological concerns about the canon and the difficulty of financing a reprinting rendered the desire impracticable. Bishop Thomas Rattray regretted this, but he reported that some met the situation by interpolation and rearrangement:

> And even some who did not use it, yet did interject a Prayer of Invocation for the descent of the Holy Ghost to bless and sanctify the Elements, to make them the Sacramental Body and Blood of Christ, and read the first prayer in the Post-Communion immediately after the Words of Institution for a Prayer of Oblation, as it was originally designed.[23]

The so-called 'Toleration Act' of 1712 gave legal sanction to non-Jacobite Anglicans who were therefore able to use the English *BCP*. Non-juring Episcopalians by contrast were under no obligation to use the English Prayer Book.[24] In the same year, at Edinburgh, the Jacobite George Seton issued a modest reprinting of the 1637 book verbatim.[25] However, the desire that the worship of the Church should aspire to the perceived primitive norms was strong on the part of some. For example, two Scottish bishops had been involved in the creation of the 1718 liturgy of the Non-jurors, Archibald Campbell and James Gadderar. Gadderar distributed copies of the 1718 rite in the diocese of Aberdeen, with its sequence of narrative–*anamnesis*–oblation–*epiclesis*–intercession. Moreover, the Scottish Liturgy included two of the 'usages' demanded by some of the English Non-jurors – the oblation of the elements and the invocation of the Spirit. All of this served to bring 1637 more centre-stage. However, because Seton's edition was expensive and scarce, editions of the Scottish Communion Office were published separately as 'wee bookies'. In these, the Scottish rite began at the offertory. A worshipper would use the English Prayer Book for the first part of the service and a 'wee bookie' for the second.[26]

The first of the 'wee bookies' was published in 1722 and reprinted in 1724. It followed 1637 almost *verbatim*. However, it appears that there was some flexibility about how the rite was used. Grisbrooke reprints changes made in a folio copy of 1637 to give the sequence: *sursum corda*, prayer of consecration, Lord's Prayer, prayer for the Church, prayers of penitence, humble access and distribution. The prayer of consecration includes an *epiclesis*, transposed to a position after the oblation:

> And here we offer and present unto thee, O Lord, these thy creatures of bread and wine, together with ourselves our souls and bodies to be a reasonable, holy and lively sacrifice

---

22 Grisbrooke cites a letter of Bishop Rattray to this effect, *Anglican Liturgies of the Seventeenth and Eighteenth Centuries*, p. 150.

23 John Dowden, *The Scottish Communion Office of 1764, New Edition* (Oxford, 1922), p. 43.

24 Dowden comments that many clergy and laity had no wish for the doctrinal emphases of 1637. Bishop Rose added an invocation to the 1662 prayer and on occasions, along with Bishop Falconar, used 1637, ibid., p. 48.

25 Gordon Donaldson, *The Prayer Book in Scotland 1549-1949* (Dundee, 1949), p. 24.

26 W. Perry, *The Scottish Liturgy: Its Value and History*, 2nd ed. (Edinburgh and London, 1922), p. 50.

> unto thee, humbly beseeching thee to send down thy holy Spirit upon us and upon these thy gifts that he may make this bread the holy Bo+dy, and this Cup the precious Blo+od of thy Christ unto us that whosoever shall be partakers of this holy communion may be fulfilled with thy grace ... [27]

Consequently, in 1735, a second 'wee bookie' was published, the title page stating 'All the parts of this office ranked in their natural order'.[28] The natural order was the perceived 'primitive order', as restored by the Non-jurors' rite of 1718. The abiding principle was to what degree the received liturgy could be adapted to accord more closely with supposed primitive norms. The second 'wee bookie' was reprinted in 1743, the same year that the Scottish bishops recommended the use of the Scottish Liturgy rather than the English order. Dowden argues that this meant 1637, in spite of the fact that 1735 was the form mainly used in preference to 1662.[29]

The Scottish interest in primitive liturgy was exemplified by the posthumous publication in 1744 of a study of the Liturgy of St James by Bishop Thomas Rattray.[30] Rattray had held the sees of Brechin and Dunkeld and had been primus from 1739 to his death in 1743. As a layman, he had allowed the use of the 1718 Non-juror rite in his private chapel.[31] In the preface, he describes the liturgy of St James as 'unquestionably one of the most ancient and valuable' liturgies extant.[32] His methodology is to compare St James with the 'Clementine' Liturgy 'which never having been used in any Church since it was inserted into the Apostolical Constitution has none of those Additions which were afterwards introduced into the other Liturgies'. This would enable St James to be 'restored to its primitive Purity'.[33] He also took into account the liturgies of St Mark, St Chrysostom, and St Basil (Byzantine) and the material from Cyril of Jerusalem's *Mystagogical Catechesis V*.

Rattray also included in his book a communion office based on his work on St James, *An Office for the Sacrifice of the Holy Eucharist, being the Ancient Liturgy of the Church of Jerusalem*. The text of the *epiclesis* ran:

> Have Mercy upon us, O Lord God, Almighty Father, have Mercy upon us according to thy great Mercy, and send down thy holy Spirit upon us, and upon these Gifts which are here set before Thee, that by his Descent upon them, he may make this Bread the holy BO+DY of thy Christ, and this Cup the precious BLO+OD of thy Christ: that they may be to all who partake of them, for the Sanctification of Soul and Body, for bringing forth the Fruit of good Works, for Remission of Sins, and for Life everlasting.

27 Grisbrooke, *Anglican Liturgies of the Seventeenth and Eighteenth Centuries*, p. 153.

28 Don, *The Scottish Book of Common Prayer 1929*, pp. 38-39.

29 Dowden, *The Scottish Communion Office of 1764*, pp. 66-67.

30 Thomas Rattray, *The Ancient Liturgy of the Church of Jerusalem* (London, 1744). The book was published anonymously.

31 H. Sefton, 'Revolution to Disruption', in Forrester and Murray, *Studies in the History of the Church of Scotland*, p. 66.

32 Rattray, *The Ancient Liturgy of the Church of Jerusalem*, p. iii.

33 Ibid., p. v.

This skilful condensing of the ancient text avoids the double invocation and omits the 'salvation history' of the Spirit; the desired effects of the invocation are also condensed.

Rattray expounded the role of the *epiclesis* in language clearly inspired by Johnson. The narrative renders the elements as instituted representatives of Christ's body and blood, they are then offered, and the *epiclesis* fully completes the consecration, effecting a change not in the substance of the elements but rather their 'Qualities, that very Body and Blood in Energy and Life-Giving Power'.[34] This compares with what he writes in his *Essay on the Nature of the Church*, where the invocation makes the bread and wine 'to be verily and indeed his Body and Blood', the Spirit 'by which the Body of Christ was formed in the womb of the blessed Virgin, and which is still united to It in heaven, descending on, and being united to these elements, and invigorating them with the virtue, power, and efficacy thereof, and making them one with it'.[35]

The effect of Rattray's book, however, was tempered by the persecution of Episcopalians following the 1745 Jacobite Rebellion. In 1755, an edition of the Scottish office was published by Bishop William Falconar, the Scottish primus. The clear influence of Rattray and the Non-jurors is seen by the adoption of the sequence narrative–oblation–invocation in the canon.[36]

Active persecution of the Scottish Non-jurors ceased after 1760, and Falconar's rite itself became the basis of a further edition produced by himself and Bishop Robert Forbes, the Bishop of Caithness, in 1764, at the request of the college of Bishops and published under the authority of the primus.[37] Dowden describes this 1764 edition as the *textus receptus*, including an exact reprint of the 8vo edition, published by Drummond of Edinburgh in successive editions of his *Historical Account*. Dowden termed it as such not because it had any definitive legal standing, but because, as the final text, it became the rite most generally used by Scottish Episcopalians. The rite begins at the exhortations. The canon includes the narrative of institution with manual acts, an oblation of the bread and wine and an invocation:

> And we most humbly beseech thee, O merciful Father, to hear us, and of thy almighty goodness vouchsafe to bless and sanctify, with thy word and holy Spirit, these thy gifts and creatures of bread and wine, that they may become the body and blood of thy most dearly beloved Son.[38]

The canon then continues with the 1662 prayer of oblation, and after that the prayer for the whole state of Christ's Church. The position of the intercessions also reflects the 'Antiochene' pattern where they are incorporated after the *epiclesis* in the

---

34 Ibid., p. xi.

35 Cited by Grisbrooke, *Anglican Liturgies of the Seventeenth and Eighteenth Centuries*, p. 142.

36 Text in Hall, *Fragmenta Liturgica Vol. 5*, p. 169. Hall wrongly attributed it to Bishop Gerard of Aberdeen, Dowden, *The Scottish Communion Office of 1764*, p. 76, fn 1.

37 Don, *The Scottish Book of Common Prayer 1929*, p. 51.

38 Dowden, reprint of 8vo edition of *The Communion-Office for the Use of the Church of Scotland, as far as the Ministration of that Holy Sacrament* (Edinburgh, 1764), pp. 13-14.

anaphora. The form for supplementary consecration begins from 'All glory ...' to '... may become the body and blood of thy most dearly beloved Son'.

The form of the *epiclesis* is significant because of the abrupt way in which it ends. It does not include any invocation of the Spirit on the worshippers or reference to the fruits of consecration in the lives of the worshippers. The form in Rattray's office includes both, and *Apostolic Constitutions 8* has the latter. It may have been that the Scottish bishops were attracted by the objectivity of *Apostolic Constitutions 8* in relation to the elements. The rite adopted the verb 'become' whereas the 1637 office read 'may be unto us' and the 1718 rite and Rattray employ 'make'. It is likely that the bishops regarded 'become' as simply synonymous with 'make'. Indeed, 'become' is a stronger verb than 'be' but could be adopted without disturbing the flow of an *epiclesis* which looks to 1637 for its form. The verb 'make' could not be introduced without a significant re-writing. As the text stands, the *epiclesis* and prayer of oblation are encompassed by the heading 'The Invocation'. Falconar and Forbes may well have judged that the fruits of communion, such as forgiveness of sins (cited in St James and *Apostolic Constitutions 8*) were there and that not too much should be made of the full stop at the end of the *epiclesis*. Nevertheless, the form adopted has received much criticism, both from Dowden and also William Perry who comments:

> Whence did Bishop Falconer (*sic*), who was the leading spirit in the revision, derive this form? Bishop Dowden says that he followed the liturgy of S. Clement (the form in Apostolic Constitutions) but not far enough. No doubt this liturgy influenced the text of 1764, but of verbal resemblance in the invocation there is hardly a trace. It seems to me that Falconer, despairing of the attempt to force into English words the Greek text of any liturgy, simply endeavoured to express in the most direct manner possible the principle of the normal liturgical invocation. He was right in eschewing the dangerous expedient of translation, but he was wrong in interpreting his models. By stopping short at the words 'they may become,' etc., he omitted what all ancient liturgies are careful to express, the purpose of the consecration. Thus the liturgy was exposed to two charges – (1) it was without ancient precedent, and (2) it was popish in appearing to countenance the doctrine of transubstantiation.[39]

That not all were happy with the 1764 form is illustrated by a modified edition of the Scottish communion office by Bishop Abernethy Drummond, Bishop of Edinburgh 1787-1806, where the *epiclesis* reads 'that they may become the spiritual body and blood ...'.[40]

The Protestant Episcopal Church of the United States of America, 1790

The background to the American Liturgy of 1790 has been thoroughly investigated by Marion Hatchett in his book *The Making of the First American Book of Common Prayer 1776-89*. A connection between Scotland and the United States of America was established when the first American bishop-designate, Samuel Seabury, having

39 Perry, *The Scottish Liturgy: Its Value and History*, pp. 51-52.

40 Dowden, *The Scottish Communion Office of 1764, New Edition*, p. 223.

been sent from Connecticut to seek consecration in England, was eventually consecrated in Aberdeen in 1784 by three Scottish bishops. A concordat was signed, whereby Seabury agreed to 'take a serious view' of the Scottish Communion Office and if judged to be agreeable to the standards of antiquity, 'give his sanction to it'.[41] While there is some evidence that Seabury equated or confused the Scottish rite with 1549,[42] in the event there is no evidence that he immediately took any action to this end on his return to America. The desire for a revised liturgy was strong, following the adoption of a Church Constitution at a convention in Philadelphia in 1785 and a committee was appointed to work on a proposed revision of the Prayer Book. This resulted in the publication of a *Proposed Book* in 1786, which included no change in the English prayer of consecration. The proposals went to State Conventions and the Maryland Convention, where Scottish influence was significant, proposed that an *epiclesis* based on the Scottish 1637 rite should be inserted before the narrative of institution. Some Scottish clergy in America had in any case been using the Scottish consecration prayer according to the various 'wee bookies'.

The Maryland proposal was supported by the Pennsylvania convention,[43] while at Boston, the influential cleric William Parker argued for the adoption of the 1764 Scottish Office. Seabury was also critical of the draft and issued an adapted version of the Scottish Office, including the 1764 *epiclesis*, to the Connecticut convocation in September 1786.[44] One contemporary witness, however, wrote that Seabury's revised rite was with '*a noble spirit rejected*'.[45] In preparation for the 1789 Philadelphia Convention, one of the Maryland Scots, William Smith, urged (at least some) delegates to adopt a prayer of consecration based on primitive models and cited the Scottish office as a good example. Seabury himself brought to the Convention his adapted version of the Scottish rite. In the end, the bishops included an *epiclesis* in the prayer of consecration, adopting the Scottish 1764 position, but amending the text in line with the proposals of Maryland and Pennsylvania which looked to 1637. The text ran:

> And we most humbly beseech thee, O merciful Father, to hear us, and, of thy almighty goodness, vouchsafe to bless and sanctify by thy word and Holy Spirit, these thy gifts and creatures of bread and wine; that we, receiving them according to thy Son our Saviour Jesus Christ's holy institution, in remembrance of his Death and Passion, may be partakers of his most blessed Body and Blood. And we earnestly ... [46]

---

41 Marion J. Hatchett, *The Making of the First American Book of Common Prayer 1776-89* (New York, 1982), pp. 42-43.

42 Ibid., p. 43.

43 Ibid., pp. 87-88.

44 A facsimile of this rite is in Samuel Hart, *Bishop Seabury's Communion-Office* (New York, 1874). Seabury's doctrine of the means of consecration followed in the Non-juring tradition, Edward P. Echlin, *The Anglican Eucharist in Ecumenical Perspective* (New York, 1968), pp. 214-216.

45 Hatchett, *The Making of the First American Book of Common Prayer 1776-89*, p. 100.

46 Text from William McGarvey, *Liturgicae Americanae* (Philadelphia, 1907), p. 240.

Thus the American eucharistic prayer followed structurally the sequence narrative–oblation–invocation in the tradition of the Scotland 1764, the Non-jurors and ultimately the 'primitive' eastern rites, but with accommodation of the English Prayer Book's emphasis on reception. It consequently includes both objective and subjective emphases. A *Standard Book* was produced in 1793, the definitive version of the American Prayer Book. Here a change was made in the *epiclesis* in that 'word' became 'Word'. This implied a change of interpretation, 'word' designating the institution narrative, and 'Word' the operation of Christ, the Word of God. Thus consecration is effected by the Second and Third Persons of the Trinity upon petition to the First. The 1892 revision of the Prayer Book did not amend the prayer of consecration.[47]

The Wesleys

At the heart of the Evangelical Revival in Britain in the eighteenth century stand the Wesley brothers, John and Charles. Their parents, Samuel and Susanna, became Anglicans by conviction during their teenage years having both come from families with strong dissenting traditions. Samuel Wesley, Rector of Epworth, espoused a 'Laudian' conception of the sacrament and celebrated a monthly communion service, uncommonly frequent for his time. Susanna combined a high regard for the sacraments with strong Puritan-inspired piety. Indeed, in a letter to John in 1732 she cites with approval a definition of Christ's presence suggested by a friend of his: 'the Divine nature of Christ is then eminently present to impart, by the operation of His Holy Spirit, the benefits of his death to worthy receivers'.[48]

The influence of the Non-jurors in the Wesley household is well documented, beginning at Epworth where Samuel Wesley was a friend of Robert Nelson, but more especially in the Oxford Holy Club through the influence of John Clayton, a close associate of Thomas Deacon.[49] Moreover, John Wesley was especially influenced by Nelson's writings, adapting extracts from *The Great Duty of Frequenting the Christian Sacrifice* for the use of students at Lincoln College. Unfortunately, there is no record of whether this association had liturgical implications, especially during

47 One further American initiative was the publication in 1895 of a prayer book of the Mexican Church of Jesus, a reforming movement which seceded from the Catholic Church and united itself to the Episcopal Church. The book drew on the work of Charles Hale, a Mozarabic scholar; see H. Boone Porter, 'Hispanic Influences on Worship in the English Tongue', in J. Neil Alexander (ed.), *Time and Community* (Washington, DC, 1990), pp. 171-184. The prayer of consecration included a single *epiclesis* after the *anamnesis*:

> … that Thou wouldst send down Thy Holy Ghost, with the fulness of Thy blessing, upon these Thy gifts and Creatures of Bread and Wine; That we, receiving them according to our Saviour Christ's Holy Institution may be partakers of his Most Blessed Body and Blood.

48 Cited by John C. Bowmer, *The Sacrament of the Lord's Supper in Early Methodism* (London, 1951), p. 20.

49 Ibid., pp. 21, 26-29; Trevor Dearing, *Wesleyan and Tractarian Worship* (London, 1966), pp. 2ff.

the mission to Georgia from 1736 to 1738. While Wesley recorded that he 'revised' the Prayer Book in March 1736, suggestions that this was to achieve conformity with 1549 or adoption of the 'usages' must remain as conjecture. Indeed, in 1736, John Wesley repudiated some of the earlier influences upon him:

> Nor was it long before I bent the bow too far the other way: (1) by making antiquity a co-ordinate (rather than subordinate) rule with Scripture; (2) by admitting several doubtful writings as undoubted evidences of antiquity; (3) by extending antiquity too far, even to the middle or end of the fourth century; (4) by believing more practices to have been universal in the ancient Church than ever were so.[50]

The role of the Spirit in the eucharist is not discussed systematically in the extant theological writings and sermons of the Wesleys. However, there are some significant pointers. John Wesley taught that the Lord's Supper was ordained 'to be a means of conveying to men either preventing, or justifying, or sanctifying grace, according to their several necessities'.[51] The work of the Spirit is central, as expounded in his sermon 'The Means of Grace': 'We allow likewise that all outward means whatever, if separate from the Spirit of God, cannot profit at all, cannot conduce in any degree either to the knowledge or love of God'.[52] The eucharistic elements thus have 'no inherent power';[53] the grace is mediated through the grace or power of the Spirit, but the elements are the channel of the grace:

> Is not the eating of that bread, and the drinking of that cup, the outward, visible means whereby God conveys into our souls all that spiritual grace, that righteousness, and peace, and joy in the Holy Ghost, which were purchased by the body and blood of Christ once shed for us?[54]

Nowhere is this conviction more eloquently stated than in his sixth discourse on the Sermon on the Mount. Commenting on the petition 'Give us this day our daily bread', Wesley observes the sacramental interpretation given by many of the Fathers, with the practice of daily reception, understanding the eucharist to be 'the grand channel whereby the grace of his Spirit was conveyed to the souls of all the children of men'.[55]

There is, however, no explicit reference to the eucharistic *epiclesis*. The nearest we have is his comment on 1 Corinthians 10:16 in John Wesley's *Explanatory Notes Upon the New Testament* where 'blessing' the cup is 'setting it apart to a sacred use, and solemnly invoking the blessing of God upon it'.[56] Similarly, in his treatise *Popery Calmly Considered*, he affirms that sacramental grace 'proceeds from the

---

50 *Works, Vol. 18*, p. 213, also cited by Bowmer, *The Sacrament of the Lord's Supper in Early Methodism*, p. 28. There is documentary evidence for Wesley's use of the mixed chalice, defended by him as late as 1749, Bowmer, ibid., pp. 92-93.

51 *Journal*, 28 June 1740, *The Works of John Wesley, Vol. 19* (ed. W.R. Ward and R.P. Heitzenrater, Nashville, 1990), p. 159.

52 *The Works of John Wesley, Vol. 1* (ed. Albert C. Outler, Nashville, 1984), p. 382.

53 Ibid.

54 Ibid., pp. 389-390.

55 'Upon our Lord's Sermon on the Mount: Discourse the Sixth', ibid., p. 585.

56 Edition cited: London: Epworth Press, 1976, p. 615.

blessing of God',[57] and in rejecting transubstantiation, echoes the familiar Anglican and Non-juring response that the Fathers called the elements 'the images, the symbols, the figure, of Christ's body and blood' but without adding the conviction that the invocation completes the consecration.

Much more significant is the collection *Hymns on the Lord's Supper* first published in 1745. The collection, prefaced by an abbreviated version of Daniel Brevint's *The Christian Sacrament and Sacrifice*, was published in the names of both John and Charles, although the latter was the chief author. Brevint's treatise, first published in 1673, does not discuss the role of the Spirit in the consecration of the elements. The Wesleys followed Brevint's chapter order and themes, but did include some accommodation of the Spirit's work. However, a cautionary word is needed. We have noted the influence of the Non-jurors with their developed epicletic theology, but the Wesleys did not view this uncritically. In their ministry in England, Wales and Ireland, we can have no doubt that they adhered faithfully to the text and rubrics of the Prayer Book. Moreover, the use of hymnody sets a broader liturgical framework than liturgical texts. So, hymns invoking the Spirit are not to be regarded as a kind of liturgical interpolation to make good what the Prayer Book omitted or only implied. Indeed, the 1745 collection includes 166 hymns which would be used selectively and comprehensively and so only occasionally. It is more likely that the Wesleys regarded them as amplifying and complementing the Prayer Book text, drawing out themes and associations which a liturgical text could not begin to incorporate. The other factor is that the condensed and poetic devices employed in hymnody make it a dangerous source for extrapolating a precise theology.[58]

A recurring theme is the concept of the Spirit as a seal. This is to confirm or bear witness to the reality of Christ's death for sinners as attested by the eucharist:[59]

Come, Holy Ghost, set to Thy seal,
Thine inward witness give,
To all our waiting souls reveal
The death by which we live.[60]

The Spirit is understood to have a clear revelatory function as evidence by the use of the verbs 'reveal', 'attest' and 'prove' in the hymn cited. Hymn 16, a prayer to the Spirit, incorporates a phrase from the *epiclesis* of *Apostolic Constitutions 8*, combined with John 14:26; the former citing the Spirit as the witness of Christ's sufferings, the later that he will bring all things to the disciples' remembrance:

Come, Thou Witness of his dying,
Come, Remembrancer Divine,
Let us feel Thy power applying
Christ to every soul and mine ...

57 *The Works of the Rev. John Wesley, Vol. 10* (London, n.d.), p. 149.

58 This danger is highlighted by John R. Parris in *John Wesley's Doctrine of the Sacraments* (London, 1963), pp. 70-71, fn. 25.

59 Quotations are from J. Ernest Rattenbury, *The Eucharistic Hymns of John and Charles Wesley* (London, 1948).

60 No. 7, v. 1; see also 10, v. 4; 75, v. 3; 89, v. 4.

The Spirit actively relates Christ's redemptive acts to the communicant so that they are personally appropriated. This thought is parallel to Charles Wesley's general hymns on the Spirit with his oft-repeated assertion that the Spirit applies the blood of Christ to the believer.[61] The application of the Spirit is clearly through the medium of the elements:

> The tokens of Thy dying love
> O let us all receive,
> And feel the quickening Spirit move,
> And *sensibly* believe.[62]

This brings out the experiential element in the brothers's thought. Believing is not merely an intellectual or cerebral activity; it engages the whole person, body and mind. The grace of God is visible and may be eaten and drunk; the Spirit can be felt or experienced. Indeed, the power inherent in the sacrament renders it as a converting ordinance as well as a confirming ordinance.

The clearest statement of the Spirit in relation to the elements is Hymn 72:

> Come, Holy Ghost, Thine influence shed,
> And realize the sign;
> Thy life infuse into the bread,
> Thy power into the wine.
>
> Effectual let the tokens prove,
> And made, by heavenly art,
> Fit channels to convey Thy love
> To every faithful heart.

J.E. Rattenbury describes this hymn as 'an exact expression of the *epiclesis* prayer' and interprets 'realize' as 'real make'.[63] Ole Borgen similarly regards this as 'similar to the *epiclesis* of the ancient church' and wishes to distinguish between the two stanzas, the first 'a prayer for the consecration of the sign' and the second 'a prayer to make this consecrated sign an effectual means of grace'. He interpreted Rattenbury as only allowing for the second, and so he interprets 'realize' as 'bring into actual existence' or make 'the elements real and sacred signs'.[64] Consequent upon the first petition, comes the second, that the grace of the sign might be received.[65] It is necessary, however, not to interpret the hymn in isolation. Hymn 66 is in certain aspects parallel in thought to 72 but is related Christologically:

---

61 J. Ernest Rattenbury, *The Evangelical Doctrines of Charles Wesley's Hymns* (London, 1941), p. 174.

62 No. 30, v. 4.

63 *Eucharistic Hymns*, p. 50, followed by Bowmer, *The Sacrament of the Lord's Supper in Early Methodism*, p. 87, fn. 1. There seem to be no linguistic grounds, however, for Bowmer's comparison of this hymn and the *epiclesis* of 1549.

64 Borgen is followed here by Daniel Stevinck, *The Altar's Fire: Charles Wesley's Hymns on the Lord's Supper, 1745* (Peterborough, 2004), p. 124.

65 Ole E. Borgen, *John Wesley on the Sacraments: A Theological Study* (Zurich, 1972), pp. 73, 75, 76.

Jesu, my Lord and God, bestow
All which Thy sacrament doth show,
And make the real sign
A sure effectual means of grace,
Then sanctify my heart, and bless,
And make it all like Thine.

It is doubtful whether too much ought to be read into the inversion of 'real sign' when compared with 72; the sense could equally be 'and make the sign real, a sure effectual sign of grace'. This would understand the sign and the grace to be in apposition. Another Christological example is number 58 where Wesley draws on the imagery of the pool of Bethesda:

Angel and Son of God, come down,
Thy sacramental banquet crown,
Thy power into the means infuse,
And give them now their sacred use.[66]

The 'empowering' of the means is for the sake of their use, in the life of the believer. The fact is that we have similar statements made both Christologically and pneumatologically. They witness to the dynamic of invocation in the eucharistic action, of the role of the Son and the Spirit, not always clearly distinguished. Moreover, all three hymns show that there is an intimate connection between the invocation and the effects desired. The Wesleys's evangelical priority is apparent in the conviction that the sacrament is not an end in itself; its power is related to the fruits of sanctification in the life of the believer. Liturgically, it seems assured that the Wesleys would have regarded the *BCP* prayer of consecration as invocatory of itself; a prayer embracing the institution to which God responds in his gracious bestowal of life through the medium of the visible elements. The role of the hymn is to provide a theological devotion, reinforcing the invocatory nature of consecration. A more systematic treatment may be apparent in Hymn 53:

O God of truth and love,
Let us Thy mercy prove;
Bless Thine ordinance Divine,
Let it now effectual be,
Answer all its great design,
And its gracious ends in me.

O might the sacred word
Set forth our dying Lord,
Point us to Thy sufferings past,
Present grace and strength impart,
Give our ravish'd souls a taste,
Pledge of glory in our heart.

66 Compare 112, where the 'Eternal Spirit' is invoked to send his blessings down, but the context confirms that Christ is being addressed.

Come in Thy Spirit down,
Thine institution crown;
Lamb of God, as slain appear,
Life of all believers Thou,
Let us now perceive Thee near,
Come, Thou hope of glory, now.

The divine 'blessing' of the ordinance is in order that it might be effectual. This is by means of 'the sacred word', the institution narrative which points us to Christ's sufferings, and the descent of the Spirit to crown the institution and reveal Christ in his fulness. It is in this context that Wesley's verb 'realize' is probably to be interpreted. The 'realization', the power implored through the Spirit and in the elements, is to enable a present experience of the living presence of Christ in and with the communicant. Both the second and third stanzas refer to spiritual blessing; both word and Spirit seek to render the eucharist effectual. It is perhaps here that we are closest to the 'Laudian' and Non-juring double focus on the institution narrative as rendering the elements as designated symbols of the body and blood and the *epiclesis* enlivening them to be the vehicles of sacramental grace. But the intensity of the personal encounter with Christ is what makes the Wesleys's approach distinctive.[67]

Finally it should be noted that John Wesley published a revision of the Prayer Book, known as his 'Abridgement', in 1784 for use in America. While there are significant changes in the communion rite, he reproduces the 1662 prayer of consecration with only minor changes to text and rubric. The revised book was subsequently published for use in Britain.[68]

The Tractarians and the Anglo-Catholic Movement

A change of emphasis is discernible in William Palmer's two volume work *Origines Liturgicae*, first published in 1832 and enlarged in 1845. Palmer's purpose was to show that the English rite was based on ancient sources; the first part of his work is a review of the liturgies of the ancient liturgical centres,[69] and the second an examination of 'the Antiquities of the English Ritual'. Palmer interprets the 'Hear us' clause as 'in the language of the primitive Church', an *epiclesis*.[70] While the explicit invocation

67 The fact that the Spirit has a clear revelatory function in the hymns may ultimately go back to the verb *apophenei* in *Apostolic Constitutions 8* which carries the sense of 'manifest', 'exhibit', 'show'.

68 *The Sunday Service of the Methodists with Other Occasional Services, 4th edition* (London, 1792).

69 Palmer occupies an important place in the quest for the 'Apostolic *anaphora*'. His research led him to the conclusion that there was not a single origin but four parental rites deriving from Apostolic times, namely the Oriental, Alexandrian, Gallican and Roman, R.C.D. Jasper, *The Search for an Apostolic Liturgy* (London, 1963), pp. 6-7; Martin Stringer, 'Antiquities of an English Liturgist: William Palmer's Use of Origins in the Study of the English Liturgy', *Ephemerides Liturgicae*, 108 (1994): 147-150.

70 W. Palmer, *Origines Liturgicae, Vol. 2*, 4th ed. (London, 1845), p. 134. Alf Härdelin observes that Palmer showed no particular interest in 1549; he was content to expound 1662 in

of the Spirit as witnessed by the Churches of Caesarea, Antioch and Alexandria with further attestation in Africa, Spain and Gaul was 'of great weight and value ... perfectly orthodox, and highly laudable', it was not essential.[71] Palmer posits two grounds: the first that there is no evidence that an *epiclesis* of the Spirit was used liturgically in Italy and Rome, and the second that 'it is not necessary in prayer to God to mention the means by which he is to accomplish the end which is prayed for'.[72] So while consecration is effected by the Spirit, explicit reference is unnecessary. The English rite is thus analogous to the Roman in this matter. Palmer argued that what was universal in all the primitive liturgies and teaching of the Fathers was the repetition of the eucharistic words of Jesus 'so that no consecration of the bread and wine could be effected without their repetition'.[73] The change of emphasis from the primitive eastern liturgies to the western and Roman tradition with the emphasis on the words of institution is most significant and set the tone for what would develop as the anglo-catholic approach.

As for the *Tracts for the Times* themselves, there is no theological discussion of the *epiclesis*. Tract 63, *The Antiquity of the Existing Liturgies*, was published in 1834 and written by Richard Hurrell Froude. Drawing on Palmer's work, Froude sets out the structure and part of the text of the Roman, Oriental (St James), Egyptian (St Mark) and Gallican forms of the eucharistic prayer. Interestingly, in his structural analysis, he cites the institution narrative as the 'commemoration of our Lord's words' and the *epiclesis* or petition for consecration as 'the Consecration' by which he means 'a prayer of consecration, that God will "make the bread and wine the Body and Blood of Christ"'.[74] He does not discuss this distinction further. Tract 81, *Catena Patrum* (1837), attributed to E.B. Pusey,[75] on eucharistic sacrifice, clearly favoured the 1549 rite, describing it as 'the genuine English Service Book'.[76] In the introductory essay preceding the catena of sixteenth-century to eighteenth-century Anglican divines,[77] Pusey commends silent prayer when the priest places the bread and wine on the altar at the offertory. The text he suggests in a footnote is Bishop

---

its own terms, *The Tractarian Understanding of the Eucharist* (Uppsala, 1965), pp. 252-253. Stringer observes that Palmer does not use the word '*epiclesis*', except in Greek; it had not yet in 1843 fully become a technical term, 'Antiquities of an English Liturgist', p. 152, fn. 30.

71 Palmer, *Origines Liturgicae, Vol. 2*, p. 136.

72 Ibid., p. 137.

73 Ibid., p. 141.

74 Tract 63, *Tracts for the Times, Vol. 2*, 4th ed. (London and Oxford, 1840), p. 7.

75 W.H. Mackean, *The Eucharistic Doctrine of the Oxford Movement* (London,1933), p. 62.

76 *Tracts for the Times, Vol. 4* (1838), Tract 81, p. 23; cf. pp. 12, 57-58. Härdelin comments that Pusey did not seek the restoration of 1549; rather, it was the key for the interpretation of subsequent revisions of the liturgy, *The Tractarian Understanding of the Eucharist*, p. 254.

77 The *catena* illustrates the fact that during this period the Tractarians drew widely on Anglican sacramental exploration. As Peter Nockles comments, Tracts 74 & 81 'included as many representatives from the receptionist school of Hooker and Waterland as from the virtualist school of Brett, Johnson and Alexander Knox', *The Oxford Movement in Context* (Cambridge, 1994), pp. 238-239.

Wilson's epicletic prayer for use after the consecration. In the main text, he goes on to give the text of the old Gallican Liturgy where oblation and invocation are combined:

> We, O Lord, observing these Thy gifts and precepts, lay upon Thine Altar the sacrifices of Bread and Wine, beseeching the deep goodness of Thy mercy, that the Holy and Undivided Trinity may sanctify these Sacrifices, by the same Spirit through which uncorrupt virginity conceived Thee in the flesh ...

Also the Gallican Christmas liturgy:

> We therefore, observing these His commandments, offer unto Thee the holy gift of our salvation, beseeching Thee that Thou wouldst vouchsafe to send Thy Holy Spirit upon these solemn mysteries, that they may become to us a true Eucharist ...[78]

While Pusey appears to suggest an epicletic prayer preceding the recitation of the narrative, authors are cited and texts quoted (such as the canon of the American liturgy) where a post- narrative invocation is attested.

It is clear that Pusey's own eucharistic thought went through a process of development. After Tract 81, one constant is the role of eucharistic words of Jesus in effecting the consecration. So in his sermon 'The Holy Eucharist a Comfort to the Penitent' of 1843 the words of institution are 'the awful words, whereby He consecrated for ever elements of this world to be His Body and Blood'.[79] In his 1857 treatise *The Real Presence of the Body and Blood of our Lord Jesus Christ*, the sacramental gift, 'the heavenly part is conveyed to us through the earthly symbol consecrated by His word of power'. In his *Eirenicon* (1865) the words of institution represent the 'immutable foundation' and that where 'there is Apostolical succession and a consecration in our Lord's words, there ... is the Eucharistic sacrifice'.[80] Pusey did have a clear doctrine of the Spirit in relation to consecration, but this is in no sense independent of the eucharistic words. In his 1853 sermon 'The Presence of Christ in the Holy Eucharist' the body and blood are given 'spiritually,[81] sacramentally, divinely, mystically, ineffably, through the operation of the word of Christ and of God the Holy Ghost'.[82] Earlier in the sermon, he adapts a quotation from John Damascene: '"... .And now askest thou, how," under these outward forms, we receive "the Body of Christ, and the Blood of Christ? The Holy Spirit cometh down and worketh what is above discourse and above all thought."'[83] So while consecration is effected by the institution, through the power of the Spirit, the emphasis is on the

---

78 *Tracts for the Times, Vol. 4*, p. 56.

79 E.B. Pusey, 'The Holy Eucharist A Comfort to the Penitent', p. 20, from *University Sermons, Vol. 1* (Oxford and London, 1879).

80 E.B. Pusey, *An Eirenicon* (Oxford and London, 1865), pp. 23, 25.

81 On the word 'spiritual', Härdelin observes that in evangelical thought, its use implied a denial of any real presence; the Tractarians, however, stressed that 'spiritual' stood in no opposition to 'real', *The Tractarian Understanding of the Eucharist*, p. 157.

82 Pusey, 'The Presence of Christ in the Holy Eucharist', p. 46, *University Sermons, Vol. 1.*

83 Ibid., p. 24; also fn. 7.

narrative. This teaching lies behind anglo-catholic dislike of the Greek sequence of narrative–oblation–invocation and the preference for a 1549-type preliminary *epiclesis* because the invocation of the Spirit becomes a prayer concerning the effect of the words of institution.

Robert Wilberforce similarly gives clear priority to the narrative of institution. The repetition of the words of Christ is essential because they are 'effective and not merely declaratory'.[84] Wilberforce sought to be inclusive of primitive tradition and so argues that the role of *epiclesis* in all the ancient liturgies except the Roman brings out the weight attached to the elements and so to the reality of the gift bestowed in them.[85] Nevertheless, the efficacy of the eucharistic words is not superseded by the *epiclesis*; in an extended discussion he argues:

> … so completely does each co-operate in that which either performs, that we cannot exclude the Holy Ghost from that action which is performed by the Son through the medium of His Priests, nor yet the Son from that which is effected by the Holy Ghost who proceeds from Him. So that it would be rash perhaps to define at what moment the act of consecration is effected, while yet it is reverent to treat it as effected when the first essential portion of it is performed.[86]

In other words, the narrative of institution is sufficient to effect consecration.[87] While Wilberforce is prone to descend into polemic, a fruitful aspect of his treatment is his attempt to see the eucharist as an action of the Trinity.

J.M. Neale provides an interesting example of a leading member of the catholic revival with a profound theological and historical interest in the Orthodox churches.[88] This is reflected in his *Sermons on the Blessed Sacrament*; sermon IV (1857), based on Exodus 16:15, includes the words:

> We all know that, as each Person of the ever-blessed Trinity has his own proper office in the work of man's redemption, so it is part of the Holy Ghost to effect the change in the elements now, as He once effected the Incarnation of the Word made Flesh. And He is indeed the Dew, so pure, so soft, coming so silently, giving life and refreshment and beauty everywhere, coming in a way that none can understand, coming invisibly, coming in the night of affliction.[89]

Neale's language that the Spirit effects the change reflects epicletic texts in the liturgies of St John Chrysostom, St James and *Apostolic Constitutions 8*; he was also an advocate of the Scottish Communion Office.

---

84 R. Wilberforce, *The Doctrine of the Holy Eucharist* (London, 1885), p. 46.

85 Ibid., p. 48.

86 Ibid., p. 244.

87 By consecration, he means the making 'sacramentally present of that very body which once became incarnate and suffered on the cross', Härdelin, *The Tractarian Understanding of the Eucharist*, p. 182.

88 See Leon Litvack, *J.M. Neale and the Quest for Sobornost* (Oxford, 1994).

89 J.M. Neale, *Sermons on the Blessed Sacrament, New Edition* (London, 1900), p. 29.

Another important aspect of this period was the production of altar missals, supplementing the Prayer Book text. P.G. Medd edited *The Priest to the Altar*, first published in 1861.[90] Here an adapted and truncated version of the *epiclesis* from *Apostolic Constitutions 8* is included as a 'secret' before the prayer of consecration as a private devotion of the priest:[91]

> Most Merciful God, look graciously upon the Gifts now lying before Thee, and send down Thy Holy Spirit upon this Sacrifice: that he may make this Bread the Body of thy Christ, and this Cup the Blood of Thy Christ.[92]

So an 'eastern' text is adapted for western theological purposes, although Medd also included in his missal the 1549 rite and the Scottish and American liturgies, thus providing texts with both 'western' and 'eastern' shapes for the *anaphora*.[93]

Orby Shipley's *Ritual of the Altar* (1870) combines the Prayer Book text with interpolations from the Roman Mass in Latin and English. These include the Roman offertory prayers including the secret *Veni sanctificator*, the Roman canon from *Te igitur* to the end of *Quam oblationem* following the prayer of humble access, and *Unde et memores* to the end of the canon following the 1662 prayer of consecration.[94] Interestingly, he describes as an 'Invocation of the Holy Ghost' both the 1662 'Hear us' clause[95] and the offertory prayers after the offering of the chalice,[96] but the *Quam oblationem* is merely cited as 'that the Oblation may become the Body and Blood of Christ'.

Devotional enrichment is illustrated by *The Priest's Book of Private Devotions* by Joseph Oldknow and Augustine Crake, first published in 1882.[97] Here the 1662 rite is supplemented at the offertory from the 1718 Non-jurors's rite:

> O almighty God, who hast created us ... Receive it, O God, as a sweet smelling savour, and send down the grace of Thy Holy Spirit upon us ...

After humble access, an *epiclesis* is adapted from the Liturgy of St James:

> Have mercy upon us, O Lord our God, after Thy great mercy, and send down upon us, and upon these Gifts lying before Thee, Thy HOLY GHOST, that He may make this bread the HOLY BODY and this cup the BLOOD of Thy Christ; that They may be to us, who partake of them for the remission of sins, and for the sanctification of soul and body unto life everlasting. Amen.[98]

---

90 P.G. Medd (ed.), *The Priest to the Altar*, 3rd ed. (London, 1879).

91 The 'Clementine' text is an alternative; the priest may say the *Te igitur* from *Sarum* instead, ibid., p. 166.

92 Ibid.

93 1549, ibid., pp. 177-201; Scotland, pp. 203-223; USA, pp. 225-244. Mark Dalby sets out the changes across successive editions in *Anglican Missals and their Canons: 1549, Interim Rite and Roman* (Cambridge, 1998), pp. 4-6.

94 Orby Shipley, *Ritual of the Altar* (London, 1870).

95 Ibid., p. vii.

96 Ibid., p. xxii.

97 The edition cited here is the Mowbray's 1906 London edition.

98 Ibid., p. 433.

The 1662 prayer of consecration is then supplemented by the 1549 canon from the *anamnesis* to the end. Once again we see a petition originally from an *anaphora* of the West Syrian type adapted to 'western' usage, although among some supplementary prayers in the appendix the 1718 Non-jurors' *epiclesis* is given in full for use 'at the canon', presumably in the 1718 position.

As well as books provided for the clergy, devotional manuals for the laity were also common. William Bright's *Ancient Collects and Other Prayers for Devotional Use* provides a variety of prayers for use of the offertory, two of which are epicletic, although addressed to different Persons of the Trinity:

> SEND forth, O Lord, we beseech Thee, the Holy Spirit, to make these present offerings Thy Sacrament unto us, and purify our hearts for its reception. (Leonine)
> WE beseech Thee, O Lord, in Thy mercy to sanctify these gifts, and having received the offering of the spiritual sacrifice, to make us a perpetual oblation unto Thee; through Jesus Christ our Lord. (Leonine)[99]

In the section 'before the consecration', a Mozarabic text includes the petition:

> ... and pray Thee to bless this Sacrifice with Thy blessing, and to sprinkle it with the dew of the Holy Spirit, that it may be to all who receive it a pure, true, and legitimate Eucharist ...[100]

In a note, Bright cites Neale's interpretation of 'legitimate' as 'effectual' rather than 'duly consecrated'. The second prayer, also Mozarabic, runs:

> BE present, be present, Jesus, Good High Priest, in the midst of us, as Thou wast in the midst of Thy disciples. Sanctify this oblation.[101]

This prayer was to appear in the 1950 rite of the Church of South India.[102]

Orby Shipley published his manual, *The Divine Liturgy*, in 1863.[103] In the preface, he writes:

> After the Offering of the Alms, the Oblation of the Elements is made. Here, persons will do well to make use of one of the Prayers for the Invocation of GOD the HOLY GHOST, that Almighty GOD would be pleased, in the language of one of them, to send down the same Most HOLY GHOST upon these Holy Gifts, that He may hallow and make this Bread the Holy BODY of CHRIST, and this Cup the Precious BLOOD of CHRIST.[104]

Shipley provides a form of *epiclesis* for each day of the week for use at the oblation of the bread and wine, preceding the prayer of consecration, drawing on translations of Eastern texts by J.M. Neale.[105]

---

99 *Ancient Collects and Other Prayers Selected for Devotional Use*, 2nd ed. (Oxford and London, 1862), pp. 140-141.

100 Ibid., p. 142.

101 Ibid.

102 See below, pp. 201, 202.

103 Orby Shipley, *The Divine Liturgy* (London, 1863).

104 Ibid., p. ix.

105 Ibid., pp. 68-73.

Similarly, W.E. Scudamore in his *Steps to the Altar* provides a preliminary *epiclesis* drawn from *Apostolic Constitutions 8* and the prayer of elevation from the liturgies of St Basil and St John Chrysostom, for use after humble access:

> *When the Priest is preparing to use the prayer of Consecration, say,*
> Most Merciful GOD, the FATHER of our LORD JESUS CHRIST, look graciously upon the gifts now lying before Thee; and send Thy HOLY SPIRIT upon this Sacrifice, that He may make this bread and this wine the Body and Blood of Thy CHRIST. O Thou, Who sittest at the right hand of the FATHER, yet art present with us, though unseen, come and sanctify with Thy Presence these Thy gifts, those who offer, and those who receive them. Amen.[106]

Finally, Bishop Walsham How in his *Holy Communion Preparation and Companion*, published in 1883, provides two prayers of invocation to be said by the worshipper between humble access and the consecration:

> *For the Blessing of the Holy Ghost.*
> O HEAVENLY FATHER, send forth the Holy Ghost to bless and sanctify this Bread and Wine, that we may behold in them the Body and Blood of Christ, and, partaking of these holy emblems, may receive forgiveness of our sins and everlasting life; through Jesus Christ our Lord. Amen.
> *Or this,*
> O GOD, send down thy Holy Spirit to bless for us these gifts of Thy hand, that receiving them with faith, we may be fed with the Bread of Life, which cometh down from heaven; through Jesus Christ our Lord. Amen.[107]

The vast majority of texts make provision for a preliminary prayer of invocation, clearly understanding the narrative of institution as the locus of the consecration. The general principle appears to be that consecration is effected in petition to the Father, through the power of the Spirit, but by the recitation of the narrative.

A final factor to be mentioned is the role of hymnody. *Hymns Ancient and Modern* was first published in 1861, with strong Tractarian involvement in its production. The first edition had no epicletic material but in the *Supplement* added in 1889, the following hymn by A.J. Mason was included:[108]

> Look down upon us, God of grace,
> And send from Thy most holy place
> The quickening Spirit all Divine
> On us and on this bread and wine.
> O may his overshadowing
> Make now for us this bread we bring
> The Body of Thy Son our Lord,
> This cup His Blood for sinners pour'd.[109]

---

106 W.E. Scudamore, *Steps to the Altar: A Manual of Devotions for the Blessed Eucharist*, 69th ed. (London: 1888).

107 H. Walsham How, *Holy Communion: Preparation and Companion* (London, 1883) p. 63. I am indebted to the Rt Revd Dr Kenneth Stevenson for this reference.

108 Mason's authorship is attested in John Julian (ed.), *A Dictionary of Hymnology* (London, 1915), p. 1579.

109 *Hymns Ancient and Modern*, 552.

However, while supplementary prayers in missals and primars were assigned a specific place, there is no such specificity for hymns. Presumably this hymn would be sung either at the offertory (which may be considered as too early) or during the distribution (which may be considered too late). It seems doubtful whether it would be sung immediately after the prayer of consecration.[110]

Nineteenth-Century Evangelicalism

The rise of the Oxford Movement was a fundamental challenge to the evangelical party in the Church of England, not least because it regarded itself as the guardian of the reformed, scriptural faith within the Church. In particular, Tractarian teaching asserting an objective presence of Christ in the eucharistic elements, a mediating and sacerdotal priesthood, and the eucharistic oblation, prompted a vigorous response. Discussion of the *epiclesis* comes as more of a by-product than a central concern but there are some notable references in evangelical sacramental writing.

William Goode, in his exhaustive study *The Nature of Christ's Presence in the Eucharist* published in 1856, summarizes the teaching of the Fathers as affirming that the body and blood of Christ are made present to the believer 'by the effectual operation of the Holy Spirit'; the Spirit enables the grace and virtue of Christ's risen body to be communicated, effecting a 'union and communion' between Christ's human nature and the communicant. Some Fathers use the language of 'change' in relation to the elements, but because they use the same language for baptism, it is clear that the elements do not change any more than the baptismal water changes, 'but only that instrumentally it worked differently from water not attended with the same Divine blessing'.[111] He rejects any notion that the 'substantial' presence of Christ is attributable to the operation of the Spirit. The Fathers are referring to a different sort of presence, namely, a

> presence to our spirits by which, through the operation of the Holy Spirit, our souls are not only enabled to behold and touch and feed upon the body and blood of Christ spiritually, but are also spiritually united to that body, so that its lifegiving efficacy and virtue are communicated to us.[112]

The Spirit therefore effects 'a real spiritual union between the human nature of Christ and the believer'.[113] Goode therefore rejects any appeal to the Greek liturgies in support to an objective change in the elements. He asserts that there is no evidence of the form of eucharistic celebration in apostolic times, the earliest liturgy is from

---

110 Anamnetic hymns such as 'And now, O Father', or 'Wherefore, O Father' would be preferred. Mason's hymn was deleted for the 1950 revision, probably because it was rarely used, but also possibly due to Gregory Dix's judgment that the *epiclesis* was a later liturgical development. The 1950 edition also deleted a further epicletic reference added in the 1916 second *Supplement*, 'Father, Who dost Thy children feed' (no. 721).

111 William Goode, *The Nature of Christ's Presence in the Eucharist, Vol. 1* (London, 1856), pp. 426-427.

112 Ibid., p. 434.

113 Ibid., p. 436.

the third century. Moreover, 'no invocation of the Holy Spirit occurs in the most ancient forms of the Roman Liturgy'.[114] The language of 'change' is not present in all the rites, but its use in some showed a strengthening of expressions used as to the effect of consecration. But as to the meaning of the change, he returns to the equivalence of baptism:

> ... the strongest terms which the Fathers use to denote a change in the Eucharistic elements are also used by them with reference to the water of baptism, in which no one supposes any other change to be made, than that from common water it becomes changed in its character, use, and effect, being consecrated to a sacred purpose, and operating, through the Divine blessing, to produce effects for which naturally it had no power.[115]

For Goode, therefore, while he is able eloquently to define the work of the Spirit in the eucharist, his terms of reference are essentially Cranmerian; the Prayer Book rite was sufficient, although doubtless he would have had no difficulty with Bucer's suggested emendation of the 1549 rite to invoke the Spirit on the worshippers only. Goode was clear that there was no biblical evidence, or sub-Apostolic evidence before the third century, for the illapse of the Spirit on the elements.[116]

Thomas Vogan stressed the role of the institution narrative, as specifying both the actions and words necessary for a valid consecration; the Church follows what Jesus said and did.[117] Specifically he argues that a eucharistic rite should embrace thanksgiving, the Lord's Prayer and the institution narrative as basic elements; other devotions could be added to these 'elementary forms' and he judged the Prayer Book order as 'a model of such devotions as befit this holy rite'.[118] Vogan regarded the doctrine of transubstantiation as an extreme form of rationalism, of speculation as to how the elements can be Christ's body and blood. An earlier manifestation of this rationalism was the theological assertion that the Spirit effected a change in the elements, and this was given liturgical expression in the *epiclesis*. For Vogan this went beyond Christ's institution:

> Our Lord said, 'This is my body, This is my blood.' He did not say, nor do his words intimate, that the bread was his body and the wine his blood, by 'a power of life sent into them,' or by a transference 'into the efficacy of His own flesh.' To assign such a mode, is, in effect, to deny the Lord's words.[119]

His most extended treatment of the *epiclesis* was largely in order to refute John Johnson's *The Unbloody Sacrifice*. Vogan rejects as unscriptural any notion that the eucharistic bread and wine constitute a sacrifice. He thus rejects Johnson's theory that the consecrated bread and wine are offered united with and replenished with the Holy Spirit:

---

114 Ibid., pp. 439-440.

115 Ibid., p. 448.

116 He held a similar position to Waterland, ibid., *Vol. 2*, pp. 963-965.

117 Thomas S.L. Vogan, *The True Doctrine of the Eucharist* (London, 1871), pp. 43-44.

118 Ibid., p. 46.

119 Ibid., pp. 49-50.

> And if the bread and wine in this union, with the presence of the Holy Ghost in, with, and working in, them, be the 'Unbloody Sacrifice' of the Eucharist, then either the Holy Ghost, impanate and invinate, is Himself a sacrifice, or part of a sacrifice with the bread and wine ...[120]

For Vogan such a theory is both impossible and unscriptural. The Holy Spirit is the gift of the Father, not a sacrifice offered to the Father. Vogan undertakes a lengthy refutation of Johnson's interpretation of the Fathers and the Greek liturgies. His own convictions are close to Goode's. While an invocation of the Spirit on the elements is ancient, it is not found in all the ancient liturgies; in this sense it is 'not Catholic'.[121] But where it does come, he stresses the fact that the invocation is for a purpose, namely the participation of the worshippers in the divine graces. The 'change' in the elements was from common to holy food; the elements are called Christ's body and blood, but,

> No infusion of the Spirit into them was imagined: no incorporation of the Spirit with them: no assumption of them into union: no impanation and invination of the Spirit. For such purposes as the invocation expressed, the bread was the body of Christ, and the wine was his blood; but, beyond this, the invocations do not seem to promote any decision.[122]

Nathaniel Dimock was anxious to assert the reformed character of the 1662 communion rite; while there had been a 'reactionary movement' in the century between 1552 and 1662 to some aspects of the Reformers's work, nevertheless:

> Still we look in vain for the restoration of such expressions as before looked most like a Corporal Presence. Still we look in vain for any Invocation of the Holy Spirit on the Elements. Still we look in vain to find in the Consecration Prayer any asking for any such inherent change in God's creatures as the Objective theory requires.[123]

He clearly regarded an *epiclesis* on the elements as tending towards an objective presence of Christ in the elements.

On a more popular level, the fact that the *epiclesis* was not on the evangelical agenda is witnessed to by the influential writing of Bishop John Charles Ryle. Again, reacting to the sacramentalism inspired by the Oxford Movement, Ryle espouses a metaphorical understanding of the eucharistic words, the bread and wine *represent* Christ's body and blood; after consecration, there is no change, no presence of Christ in or with them whatsoever. The presence Christ mediates is a spiritual presence imparted to the faithful communicant. The Prayer Book petition, 'grant that we receiving ... may be partakers' was sufficient.[124]

---

120 Ibid., pp. 423-424.

121 Ibid., p. 436.

122 Ibid., p. 437.

123 N. Dimock, *Papers on the Doctrine of the English Church Concerning the Eucharistic Presence* (London, 1911), p. 302.

124 John Charles Ryle, *Knots Untied* (ed. G.E. Duffield, London, 1904), pp. 162-163; *Expositionary Thoughts on the Gospels: St. Matthew* (Cambridge, n.d.), pp. 355-357.

Christopher Cocksworth observes that the evangelical reaction to the spread of Tractarian and Ritualist theology was to meet creativity with defensiveness, and that Ryle was influential in rejecting the contemporary moves to make the eucharist more central to the worship of the Church.[125] Liturgically, the fact is that the Prayer Book rite both expressed and protected evangelical theological concerns, thus setting the background for the strong evangelical 'no change' lobby when liturgical revision was undertaken in the early twentieth century.

Conclusion

The eighteenth and nineteenth centuries reveal four major trends in relation to Anglican understanding of consecration.

The moderate, broad view, identified with central churchmanship, exemplified by Waterland's *A Review of the Doctrine of the Eucharist*, which continued to sell widely well into the nineteenth century, was content with 1662 as it stood, had no particular desire for an overt *epiclesis*, and understood consecration to be effected by the rehearsal of the eucharistic words in the context of prayer.

Evangelical Anglicans in the main did not follow the sacramental emphasis of the Wesleys but tended to be Cranmerian in their eucharistic theology, rejecting any notion of an objective presence of Christ in the elements. They were also content with the 1662 rite as agreeable to Christ's institution, understanding consecration as the setting aside of the elements for a holy use. It is fair to say that any notion of *epiclesis* was not on their agenda, except in relation to debate about the theology of the Fathers, and, in its own right, noticeably absent from their writings.

The heirs of the Non-jurors and the Scottish and American traditions, although mindful of the fact that the 'apostolic' premises in relation to *Apostolic Constitutions 8* and St James espoused by their forebears had been shown to be spurious, nevertheless still held that the eastern pattern of the *anaphora* accorded with primitive and even apostolic practice, and continued to press the claims of a consecratory *epiclesis* in the 'Antiochene' position if Anglican worship was truly to be primitive and catholic.

The Tractarians and the devotees of the Oxford Movement by contrast, while being concerned fundamentally with defending the real presence of Christ in the eucharistic species, built their case on the inviolability of the eucharistic words of Jesus. While they by no means rejected the role of the Spirit in the eucharist, they reasserted the western identity of the Church of England with an understanding of consecration on solidly Christological terms, centred on the rehearsal of the institution narrative and according with Roman practice.

The division of opinion in the ranks of 'high church' or 'catholic' Anglicans over consecration and the role of the Spirit can be illustrated by W.E. Scudamore's influential *Notitia Eucharistia*, where he argued that an *epiclesis* on the elements is not necessary[126] and E.S. Ffoulkes's *Primitive Consecration of the Eucharistic*

125 Cocksworth, *Evangelical Eucharistic Thought in the Church of England*, pp. 85-87.

126 W.E. Scudamore, *Notitia Eucharistia*, 2nd ed. (London, 1876), p. 591. Scudamore also rejected consecration by the narrative alone, stressing the role of prayer.

Oblation, where in an exhaustive historical survey, he made a trenchant appeal for the restoration of the *epiclesis* in the Roman and Anglican Churches.[127] In the meantime, interest in historic eucharistic texts continued to be nurtured by liturgical scholarship. So, C.A. Swainson published his study *The Greek Liturgies: Chiefly from Original Authorities* in 1884, and F.E. Brightman the first volume of his magisterial *Liturgies Eastern and Western* in 1896. Moreover, the outward appearance of Anglican worship was changing, not only through the popularization of hymnody but also through the ritual and ceremonial innovations of the Oxford Movement. As the desire for Prayer Book revision gained strength, the scene was set for the inevitable battleground over eucharistic theology in which the question of the *epiclesis* was well to the fore.

---

127 E.S. Ffoulkes, *Primitive Consecration of the Eucharistic* (London, 1885).

Chapter 4

Pan-Anglican Reports and Statements

The Lambeth Conference

The Lambeth Conference first met in 1867 and the 1998 Conference was the thirteenth such gathering. The Lambeth Conference resolutions and reports are not binding upon the Anglican Communion; they are simply conferences 'of those Anglican bishops whom the Archbishop of Canterbury chooses to invite'.[1] The first five Lambeth Conferences (1867-1908) all affirmed that the 1662 *Book of Common Prayer* remained the norm for the worship of the Anglican Communion while accepting that adaptation of the liturgy for the particular circumstances of each Church was acceptable provided that it was not inconsistent with the spirit and principles of 1662.[2] It was the Lambeth Conference of 1920 that represented a change in emphasis. Resolution 36 affirmed:

> While maintaining the authority of the Book of Common Prayer as the Anglican standard of doctrine and practice, we consider that liturgical uniformity should not be regarded as a necessity throughout the Churches of the Anglican Communion. The conditions of the Church in many parts of the Mission Field render inapplicable the retention of that Book as the one fixed liturgical model.[3]

The Conference recognized that the growth in self-consciousness of indigenous Churches rendered inapplicable the principle of uniformity as set out in the *BCP* preface. Therefore the missionary Churches were given the liberty to adopt new uses. The committee on 'Missionary Problems' set out four criteria for liturgical revision: there should be a 'Scriptural and Catholic balance of Truth'; due consideration given to the precedents of the early Church; the observation of such limitations as may be imposed by higher synodical authority; and awareness of the possible effect such revision may have on other parts of the Anglican Communion.[4] The Conference also empowered the Archbishop of Canterbury to appoint a 'Committee of students of liturgical questions' to advise on liturgical revision.[5] The 1930 Conference reiterated the approach of 1920, while Lambeth 1948 was, if anything, more cautious, insisting

---

1 C.O. Buchanan, *Lambeth and Liturgy 1988* (Bramcote, 1989), p. 3.

2 Randall T. Davidson (ed.), *The Five Lambeth Conferences* (London, 1920).

3 *The Lambeth Conferences 1867-1930* (London, 1948), p. 45.

4 Ibid., p. 84.

5 Resolution 38, ibid., p. 45; the work of the committee of experts was to have special reference to holy communion, ibid., p. 84.

that revisions of the Prayer Book should be in accordance with the doctrine and accepted liturgical worship of the Anglican Communion.[6]

Prayer Book revision was, however, firmly on the Lambeth 1958 agenda. Preparatory reports were prepared by the Church of England Liturgical Commission and a Select Committee of the Church of India, Pakistan, Burma and Ceylon (CIPBC).[7] A third document, *Anglican Prayer Books: A Scottish View*,was circulated privately but later derestricted.[8] The Conference report on Prayer Book revision was written by a sub-committee of the committee entitled 'Progress in the Anglican Communion'. The secretary was Dr Leslie Brown, Bishop of Uganda, the main drafter of the 1950 Church of South India (CSI) rite, and the influence of the CSI rite is apparent in the text. The report noted that in the past, 1662 had remained the basic pattern for Anglican liturgical revision. The sub-committee affirmed, however, the principle of local autonomy enshrined in Article XXXIV, and developments in liturgical scholarship, especially in relation to the worship of 'the primitive Church'. The report therefore set out features of the Prayer Book liturgies regarded as essential to safeguarding Anglican unity and maintaining traditional doctrinal emphasis, with a list of modifications or additions for the further recovery of elements of the worship of the primitive church.[9] The Report also included comments on the main services, including a section on holy communion. On the *epiclesis*, the sub-committee reported:

> Whether or not an invocation of the Holy Spirit upon the worshippers or upon the elements or both is to be included in the Prayer of Consecration, it is to be remembered that the Holy Spirit informs and vivifies the whole Rite and that the so-called Collect for Purity has in consequence a profound theological significance.[10]

This was a clear exercise in 'fence-sitting' but hardly surprising given the inconclusive treatment of the *epiclesis* by the CIPBC report and the trenchant defence of the *epiclesis* on the elements by the Scottish report; it was too divisive a question to handle.[11] The sub-committee then included a section on consecration which at least suggested a new tack:[12]

> We desire to draw attention to a conception of consecration which is scriptural and primitive and goes behind subsequent controversies with respect to the moment and formula of consecration. This is associated with the Jewish origin and meaning of *eucharistia* and may be called consecration through thanksgiving.[13]

---

6 *The Lambeth Conference 1948* (London, 1948), p. 46.

7 *Prayer Book Revision in the Church of England* (London, 1957) and *Principles of Prayer Book Revision* (London, 1957). The first report did not discuss the *epiclesis*. For the treatment of the *epiclesis* in the second report, see p. 197 below.

8 *Anglican Prayer Books: A Scottish View* (London, 1958).

9 *The Lambeth Conference 1958* (London and Greenwich CT, 1958), pp. 2, 78-81.

10 Ibid., p. 2.85.

11 Colin Buchanan commented, 'The single passing mention of the epiclesis in the Lambeth Report shows how far that particular controversy had ceased to be a live issue', *MAL*, p. 17. The CIPBC and Scottish reports, however, give it rather more prominence.

12 The sub-committee was clearly drawing on Dix here.

13 Ibid.

The report then included quotations from1 Timothy 4:4, 5 and Louis Bouyer's *Life and Liturgy* in support of this emphasis on the role of thanksgiving in consecrating the elements.[14] Resolution 75 of the Conference commended the report of the sub-committee to the Anglican Communion, but resolution 73 represented the parting of the ways by asserting that the *BCP* was no longer the main focus of liturgical revision but: 'the chief aim of Prayer Book Revision should be to further that recovery of the worship of the Primitive Church which was the aim of the compilers of the first Prayer Books of the Church of England'.[15] Resolution 76 requested the Archbishop of Canterbury to appoint a committee to make recommendations about the structure of the holy communion service for those Provinces undertaking revision 'which would both conserve the doctrinal balance of the Anglican tradition and take account of present liturgical knowledge'.[16]

Lambeth 1968 did not include any section on liturgy,[17] while in 1978, growing ecumenical agreement on the structure of the eucharistic prayer was commended without specifying details.[18] At Lambeth 1988, the eucharist was considered only in general terms,[19] and the 1998 Conference did not include direct discussion of liturgical matters. However, the Section 1 Report on the environment recognizes that 'by the sacramental presence of the Spirit, creation is endowed with sacred value and dignity', and that the eucharistic elements themselves become means of grace, and receive new meaning and status, even if the Report goes on to relate this more to eucharistic offering than the invocation of the Spirit.[20] Resolution 4.12 urges that new liturgical texts and practices should be consonant with accepted ecumenical agreements reached in multilateral and bilateral dialogues, and that the Primates should encourage this in consultation with the International Anglican Liturgical Consultation (IALC).[21]

The 'Pan-Anglican Documents'

The first so-called 'Pan-Anglican Document' fulfilled resolution 76 of the 1958 Lambeth Conference. A sub-committee of the liturgical consultation following the 1963 post-Lambeth Anglican Congress in Toronto was commissioned to draft it.

---

14 It could also have pointed to the principles underlying the 1924/29 South African rite.

15 Ibid., p. 1.47. Whether this is an accurate observation on the Reformers is questionable. The main issue in 1552 was whether the rites were scriptural and so 'primitive' in this sense.

16 Ibid., p. 1.48.

17 Except for a survey of liturgical revision in its preparatory papers, *Lambeth Conference 1968: Preparatory Information* (London, 1968), pp. 35-70.

18 *The Report of the Lambeth Conference 1978* (London, 1978), pp. 35-70.

19 *The Truth Shall Make You Free: The Lambeth Conference 1988* (London, 1989), pp. 73-74. Resolutions 22 and 47 continued to give encouragement to liturgical inculturation.

20 *The Official Report of the Lambeth Conference 1998* (Harrisburg, 1999), pp. 90-91; cf Resolution 1.8, ibid., p. 379.

21 Ibid., p. 379, reflecting p. 263 (Section IV Report, 'Called to be One').

The membership was Archbishop L.W. Brown (Uganda), Bishop C.K. Sansbury (Singapore), Archbishop H.H. Clark (Canada), and Dr Massey Shepherd (USA). The document, dated 1965, set out a proposed structure of the eucharistic rite with further advice on contents. The section on the eucharistic prayer included nothing explicit on the *epiclesis*: 'The consecration prayer should be in the form of a thanksgiving for creation and for God's mighty acts in Christ and in sending the Holy Spirit. There should be a recital of the words and acts of the Lord at the last supper and a prayer for the communicants.'[22]

A second document was produced in 1970 at the suggestion of the Anglican liturgical consultation following Lambeth 1968. It was drafted by Leslie Brown (now Bishop of St Edmundsbury and Ipswich) and R.C.D. Jasper, chairman of the Church of England Liturgical Commission, in consultation with the drafters of the 1965 document. The second document suggested a fuller structure and contents, including the listing of five basic elements for the eucharistic prayer. The first four were *sursum corda*, preface, narrative and *anamnesis*; the fifth read: 'The prayer that through the sharing of the bread and wine and through the power of the Holy Spirit we may be made one with our Lord and so renewed in the Body of Christ.'[23]

This final section clearly envisages a form of congregational *epiclesis*, and in this sense is a step beyond the 1965 document. The consultation also discussed the question of supplementary consecration. The members of the consultation were against a simple repetition of the narrative, and raised the issue of whether further words were required at all. What is clear is that the question of an *epiclesis* was not on the table; the dominant theory of consecration was clearly consecration by thanksgiving.[24] While it is difficult to gauge the exact influence of these two documents on Anglican eucharistic revision, it is unlikely that they fulfilled to any great degree the function hoped for in resolution 76 of Lambeth 1958.[25]

The International Anglican Liturgical Consultations

The International Anglican Liturgical Consultation (IALC) began in 1985 as a gathering of Anglican liturgists attending the bi-annual conference of (the ecumenical) Societas Liturgica. The Consultation, now normally held every four years, became recognized by the Anglican Consultative Council (in 1987) and the Primates's Meeting as the official network for liturgy in the Anglican Communion

---

22 The background to and text of the document are given in R.T. Beckwith, 'The Pan-Anglican Document', in *MAL*, pp. 22-32.

23 The text is reproduced in *Partners in Mission* (London, 1973) pp. 70-73 and in *FAL*, pp. 26-31.

24 *Report of the Liturgical Consultation Held at Church House, Westminster 27, 28.8.68*, section 9. The report affirmed that for 'supplementary consecration' additional words should 'not appear to be consecratory' and offered two suggestions: 'Take, O Lord, this bread also to this holy use' and 'In thankful remembrance of God's mighty acts and redemption of the world by our Lord Jesus Christ, we pray that this bread may be unto us the body ...'.

25 Roger Beckwith, 'The Pan-Anglican Document', *The Churchman*, 88 (1974): 54-57.

to resource the Churches and communicate about liturgy across the Communion. The fifth Consultation, on the eucharist, was held in Dublin in 1995, preceded by a preparatory conference in Untermarchtal in Germany in 1993.

The Dublin Consultation agreed nine principles and recommendations. The sixth of these was related to the eucharistic prayer and matters of consecration:

> 6. In the eucharist, we encounter the mystery of the triune God in the proclamation of the word and the celebration of the sacraments. The fundamental character of the Eucharistic prayer is thanksgiving, and the whole Eucharistic prayer should be seen as consecratory. The elements of memorial and invocation are caught up within the movement of thanksgiving. More recent theological work on the eucharist has stressed the role of the Spirit in the eucharistic action.[26]

This was further amplified by the five 'Working Group Papers', embracing eucharistic theology; ministry and order; the structure of the eucharist; ritual, language and symbolism; and liturgical and eucharistic renewal. In the eucharistic theology paper there was a strong plea that the eucharistic rite in general, and the structure of the eucharistic prayer in particular, should be explicitly Trinitarian. Hence:

> The Western eucharistic rites have not always given full expression to our Trinitarian faith. The classical forms of the eucharistic prayer in the East have an explicitly Trinitarian structure which became lost in the West. It is not found in the Roman Canon, nor was it part of the awareness of most of the Reformers.[27]

The crucial issue of structure had been raised by Thomas Talley in a seminal paper at the Untermarchtal conference.[28] In an analysis of early eucharistic prayers, Talley set out a convincing case that there is 'a rather consistent pattern of thanksgiving followed by supplication',[29] in which the *epiclesis* forms a significant element in the supplication. This overcomes some of the problems posed by a single and often narrowly consecratory *epiclesis* before the institution narrative, or a double or 'split' *epiclesis*, enveloping the narrative of institution. So the Dublin paper reflected this understanding:

> The restoration of a Trinitarian structure for the eucharistic prayer in historic as well as contemporary Anglican texts has included the restoration of an invocation (epiclesis) of the Holy Spirit. Modern scholarship understands the 'deep structures' of the prayer to embrace thanksgiving and supplication. In the Jewish models from which the Christian prayers grew, the supplication is for the restoration of Jerusalem or the future of Israel. In early Christian prayers, this becomes prayer for the gathering of the Church into the kingdom. The link between this eschatological perspective and the work of the Spirit is made explicit in Romans 8. In Christian prayer, therefore, the supplication becomes an explicit invocation of the Holy Spirit. The epiclesis later came to be interpreted as an

---

26 David R. Holeton (ed.), *Our Thanks and Praise: The Eucharist in Anglicanism Today* (Toronto, 1998), p. 262.

27 Ibid., p. 266.

28 David R. Holeton, *Revising the Eucharist: Groundwork for the Anglican Communion* (Bramcote, 1994). See further below on pp. 222–225.

29 Ibid., p. 19.

> invocation upon the elements of bread and wine or upon the communicants or both, but it is better understood in its earliest forms as invoking the Spirit upon the whole life of God's people as expressed in the eucharistic action. Difficulties which many Anglicans have felt with an epiclesis in this part of the eucharistic prayer may be transcended if the invocation avoids a narrow focus on the elements or the communicants. The thanksgiving and proclamation section with its twin foci of God as creator and redeemer may be opened up towards supplication for the fulfilment of God's promise through the work of the Spirit. The recovery of the epiclesis thus enables the church to enter into the full Trinitarian pattern of eucharistic praying. The assembled community is gathered into the whole sweep of the Triune God's work in creation, redemption, and promise. Thus we are given a vision of the transformation of the whole creation.[30]

Indeed, the whole drift of the theological section is to avoid narrow understandings of both the *epiclesis* and narrative of institution as formulae for consecration.

In the paper on the structure of the eucharist, a kind of updated 'Pan-Anglican document', three outline structures for the eucharistic prayer are provided; all of them place the *epiclesis* after the *anamnesis* in conformity to the thanksgiving–supplication model, even if the outlines are described merely as 'a common arrangement'.[31] One structure allows the possibility of a 'Thanksgiving for the work of the Spirit' to precede the *epiclesis*:

> Dialogue
> Thanksgiving for Creation
> Sanctus
> Thanksgiving for Redemption
> Institution Narrative
> Anamnesis
> Thanksgiving for the Work of the Spirit
> Epiclesis
> Supplication for the Assembly and the Mission of the Church
> Doxology and Amen.[32]

The Influence of Lambeth, the Pan-Anglican documents and the IALC

It is possible to categorize the approaches to liturgical revision in the Lambeth Conferences and Pan-Anglican documents and consultations under four phases:

1867-1910

The presupposition was that the 1662 *Book of Common Prayer* remained the liturgical norm and would simply be adapted to local circumstances. So long as 1662 was regarded thus, it is unsurprising that the question of the *epiclesis* did not figure prominently. Nevertheless, the Scottish/American eucharistic tradition with its

30 Holeton, *Our Thanks and Praise*, p. 267.
31 Ibid., p. 287.
32 Ibid., pp. 287-288.

explicit *epiclesis* was clearly regarded as an acceptable variant and it did influence those Churches where American missionary activity was strong.

1920-1948

The principle of local revision was accepted, but 1662 remained the standard of doctrine and practice, against which revisions were measured. Here adaptations of the *Book of Common Prayer* rite attempted particularly to restore 'primitive' elements with an integrated eucharistic prayer, but with no unanimity about a consecratory *epiclesis* as witnessed in disputes in England and South Africa, and in the inconclusive treatment of the *epiclesis* in the CIPBC report prepared for Lambeth 1958, and in the section on the *epiclesis* in the 1958 report on the *BCP*.

1958-1978

In this period1662 was no longer regarded as the liturgical norm, but Provinces and Churches were encouraged to make revisions in the light of liturgical scholarship and particularly with regard to the worship of the primitive church, and local cultural propriety. One particularly important development was the stress on the role of thanksgiving in eucharistic consecration. This stress on thanksgiving included (as in both 'Pan-Anglican documents') praise for the gift of the Spirit in the preface but rather eclipsed the question of a consecratory *epiclesis*, although the second 'Pan-Anglican document' recommended a congregational *epiclesis*. During this period, eucharistic revision in both the Anglican Communion (where England and North America were particularly influential) and other Churches (especially the reforms of Vatican II), ecumenical dialogue on the nature of the eucharist, and emerging ecumenical convergence among liturgical scholars also influenced thinking and practice.

1988 onwards

Lambeth 1958 was the last conference where detailed comments on Anglican eucharistic rites were included, and the principle of local liturgical autonomy has meant that subsequent Conferences have concentrated more on general principles in worship. However, exploration of how agreed ecumenical statements might relate to liturgical text and practice is slowly beginning to emerge. The growing influence and importance of the IALC, and Paul Gibson's pioneering work as Coordinator for Liturgy for the Communion has led to the enunciation, through the IALC's statements and findings, of principles and guidance to 'inform the Communion during the next stage of revision and renewal'. This has enabled a theologically grounded body of contemporary liturgical expertise to emerge, taking account of the cultural diversity of the Communion and the setting of Anglicanism in the wider ecumenical context.

Chapter 5

Ecumenical Exploration

Anglican–Roman Catholic International Commission

The Anglican–Roman Catholic International Commission (ARCIC) was formed in 1970, following a meeting in 1966 between Pope Paul VI and Archbishop Michael Ramsey. The report of a Joint Preparatory Commission was endorsed by the 1968 Lambeth Conference, ensuring that ARCIC was recognized as an official commission of the Anglican Communion rather than particular Provinces. The first fruits of the Commission was the publication of the 'Agreed Statement on Eucharistic Doctrine' (popularly known as the 'Windsor Statement') in 1971.[1] The role of the Holy Spirit is the eucharist is a significant feature of the 'Windsor Statement'. Section II, 'The Mystery of the Eucharist' includes the following general statement: 'Christ through the Holy Spirit in the eucharist builds up the life of the Church, strengthens its fellowship and furthers its mission.'[2] Section III, 'The Presence of Christ', is more explicit in its discussion of the eucharistic prayer: 'Through this prayer of thanksgiving, a word of faith addressed to the Father, the bread and wine become the body and blood of Christ by the action of the Holy Spirit, so that in communion we eat the flesh of Christ and drink his blood.'[3]

It is significant that the whole eucharistic prayer is regarded as effecting consecration and that consecration and reception are here kept in close proximity. This is followed by a paragraph related to the Church's mission:

> The Lord who thus comes to his people in the power of the Holy Spirit is the Lord of glory. In the eucharistic celebration we anticipate the joys of the age to come. By the transforming action of the Spirit of God, earthly bread and wine become the heavenly manna and the new wine, the eschatological banquet for the new man: elements of the first creation become pledges and first fruits of the new heaven and the new earth.[4]

While the 'Windsor Statement' does not flinch from using the language of 'becoming' in relation to the effect of consecration, it stops short of the language of 'change', which is discussed not in the main text but in a footnote. Indeed, the verb 'transform' is a broad term allowing some theological space.[5] The transformation of the elements and the

1 Quotations are taken from Anglican–Roman Catholic International Commission. *The Final Report* (London, 1982).

2 Ibid., p. 12.

3 Ibid., p. 16.

4 Ibid.

5 *The Response to the Final Report of ARCIC I by the Roman Catholic Bishops Conference of England and Wales* (1985), however, cites the use of 'become' and the

community is moreover related eschatologically as pledge and promise of God's future for his people. The Statement does not offer any liturgical guidance to the Churches. However, from the quotations above it would appear to envisage some statement within the eucharistic prayer of the role of the Spirit in effecting consecration. The new eucharistic prayers of the 1969 Roman *Sacramentary* had indeed introduced an *epiclesis* of the Spirit on the elements in the eucharistic prayers II, III and IV. However, the Tridentine canon, eucharistic prayer I of the new missal and the communion rite of the *Book of Common Prayer* (1662) have no *epiclesis* of the Spirit at all. The theological articulation of the role of the Spirit in the eucharist, therefore, need not demand liturgical expression.[6] The last quotation above expresses the role of the Spirit in transforming the elements. It would, however, be unfair to the Statement to suggest that, where there is an *epiclesis*, it would imply a notion of 'consecration by formula'. Section II of the Statement affirms that it is in the whole action of the eucharist that the gift of Christ is received: 'In the whole action of the eucharist, and in and by his sacramental presence given through bread and wine, the crucified and risen Lord, according to his promise, offers himself to his people.'[7]

In the light of responses to the Windsor Statement, a further *Elucidation* was published in 1979. This included the statement: 'His body and blood are given through the action of the Holy Spirit, appropriating bread and wine so that they become the food of the new creation already inaugurated by the coming of Christ.'[8] However, here the Commission explicitly denies that such language implies a material change in the elements. Rather, 'What is here affirmed is a sacramental presence in which God uses realities of this world to convey the realities of the new creation: bread for this life becomes the bread of eternal life.'[9] It also sought to affirm that the goal of eucharistic participation is the transformation of the people of God: 'The ultimate change intended by God is the transformation of human beings into the likeness of Christ. The bread and wine *become* the sacramental body and blood of Christ in order that the Christian community may *become* more truly what it already is, the body of Christ.'[10]

Once again, the language of consecration is intimately linked to reception. Liturgically, this would imply that a petition for the consecration of the elements would be incomplete without a complementary statement of the spiritual consecration and empowering of the Church. The Elucidation also sought to hold together differing perceptions of eucharistic presence, maintaining that eucharistic doctrine needed to

---

transforming action of the Spirit and the language of change in the footnote as affirming 'the substantial nature of the change of the bread and wine …', cited by Christopher Hill and Edward Yarnold (eds), *Anglicans and Roman Catholics: The Search for Unity* (London, 1994), p. 99.

6 The 'Windsor Statement' did in fact directly influence the Church of England Series 3 rite (see pp. 149, 150 below).

7 Ibid., p. 13.

8 Ibid., p. 21.

9 Ibid.

10 Ibid., p. 22.

affirm both the association of Christ's presence with the consecrated elements and the presence of Christ in the heart of the believer through reception by faith.[11]

The official *Response of the Holy See* to the Final Report of ARCIC 1 raised issues concerning eucharistic sacrifice, presence and reservation of the consecrated species. On presence, the *Response* sought clarification that 'Christ in the Eucharist makes himself present sacramentally and substantially when under the species of bread and wine these earthly realities are changed into the reality of his Body and Blood, Soul and Divinity'.[12] In response, *Clarifications on Eucharist and Ministry*, published in 1994, affirmed belief 'in the presence of the living Christ truly and really in the elements', while defending the methodological legitimacy 'of fresh ways of expressing this change even by using new words, provided that they kept and reflected what transubstantiation was intended to express'.[13]

Anglican–Orthodox Dialogue

Formal Anglican–Orthodox theological dialogue was initiated by the 1930 Lambeth Conference. Following discussion with the Pan-Orthodox delegation at Lambeth, an Anglican–Orthodox Joint Doctrinal Commission was appointed by the Archbishop of Canterbury and the Oecumenical Patriarch and met in 1931.[14] The Commission did not have enough time to discuss the eucharist in any detail and in their report, discussion of the sacraments is mainly limited to their number.[15] The Commission regarded the material on the eucharist in the *Résumé* and *précis* of the committee of Anglican Bishops and the Orthodox delegation at the 1930 Lambeth Conference as a sufficient starting point; but while this discussed eucharistic sacrifice and presence, it did not discuss how the eucharistic presence was effected.[16] A further initiative occurred in 1935 when an Anglican delegation was invited to a conference in Bucharest at the invitation of the Holy Synod of Romania.[17] The conference issued a statement, including the following three clauses:

---

11 Ibid.

12 *Response of the Holy See to The Final Report of the Anglican–Roman Catholic International Commission, 1982* (London, 1991), p. 9.

13 *Clarifications of certain aspects of the Agreed Statements on Eucharist and Ministry of the First Anglican-Roman Catholic International Commission* (London, 1994), pp. 6-7.

14 Colin Davey, 'Anglican–Orthodox Dialogue 1920-76', in Kallistos Ware and Colin Davey (eds), *Anglican–Orthodox Dialogue: The Moscow Agreed Statement* (London, 1977), pp. 7-9.

15 'Report of the Joint Doctrinal Commission', *Lambeth Occasional Reports 1931-38* (London, 1948), pp. 54-57.

16 Ibid., pp. 92-94, 104-105. The *epiclesis* was touched upon minimally in the report on day 3 of the discussions. The main thrust of the debate was, however, to what extent Anglicans believed in the real presence of Christ in the eucharist, ibid., pp. 104-105.

17 This delegation was strictly speaking a Church of England delegation, supplemented by two 'Assessors' from Ireland and the USA, Davey, 'Anglican–Orthodox Dialogue 1920-76', p. 10.

3. The sacrifice on Calvary is perpetually presented in the Holy Eucharist in a bloodless fashion (ἀναιμάκτως) under the form (Rumanian, *sub chipul*) of bread and wine through the consecrating priest and through the work of the Holy Ghost in order that the fruits of the Sacrifice of the Cross may be partaken of by those who offer the Eucharistic sacrifice, by those for whom it is offered, and by those who receive worthily the Body and Blood of the Lord.

4. In the Eucharist the bread and wine become by consecration (μεταβολή) the Body and Blood of our Lord. How? This is a mystery.

5. The Eucharistic bread and wine remain the Body and Blood of our Lord as long as these Eucharistic elements exist.[18]

While this statement does not say very much about the *epiclesis*, sections 3 and 5, however acceptable to the Anglican delegation, would be doctrinally sensitive for many Anglicans. The agnosticism of the 'how' in section 4 would likely command wide support, although the verb 'become' may well be considered as too realist. A further conference was held in 1956 between the Church of England and the Russian Orthodox Church, but without explicit reference to the significance of the *epiclesis*.[19] The decision to resume full Pan-Anglican, Pan-Orthodox discussions derives from a meeting between the Archbishop of Canterbury and the Oecumenical Patriarch of Constantinople in 1962. Preparations for the dialogue were undertaken by both traditions, including a meeting in 1975 in London to discuss the *epiclesis*.[20] The Moscow Conference of 1976 adopted an 'Agreed Statement', including a full section on the eucharistic *epiclesis*. Because of its importance, it is quoted in full:

VII The Invocation of the Holy Spirit in the Eucharist

29. The Eucharist is the action of the Holy Trinity. The Father gives the Body and Blood of Christ by the descent of the Holy Spirit to the Church in response to the Church's prayer. The Liturgy is this prayer for the eucharistic gifts to be given. It is in this context that the invocation of the Holy Spirit should be understood. The operation of the Holy Spirit is essential to the Eucharist whether it is explicitly expressed or not. When it is articulated, the *Epiclesis* voices the work of the Spirit with the Father in the consecration of the elements as the Body and Blood of Christ.

30. The consecration of the bread and wine results from the whole sacramental liturgy. The act of consecration includes certain proper and appropriate moments – thanksgiving, anamnesis, *Epiclesis*. The deepest understanding of the hallowing of the elements rejects any theory of consecration by formula – whether by Words of Institution or *Epiclesis*. For the Orthodox the culminating and decisive moment in the consecration is the Epiclesis.[21]

18 'Report of the Conference held from Saturday, June 1st, to Saturday, June 8th, 1935', *Lambeth Occasional Reports 1931-38*, p. 197.

19 H.M. Waddams (ed.), *Anglo-Russian Theological Conference, Moscow, July 1956* (London, 1957).

20 *Anglican Orthodox Dialogue: The Moscow Agreed Statement*, pp. 18-36.

21 This last reference to 'Epiclesis' is not italicised.

> 31. The unity of the members of the Church is renewed by the Spirit in the eucharistic act. The Spirit comes not only upon the elements, but upon the community. The *Epiclesis* is a double invocation: by the invocation of the Spirit, the members of Christ are fed by his Body and Blood so that they may grow in holiness and may be strong to manifest Christ to the world and to do his work in the power of the Spirit. 'We hold this treasure in earthen vessels.' The reception of the Holy Gifts calls for repentance and obedience. Christ judges the sinful members of the Church. The time is always at hand when judgement must begin at the household of God (2Cor. [*sic*] 4.7, I Pet. 4.17).
>
> 32. Although *Epiclesis* has a special meaning in the Eucharist, we must not restrict the concept to the Eucharist alone. In every sacrament, prayer and blessing the Church invokes the Holy Spirit and in all these various ways calls upon Him to sanctify the whole of creation. The Church is that Community which lives by continually invoking the Holy Spirit.[22]

The Statement thus affirms that the eucharist is an action of the Trinity, the *epiclesis* has to be understood in the context of supplication for the sacramental gift of Christ; that consecration is a movement rather than a 'moment', and that the action of the Spirit is in relation to the community as well as the elements. The statement in paragraph 31 that the Spirit 'comes ... upon the elements' is bold from the standpoint of Anglican evangelical concerns, but the rest of the paragraph stresses the work of the Spirit in the communicants. The last sentence in paragraph 30 is unusual in 'agreed' statements of this kind – it affirms the Orthodox understanding of the role of the *epiclesis* in consecration, but is silent about Anglican perspectives in this matter. In a short commentary on the Moscow Agreed Statement, Archimandrite Kallistos Ware, drawing on the Minutes, commented thus on eucharistic rites lacking an *epiclesis* of the Spirit:

> .... the delegates at Moscow did not condemn those which lack an *Epiclesis* of the Eastern type, but they simply assert in the Agreed Statement that the operation of the Spirit is essential to the Eucharist, 'whether it is explicitly expressed or not' ... As Bishop Terwilliger put it, 'Consecration is always the work of the Holy Spirit, whatever the liturgical text says'; Anglican rites 'could not be expected to conform' literally and word-for-word to Eastern models.[23]

The Moscow Agreed Statement was discussed at a meeting of the [Pan-Orthodox] Joint Theological Commission for dialogue between Orthodox

---

22 *Anglican–Orthodox Dialogue: The Moscow Agreed Statement*, pp. 90-91. Sections 31 and 32 of the Statement are influenced by a discussion paper delivered in July 1975 by Anglican delegate, Bishop R.E. Terwilliger (suffragan Bishop of Dallas) entitled 'The Epicletic Church': 'in one form or another, Eucharistic consecration is the Spirit's work … by the invocation which the Church continually makes in the eucharist, no matter what words are actually used …The epiclesis ought to be a double epiclesis whereby by the invocation of the Spirit the Body of Christ eucharistic creates the Body of Christ ecclesial to be the Body of Christ in the world.' Anglican/ Orthodox Joint Doctrinal Discussions, unpublished paper (AO/JDD.101), p. 4.

23 Kallistos Ware, 'The Moscow Conference 1976'. in *Anglican–Orthodox Dialogue: The Moscow Agreed Statement*, p. 70.

and Anglicans. It reported specifically on the subject of the *epiclesis* and the 1935 Bucharest formula. On the former, it declared that the reference in paragraph 30 of the Moscow Statement was inexact in its use of the word 'formula' as the Orthodox do not regard the *epiclesis* as a 'formula' if this implies that the *epiclesis* is regarded in 'a legalistic and mechanical fashion, as a prescribed form of words necessary for the valid performance of the consecration'. As for the latter, it expressed the reservations felt by certain Anglicans about the wording of the Bucharest agreement without specifying what those reservations were. But it can scarcely be doubted that this would include strong evangelical reservations about sections 3-5 of the Bucharest text.[24] In contra-distinction, Kallistos Ware reports that many if not all of the Orthodox delegation wished for a stronger reaffirmation of the Bucharest Statement.

The issue of the ordination of women to the priesthood threatened any further work between the two Communions from 1977. However, after initial difficulties, the Anglican–Orthodox Joint Doctrinal Commission continued its work in 1980. This led to the publication of 'The Dublin Agreed Statement 1984', completing the second phase of Anglican–Orthodox dialogue.[25] While the Statement included a section on 'Worship and Tradition' there was no explicit discussion of eucharistic consecration. However, the Statement also included an epilogue seeking to summarize the progress made in Anglican–Orthodox dialogue since 1973. This included the following paragraphs:

> 110. (c) We are agreed in attaching cardinal importance to the action of the Holy Spirit in the Eucharist, as also throughout the entire life of the Church. In the Orthodox eucharistic liturgy this is an invocation (επικλησις) of the Holy Spirit; in some Anglican liturgies there is no such explicit *epiclesis*, but all Anglicans are agreed that the operation of the Holy Spirit is essential to the Eucharist.
>
> 111. (d) We are agreed that through the consecratory prayer, addressed to the Father, the bread and wine become the Body and Blood of the glorified Christ by the action of the Holy Spirit in such a way that the faithful people of God receiving Christ may feed upon him in the sacrament. But we have not yet discussed in detail what is the nature of the ineffable change effected through the consecratory prayer, nor have we considered how far the Eucharist may be regarded as a sacrifice.[26]

Section 111 is careful to relate consecration to reception, so as not to negate the Anglican reformed emphasis that the eucharistic gift is received through faith. The fact that the nature of the 'change' is not included in the statement reveals that it falls short of full agreement on the nature of eucharistic consecration.

The third phase of dialogue, from 1989 to 2006 culminated in the publication of *The Church of the Triune God*. The only explicit reference to *epiclesis* is in the context of the ordination prayer for priests.[27] The Report does not include a discrete section

24 Ibid. pp. 92-93.

25 *Anglican-Orthodox Dialogue: The Dublin Agreed Statement 1984* (London, 1984).

26 Ibid., p. 47.

27 *The Church of the Triune God* (London, 2006), p. 73.

on the eucharist. However, it does include significant discussion of pneumatology and the role of the Spirit in eschatology, both of which may be applied to eucharistic doctrine, and, in a section on priesthood, it includes the statement:

> In the eucharistic prayer, the offering of praise and thanksgiving for the mighty deeds of God, culminating in the sacrifice of the paschal mystery, is offered for all creation. Received by the Father, the gifts of bread and wine are returned in the Holy Spirit as Christ's risen life, his body and his blood, the bread of heaven and the cup of salvation.[28]

So, the outstanding issues from Dublin are still to be explored in depth.

Anglican–Lutheran Dialogue

The progress of international Anglican–Lutheran relations from 1972 to 2002 is evident from the report *Growth in Communion*, issued by the Anglican-Lutheran International Working Group.[29] With regard to the eucharist, certain documents have proved to be particularly influential during this period.

The 'Pullach Report', 1972

Formal Anglican–Lutheran dialogue was initiated by the Lambeth Conference and the Lutheran World Federation in 1968. The Anglican–Lutheran International Commission met from September 1970 to April 1972 and published its report (popularly known as the 'Pullach Report') in 1972.[30] It included a statement on eucharistic presence:

> 68 Both Communions affirm the real presence of Christ in this sacrament, but neither seeks to define precisely how this happens. In the eucharistic action, including consecration and reception, the bread and wine, while remaining bread and wine, become the means whereby Christ is truly present and gives himself to the communicants.

The word 'consecration' is defined in a footnote as 'the setting apart of the elements, the recitation of the thanksgiving with the words of institution and the invocation of the Holy Spirit, whether explicit in the liturgical words or not'.[31] The Anglican Consultative Council and the Executive Committee of the Lutheran World Federation responded to the 1972 Report by recommending continuing regional dialogue in Europe, North America and Tanzania.

---

28 Ibid., p. 72.

29 The text is included in *Anglican–Lutheran Agreements* (Geneva, 2004), pp. 275-338.

30 *Anglican–Lutheran International Conversations: The Report of the Conversations 1970-1972* (London, 1973).

31 Ibid., pp. 16–17.

Lutheran–Episcopal Dialogue, 1969-1980

The dialogue was undertaken in two phases between 1969 and 1980 by the Episcopal Church (USA) and three main-line Lutheran Churches: the American Lutheran Church, the Association of Evangelical Lutheran Churches and the Lutheran Church in America.[32] The dialogue culminated in the publication of *Lutheran–Episcopal Dialogue: Report and Recommendations* which included five 'Joint Statements', the third of which is entitled 'Joint Statement on Eucharistic Presence', and includes the following:

> Throughout Western Christianity, the Words of Institution (*Verba Christi*) have been generally seen as the focus of the consecration, although all would acknowledge that the presence of the Holy Spirit is essential to the Eucharist whether or not it is explicitly expressed. Eucharistic prayer encompasses proclamation, remembrance, and supplication. Within the framework of this thanksgiving, the Church proclaims its faith through the memorial of Christ in the events of salvation history and the supplication of the Holy Spirit to build up the unity of God's people through faithful reception of the body and blood of Christ.
>
> The Church's celebration of the Eucharist rests upon the Word and authority of Christ, who commanded his disciples to remember him in this way until his return ...
>
> The Lord who comes to his people in the power of the Holy Spirit and by means of his Word 'in, with, and under' the forms of bread and wine enables all Christians to avail themselves of the benefits of his saving death and life-giving resurrection.[33]

Footnote 3 at the end of the statement outlines further areas for dialogue in the quest to find 'sufficient agreement', including the theology of consecration and its practical consequences in regard to the elements, and further clarification of the doctrine of the Real Presence.[34] A significant feature of this statement is the close association of 'Word' and 'Spirit'. Although the concept of 'Word' is sometimes used to designate the 'word of God' in general, and the capitalization of 'Word' in Episcopal Liturgies is understood as a reference to Christ, in this statement the primary reference is the narrative of institution. The statement, however, also clearly affirms the role of the Spirit in consecration, although Lutheran theological and liturgical sources would tend to suggest that the narrative of institution is primary.

Anglican–Lutheran European Regional Commission (ALERC) Report, Helsinki, 1982

The Commission met from 1980 to 1982 and its report, *Anglican–Lutheran Dialogue: The Report of the European Commission*, was published in 1983. In the section of

---

32 The three Churches united in 1987 as The Evangelical Lutheran Church in America.

33 *Lutheran–Episcopal Dialogue: Report and Recommendations* (Cincinnati, 1981), p. 27.

34 Ibid., p. 29.

the report concerning the eucharist, the following statement about consecration is made:

> 28 Although Christ is present and active in the entire eucharistic celebration, Anglicans and Lutherans have also affirmed a particular sacramental presence of Christ ... In virtue of the living Word of Christ and by the power of the Holy Spirit the bread and wine are the sacrament of Christ's body and blood. In the Lord's Supper, Jesus Christ, true God and true man, crucified, risen and ascended, is truly present in his body and blood under the elements of bread and wine ... Under these elements Christ comes to us order to renew our entire being.[35]

We note the same reference to 'Word' and 'Spirit' as in the American conversations. The report also affirms that while historically both traditions have understood the effects of communion principally in terms of the forgiveness of sins, contemporary understanding would also stress the building up of the community of the Church, and the strengthening of faith, hope, witness and service in Christian living.[36] While the Report does not discuss liturgical implications, such fruits of communion are often liturgically expressed in the 'communion' aspect of the *epiclesis*.[37]

The Niagara Report, *1987, and The Porvoo Common Statement, 1992.*

The Niagara Report, by the Anglican–Lutheran International Continuation Committee, while focusing on the issue of episcope, included a brief statement on eucharistic presence: 'We believe that the Body and Blood of Christ are truly present, distributed and received under the forms of bread and wine in the Lord's Supper.'[38]

This statement is amplified in *The Porvoo Common Statement* of the Anglican Churches of Great Britain and Ireland and the Nordic and Baltic Lutheran Churches, which continues: 'In this way we receive the body and blood of Christ, crucified and risen, and in him the forgiveness of sins and all other benefits of his passion.'[39] This has proved determinative for subsequent statements, which draw on *Niagara* and *Porvoo*, but without any further elaboration of the role of the Spirit.[40] The influence of the World Council of Churches 'Lima Text', *Baptism, Eucharist and Ministry*, has evidently also been important in the various regional dialogues around the world.

---

35 *Anglican–Lutheran Dialogue: The Report of the European Commission*, p. 12.

36 Ibid.

37 'The Porvoo Common Statement' from conversations between the British and Irish Anglican Churches and the Nordic and Baltic Lutheran Churches draws on the work of ALERC as well as the 'Lima Statement' and the Churches's response to it; see *The Porvoo Common Statement* (London, 1993), pp. 16–17.

38 *Anglican–Lutheran Agreements*, p. 106.

39 Ibid., p. 162.

40 See for example, 'The Reuilly Common Statement' (British and Irish Anglicans and French Lutheran and Reformed Churches), 1999, section 31(g); *Called to Common Mission* (Evangelical Lutheran Church in America and The Episcopal Church), 1999, 2000, section A50; *Common Ground* (The Anglican Church of Australia and The Lutheran Church of Australia), 2001, section 15. Texts in *Anglican–Lutheran Agreements*, pp. 219-220, 232, 257.

Anglican–Reformed Dialogue

The Anglican–Reformed International Commission was set up under the auspices of the World Alliance of Reformed Churches and the Anglican Consultative Council in 1981. It published its report in 1984,[41] which included a statement on the *epiclesis*:

> 68 (d) Our being united to Christ in his offering of himself to the Father is a work of the Holy Spirit. The prayer of invocation (*epiklesis*) is therefore a proper part of the eucharistic action. 'The Church prays to the Father for the gift of the Holy Spirit in order that the eucharistic event may be a reality: the real presence of the crucified and risen Christ giving his life for all humanity' (BEM, p. 13, para. 13). The Eucharist is a making present of the once-for-all sacrifice of Christ. Joined to Christ in that sacrifice, the Church makes an acceptable offering of itself in thanksgiving to the Father. We therefore invoke the gift of the Spirit from the Father to sanctify both us and the elements of bread and wine, so that in our eating and drinking we may be united with the one sacrifice of Jesus. 'Sanctified by his Spirit, the Church, through, with and in God's Son Jesus Christ, offers itself to the Father. It thereby becomes a living sacrifice of thanksgiving through which God is publicly praised' (WARC/RC, Section 81).[42]

The next section of the report begins: 'The presence of the Spirit is the foretaste, pledge and first-fruits of God's coming kingdom.'[43] This report clearly understands the role of Spirit as, in John McKenna's phrase, 'realizing' the eucharist in the sense that it is the work of the Spirit to mediate and confirm or assure the communicant of Christ's presence in the eucharistic event. The Spirit is understood as the means of union between the Church on earth with Christ in his vicarious offering of himself to the Father in heaven. In this sense it represents the dynamic understanding of union with Christ's (?eternal) sacrifice through the power of the Spirit characteristic of 'high Calvinist' theology. While this is 'reformed' theology, looking back to Calvin, it has not been a position adopted, for example, by the evangelical tradition in Anglicanism, part of which at least would also question the reference to the invocation of the Spirit on the elements.

Anglican–Baptist Dialogue

International conversations between the Anglican Communion and Baptist World Alliance were initiated in 2000, and the first report of the process was published in 2005. Discussion on the eucharist has not been extensive apart from some initial exploration of eucharistic presence, the meaning of 'sacrament' and 'ordinance', eucharistic presidency and Eucharistic hospitality. On presence, the report states:

> Like other Reformed groups, Baptists have refused to locate the presence of the Christ in the elements in any restrictive way, finding the presence of the crucified and risen Christ in the whole event of the meal and in the gathered congregation. They have also declined to identify

41 *God's Reign and Our Unity: The Report of the Anglican–Reformed International Commission 1981-1984* (London and Edinburgh, 1984).

42 Ibid., p. 42.

43 Ibid.

> any change in the bread and wine other than a change in significance in the special use to which the elements are being put.[44]

As yet, there has been no application to pneumatology or exploration of the role of the Holy Spirit in the eucharistic celebration.

Responses to *Baptism, Eucharist and Ministry*

The World Council of Churches published *Baptism, Eucharist and Ministry* (*BEM*) in 1982.[45] Popularly known as 'the Lima Text', it was drafted by the Faith and Order Commission and represented work undertaken by the Commission over a fifty year period. Part II of the section on the eucharist includes the following paragraphs on 'The Eucharist as Invocation of the Spirit':

> 14. The Spirit makes the crucified and risen Christ really present to us in the eucharistic meal, fulfilling the promise contained in the words of institution. The presence of Christ is clearly the centre of the eucharist, and the promise contained in the words of institution is therefore fundamental to the celebration. Yet it is the Father who is the primary origin and final fulfilment of the eucharistic event. The incarnate Son of God by and in whom it is accomplished is its living centre. The Holy Spirit is the immeasurable strength of love which makes it possible and continues to make it effective. The bond between the eucharistic celebration and the mystery of the Triune God reveals the role of the Holy Spirit as that of the one who makes the historical words of Jesus present and alive. Being assured of Jesus' promise in the words of institution that it will be answered, the Church prays to the Father for the gift of the Holy Spirit in order that the eucharistic event may be a reality: the real presence of the crucified and risen Christ giving his life for humanity.
>
> 15. It is in virtue of the living word of Christ and by the power of the Holy Spirit that the bread and wine become the sacramental signs of Christ's body and blood. They remain so for the purpose of communion.
>
> 16. The whole action of the eucharist has an 'epikletic' character because it depends upon the work of the Holy Spirit. In the words of the liturgy, this aspect of the eucharist finds varied expression.
>
> 17. The Church, as the community of the new covenant, confidently invokes the Spirit, in order that it may be sanctified and renewed, led into all justice, truth and unity, and empowered to fulfil its mission in the world.
>
> 18. The Holy Spirit through the eucharist gives a foretaste of the Kingdom of God: the Church receives the life of the new creation and the assurance of the Lord's return.[46]

---

44 *Conversations Around the World: The Report of the International Conversations between The Anglican Communion and The Baptist World Alliance* (London, 2005), p. 56.

45 *Baptism, Eucharist and Ministry* (Geneva, 1982).

46 Ibid., p. 13.

The 'Lima Text' includes a commentary on sections 14 and 15. On 14 it notes that there is an 'intrinsic relationship' between the narrative of institution and the *epiclesis* and continues:

> In the early liturgies the whole 'prayer action' was thought of as bringing about the reality promised by Christ. The invocation of the Spirit was made both on the community and on the elements of bread and wine. Recovery of such an understanding may help us overcome our difficulties concerning a special moment of consecration.[47]

The commentary on 15 notes that in church history, different attempts have been made to explain the nature of Christ's presence in the eucharist, and that some traditions 'assert a change wrought by the Holy Spirit and Christ's words' so that the elements are no longer ordinary bread and wine but Christ's body and blood.[48] The section on the eucharist also includes a discussion of the celebration of the eucharist, including a list of elements traditionally found in eucharistic liturgy. Among them it cites:

> the invocation of the Holy Spirit [*epiklesis*] on the community, and the elements of bread and wine (either before the words of institution or after the memorial, or both; or some other reference to the Holy Spirit which adequately expresses the 'epikletic' character of the eucharist) ...[49]

In publishing the 'Lima Text', the Faith and Order Commission invited official responses from the Churches, and these responses have been collated into a series of

---

47 Ibid.

48 Ibid.

49 Ibid., p. 16. David Wright argues that it would have been better to speak of a 'spiritual', 'pneumatic' or 'pentecostal' character of the eucharist rather than the word 'epikletic', a term virtually impossible to disentangle from historic debates about the 'moment of consecration', 'The Lima Report: *Baptism* and *Eucharist* Compared', *Theology*, 87 (1984): 334. Max Thurian composed a liturgy known as 'the Eucharistic Liturgy of Lima' as an illustration of *BEM*. He includes a preliminary *epiclesis*:

> Upon your eucharist send the life-giving Spirit, who spoke by Moses and the Prophets, who overshadowed the Virgin Mary with grace, who descended upon Jesus in the river Jordan and upon the Apostles on the day of Pentecost. May the outpouring of this Spirit of Fire transfigure this thanksgiving meal that this bread and wine may become for us the body and blood of Christ.
> *Veni Creator Spiritus!*

And also a second *epiclesis* upon the worshippers. Text from: *The Eucharistic Liturgy: Liturgical Expression of Convergence in Faith Achieved in Baptism, Eucharist and Ministry* (Geneva, 1983), pp. 20, 22. The salvation history of the Spirit in the first *epiclesis* was inspired by the liturgy of St James; the verb 'transfigure' was intended to understand consecration in a 'sacramental and mystical manner', and reference to the Spirit 'accomplishing' the words of Christ was to affirm the unity of Son and Spirit, the latter making words spoken historically 'alive and contemporary'. The second *epiclesis* focusses on unity and the anticipation of the coming Kingdom. From the introduction by Max Thurian, ibid., pp. 8-10.

books entitled *Churches Respond to BEM*; the contributions include Churches of the Anglican Communion.[50] A number of Anglican churches made explicit reference to the section of the 'Lima Text' on the *epiclesis*. For example, the Church of Ireland response was critical of the suggestion that in the liturgy there should be an *epiclesis* on the community *and* the elements,[51] while the Anglican Church of Australia cited the absence of explicit reference to the *epiclesis* in the New Testament.[52] By contrast, the responses from Aotearoa-New Zealand, England and South Africa welcomed the *double* emphasis on both elements and community.[53] The Canadian response, while commending the epicletic emphasis on the role of the Spirit, and that the sacraments are 'prayer-actions and not mechanical means of grace', noted that there were continuing questions such as the relationship of the *epiclesis* to Christ's presence in the eucharist. The Church in Wales noted that it needed to consider the role of the Spirit in consecration as historically its rites had emphasized the institution narrative.[54]

Conclusion

All of the formal statements wish to expound the mystery of the eucharist in a fully Trinitarian context and so affirm the role of the Spirit in the eucharistic action. All agree that in the wider context of the whole eucharistic rite and the administration of the sacrament and the narrower context of the eucharistic prayer the elements 'become' the Body and Blood of Christ by the action of or power of the Holy Spirit whether this is explicitly stated or not. The dialogues with Lutherans stress the role of the active Word of Christ in conjunction with the power of the Spirit as the means of consecration. This suggests that the narrative of institution is inviolable. The American statement understands the *epiclesis* as a supplication to build up the unity of the Church through reception. The ARCIC and AOD statements are careful to hold together the objective and subjective movements in relation to eucharistic presence, both the objective gift of Christ's body given in the sacrament and the subjective reception of that gift by faith by the communicant. This can be regarded as a specifically Anglican contribution to ecumenical eucharistic theology. *The Emmaus Report* of the 1987 Anglican Ecumenical Consultation draws special attention to this principle, and cites official responses to ARCIC. from New Zealand and South Africa which both affirm this understanding. So the response of the Theological Commission of the Church of the Province of Southern Africa

---

50 Max Thurian (ed.), *Churches Respond to BEM: Official Responses to the 'Baptism, Eucharist & Ministry' Text, Volumes I-VI* (Geneva, 1986-1988).

51 Ibid., *Vol. 1*, pp. 66-67.

52 Ibid., *Vol. 2*, p. 34.

53 Ibid., *Vol. 2*, p. 66; *Vol. 3*, p. 45; *Vol. 3*, p. 103. See also, *Baptism, Eucharist & Ministry 1982-1990: Report on the Process and Responses* (Geneva, 1990), where it is noted that some Lutheran and Anglican responses doubt or reject a 'constitutive' approach, invoking the Spirit on the elements.

54 Thurian, *Churches Respond to BEM, Vol. 2*, p. 39; *Vol. 3*, p. 85.

welcomes the clear statement in section 7 of the *Elucidation* that the two movements are complementary:

> We believe that this is the correct position to take and that it accords fully with the Anglican tradition as found in the S.A.P.B. words of invitation 'Draw near and receive the Body and Blood of Our Lord Jesus Christ, which were given for you, feed on him in your hearts by faith with thanksgiving'; words which epitomise the teaching of the Book of Common Prayer, Articles and Catechism on this subject.[55]

It urges Anglicans to be 'true to this formulary, regardless of which side of it they feel drawn to'.[56]

The Anglican Church of Australia's response to *BEM*, however, notes that those within the Anglican tradition who understand Christ's presence as being specially found in faithful reception of the elements do not find their position clearly stated in the 'Lima Text'.[57] Indeed, in this connection *The Emmaus Report* draws attention to the difficulty felt by provinces such as Ireland about an *epiclesis* on the elements: 'the Church of Ireland is not alone in suggesting that the appeal for the restoration in the liturgy of the invocation of the Spirit on both the community and upon the elements goes beyond Anglican tradition as the tradition has been expressed in their own formularies'.[58]

The concern here again probably arises from Anglicans wishing to affirm worthy reception as the central dynamic of eucharistic participation. Naturally Anglicans who understand the locus of the presence of Christ to be the heart of the believer through worthy reception and not the elements *per se* will be suspicious of petitions which might appear to place the emphasis on the elements at the expense of reception, or more accurately on a petition which appears to make the action of the Spirit terminate on the elements independent of reception. Such concerns do not appear to have been given much attention in the Anglican–Reformed statement, while the Church of England response to *BEM* on the part of the Board for Mission and Unity gives no indication that while the 'epicletic' character of the eucharistic action would be widely accepted, how this is expressed in relation to the elements and the position of the *epiclesis* are still areas of dispute in England.

All of the statements are concerned to express the role of the Spirit in renewing and transforming the eucharistic community, equipping them for mission and service. Many of the texts allude to the eschatological dimension of the eucharist so that the transformation of the gifts and community becomes a pledge of the eschatological renewal of all creation.

The official Anglican ecumenical dialogues which we have been considering are all agreed theological statements with no specific liturgical brief. Liturgical questions arise in the context of theological exploration or where a theological

---

55 From the Southern African Anglican Theological Commission Report on the *Final Report* of ARCIC, II. 1.3, cited in *The Emmaus Report: A Report of the Anglican Ecumenical Consultation 1987* (London, 1987), p. 61.

56 Ibid.

57 Ibid., p. 131.

58 Ibid., p. 130.

principle is stressed through the medium of liturgy as in the place of the *epiclesis* in the Orthodox tradition. *BEM* represents a survey of theology and practice noting unitive categories but also points of divergence. None of the documents suggest liturgical texts to illustrate the theology (with the exception of Max Thurian's unofficial 'Lima Liturgy').

The Anglican ecumenical statements are important, however, as a primary medium in which Anglican theologians representing the Anglican Communion are working theologically together. The statements therefore set out markers which the writers of liturgies ought to take seriously. As such, the statements suggest four principles for liturgical reform:

1. While more than one document asserts the role of the Spirit in the eucharist whether the liturgical texts express it or not, the 'or not' phrase suggests that this is in part recognition of the invisibility of a rich theology of the Spirit in historic western liturgical texts. The clear implication of the statements is that the role of the Spirit ought to be expressed much more centrally in Anglican eucharistic texts, and in the eucharistic prayer in particular.
2. As stated above, the Anglican tradition historically has sought to maintain a balance between objective and subjective movements in relation to the presence of Christ. The liturgical articulation of the work of the Spirit can assist here in expressing the truth that Christ is present through the power of the Spirit in the objective gift of his body and blood and is received by faith through the power of the Spirit operating in the life of the communicant. A single *epiclesis* embracing both movements is more likely to assist theological clarity than a 'split' *epiclesis* where textually petitions relating the Spirit to the elements and the worshippers are often remote from each other.
3. The nature of the language of the *epiclesis* remains doctrinally sensitive especially in relation to the elements.
4. The methodology of 'agreed statements' has proved to be fruitful theologically and ecumenically and the same principle should hold fast for liturgical texts both within Provinces and across the Anglican Communion.

Chapter 6

The 1928 Prayer Book: 'Eastern' or 'Western' Identity?

Introduction

The process of Prayer Book revision was initiated by the findings of the 1906 Royal Commission on Ecclesiastical Discipline. Among its recommendations was that Letters of Business should be issued to the Convocations regarding modifications in the existing law relating to the conduct of Anglican worship. The Royal Letters of Business were issued to the Convocations on 10 November 1906. They were instructed to consider and agree any modifications to the law relating to the conduct of Divine Service and to the ornaments and fittings of churches. After such consideration, the Convocations were instructed to present a report to the Crown.[1]

Theological Writing 1900-1920

Charles Gore

Gore published his important book *The Body of Christ* in 1901. In the final chapter he evaluates the 1662 rite in the light of what he understood as the 'primitive type' of the *anaphora,* namely a basic structure of *sursum corda*, thanksgiving for creation and redemption with the *sanctus*, institution narrative, *anamnesis* and oblation, and then 'the invocation of the Holy Spirit, or of the divine power' to consecrate the bread and wine 'to be the body and blood of Christ for the reception of the faithful'.[2] Gore found all these elements to be present adequately enough in 1549 but laments the absence of a verbal *anamnesis* and reference to the work of the Spirit in the prayer of consecration of 1662.[3] His support for an invocation arises from his opposition to any polarization between the material and the spiritual in the sacraments by analogy with the relationship between the physical body and the soul or personality,[4] and his understanding of the 'scriptural principle' that it is the role

1 Convocation of Canterbury, *The Chronicle of Convocation*, November, 1906, p. 332. It is salutary to note that the Royal Letters of Business were essentially concerned with rubrics and ornaments. The background is well documented in Donald Gray, *The 1927-28 Prayer Book Crisis: 1. Ritual, Royal Commissions, and Reply to the Royal Letters of Business* (Norwich, 2005).

2 Charles Gore, *The Body of Christ* (London, 1901), p. 281.

3 Ibid., p. 284. He quotes the 1549 *epiclesis* with approval on p. 233.

4 Ibid., pp. 37-38.

of the Spirit to communicate the life of Christ to the Church.[5] Moreover, the Spirit is rightly understood as the agent of consecration, as the majority of liturgies from before the end of the fifth century bear witness.[6]

Darwell Stone

As a leading theologian of the anglo-catholic party, Stone's writings were particularly influential. He published a short work *The Holy Communion* in 1904 and his massive two-volume treatise *A History of the Holy Eucharist* in 1909. His first book includes a discussion of the historic doctrines of consecration in east and west with the assertion that the Church of England is 'committed to the ordinary Western opinion that the words of institution are by themselves sufficient to effect the consecration'.[7] His longer study follows a particular methodology in that he is concerned 'to tabulate and classify facts' but not to pass judgement on them.[8] There is consequently a lack of discussion of the *epiclesis* even in the eastern liturgies.[9] His chief interest appears to be more the fact of consecration than the method. Given his conviction that the Church of England embraced the western tradition of consecration, it is easy to see from his massive treatment of the history of the eucharist in the west why he should regard the view of consecration by invocation of the Spirit as wholly alien.[10]

W.C. Bishop

Bishop, writing in 1908, argues that the eastern tradition of the *anaphora* is nearer to the primitive form of the eucharistic prayer.[11] He first of all draws attention to the accounts of the Last Supper which set eucharistic consecration in the context of thanksgiving, and where the eucharistic words of Jesus are words of administration rather than consecration. Examining the eastern rites, he sees the role of the narrative as being the authority for the performance of the rite with the *epiclesis* as a prayer that the supernatural gift of Christ's body and blood will be bestowed. Drawing on a study previously published in *The Church Quarterly Review*,[12] he argues that the

5 Ibid., pp. 77ff. In quoting from *Apostolic Constitutions 8*, he expounds the verb ἀποφήνῃ with the similar ἀναδεικνύναι as carrying 'not only the idea of making the elements to be what they were not before, but also the idea of revealing or declaring what they have become to the faithful'.

6 Ibid., pp. 102, 186.

7 Darwell Stone, *The Holy Communion* (London, 1904), pp. 228-229.

8 Darwell Stone, *A History of the Doctrine of the Holy Eucharist*, Vol. 2 (London, 1909), p. 648.

9 Ibid., Vol. 1, p. 87.

10 Stone's *History* was reviewed by Arthur Headlam in his article 'The Eucharist in History', *The Church Quarterly Review*, 70 (1910): 29-63. Headlam warned that it was misguided to make hard divisions between the spiritual and the material.

11 W.C. Bishop, 'The Primitive Form of Consecration of the Holy Eucharist', *The Church Quarterly Review*, 66 (1908): 385-404.

12 W.C. Bishop, 'The Mozarabic Rite', *The Church Quarterly Review*, 63 (1907): 298-322.

Gallican rite originally possessed an *epiclesis* approximating to the eastern type, and that the *Supplices te* of the Roman rite supplanted an original invocation by analogy with the position and form of the *epiclesis* in the consecration of the font in the Gregorian and Gelasian sacramentaries. A possibly earlier form of the *epiclesis* may be found in the early Gallican tradition, that God would send his Spirit upon the sacrifice (a form not too far removed from that in the *Egyptian Church Order* as yet unrecognized as the *Apostolic Tradition*). Bishop's conclusion was that the primitive form of the consecration is reflected in the eastern pattern of narrative, *anamnesis*, invocation.[13]

R.M. Woolley

Writing in 1910, Woolley sought to assemble all the extant textual evidence for the development of the *epiclesis*. His contention is that originally the whole *anaphora* and not just a part of it effected consecration, and that the pristine *epiclesis* was a petition that the worshippers may share in 'the full grace and virtue of the Holy Sacrament'.[14] The crucial change in the role of the *epiclesis* came in the middle of the fourth century, coinciding with the dogmatic definitions of the person of the Spirit in the wake of the Arian controversy. So to the petition for worthy communion was added a 'direct reference to the sanctifying work of the Holy Spirit in the consecration of the elements' so that the *epiclesis* became a consecratory formula.[15]

W.H. Frere

Frere published his influential book *Some Principles of Liturgical Reform* in 1911. He sets out the historic divide between east and west and argues that at the present time it would be inopportune for the Church of England to consider the reintroduction of an *epiclesis* of the Holy Spirit in either its eastern or preliminary position. He did state, however, that the 1662 canon was 'more Roman than Rome' in its emphasis on the role of the eucharistic words in effecting consecration. This led Frere to suggest a rearrangement of the 1662 material to restore something like a composite eucharistic prayer, namely, the comfortable words and prayer of humble access followed by the sequence, *sursum corda*, preface and *sanctus*, consecration prayer, prayer of oblation and Lord's Prayer.[16]

---

13 Peter Hinchliff makes the observation that Bishop was 'concerned more with the "form" or pattern of the anaphora than the theology of consecration', *The South African Liturgy* (Cape Town, 1959), p. 18. Bishop, recognizing 'low church' concerns suggested texts such as 'that they may become *unto us* the Body and Blood of Christ' or 'that they may become unto us *the spiritual food* of the Body and Blood of Christ', 'The Prospects and Principles of Prayer-Book Revision', *The Church Quarterly Review*, 71 (1910): 97-119.

14 Reginald Maxwell Woolley, *The Liturgy of the Primitive Church* (Cambridge, 1910), p. 96.

15 Ibid., p. 111.

16 W.H. Frere, *Some Principles of Liturgical Reform* (London, 1911), p. 191. His suggestion for a rearranged canon was largely followed by Athelstan Riley, *Prayer Book Revision* (London and Oxford, 1911). Frere's scheme was also commended by E.G.P. Wyatt

J.H. Srawley

Srawley published *The Early History of the Liturgy* in 1913, a survey of the development of the eucharistic liturgy during the first six centuries. He makes a distinction between a developed *epiclesis* of the Holy Spirit upon the elements and the earlier and more diverse forms of invocation. He argues that while the earliest eucharistic prayer was a thanksgiving over the elements, by the fourth century an invocation of some sort is found in all available eastern sources while there are references to an invocation in some western texts. However, the form and contents of the invocations differ widely. Not all invocations are related to the Spirit; for example, the references in Irenaeus, Justin and Sarapion are to an invocation of the 'Word' or *Logos*, while Augustine, Ambrose and the Roman canon are silent in relation to the Spirit. Where the Spirit is cited, the *epiclesis* in the *anaphora* of Addai and Mari and the *Ethiopic Church Order* primarily request that the blessings of the sacrament may be secured for the worshippers, while in Cyril of Jerusalem, Sarapion and *Apostolic Constitutions 8* the prayer is that 'the elements may be made, or become, or be shewn as, the Body and Blood of Christ'.[17] He argues that the invocation of the Spirit was not a native or original feature of western liturgy.

F.E. Brightman

Brightman published his magisterial two-volume work *The English Rite* in 1915.[18] While the work does not attempt theological evaluation, Brightman cites the liturgy of St Basil as a possible source for Cranmer's 1549 *epiclesis*,[19] especially the invocation of the Spirit and the verbs 'bless and sanctify', while he ascribes the invocation of the word to Augustine's sermon ccxxvii and the words '*sanctificatus per verbum Dei*', with allusion to 1 Timothy 4:5.[20] For Brightman, Cranmer's purpose was to combine 'the Eastern and Western conception of the "form" of consecration by the addition of the Invocation of the Holy Ghost, while avoiding the difficulties this might involve for a western, by placing the Invocation before, instead of after, the recital of the Institution'.[21] Brightman's conclusions thus gave encouragement to those who would argue that the restoration of an *epiclesis* ought not to be at the expense of the centrality of the institution narrative for a Church that was part of western Christendom.

---

in his book *The Eucharistic Prayer* (London, 1914), and by T.A. Lacey who in 1912 issued a new edition of an earlier work, *Liturgical Interpolations and the Revision of the Prayer Book* (London, 1912).

17 J.H. Srawley, *The Early History of the Liturgy* (Cambridge, 1913), p. 209.

18 F.E. Brightman, *The English Rite*, Vols 1 & 2 (London, 1915).

19 Ibid., Vol. 2, p. 692. He was later, in 1927, to revise this view, citing western sources where the Spirit is linked to consecration.

20 Ibid., Vol. 1, p. cvii.

21 Ibid., Vol. 1, p. cvi.

W.J. Sparrow Simpson

Sparrow Simpson published *The Prayer of Consecration* in 1917.[22] His purpose was to set out criticisms made of alleged defects in the 1662 prayer of consecration, especially with regard to the nature of consecration and the eucharistic offering. In essence, he provides a historical survey from the sixteenth to the twentieth centuries, to illustrate discontent with the rite. He does little evaluation of the criticisms; indeed, the impression given during the survey is that he approves of an *epiclesis* regardless of its position in the canon. This, however, is misleading, for the whole exercise is carried out with a view to the restoration of 1549. He suggests that the wisest course is to seek to combine the western stress on the eucharistic words with the eastern emphasis on invocation.[23] It is clearly his conviction that 1549 did that by a preliminary invocation leading into the narrative, accommodating an eastern insight into an essentially western framework.

J.W. Tyrer

Tyrer's important work *The Eucharistic Epiclesis* was published in 1917. It is a study of the *epiclesis* in the first four centuries and his purpose is to assemble the Patristic material and allow it to speak for itself.[24] Tyrer does not discuss whether the *epiclesis* is *the* necessary form of consecration nor does he relate his findings to Prayer Book revision. In particular, he replies to Edmund Bishop's essay 'Moment of Consecration' in R.H. Connolly's *The Liturgical Homilies of Narsai* (1909).[25] Bishop had argued that the earliest form of *epiclesis* was an invocation of Christ as Word; the invocation of the Spirit was a later development in the context of the outbreak of the Pneumatomachian controversy in 360.[26] Tyrer discusses the form of *epiclesis* in 'the three earliest extant Eucharistic forms which can be dated with any certainty':[27] Sarapion, *Mystagogical Lecture 5* of Cyril of Jerusalem and the so-called *Egyptian Church Order*, all three to be dated before 360. He airs the possibility that in Sarapion, a text apparently supporting Bishop's position, the invocation of the Word may have been a personal initiative arising from his 'intense devotion to the Godhead of our Lord'.[28] More importantly Cyril's text, which Tyrer dates in 348 and where the *epiclesis* of the Spirit is 'the form of consecration',[29] gives no indication that the *epiclesis* is a recent innovation, and probably predated Sarapion. The most significant factor however was that the quest for 'the primitive eucharistic prayer' gained fresh impetus from the publication in 1916 of R.H. Connolly's *The So-Called Egyptian*

22 W.J. Sparrow Simpson, *The Prayer of Consecration* (London, 1917). Gore in the foreword again asserted his support of a reordering of 1662 or better still, the authorization of 1549, p. iii.

23 Ibid., p. 17.

24 J.W. Tyrer, *The Eucharistic Epiclesis* (London, 1917), p. 3.

25 R.H. Connolly, *The Liturgical Homilies of Narsai* (Cambridge, 1909).

26 Ibid., Appendix vi, pp. 138-141.

27 Tyrer, *The Eucharistic Epiclesis*, p. 28.

28 Ibid., p. 34.

29 Ibid., p. 35.

Church Order and Derived Documents,[30] which identified the *Egyptian Church Order* with the *Apostolic Tradition* attributed to Hippolytus. Tyrer is one of the first writers to give special attention to Connolly's research. He dates it 'not later than 235',[31] and so bearing witness to a Spirit-*epiclesis* over a century before Sarapion's text. Tyrer judged that the only evidence in support of a 'word' *epiclesis* was the reference in Athanasius, 'the Word descends on the bread and the cup, and it becomes his body', also from the second quarter of the fourth century.[32] He argues that a Spirit *epiclesis* was known at Jerusalem in the first quarter of the fourth century, probably in N. Africa in the middle of the third, and also in the third century in *Didascalia*, the writings of Origen, as well as in the liturgical text of *Egyptian Church Order*.

W. Lockton

Lockton, writing in *The Church Quarterly Review*,[33] reflects the view that the so-called *Egyptian Church Order* provides the earliest complete eucharistic prayer, and that it was 'an elaboration of a Jewish grace to be said before meat', alluded to in 1 Timothy 4:3-5.[34] Drawing on Connolly's work, he dates it to the early part of the third century. He regards the *epiclesis* of Hippolytus as an insertion, interrupting the flow of the prayer. Lockton lays special emphasis on the Jewish origins of the eucharistic prayer, and that consecration is effected by thanksgiving. The *epiclesis* is a later addition, although the epicletic petition for the unity of the Church is an early development traceable to the *Didache*, and expanded in Hippolytus. Lockton's purpose is to defend 1662; the sequence from *sursum corda* to the prayer of consecration effected consecration by thanksgiving, culminating in the narrative of institution, 'as in the earliest days' of the Church.[35] He also appealed to the collect for purity as a kind of *epiclesis* over the whole rite.[36]

Suggestions for Liturgical Revision

In 1913 and 1914, Mowbrays published two books with suggestions for liturgical revision. The first was an anonymous service book entitled *A Prayer Book Revised* with a preface by Charles Gore, now Bishop of Oxford.[37] Here the invocation of the 1637 Scottish *BCP*, drawing on 1549, is used in the communion service,

---

30 R. Hugh Connolly, *The So-Called Egyptian Church Order and Derived Documents* (Cambridge, 1916).

31 Tyrer, *The Eucharistic Epiclesis*, p. 70. Bishop regarded the presence of the *epiclesis* in the *Egyptian Church Order* as an indication of a late date for that document, Connolly, *The Liturgical Homilies of Narsai*, p. 144.

32 Tyrer, *The Eucharistic Epiclesis*, p. 52.

33 W. Lockton, 'The Eucharistic Prayer', *The Church Quarterly Review*, 86 (1918): 305-332.

34 Ibid., p. 310.

35 Ibid., p. 332.

36 Lockton's article found episcopal support from Bishop Knox of Manchester in *The Proposed Changes in the Prayer of Consecration* (London, 1918).

37 The author was Percy Dearmer, see Hinchliff, *The South African Liturgy*, p. 84.

reflecting Gore's admiration for 1549. The second, *A Revised Liturgy* was written by B.W. Randolph.[38] Again, the 1549 invocation was restored. Both books were criticized by W.C. Bishop because of the position of the *epiclesis*, in that they followed 'Cranmer's half-hearted attempt at following the Greek liturgies'.[39] Bishop argued that if the Church of England was to follow antiquity, it must 'add a proper Invocation *after* the words of Institution'.[40]

W.H. Frere

In 1920, Frere drew attention to the form of the *epiclesis* in the 1919 South African liturgy. He was well aware of the controversial nature of an apparently consecratory *epiclesis*. He commended the form

> we humbly beseech thee to pour thy Holy Spirit upon us and upon these thy gifts, that he may hallow this oblation, and that all we who are partakers of this holy communion may worthily receive the most precious Body and Blood of thy Son, and be fulfilled with thy grace and heavenly benediction

on the basis that it was drawn from the less explicit Gallican rites (in comparison to the Greek forms). So it was an example of a non-Roman western text and he regarded the phrase 'that he may hallow this oblation' as 'reticent' and 'non-controversial'.[41]

Liturgical Revision in Convocation 1900-1920

Convocation of Canterbury

The revision of the communion office was first considered by the Lower House of the Convocation of Canterbury in 1910. It requested that 'a service on the lines of the Scottish Communion Office be provided as an alternative'.[42] However, when the House met in July 1911, a motion than an alternative order should be drawn up based on 1549 and the Scottish and the American offices was lost by 47 votes to 32.[43]

Convocation of York

The joint committee of the Lower House meeting in February 1912 passed the following resolution with regard to the canon:

---

38 B.W. Randolph, *A Revised Liturgy* (London, 1914).

39 W.C. Bishop, 'Progress in Prayer Book Revision', *The Church Quarterly Review*, 78 (1914): 93.

40 W.C. Bishop, 'Prayer Book Revision: The Present Stage', *The Church Quarterly Review*, 80 (1915): 358-393.

41 W.H. Frere, 'The New South African Liturgy', *The Church Quarterly Review*, 90 (1920): 367-374.

42 *Report of a Committee of the Lower House on the Royal Letters of Business (No. 447)*, resolution 54a.

43 Ibid., p. 367.

> The Committee approve of the principle of the restoring of the Epiklesis (or Invocation of the Holy Spirit) in the Prayer of Consecration.
>
> The Committee are of the opinion that it is desirable that the Prayer of Oblation and the Lord's Prayer should be placed immediately after the Prayer of Consecration.[44]

This was accepted by the Lower House.[45] However, at the July meeting of the Upper House, a motion by the Bishop of Manchester, Dr E.A. Knox, for no change in the prayer of consecration was carried by six votes to one.[46]

Convocation of Canterbury

Meanwhile, a committee of the Lower House of Canterbury had met to consider the question of the canon in 1914. Its report rejected the restoration of 1549 as an alternative to 1662. Instead, it proposed a rearrangement of the Prayer Book rite, as had been suggested by Frere.[47] This was accepted by 79 votes to 8,[48] and it appeared in Report 487. The Report was debated in the Upper House in April 1915 but rejected by 15 votes to 5, and while the issue of whether there should be an alternative order to 1662 see-sawed between the Houses during the period 1915 to 1918 there was little discussion of the *epiclesis*.[49]

What was at issue was the restructuring of the canon. A conference of members of the Houses of both Convocations meeting in October 1918 proposed a conference on the structure of the eucharistic prayer.[50] It met in the same month but could not reach agreement on the canon. A second conference assembled at Lambeth Palace on 2 May 1919.[51] After discussion, the following proposals, made by the Bishop of Ripon, Dr T.W. Drury, and seconded by Frere, were accepted:

1. That the Prayer of Oblation be not moved from its present position;
2. That the Prayer of Humble Access be moved so as to follow immediately after the Comfortable Words;
3. That the Lord's Prayer be placed after the Prayer of Consecration, and immediately before the Communion;

---

44 *Report of the Committee of the Royal Letters of Business, Lower House (No. 227)*, 1912, p. xxiv.

45 *Report of the Joint Committee of the Two Houses of the Convocation of York (No. 302)*, 1915, p. xl.

46 *Journal of Convocation*, 1915, p. 316.

47 See R.C.D. Jasper (ed.), *Walter Howard Frere: His Correspondence on Liturgical Revision and Construction* (London, 1954), pp. 57-58.

48 Convocation of Canterbury, Lower House, *Report of the Committee (No. 480)*, pp. 2, 9, 10; *Chronicle of Convocation*, 1914, p. 161.

49 The Convocation of Canterbury proposed a canon in 1918 taking up the 1914 rearrangement but with the addition of the 1549 *anamnesis*, *Chronicle of Convocation*, 1918, pp. 137-167.

50 *Report of Committee on the Royal Letters of Business (No. 335)*, 1919, p. xvi.

51 Ibid., pp. xvi-xvii.

4. That the Words of Institution be followed by –
   (a) An Act of Remembrance;
   (b) An Act of Thanksgiving;
   (c) A Prayer for the Holy Spirit.[52]

A committee, chaired by Drury, was appointed to draft the wording and when the conference reassembled at Church House in November, the following *epiclesis* (following the *anamnesis*) was agreed:

> And we pray thee of thine almighty goodness to send upon us and upon these thy gifts thy holy and blessed Spirit, who is the Sanctifier and the Giver of life, to whom with thee and thy Son Jesus Christ be ascribed by every creature in earth and heaven all blessing, honour, glory, and power, now henceforth and for evermore. *Amen.*[53]

This was duly reported in the Royal Letters of Business Report 529 (1920).[54]

Convocation of York

The Lower House of the Convocation of York met on 11 February 1920. Frere reported on the conference at Lambeth and moved a motion that the recommendations of the conference be accepted. On the *epiclesis*, he hoped that what was proposed might act as a bridge between the Christian east and west. While members of the committee recognized that the epicletic text was a compromise, nevertheless he thought it was a compromise of hope. To an objection that it was unscriptural to invoke the Spirit on inanimate objects, Frere replied that the Spirit brooding upon the face of chaos should remove any question of the Spirit's relationship with matter. In the end, Frere's motion was carried by 34 votes to 29.[55] The Upper House also met on 11 February to consider the proposals for an alternative canon. Drury reiterated the point that in 1662 from the collect for purity to the end there was no petition for the gift of the Spirit, but it was by the operation of the Spirit that the Lord's presence was mediated at communion. In his view, the petition was comparable with the petition in the baptism service: 'Sanctify this water to the mystical washing away

52 Ibid., pp. xvii-xviii. Jasper, in *Walter Howard Frere: His Correspondence*, sets out letters between Frere and Drury in preparation for the conference, including suggested texts for the *epiclesis*, pp. 66-67, 72-73.

53 *Report of Committee on the Royal Letters of Business (No. 335)*, 1919, p. xviii. Drury's contribution is important because he belonged to the evangelical wing of the Church and was an able liturgist. He argued that in the 'Hear us' clause of 1662, 'we are most truly praying for the presence and help of the Holy Spirit, for it is only by the Holy Spirit that we can feed on Christ. It is He who, coming down upon the recipients in His gracious power, brings the presence of Christ into their hearts, not indeed through material channels of bread and wine, but yet so that in the use of them every faithful recipient is made partaker of His blessing'. T.W. Drury, 'The Lord's Supper', in Henry Wace (ed.), *Church and Faith* (Edinburgh and London, 1899), p. 195.

54 Convocation of Canterbury, *Report 529*, 1920, p. 4. The text of the *epiclesis* had gone through a number of drafts, with Frere and Drury working closely together.

55 Convocation of York, *Minutes of the Lower House*, 1920, p. 3.

of sin'.[56] There was, however, strong opposition to the proposed text from Bishop Knox that the proposed *epiclesis* suggested an assimilation to the doctrine of the eastern Church and Frere's suggestion that the rite would be a 'bridge' between the eastern and western Churches was weighted on the eastern side and suggested adoration. When it came to the vote, an amendment by Knox 'not to alter the structure and sequence of Holy Communion' was rejected by a casting vote from the Archbishop of York, Dr C.G. Lang. However an amendment from Bishop F.J. Chavasse of Liverpool to delete 'and upon these thy gifts' from the conference text was accepted by four votes to three, thus relating the *epiclesis* solely to the worshippers. [57]

At the meeting of the full Convocation on 29 April 1920 Archbishop Lang drew attention to the small majorities for the amendments to the conference canon in the Upper House and was anxious that Synod should have the opportunity to discuss whether they expressed its mind.[58] Knox proposed a 'no change' amendment; he reiterated his concerns about eastern theology and piety, and that the *epiclesis* was a late development,[59] and the amendment was carried by 28 votes to 25. The 'no change' lobby had it.[60]

Convocation of Canterbury

The Upper House met on 11 February 1920. The Bishop of Gloucester, Dr E.C.S. Gibson, in introducing the text of the conference *epiclesis*, drew attention to the parallel in the baptism service as the justification for the descent of the Spirit upon the gifts.[61] The bishops were largely in agreement as voting 14–2 in favour. The Lower House met on 12 February. While Henry Wace articulated evangelical concerns about an invocation on the elements, other issues were that the proposed prayer had in effect a double-invocation, the minimalist form of the Prayer Book before the narrative and the form invoking the Spirit after, while others regarded the latter form as not being specific enough. Srawley sought to answer such criticisms:

> … the Conference finally went back for guidance to some of the other Western, non-Roman forms, in which there was a reference to the work of the Holy Spirit in a much less direct form, praying for his coming upon the gifts and upon the worshippers, and praying for gifts of grace and blessing for those who were communicants. The way in which the Conference attempted to do without any repetition of the previous Invocation was by dwelling upon the two great forms of the operation of the Holy Spirit as the Sanctifier and the Giver of Life.

---

56 *Journal of Convocation*, 1920, pp. 22-26.

57 Ibid., pp. 56-57.

58 *Journal of Convocation*, 1920, pp. 211-212.

59 Ibid., pp. 213-216.

60 Ibid. For Knox's personal account of this episode, see E.A. Knox, *Reminiscences of an Octogenarian 1847-1934* (London, 1934), p. 317.

61 *Chronicle of Convocation*, 1920, pp. 66-69.

> To say that the Invocation was colourless because it did not go on to refer to the elements, and to pray that the elements might become to us the Body and Blood of Christ, was really beside the mark, in face of the fact that the Conference decided to retain the Invocation to that effect which was in the existing Book.[62]

In the end the proposals of Report 529 were accepted by the Upper and Lower Houses and duly incorporated in Report 533.[63]

It was thus on 29 April 1920, that the official reply to the Royal Letters of Business was signed by the Archbishops and the Prolocutors. The Convocations of York and Canterbury had not reached agreement on the eucharistic prayer, Canterbury alone agreeing to its restructuring. The proposals now passed to the newly empowered National Assembly of the Church of England under the terms of the Church of England Assembly (Powers) Act, 1919.

Theological Writing 1921-25

T. Herbert Bindley

Writing in *Theology* in 1921, Bindley argues that the *epiclesis* in Hippolytus was not upon the elements but rather the oblation of praise and thanksgiving.[64] He follows Srawley's suggestion in differentiating between 'invocation' and '*epiclesis*', the latter being a petition for the Spirit to effect a change in the elements. This was unknown before Cyril of Jerusalem, and therefore from a historical point of view, neither 'historical' nor 'catholic'.[65] He then argued that the petition for consecration in 1662, relating to the worshippers' communion, 'approaches more nearly to that of the Apostolic Anaphora, as we get in Hippolytus, than any other'.[66] The real defect in 1662 was its lack of stress on thanksgiving.[67]

E.C.F. Atchley

Atchley's article in the August 1921 edition of *Theology* was clearly a response to Bindley.[68] Atchley is concerned to give a survey of references to the eucharistic *epiclesis* from the post-New Testament period to the middle of the fourth century. He also attempts to show that the popular criticism that before the middle of the fourth century the roles of the second and third Persons of the Trinity are not sufficiently

---

62 Ibid., pp. 159-160.

63 *Proposals for the Revision of the Book of Common Prayer as Approved by the Convocation of Canterbury*, April 1920.

64 T. Herbert Bindley, 'The Structure of the Early Liturgies and Some Recent Proposals for the Revision of the English Rite', *Theology*, 2 (1921): 14-22, 80-85, 130-140.

65 Ibid., p. 85.

66 Ibid., p. 135.

67 Bindley here anticipates the later stance of Ratcliff and Dix, although his suggestion that the shape of the prayer of consecration should be thanksgiving, *anamnesis*, narrative, was idio-syncratic, ibid., p. 136.

68 Cuthbert Atchley, 'The Epiclesis', *Theology*, 3 (1921): 90-98.

differentiated may be an exaggeration. For him, it was rather that before the fourth century the role of the Spirit *as the specific agent of sanctification on earth, of both persons and things* was not defined.[69] He criticizes Srawley's attempt to distinguish between '*epiclesis*' and 'invocation'. Rather he shows the great fluidity of forms of *epiclesis* by distinguishing eleven types.[70] He regards the *Logos-epiclesis* as probably being earlier than the Spirit-*epiclesis* but with the growing realization of the personality of the Spirit, it came to be held 'that He was the Instrument of the Incarnation, and of the parallel case of the Eucharistic Presence, of our Lord'.[71] Atchley did not relate his findings to the issue of Prayer Book. However, he was clearly writing in support of those who wished to see a restoration of the *epiclesis* on the grounds of the primitive practice of the Church, and his eleven categories underlined the fact that such an *epiclesis* need not be the full-blown Greek type.

E.C. Trenholme

Trenholme illustrates anglo-catholic concerns in articles in *Theology* and *The Church Quarterly Review*.[72] His concern was for the authorization of a canon as proposed by the Convocation of Canterbury in 1918. He regards Hippolytus as the nearest extant *anaphora* to the original 'parent form, near to the time of the Apostles'. However, he does not argue for the restoration of a Hippolytan *epiclesis* on the basis that this is sufficiently covered by the petition for consecration in the 1662 canon. He would not be opposed to the restoration of the 1549 petition which explicitly mentions the Holy Spirit. In Trenholme's writing we see a concern to preserve the 'western' tradition of consecration.

W.H. Frere

Frere published his book *The Primitive Consecration Prayer* in 1922.[73] It is essentially a study of the *anaphora* in *Apostolic Tradition*.[74] He understands the ground-plan of the 'primitive anaphora' as containing three movements: 'We thank thee ... We offer unto thee ... We ask thee to send thy Holy Spirit ... '.[75] As for the *epiclesis* in Hippolytus, Frere regards it as 'brief and primitive', and he defends the text against charges that it was a later interpolation. He interprets it as an invocation upon the elements. Its position after the *anamnesis* is regarded as natural given the credal progression of thought.

---

69 Ibid., p. 96.

70 Ibid., p. 97.

71 Ibid., p. 98.

72 E.C. Trenholme, 'The Canon of the Liturgy', *Theology*, 3 (1921): 99-104; 'Liturgies Old and New', *The Church Quarterly Review*, 93 (1921): 68-85 and 'The Urgency of Eucharistic Revision', *Theology*, 4 (1922): 311-314.

73 W.H. Frere, *The Primitive Consecration Prayer* (London, 1922).

74 Based on a comparison of the use of *AT* in the Greek text of *Apostolic Constitutions 8* with the Latin 'Verona' text.

75 Frere, *The Primitive Consecration Prayer*, p. 12.

T.W. Drury

Drury resigned as Bishop of Ripon in 1920. After this he played no further part in Prayer Book revision before his death in 1926, save for an article in *The Church Quarterly Review* in 1923. Drury wishes to commend what he regards as the primitive form of the *epiclesis* which did not pray for an absolute change in the elements but rather sanctified them to a holy use that they might be the vehicle of blessings promised to the communicant.[76] For this reason he was keen to promote the verb 'sanctify' and the phrase 'upon us and upon these gifts'. He regarded the eastern position for the *epiclesis* as the most primitive. He interprets the 1552/1662 petition for consecration not as a rejection of the 1549 formula but as a reaction to catholic interpretations put upon 1549. However, he regrets that apart from the collect for purity the role of the Spirit is marginalized liturgically in 1662.

J.W. Tyrer

In January 1923, R.H. Connolly published an article in the *Downside Review* entitled 'The Meaning of ἐπίκλησις', in which he argued that the words 'invoke' or 'invocation', when used in early Christian literature, designate a formula involving the use of names, rather than the idea of making a petition. Tyrer's article is a reply to Connolly defending the traditional interpretation.[77] Building on a quotation from Origen (as cited by Rufinus) where *invocare nomen Domini* has the same meaning as *orare Domini*, Tyrer examines references in the *Septuagint* and New Testament where the verb ἐπικαλειν means to 'invoke' or 'appeal', with no special emphasis on the divine Name. In response to Connolly's statement that he knew of no *ante*-Nicene reference where ἐπίκλησις signifies petition, Tyrer assembles four pages of quotations and proceeds to show the association between ἐπίκλησις and petition, and that when ἐπίκλησις is used of the eucharist it either means the whole consecration prayer or, later, a formula within it, but always it denotes a prayer. So he concludes that the 'normal' meaning of ἐπικαλεισθαι, *invocare* is to 'petition' or 'appeal' and of ἐπίκλησις, *invocatio* is, when used of a religious formula, is 'petition' or 'appeal'.

Tyrer's contribution to the debate over Prayer Book revision came in 1924.[78] It is a robust defence of the 1549 *epiclesis*. Drawing on Gasquet and Edmund Bishop, he regards the 1549 invocation as a combination of Greek and Latin formulae, suggesting a reconciliation between east and west and safeguarding the principle that consecration is the work of God through the Spirit. He suggests that an understanding of the Spirit as the agent of sanctification is both primitive and catholic. Although Tyrer regards an invocation after the *anamnesis* as occupying the 'more usual place',

76 T.W. Drury, 'The *Epiclesis* in the Service of Holy Communion', *The Church Quarterly Review*, 97 (1923): 4-5.

77 J.W. Tyrer, 'The Meaning of ἐπίκλησις', *The Journal of Theological Studies*, 25 (1924): 139-150.

78 J.W. Tyrer, 'The English Canon of 1549 and Its Invocation', *Theology*, 9 (1924): 259-265.

the 1549 position was acceptable, not least because it could be used both by those who regard the invocation as the chief element in consecration and also by those who look to the institution narrative.

J. Armitage Robinson

In contrast to Tyrer, Robinson closely follows Connolly's theory.[79] So invocation 'is primarily a matter of the naming of a powerful Name and the recital of appropriate attributes of the deity involved'.[80] Applied to the eucharist, Robinson argues that from the second century consecration of the eucharist was believed to be effected by *epiclesis* – 'not a petition for the coming of the Blessed Trinity upon the elements of bread and wine, but a naming of the Sacred Name of God by way of consecration'.[81] Again, he follows Connolly in drawing attention to the fact that in the early liturgies the naming of the Trinity in the doxology of the thanksgiving was the earliest form of this invocation. The writings of Cyril of Jerusalem, however, demonstrate a wholly new development in the explicit invocation of the Spirit to change the bread and wine, so that the general '*epiclesis*' became 'the *Epiclesis*'. For Robinson, this was a deviant development that became characteristic of the eastern Churches.[82] Robinson argues that the western Churches never adopted an *epiclesis* of eastern type and in his article he repeats the substance of his speech at the Church Assembly in 1923 (see below) in asserting the essential western identity of the Church of England in which consecration is understood in Christological rather than pneumatological terms.

F.E. Brightman

Brightman replied to Robinson's article in a letter published in *Theology* in July, 1924. He agrees that it was undesirable to introduce an invocation, unless the 1549 position was adopted. However, he is critical of definitions used by Robinson and Connolly and their stress on the association with the divine Name. Rather he understands *epiclesis* as having a number of meanings: a general meaning – 'a calling to' or 'in'; and two specific meanings – 'a calling on to' a person or thing or a 'calling over', given that Origen, for example, regarded consecration as a 'praying over the bread'.[83] He therefore judges that Robinson is not justified in translating *epiclesis* as 'invocation of the Divine Name'.[84] Brightman is also critical of Robinson's hard and fast distinction between eastern and western ideas of

79 J. Armitage Robinson, 'Invocation in the Holy Eucharist', *Theology*, 8 (1924): 89-100. He states in a footnote that he and Connolly were 'collaborating on the subject'.

80 Ibid., p. 91.

81 A.E. Burn continued the lively debate in *Theology* by supporting Robinson's argument for a canon without an *epiclesis* on the elements. 'Invocation in the Holy Eucharist', *Theology*, 8 (1924): 317-321.

82 Robinson had already made his opposition to a consecratory *epiclesis* clear in 1920 – 'The "Apostolic Anaphora" and the Prayer of St. Polycarp', *The Journal of Theological Studies*, 21 (1920): 97-105.

83 F.E. Brightman, 'Invocation in the Holy Eucharist', *Theology*, 9 (1924): 34-35.

84 Ibid.

consecration. For example, the *Didascalia* witnesses to consecration by invocation of the Spirit a century before the idea was suggested of consecration by the narrative; the role of Christ as consecrator is attested by John Chrysostom; both eastern and western divines attest to the operation of the Spirit in the eucharist; and there is evidence for an invocation of the Spirit in Africa, and in the Gallican rites of Gaul and Spain.[85] For Brightman, 1549 with its 'indefinite' invocation before the narrative witnesses to the fact that 'the "word" of institution is operative through the Eternal Spirit'.[86]

W.O.E. Oesterley

Oesterley made a distinctive contribution to the *epiclesis* debate by suggesting that the origins of the Christian invocation lay in the Jewish concept of *Shekhinah*, or the divine presence in the midst of God's people.[87] In Rabbinic thought the *Shekhinah* expressed God's immanence, a theme readily applicable to Christian experience both in a Christological sense, 'For where two or three are gathered in my name, there am I in the midst of them' (Matt. 18:20), and John 1:14 with its allusion to the Tabernacle, and pneumatologically in the Pentecost event. By this exposition, Oesterley is able to suggest biblical origins for the *epiclesis*, but also that in its earliest form, the *epiclesis* was essentially the invocation of the Spirit or the Word or the Trinity upon the worshippers, the Divine Presence among the assembly.[88] The invocation upon the elements was a later development.

Proposals for Liturgical Revision, 1921-25

In an attempt to resolve the *impasse* on the canon, a committee of the National Assembly representing the bishops, clergy and laity, appointed a sub-committee to take matters forward.[89] Following a suggestion by Srawley,[90] it drafted a composite eucharistic prayer along the lines of the 1918 Canterbury proposal and it duly appeared in the report of the full committee, N.A. 60. In receiving the report, the Church Assembly affirmed the following:

> It is not desirable at present to seek to introduce into the text of the existing Book of Common Prayer any of the changes now recommended; but that a supplementary volume should be provided, as well as a schedule of permissive variations from the existing book

85 Ibid., pp. 36-39.

86 Ibid., p. 40. Robinson reasserted his position in a letter in *Theology* in September, 1924, drawing attention to Connolly's reply to Tyrer in *The Journal of Theological Studies*, 25 (1924) and asked again, 'When first is the Holy Spirit spoken of as consecrating things as distinct from persons?'

87 W.O.E. Oesterley, *The Jewish Background of the Christian Liturgy* (Oxford, 1925), ch. ix.

88 Ibid., pp. 228-230.

89 Jasper, *Walter Howard Frere: His Correspondence*, pp. 83-84.

90 Ibid., pp. 84-85.

of Common Prayer, to be sanctioned by authority for optional use for such period as may hereafter be determined.[91]

Thus, when the House of Bishops accepted the report, they incorporated it in the form of a full text, in *The Church of England Revised Prayer Book (Permissive Use) Measure* (N.A. 84) in 1923.[92] This principle of 'a supplementary volume' opened the way for individuals and pressure groups to issue their own 'alternative books'. The first was by J.N. Dalton,[93] who looked to 1549 and incorporated a preliminary *epiclesis*, combining elements of 1549 and 1552. This was followed by the coloured books – green, grey and orange (yellow). The 'Green Book',[94] first published in October 1922 by the Church Union, carried the anglo-catholic proposals.[95] The canon reproduced the 1549 preliminary *epiclesis* (but without black crosses). The *anamnesis* also included an oblation of the bread and cup. The preliminary *epiclesis* accorded with the catholic understanding of the narrative of institution as a consecratory formula.[96]

The 'Grey Book'[97] included in part 1, issued in April 1923, the 'Order for Communion'. Published by the Life and Liberty Movement, the foreword was written by William Temple, Bishop of Manchester. Temple indicates that there was not unanimity as to the structure of the prayer of consecration although there was agreement about the constituent elements. The *epiclesis* follows the *anamnesis*:

> Hear us, O merciful Father, we most humbly beseech thee, and with thy Holy Spirit bless and sanctify both us and these thy gifts of Bread and Wine, that we receiving them according to thy Son our Saviour Jesus Christ's holy institution may be partakers of his most blessed Body and Blood, unto the fulfilment of the Kingdom of heaven.

An anonymous commentary on the 'Grey' rite, acknowledging that the *epiclesis* was a departure from N.A. 84, defends its inclusion on theological rather than historical or ecumenical grounds so that 'mechanical efficacy' is not attributed to the words of institution, and that the whole sacramental action depends for on being 'in the Spirit'.[98] It also asserts that the 'Grey' *epiclesis* falls short of the 'transubstantiationalist'

---

91 *National Assembly of the Church of England, Report 60*, p. 7.

92 *National Assembly of the Church of England: Revised Prayer Book (Permissive Use) Measure, 1923.*

93 J.N. Dalton, *The Book of Common Prayer* (Cambridge, 1920).

94 *A Suggested Prayer Book* (London, 1923).

95 R.C.D. Jasper cites Darwell Stone and N.P. Williams as the main drafters in *The Development of the Anglican Liturgy*, p. 115.

96 The 'Green' canon received some support from E.C. Trenholme in his article 'The Revision of the Prayer Book', *The Church Quarterly Review*, 97 (1923): 34-48. He was opposed to an *epiclesis* in the eastern position.

97 *A New Prayer Book* (London, 1923); Jasper cites the main authors as Percy Dearmer, R.G. Parsons, F.R. Barry, Leslie Hunter, F.W. Dwelly and Mervyn Haigh, *The Development of the Anglican Liturgy*, p. 115.

98 *The Sacrifice of the Communion*, 2nd ed. (London and Oxford, 1923), p. 11.

petitions of the Greek liturgies, placing more emphasis, following Hooker, on what is imparted through reception.[99]

In introducing the 'Grey Book' proposals to the House of Clergy in November 1923, one of its drafters, R.G. Parsons, suggested that evangelicals and catholics might find the eastern liturgical tradition to be a greater basis of unity than the western. He may have been correct with regard to more 'liberal' evangelicals and catholics but hardly for conservatives. Interestingly, he argued that the basis of the 'Grey Book' form was that the Spirit was operative in the whole act of consecration and 'that it is in response to the prayer of consecration rather than as a result of the retention of any particular words that consecration is completed', another indication of an approach that would characterize Church of England thinking about the eucharistic prayer in the 1960s and 1970s.

The 'Orange Book',[100] published by the Alcuin Club and drafted principally by Frere,[101] sought to bring together the proposals from N.A. 84, the 'Green Book' and the 'Grey Book'.[102] Two forms of the canon are set out with commentary. The first uses the text of N.A. 84 as its basis, but adds an *epiclesis* in the form of the 1920 Canterbury proposal:

> And here we offer and present unto thee, O Lord, ourselves, our souls and bodies to be a reasonable holy and living sacrifice unto thee: and we pray thee of thine own almighty goodness to send upon us, and upon these thy gifts, thy holy and blessed Spirit, who is the Sanctifier and the Giver of life; humbly beseeching thee that all we who are partakers of this holy Communion may be fulfilled with thy grace and heavenly benediction.[103]

The second canon is based on the 'Green Book' canon, following its structure but making some changes in wording, one of which was the omission of Cranmer's 1549 phrase 'with thy Holy Spirit and word' from the preliminary invocation.[104] For supplementary consecration, the formula for the first canon included narrative and *epiclesis*; the second only the narrative.

The proposals in N.A. 84 and the suggestions in the various books were then referred back to the Houses of Clergy and Laity.

The House of Clergy

When the House of Clergy came together at Church House, Westminster, on 13 November 1923, the first concern was whether the canon of 1662 should be

---

99 Ibid., pp. 11-12. Positive support for the 'Grey' canon also came in Francis C. Eeles, *Prayer Book Revision and Christian Reunion* (Cambridge, 1923).

100 *A Survey of the Proposals for the Alternative Prayer Book* (London, 1923). The 'Orange Book' was in three volumes.

101 Jasper, *The Development of the Anglican Liturgy*, p. 116.

102 Although it appears to be not so much a genuine survey as Frere attempting to steal a march!

103 *A Survey of the Proposals for the Alternative Prayer Book*, p. 37.

104 The commentary criticizes the invocation of the Spirit before the narrative without any form of invocation to follow it. Ibid., p. 40.

altered at all. An amendment to N.A. 84 proposed by Canon E. Grose-Hodge, an evangelical, that the communion service should remain unaltered after the prayer for the church militant was lost by 189 votes to 43.[105] But perhaps it was a statement by Dean Wace that most accurately summed up evangelical desires:

> There are things that we did want in this Revision of the Prayer Book. We did want some obsolete things altered; we did want new prayers introduced; we did want a certain amount of elasticity, but when we went into the matter we went into it with the deep intention of not doing anything to shake the position or doctrine of the Church of England in any particular way. Touch this Consecration Prayer and you will do that.[106]

Given that the House of Clergy rejected the 'no change' motion with regard to the canon, an unofficial conference was held in the Jerusalem Chamber of Church House on 13 November. As well as the Members-in-Charge of the Measure,[107] the 'Green Book' was represented by Darwell Stone and B.J. Kidd, the 'Grey Book' by C. Hepher and F.C.N. Hicks, the 'Yellow' (Orange) by G.W. Hockley and the C.E. Lambert, and the evangelicals by Wace and Grose Hodge.[108] While the conference was agreed that if possible there should be only one form of the canon in the 'Alternative Book', in the end it reached the conclusion that two forms would have to be allowed.

The following day Dean Norris of York, in opposition to the mind of the conference, moved that there should be only one Canon in the Alternative Book, and that for the purpose of discussion the second form in the 'Yellow Book' be considered.[109] However, there were strong advocates for the Grey canon, and for the restoration of the 1549 'Holy Spirit and word' phrase.[110] Armitage Robinson, in an important speech, referred to the desire in some parts of the Church for an *epiclesis* approximating to the eastern rite. But, he argued, in the eastern texts the purpose of the *epiclesis* is to effect a *change* in the elements; this could not be the purpose of those who see it as 'a calling down of the Holy Spirit "upon ourselves and upon the gifts" *with a view to a profitable Communion*'. He then criticized an invocation upon the gifts. He asked when the Holy Spirit is thought of in the Christian Church as consecrating things rather than persons?[111] He could find no New Testament evidence for it. Rather, he defended the western stress on the eucharistic words.[112] In

105 *House of Clergy Debates Transcript: Prayer Book Revision*, Vol. 2, Autumn, 1923, p. 52.

106 Ibid., p. 36.

107 E.A. Burroughs, A.F. Kirkpatrick, The Archdeacon of Wisbech, S.L. Ollard, R.G. Parsons and Guy Rogers.

108 House of Clergy, *Minutes of Proceedings*, Nov. 13-15, 1923, p. 5. The chairman (Dean of Westminster, H.E. Ryle) and vice-chairman (Dean of York, W.F. Norris) of the House of Clergy were also in attendance.

109 Ibid., p. 6. The desirability of only having one canon is evident; the problem was that members wanted different ones!

110 *House of Clergy Transcript*, pp. 108-116.

111 *Transcript*, p. 119.

112 Ibid., pp. 120-122. Robinson's opposition to an invocation of the Spirit upon the elements was long standing; T.E. Taylor, *J. Armitage Robinson: Eccentric, Scholar, Churchman* (Cambridge, 1991), p. 71.

what was becoming a somewhat polarized debate, Srawley defended the possibility of allowing two forms of canon, the second following the lines of the 'Grey Book', even though his own sympathies were with the western form of consecration.[113] With regard to Christian unity, he pointed out that some Churches in communion with Rome have eastern rites, and that other Anglican provinces have their own variants.[114] However, it was clear that there were acute sensitivities about having more than one form of canon.

In the end, part 1 of Norris's motion was carried by 192 votes to 11. The second part was withdrawn. Consequently, it was suggested that the Jerusalem Chamber conference should meet again.[115] The second meeting of the conference found it impossible to implement the resolution that there should be but one alternative canon. Two canons were drafted, one based on the 'Yellow' (Orange) and 'Green' book and the other on the 'Grey'. The first new canon also omitted the phrase 'and with thy Holy Spirit and word' from its preliminary *epiclesis*:

> Hear us, O merciful Father, we most humbly beseech thee, and vouchsafe to bless and sanctify these thy gifts and creatures of Bread and Wine, that they may be unto us the Body and Blood of thy most dearly beloved Son, Jesus Christ.[116]

The second canon reproduced the *epiclesis* of the 'Grey Book' with the omission of the phrase 'unto the fulfilment of the Kingdom of heaven'.[117] The House re-convened on 15 November. After the chairman explained the course of action adopted by the conference, the first form was introduced by Darwell Stone and Lambert and the second by Parsons and J.V. MacMillan (Archdeacon of Maidstone). The first form was most significant for its use of the 1549 *anamnesis* rather than an oblation of the bread and cup. Stone, commenting on the second canon, stated that it was not acceptable as the only alternative to the *BCP* because 'it depends for its value upon that theory of Consecration which is associated with the Eastern Church'.[118] Lambert compared the invocation in the first form to 'the Grace before the Heavenly Banquet'. It is no longer an *epiclesis* as in the 'Green Book' and 1549 and so is faithful to the western tradition. The phrase 'may be unto us the Body ... ' is capable of a 'receptionist' understanding as well as a view that would identify outward sign and the gift signified. It is thus 'patient of those two historical interpretations both of which since the Reformation have had their representatives within the limits of the Church of England'.[119]

In introducing the second canon, Parsons again returned to the ecumenical question. As well as being a bridge between Rome and Orthodoxy, the Church of England stands between Rome and the Protestant Churches. He argued that the second canon would appeal more to the Churches of the Reformation, and that it stresses the

---

113 *Transcript*, p. 139.
114 Ibid., pp. 140-141.
115 *Minutes*, pp. 6-7.
116 Dean Wace stated his opposition to the proposed 'Green' form, *Minutes*, pp. 8-9.
117 Ibid., pp. 12-14.
118 *Transcript*, p. 246.
119 Ibid., pp. 249-251.

spiritual nature of consecration.[120] MacMillan stated that the 'Grey Book' had much support, and was in line with revision in other Anglican provinces, and he made a plea for alternative canons so that the Church could experiment with them.[121]

Evangelical reactions to the question can be illustrated by Grose-Hodge's speech, originally part of the 'no change' lobby but now willing to accept alternative canons for two reasons: the spirit of willingness at the conference to surrender points for the good of all and because diversity was better than a spirit of suspicion and division. This contrasts with the view of Wace, unable to agree with either canon, the first because it taught 'catholic doctrine'; the second because the compilers had a liberal view of God in their understanding of the God of the Old Testament.[122]

A motion that the two forms of the canon be generally approved was passed by a large majority.[123] Detailed discussion of the two canons was due to take place in the July 1924 sessions of the House of Clergy. [124] At the meeting of the House, canon I was accepted without alteration.[125] In canon II, the Revd W.H. Norman moved to omit the words 'and with thy Holy Spirit' from the *epiclesis* on the basis that they were not based on Scripture. A vigorous debate ensued;[126] the amendment was eventually lost, and the paragraph accepted without alteration.[127] The House of Clergy amendments were duly published in C.A. 158 in March 1925.[128]

The House of Laity

Debates in the House of Laity were of a rather different order. By far the vast majority of members were content with the 1662 service as it stood. The major concerns were over reservation and the Ornaments Rubric and this is reflected in the voting sequence. The House rejected motions for the acceptance of the clergy proposals in C.A. 158, and for an alternative form based on 1549. In the end, the following motion was accepted by a large majority:

> That while this House believes that the great majority of the Laity are satisfied with the present service of Holy Communion, the House will nevertheless agree to the insertion by the Bishops in the Prayer Book of one alternative form containing provision for Vestments and Reservation for the Sick only, if in their opinion this will promote peace and order in the Church.[129]

---

120 Ibid., pp. 254-259.

121 Ibid., pp. 260-262.

122 Ibid., pp. 268-272, 278-282.

123 *Minutes*, pp. 14-15.

124 Concern about alternative canons is illustrated by E.G. Selwyn, 'Further Plea for a Single Revised Liturgy', *Theology*, 9 (1924): 2.

125 *Minutes*, pp. 21-22.

126 *Transcript*, pp. 272-282.

127 *Minutes*, p. 23.

128 *Amendments Made By the House of Clergy in the Revised Prayer Book (Permissive Use) Measure 1923* (London, 1925), pp. 76-79.

129 House of Laity, *Minutes of Proceedings*, 1925, p. 9.

While some anglo-catholic members of the House were concerned to preserve a western view of consecration, the *epiclesis*, let alone its position, was largely a non-issue.

The House of Bishops

The bishops began their own deliberations on eucharistic revision in 1926. This began with a meeting with members of the House of Clergy on 14 January.[130] Srawley outlined the differences between the two canons proposed by the House of Clergy,[131]and a general discussion ensued. During it, Frere, now Bishop of Truro, asked if the committee had considered suggesting a single prayer with two alternative invocations, the first from the 'Green' Book and the second from the 'Grey', only one of which would be used. His suggestion was somewhat brushed aside by Archbishop Davidson on the basis that there would not be a 'unified Canon'.[132]

Discussion on the issue of the canon continued on Friday, 18 June 1926. The bishops had five texts before them: the canon from N.A. 84; the two proposals from the House of Clergy in C.A. 158, a further suggestion from the Members-in-Charge, and a fifth form, the fruits of a conference called by the Bishop of Winchester, Dr F.T. Woods, at Farnham Castle in April.[133] The Farnham conference produced a canon with a double invocation. After the opening paragraph (the beginning of the 1662 prayer of consecration), the first invocation reads:

> Hear us, O merciful Father, we most humbly beseech thee, and vouchsafe to bless and sanctify these thy creatures of bread and wine, that they may be unto us the Body and Blood of thy Son our Saviour Jesus Christ, to the end that all who shall receive the same may be made partakers of his life.

This was followed by the narrative, *anamnesis*, part of the 1662 prayer of oblation, and then the second invocation and doxology:

> And humbly offering ourselves unto Thee, O Father Almighty, we pray thee to accept this oblation of thy Church, through the ministry of our great High Priest, that in the power of thy life-giving Spirit all we who are partakers of this Holy Communion may be fulfilled with thy grace and heavenly benediction. Through Jesus Christ our Lord, by whom ...[134]

---

130 *House of Bishops, Minutes of Proceedings*, 14 January 1926, p. 54. The clergy present were: W.F. Norris, K.F. Gibbs, B.J. Kidd, R.G. Parsons, A.G. Robinson and J.H. Srawley.

131 *House of Bishops Debates Transcripts, Prayer Book Revision Vol. 4*, Spring, 1926, p. 428.

132 *Transcript*, p. 428.

133 Bishop Woods informed the House of the membership of the conference when he introduced the 'Farnham Canon', *House of Bishops Debates Transcripts*, Summer, 1926, p. 363. See also Jasper, *Walter Howard Frere: His Correspondence*, pp. 103-104.

134 According to Srawley, Parsons was the principal drafter of the Farnham canon, Jasper, *Walter Howard Frere: His Correspondence*, p. 104.

The canon proposed by the Members-in-Charge of the Measure (Frere, W.O. Burrows, Guy Warman and T.B. Strong) took up Frere's earlier suggestion of including two invocations, one before the institution and one after, only one of which should be used. The two invocations read:

> I * Hear us, O merciful Father, we most humbly beseech thee, and vouchsafe to bless and sanctify these gifts and creatures of bread and wine, that they may be unto us the Body and Blood of thy most dearly beloved Son Jesus Christ.
>
> II * Hear us, O merciful Father, we most humbly beseech thee, and with thy Holy Spirit bless and sanctify both us and these thy gifts of bread and wine; that we receiving them according to thy Son our Saviour Jesus Christ's holy institution may be worthy partakers of his most blessed Body and Blood.

Dr Strong introduced the various suggestions to the House. Commenting specifically on the canon of the Members-in-Charge, he outlined the dispute regarding the *epiclesis*, citing the views of Armitage Robinson. He drew attention to the provision of alternative clauses for the *epiclesis*, and while expressing his dissatisfaction with this as a solution to the *impasse*, indicated that the Members put it forward 'tentatively, with a view to seeing what the House will say about it'.[135]

Some members of the House were evidently alarmed by this provision of alternative clauses. Frere defended it on the grounds that it represented the only possibility of making a single canon, because of the almost irreconcilable differences about the role of the *epiclesis*:

> It is a division which has divided the East from the West for the last 400 years, at any rate so far as the Roman world in concerned. The Latin world on the whole, down to about the 8th or 9th century, agreed with the Eastern world. It is a question really of Rome against the rest of the world. Our Prayer Book at present falls within the Roman line, that is to say, it gives you nothing else but the words of institution, and no invocation of the Holy Spirit at all.[136]

Frere outlined what he regarded as the illogical position of a preliminary *epiclesis* and how attempts to locate a consecratory *epiclesis* there in the Roman, Alexandrian and Scottish Episcopal (1637) rites all failed. If the Church was to have just one alternative canon, he concluded, the Members-in-Charge suggestion was the only solution.[137]

Dr Woods then introduced the 'Farnham Canon'. On consecration, he tried to steer the debate away from 'moments' of consecration:

> I am anxious for a Canon in my Prayer Book in which it shall be plain that the whole action or the whole prayer is involved in consecration, and in no particular sentence therein.[138]

135 *Transcript*, p. 355.
136 Ibid., p. 357.
137 Ibid., pp. 356-359.
138 Ibid., p. 361.

The drafters were clear that there should be a reference to the Spirit but feared that such were the difficulties that no specific mention should be made of the Spirit in the preliminary invocation. Evangelical members of the conference, unhappy with the phrase 'may be unto us the Body and Blood' without further qualification, were content with the addition of 'to the end that all who shall receive the same may be made partakers of his life'. The reference to the Spirit in the second *epiclesis* was described as 'unexceptionable, understandable, and inspired'.[139]

A general debate in the House of Bishops on the proposed canons took place on Saturday 16 June. There were, of course, differing viewpoints. For example, Bishop W.G. Whittingham of St Edmundsbury and Bishop E.W. Barnes of Birmingham were critical of the *epiclesis*, the former rejecting an invocation of the Spirit on material things, and the latter on 'Modernist' grounds that there can be no 'objective' consecration of the elements. By contrast, William Temple of Manchester, Guy Warman of Truro and Cyril Garbett of Southwark defended the *epiclesis* on the grounds that consecration is essentially spiritual, an action of the Spirit.[140]

In response, Dr Lang, seeking to combine and simplify the two proposed canons, suggested that on the basis of the debate, most bishops favoured some sort of *epiclesis*. The House had to decide about position and he judged that it should probably come after the *anamnesis*, especially in the light of revision in other Provinces. His suggestion was that the preliminary invocation should be omitted in both canons, a joint *anamnesis* should be agreed, followed by an *epiclesis*. An unspecified group with whom he was working had considered a suitable text for the *epiclesis*. They had tried to consider those who looked to the form of words in 1549 and evangelical concerns that the text should state what is the nature and purpose for which the elements are received. In the end two texts were circulated:

> Hear us, O merciful Father, we most humbly beseech Thee, and with Thy holy and life-giving Spirit vouchsafe to bless both us and these Thy gifts of bread and wine; that they may be unto us the Body and Blood of Thy most dearly beloved Son Jesus Christ, to the end that all who receive the same may be sanctified both in body and soul.

or:

> Hear us, O merciful Father, we most humbly beseech Thee, and with Thy Holy Spirit bless and sanctify both us and these Thy gifts of Bread and Wine that they may be unto us the Body and Blood of Thy Son our Saviour Jesus Christ to the end that all who receive the same may be strengthened and refreshed in body and soul.

Both forms contained the phrase 'that they may be unto us the Body and Blood' from 1549. The first form used only the verb 'bless' because 'sanctify' appears further on in the petition. The proposed structure would be: beginning of the 1662 prayer of consecration (slightly adapted), narrative of institution, *anamnesis*, *epiclesis* and prayer of oblation (slightly adapted). There was clearly some confusion about the proposed structure of the canon and in view of this Dr Burrows suggested that when

139 Ibid., pp. 364-367.
140 Ibid., pp. 387-434.

the House reconvened, the canon proposed by the Members-in-Charge should be considered paragraph by paragraph.[141]

The first issue for the bishops in relation to the *epiclesis* when they reconvened on 21st June was the preliminary invocation of the Members-in-Charge canon. Archbishop Lang moved its omission in anticipation of finding an agreed formula for an *epiclesis* after the *anamnesis*, rehearsing his arguments from the previous Saturday.[142] Dr A.F. Winnington-Ingram was sensitive to the fact that the second invocation as it stood still called the elements 'bread and wine' after 'the words of consecration', that is, the institution narrative. The bishops would have to justify this to certain sections of the Church.[143] Dr Woods reiterated his conviction that 'consecration is concerned with the whole prayer and not with particular words', and so he supported the later position. Dr Strong agreed; he disliked a preliminary invocation not only because it is unusual in liturgical tradition but also because he maintained that the real mischief of the Roman system was that 'the whole conception of the Sacrament is in terms of time and material considerations'.[144] He agreed that the whole prayer effects consecration.[145] Dr E.A. Burroughs argued that as the narrative sets out the justification for the eucharistic prayer, it is more appropriate for the petition for consecration to follow it.[146] When put to the vote, Lang's amendment was carried *nem. con.*[147]

The bishops then discussed the narrative of institution and the *anamnesis*. Dr Lang moved the insertion of an *epiclesis* after the *anamnesis*. He drew attention to the two forms he circulated previously, and moved that the first form should be considered as a basis.[148] The Bishop of Gloucester, Dr A.C. Headlam, in seconding the proposal, commented that the major theological reason for such a form of invocation in this place was that the strong statements 'This is my Body which is given for you', 'This is my Blood of the new Testament', required explanation of their purpose lest they are interpreted in an extreme sense and so be taken to justify extra-liturgical use. The role of the *epiclesis* was to limit the meaning of the phrases, and he cited part of the *epiclesis* from the Liturgy of St John Chrysostom as an example.[149] Dr Warman agreed but criticized the phrase 'may be unto us' on the basis that it did not limit the meaning sufficiently. Various amendments were suggested to the text and by now the House was getting lost in a sea of them; the essential issue was whether to use Lang's text or the Garbett/Members-in-Charge text as a basis. Lang was concerned

141 Ibid., p. 459.

142 Ibid., pp. 466-468.

143 Ibid., p. 463.

144 T.B. Strong, in *Eucharistic Doctrine* (London, 1924), wished, on the basis of the Incarnation, to reject any notion that the 'spiritual' and the 'material' should be utterly separated, p. 16, fn. 1.

145 *Transcript*, pp. 468-469.

146 Ibid., pp. 469-470.

147 Ibid., p. 470; *House of Bishops, Minutes of Proceedings 1921-1927*, Monday 21 June, 1926, p. 34.

148 *Transcript*, pp. 480-482; *Minutes*, p. 35.

149 *Transcript*, pp. 483-484. Headlam's views on the canon had changed over time; see Ronald Jasper, *Arthur Cayley Headlam* (London, 1960), pp. 181-184.

that if his text was not the basis, the words 'may be unto us' would be lost. They had appeared in the first canon accepted by the House of Clergy, and while he recognized that some evangelicals had expressed concern about the phrase, the real difficulty lay with the more catholic clergy and he was fearful that it would be much more difficult to secure their loyalty if this phrase were omitted.[150] Frere supported him because his formula also included 'a definition of the purpose of Consecration', the very concern which Burroughs had raised; Frere argued that the words of institution required further definition to 'diminish the opportunity of misunderstanding'. He also suggested that the word 'we' should be inserted after 'all' so that it is clear that the petition refers to one class of people.[151] After further discussion, Lang's form was carried and the House adjourned.[152]

On resumption, the Bishop of Bristol, Dr G. Nickson, moved an amended version of the Lang formula:

> Hear us, O merciful Father, we most humbly beseech thee, and with thy Holy and Life-giving Spirit bless and sanctify both us and these thy gifts of bread and wine, that they may be unto us the Body and Blood of thy Son Jesus Christ to the intent that receiving the same we may be strengthened and refreshed both in body and soul.[153]

In discussion, he acknowledged that the omission of 'vouchsafe to' before 'bless and sanctify' was not deliberate and so it was restored. His proposal restored the couplet 'bless and sanctify' and avoided repetition of 'sanctify' by changing the final clause to 'strengthened and refreshed'. The substitution of 'strengthened and refreshed' was agreed *nem. con.* Bishop Woods moved that the phrase 'thy Son our Saviour Jesus Christ' from the Farnham canon (but deriving from the American rite) should replace both Lang's and Nickson's suggestions. This was carried *nem. con.*[154] The bishops agreed to retain 'receiving the same' rather than 'receiving them' as suggested by Dr Burrows. Dr Barnes clarified the point that a comma should come after 'our Saviour Jesus Christ'. The final form was:

> Hear us, O merciful Father, we most humbly beseech thee, and with thy Holy and Life-giving Spirit vouchsafe to bless and sanctify these thy gifts of bread and wine, that they may be unto us the Body and Blood of thy Son our Saviour Jesus Christ, to the intent that receiving the same we may be strengthened and refreshed both in body and soul.[155]

The bishops also completed work on the other sections of the canon so that the new canon was substituted for the one proposed in N.A. 84. The two forms proposed by the House of Clergy were not moved.[156] The House also considered the form of supplementary consecration at its June meeting. Dr Warman introduced a draft proposal on behalf of the Members-in-Charge to include both the words of institution

---

150 *Transcript*, pp. 497-499.
151 Ibid., pp. 501-502.
152 Ibid., p. 505; *Minutes*, p. 35.
153 *Transcript*, p. 506.
154 Ibid., p. 510; *Minutes*, p. 36.
155 *Minutes*, pp. 35-36.
156 *Ibid.*, pp. 36-37.

and the *epiclesis* from the new canon for supplementary consecration in either kind or both kinds. This was agreed.[157]

The Prayer Books of 1927 and 1928

The bishops met again in January 1927. One issue regarding the *epiclesis* was outstanding. Dr Lang argued for the substitution of 'to the end that' for 'to the intent that' on the basis that it would be irreverent to suggest that God had an intention in mind. Frere produced a catena of quotation from the Prayer Book to illustrate his conviction that 'to the end' indicates divine action and 'to the intent' human action. The amendment 'to the end that' was carried by 15 votes to 9.[158] The bishops completed their work on the entire programme of revision and their draft book was issued to the Convocations on 7 February 1927.[159]

That the proposals for the canon would not please anglo-catholics was self-evident. Such was the hostility of the reaction that Bishop Woods called an unofficial conference of bishops and representatives of the anglo-catholic party on 18 February to discuss the proposed canon and other contentious issues. Although he could not attend the conference, Frere continued to press that the only way out of the *impasse* was to have alternative clauses for the invocation.[160] At the conference, however, Frere's suggestion was rejected. In Woods's report, he simply notes that the alleged departure from western tradition was a cause of 'regret' to some. In a letter to Frere, his judgement was that on the whole the conference 'did not feel the difficulty about the Epiclesis and the alleged departure from Western tradition as keenly as you do'.[161]

The Lower Houses met to consider the proposals in February 1927. The fact that the *epiclesis* in the proposed prayer of consecration was controversial can be illustrated by the six proposed amendments in the Lower House of the Convocation of Canterbury.[162] Although all were lost or withdrawn, nevertheless they illustrated that the proposed text was hardly a focus of unity. The issues concerned the position of the *epiclesis* and the reference to the Spirit. For example, Darwell Stone, supported by Armitage Robinson, requested a preliminary invocation only, without reference to the Spirit. This was lost by 83 votes to 70, a majority of only 13. Srawley unsuccessfully tabled a motion for alternative clauses. The House did, however, agree to a resolution proposed by E.G. Selwyn to request a form nearer

157 *Transcript*, pp. 672-674; *Minutes*, p. 51. The rubric was subsequently amended at the October 1926 meeting of the House of Bishops.

158 *House of Bishops Debates Transcripts, Prayer Book Revision Vol. 8*, Spring, 1927, pp. 318-322.

159 *Book Proposed to be Annexed to the Prayer Book Measure 192-* (London, Oxford and Cambridge, 1927).

160 See his letter to J.H. Srawley on 15 February 1927 in Jasper, *Walter Howard Frere: His Correspondence*, p. 115.

161 Jasper, *Walter Howard Frere: His Correspondence*, pp. 119-121.

162 There were no proposals on the *epiclesis* from the Lower House of York.

to that of the Episcopal Church of Scotland.[163] To this resolution was added a memorandum in which Selwyn made two criticisms of the proposed text. While he agreed with Armitage Robinson that an *epiclesis* was not necessary, nevertheless, he was concerned that the proposed text needed amendment. His first criticism was that in the Phrase 'with thy holy and life-giving Spirit', 'with' in this context is an ablative of the instrument, 'properly applicable to a thing, but not to a person'. This would suggest that the Spirit 'is an effluence or power of the Godhead, rather than God Himself in personal activity'. He suggested the substitution of 'by' or 'through' or 'by the grace of'. His second objection was to the phrase 'bless and sanctify both us and these thy gifts of Bread and Wine, that they may be to us ... '. He wished to distinguish between the Holy Spirit's consecration of 'persons' and 'things'. He argued that the eastern liturgies made clear the distinction by adding further verbal clauses relating to the consecration of the elements (bless, sanctify, change, etc.) only after the petition that the Spirit may come upon the worshippers and gifts together, as in the Scottish Office though 'at the expense of a certain cumbrousness'. The bishops' text was too compressed.[164]

The Lower House of Canterbury effectively failed to reach a conclusion on the issue. While they presented no recommendation to the bishops on the *epiclesis*, they did register widespread unease. This prompted the bishops to appoint a small doctrinal committee from within their ranks.

The House of Bishops met on 4 March. The Archbishop of Canterbury outlined three possible responses to the dispute about the *epiclesis*: to leave things as they are; to change the position; to change the wording. Bishop Headlam, on behalf of the doctrinal committee, reported on the issues raised by the 'Selwyn Memorandum'. Various suggestions for amendment were made in response,[165] but the doctrinal committee's recommendation that the wording of the *epiclesis* should be retained with the small grammatical change of 'we, receiving the same ... ' was carried *nem. con.*[166]

With regard to the position of the *epiclesis*, Frere drew attention to the amendments presented to the Lower House of Canterbury. He reminded the House of the small majority which defeated Darwell Stone's request for a preliminary invocation (83–70). But he was more concerned with Srawley's suggestion of alternative clauses either before or after the narrative of institution. There had been no vote on this in the Lower House but the 'noes' clearly won. Frere commended Srawley's suggestion as 'the thing which is most likely at the present moment to bring peace and reconciliation'. He pointed out that the suggestion had been made at an early stage by the Members-in-Charge but had been rejected then because all efforts were directed to a single canon. History had shown, as had a vote of 83–70, that a canon without such an alternative would not bring peace. He therefore moved as an amendment: 'That an alternative clause be provided allowing some form of

163 *Chronicle of Convocation*, 1927, p. 68.

164 Ibid., pp. 68-69. See also E.G. Selwyn, 'Prayer Book Revision', *Theology*, 14 (1927): 165-166.

165 *Transcript*, pp. 222-231.

166 *Minutes*, p. 19; *Transcript*, p. 232.

Invocation to be said before, instead of after, the recital of the Institution.'[167] Frere also commented that there were two legitimate views of consecration; when they are put into opposition, misfortune is always the result. The primitive Church for a while did hold both together and the same is true in Scotland and South Africa where 1662 and alternative forms stand side by side. However, there was clear opposition to Frere's suggestion, and some bishops were clearly having difficulty in following the line of argument, and after speeches by Headlam, Temple and Lang in favour of the bishops's canon, Frere's motion was put and lost by 31 votes to 3.[168]

The bishops presented the final form of the Book to the Convocations on 29 March; although other amendments had been accepted, the canon was unchanged. The Convocations voted decisively in favour of the proposed Book.[169] In the light of this, E.G. Selwyn took a conciliatory line in the May edition of *Theology*.[170] While reiterating his desire for a 'Western canon' and citing the views of Atchley, Armitage Robinson, Brightman and Tyrer in previous editions of the journal in favour of such a course,[171] he made a case for the catholicity of the 1927 prayer. For example, he argued that the *epiclesis* was 'unequivocal in its witness to the objective aspect of Consecration, which carries with it the truth of the Real Presence'.[172] While he regarded the concept of consecration in the prayer to be debatable, nevertheless, in his view the *epiclesis* was not eastern in type; the invocatory formula was 'simply an *allusion* to the Holy Spirit as co-operating with the Father in the whole action of consecration and communion',[173] and the fact that the *anamnesis* describes the gifts as 'holy' before the invocation suggests that the elements are already in some sense consecrated. Further support for the Book came in a series of published lectures given at King's College, London. For example, Evelyn Underhill argued:

> For surely the Epiklesis simply affirms the principle that the Spirit of God is at all times and under all dispensations, whether in union with Our Lord's Incarnate Life or not, still the only source of supernatural life and transfiguration and that the Spirit can and does make matter itself the direct vehicle of grace.[174]

---

167 *Minutes*, p. 19.

168 *Minutes*, p. 19; *Transcript*, pp. 237-256.

169 The voting was: Canterbury, Upper House 21–4, Lower House 168–22; York, Upper House unanimous, Lower House 68–10, *Acts of the Convocations of Canterbury and York* (London, 1948), p. 62.

170 E.G. Selwyn, 'The New Prayer of Consecration', *Theology*, 14 (1927): 242-246.

171 Although in Atchley's case it was the fact that he argued that the *logos-epiclesis* was an earlier form than the Spirit-*epiclesis* that is cited by Selwyn. Atchley did not comment on the Prayer Book revision issue, but his article in general could easily be taken to support the 1927 canon.

172 Selwyn, 'The New Prayer of Consecration', p. 244.

173 Ibid., p. 244. He argued this on the basis of the words '*with* Thy holy Spirit', rather than 'through' or 'by', ibid., fn.

174 E. Underhill, 'The Essentials of a Prayer Book,' in H. Maurice Relton (ed.), *The New Prayer Book* (London, 1927), p. 59.

The Proposed Book was presented to the National Assembly of the Church of England for final approval in July 1927.[175] As the National Assembly gathered, the July edition of *The Church Quarterly Review* carried articles by Headlam defending the new book and Brightman attacking it.[176]

Brightman's article was in fact a reply to a charge delivered by Headlam to the clergy and churchwardens of the Diocese of Gloucester in April.[177] In his charge, Headlam had sought to defend the notion of a 'spiritual' presence of Christ in the sacrament while condemning all 'materialistic' interpretations, and he criticized the Roman canon and 1662 for suggesting a mechanical view that consecration is effected by formula. The *epiclesis* in the new canon emphasized the fact that holy communion is essentially a spiritual action, 'the whole action is in the realm of the Spirit, and there is nothing material or mechanical'.[178]

In his article, Headlam sought to defend the structure of the canon by making reference to the 'the primitive and most Catholic form' of the eucharistic prayer (he did not cite any texts or authorities), American and Scottish Anglican rites, the liturgy of Jeremy Taylor, the Westminster *Directory* and the 1884 *Euchologion* of the Church Service Society. He stressed that the new rite 'does not give the opportunity of limiting the consecration to any particular portion of the service' but that 'in and through these Gifts, sanctified by His Holy Spirit for this purpose, Christ Himself gives us the spiritual food of His Body and Blood'.[179]

Brightman, by contrast, regarded the new canon as a 'tardy' attempt to restore what was lost in 1552 and its structure as 'a gratuitous departure from our tradition, containing as it does an Invocation of the Holy Ghost following after "the recital of the Institution"'.[180] For him, fidelity to western tradition was all important. In response to Headlam, Brightman sought to demonstrate that the role of the Spirit as the 'agent' of consecration was as important in the west as in the east. The rite of 1549 made explicit in its invocation what was implicit in the Roman rite, and he argued that 'both the position and the matter of the Invocation of 1549 are thoroughly in accordance with Western tradition'.[181] As far as the wording of the text is concerned, he was critical of the fact that the petition asks that gifts previously described as holy in the *anamnesis* should now be sanctified and blessed.[182]

---

175 *National Assembly of the Church of England: Book Referred to in the Prayer Book Measure*.

176 A.C. Headlam, 'A Defence of the New Prayer Book'; F.E. Brightman, 'The New Prayer Book Examined', *The Church Quarterly Review*, 104 (1927): 199-218, 219-252.

177 It was subsequently published as *The New Prayer Book* (London, 1927).

178 Ibid., p. 71.

179 Headlam, 'A Defence of the New Prayer Book', p. 214.

180 Brightman, 'The New Prayer Book Examined', p. 236.

181 Ibid., p. 241. This was a revision of his position in *The English Rite*. Now Brightman's conclusion is: 'The Invocation of 1549 therefore is Western in its whole substance, and it might quite well have been put together without any reference to the East. And all the East in fact contributed was the words "to bless and sanctify these gifts," derived from the Invocation of S. Basil.' Ibid.

182 Ibid., pp. 244-245. For correspondence between Brightman and Headlam, see Jasper, *Arthur Cayley Headlam*, pp. 186-187. It reveals that while Brightman had been part

The National Assembly debated the book on 5, 6 July. Many of the old arguments were rehearsed,[183] but despite such concerns, the new Book was passed decisively and so passed to Parliament.[184] It became then universally known as 'the Deposited Book' on the grounds that it was deposited with the Clerk of the Parliament rather than annexed to the Prayer Book Measure.

Opposition to the Deposited Book and to its eucharistic contents in particular continued unabated. For example, anglo-catholic concerns are well summarized by Sparrow Simpson, who made a plea for the authorisation of the 1549 canon as it was a synthesis of the historic east–west divide, without compromising the western stress on the words of Christ as the means of consecration.[185] From the evangelical wing of the Church, the most persistent voice against the book was Bishop Knox. In a succession of pamphlets Knox railed against reservation, the *anamnesis* as implying an oblation of the bread and wine, and the *epiclesis* as implying an objective change in the elements.[186] Another highly publicized voice in opposition was that of Dr Barnes, the Bishop of Birmingham. On 'modernist' premises, he objected to the *epiclesis* on the grounds that it suggested that 'a particular form of words effects a miraculous change in the bread and wine',[187] while his conviction that 'you cannot endow dead matter with spiritual qualities'[188] drew a strong response from William Temple: 'Our experience quite apart from religion is already so rich in instances of the interpenetration of matter by spirit that I cannot see the smallest objection to believing that the Holy Spirit will use matter as part of His plan for the most sacred purposes of our spiritual life.'[189]

The Deposited Book came to the House of Lords on Monday, 12 December, and the debate lasted for three days. Archbishop Davidson set the tone for the debate by stating that the floor of the House was not the right place to enter into 'such profound doctrines as the presence of the Lord'.[190] The *epiclesis* did not figure prominently in the debate. However, the case for the Book was well made and it was passed by 241 votes to 88.[191] The Book came to the Commons on 15 December. Here the tone of the debate was far more hostile. The alternative order for holy communion and reservation in particular were roundly criticized, and the word 'transubstantiation'

---

of an Advisory Committee of Liturgical Experts appointed to advise on revision, its role was marginal.

183 Jasper, *Walter Howard Frere: His Correspondence*, p. 124.

184 The voting was House of Bishops, 34–4; House of Clergy, 253–37; House of Laity 230–92, Jasper, *Walter Howard Frere: His Correspondence*, p. 129.

185 W.J. Sparrow Simpson, 'The Eucharistic Canon: Why the Invocation Should Come First' in Darwell Stone (ed.), *The Deposited Prayer Book* (London, 1927).

186 His fullest treatment is in E.A. Knox, *The Unscriptural Character of the Alternative Consecration Prayer* (London, 1927).

187 John Barnes, *Ahead of His Time: Bishop Barnes of Birmingham* (London, 1979), p. 188.

188 For the background to this phrase see F.A. Iremonger, *William Temple: Archbishop of Canterbury* (London, 1948), pp. 347-348.

189 William Temple, *A Plea for the New Prayer Book* (London, 1927), pp. 23-24.

190 *The Parliamentary Debates (Official Report)* 69/4, House of Lords, 1927, p. 783.

191 Ibid., p. 967.

figured prominently in the debate. The canon was rarely referred to; there was rather the implication that it taught transubstantiation and that reservation meant adoration. The Commons defeated the Book by 238 votes to 205.[192]

In the light of the defeat, the bishops undertook certain proposed changes in January 1928 (set out in Report C.A. 252), but there were no new proposals for the canon. In response, the Houses of Clergy and Laity meeting in February 1928, passed the following resolution in relation to the canon: '25. "That the House of Clergy respectfully requests the House of Bishops to consider the possibility of changing the form of Invocation in the Prayer of Consecration."'[193]

The House of Bishops met on 7 March 1928. The mood of the House, however, was that there was insufficient time to revisit the canon, and so no action was taken on the resolution.[194] This provoked Frere to withdraw his support for the new Book. He was troubled by a number of issues, and the canon figured prominently among them:

> The Roman type of liturgy has prevailed in the English Church from St. Augustine's time till now; and I think it unfair that no form of Canon should be provided for those who wish to keep it, or who for other reasons dislike an Epiclesis. Peace and contented worship can hardly be secured while the desire of so large a class of worshippers is ignored or refused.[195]

The revised Book was presented to the Convocations on 28 and 29 March 1928, and to the Church Assembly on 26 and 27 April. The dominant issue was reservation and again the Book received significant endorsement.[196] Before the Commons debate, and in the light of the Protestant opposition in the Commons in 1927, Archbishop Davidson published a booklet *The Prayer Book: Our Hope and Meaning*. He argued that the alternative communion did not betray Reformation principles, that it looked 'not towards but away from the doctrine of Transubstantiation',[197] and that the *epiclesis* contained more theological safeguards than 1549.[198] However, Sir William Joynson-Hicks, the Home Secretary, set out Protestant objections in his book *The Prayer Book Crisis*, citing the *epiclesis* as an expression of a belief in the 'Presence of Christ in the consecrated Bread and Wine'.[199]

The House of Commons debate took place over 13, 14 June. This time there was more explicit reference to the *epiclesis*; for example, the Duchess of Athol

192 *Parliamentary Debates (Official Report)*, 211/10, House of Commons, 1927, p. 2652.

193 *Report C.A. 257, Amendments made and Resolutions passed by the Houses of Clergy and Laity*, p. 10.

194 *Minutes*, p. 18.

195 Jasper, *Walter Howard Frere: His Correspondence*, p. 150.

196 Convocations: Canterbury, Upper House, 20–6; Lower House, 126–48; York, Upper House, unanimous; Lower House, 50–19. Church Assembly: Bishops 32–2, Clergy 183–59, Laity 181–92, *Report of Proceedings*, p. 110.

197 *The Prayer Book: Our Hope and Meaning by the Archbishop of Canterbury* (London, n.d.), p. 27.

198 Ibid., pp. 43-44.

199 Sir William Joynson-Hicks, *The Prayer Book Crisis* (London, 1928), p. 176.

(Church of Scotland) pointed out that the changes in the communion office brought the Church of England into line with the Presbyterian communion and so lead the Church further from Rome.[200] However, the objections from the previous December were still as strong and, although the speeches made in favour of the Book were vastly superior at the second debate, it was defeated by 266 votes to 220.[201]

After 1928: The *Epiclesis* Debate Continues

The decade between 1928 and the outbreak of the Second World War saw a continuing debate concerning the nature of the *epiclesis*, not least in the pages of *Theology*.[202] The most significant contributions were from Gabriel Hebert, Gregory Dix, Cuthbert Atchley and Walter Howard Frere.

Gabriel Hebert

For Hebert, the pattern of redemption was the starting point; first, Christ gave himself vicariously for humanity; second, this is then actualized in the life of the Church through the Spirit.[203] The eucharist, as 'the liturgical representation of God's redeeming work' must include both aspects, namely the pleading of 'the one sacrifice of Christ, and the continual offering-up of the Church' through the Spirit. This balance, he argues, is clearly seen in Hippolytus; the *anamnesis* is a presenting and pleading of the sacrifice of Christ, but the 'oblation' in the *epiclesis* cannot be the oblation of the bread and wine, which would be expressed in the plural, but of the Church herself. So the Spirit is invoked upon the Church; the *epiclesis* does not consecrate the elements. However, in the east a development took place, rightly emphasizing the role of the Spirit in consecration but at the expense of insufficiently expressing the role of the Son. The western tradition, seen especially in the Roman canon, retained the emphasis: 'that Christ is the High Priest and Consecrator in every Eucharist, pleading His own sacrifice and offering up the Church with Himself'. Hebert therefore argues that there ought to be a form of canon which expresses the role of the Son and the Spirit, but 'which shall preserve the consecratory character of the Dominical Words'. His solution therefore is a split *epiclesis*, with the suggested texts:

> Hear us, O merciful Father, we most humbly beseech thee, and with thy Holy Spirit vouchsafe to bless and sanctify these thy creatures of bread and wine according to our Saviour Jesus Christ's holy institution, who in the same night ...

---

200 *Parliamentary Debates (Official Report)*, 218/6, 1928, p. 1217.

201 Ibid., p. 1320.

202 Athelstan Riley, 'The Liturgy of 1928', *Theology*, 19 (1929): 44-46; H.T. Knight, 'Eucharistic Doctrine', *Theology*, 21 (1930): 202-205; K.D. Mackenzie, 'The Way Out from Liturgical Chaos', *Theology*, 26 (1933): 88-93; W.K. Lowther Clarke, 'The Epiclesis in the 1549 and 1928 Rites', *Theology*, 26 (1933): 93-97. A major study by an Australian, John Blomfield, was published posthumously in 1930, *The Eucharistic Canon* (London and New York, 1930). A detailed study of Patristic sources led him to commend an eastern consecratory *epiclesis*; sadly, it appeared too late to influence the Prayer Book debate.

203 A.G. Hebert, 'The Meaning of the Epiclesis', *Theology*, 27 (1933): 198-210.

and (following the narrative and *anamnesis*):

> And we beseech thee to pour thy Holy and life-giving Spirit on us and on thy whole church, that all we who are partakers of this holy communion may be fulfilled with thy grace and heavenly benediction, and be made one body with thy Son our Saviour Jesus Christ, that he may dwell in us and we in him: that so our sacrifice of praise and thanksgiving may be acceptable unto thee, and that by the merits and death of thy Son ...[204]

For Hebert, this provides a much wider understanding of the role of the *epiclesis* than simply the consecration of the elements.

Gregory Dix

Dix took up Hebert's assertion that the *epiclesis* is not primarily regarded as effecting consecration.[205] Describing himself as an 'unrepentant Western', he undertook a defence of the western view of consecration. Dix rejected Hebert's argument that the singular 'oblation' in the *epiclesis* of *Apostolic Tradition* ruled out a reference to the bread and wine. For Dix, the invocation in Hippolytus does refer to the elements, though it is not strictly consecratory. He then sets out the substance of the argument, later expounded in full in his book *The Treatise on the Apostolic Tradition of St. Hippolytus of Rome*, that the *epiclesis* attested by the Latin Verona text was a later interpolation, and that the text of *Testamentum Domini*, without the *epiclesis*, is more likely to reflect the original Greek text. What was important, Dix argued, was the utterly Christological emphasis in Hippolytus, and that 'the primitive universal tradition of Christendom viewed the Eucharist as an operation of the Logos, often designated Holy "Spirit"'.[206] In Syria, references in the *Didascalia*, and the Gnostic *Acts of Judas Thomas* show signs of what would eventually give rise to a consecratory *epiclesis* of the Spirit, but Cyril of Jerusalem in AD 348 is the first clear testimony. Dix cites a *catena* of Patristic authorities to demonstrate the complementarity of 'Word' and 'Spirit', while contending that in the references to consecration in Irenaeus, Tertullian, Cyprian and Hippolytus, 'the whole emphasis is placed on the unseen action of the heavenly High Priest, the Logos, the Second Person of the Trinity'.[207] Thus, the theological heart of the primitive eucharist is the action of Christ in offering himself through the eucharistic memorial. The emphasis is not so much on a real presence of Christ in the elements but a making present of the 'real sacrifice' in which the Church participates through faith. After 381, however, attributes previously ascribed to the Logos are transferred to the Spirit and it is then that references to the Spirit as consecrator multiply. Dix regards the unfortunate consequence of this eastern development as 'casting doubt upon the validity' of all

---

204 Ibid., pp. 209-210. He was supported by Hugh Cecil, *The Communion Service as it Might be* (London, 1935), pp. 46-47.

205 Gregory Dix, 'The Origins of the Epiclesis', *Theology*, 27 (1934): 125-137; 28 (1934): 187-202.

206 Ibid., p. 202.

207 Ibid., pp. 189-193.

eucharists before about A.D. 330'.[208] Dix closed his article by touching on Prayer Book revision:

> I would plead for a truce to the persistent suggestions that the rite of 1662 ... needs supplementing with an epiclesis, at least until the matter has been more adequately surveyed. It may well turn out to be not the least of the blessings of the events of 1927-28 that *Ecclesia Anglicana* was prevented from committing herself by a piece of false archaeology to a practice as un-Scriptural and unprimitive as it is historically un-English.[209]

Cuthbert Atchley

Responding to Dix in *Theology*,[210] Atchley defended the integrity of the text of *Apostolic Tradition*, and took issue with Dix's understanding of the development of theories of consecration. However, in 1935 Atchley published his definitive work *On the Epiclesis of the Eucharistic Liturgy and in the Consecration of the Font*. Here, he rejects the theory of Connolly and Robinson that the *epiclesis* is essentially the invocation of the power associated with a divine name, in favour of the more general meaning from biblical and classical sources 'to call upon', 'recite over', 'pray'.[211] Atchley's theory is that the eucharistic consecration is effected essentially by prayer and that by the third century there is clear evidence of an invocation of the Spirit on the elements. In the fourth century, the language of 'change' is employed in relation to the effect of the invocation, and it is only in the fifth century that the Spirit is invoked upon the communicants.[212] For example, in his discussion of the *epiclesis* in *Apostolic Tradition* (which he believes is authentic) he interprets the reference to the oblation as meaning the eucharistic elements. He rejects as 'mistaken and untheological' any suggestion that a distinction ought to be made between the developed eastern *epiclesis* and the kind found in Hippolytus; the eastern forms are simply more explicit.[213] He regards the *anaphora* of *Apostolic Tradition* as being of the 'normal type', the Roman canon alone being the great exception. He argues that the *epiclesis* in *Apostolic Tradition*, a reference to the Spirit in a letter from Pope Gelasius to Elpidius at the end of the fifth century, and the form of the consecration of the chrism on Maundy Thursday and of the font on Easter Eve, constitute evidence that the Roman canon originally included an *epiclesis* of the Spirit which, for reasons unknown, was eliminated and replaced by *Supplices te rogamus* before the end of the sixth century.[214] Atchley also includes a survey of sixteenth- and seventeenth-century English divines, both Laudian and Puritan, citing references to consecration being effected by invocation.

208 Ibid., p. 202.

209 Ibid.

210 Cuthbert Atchley, 'The Epiclesis: A Criticism', *Theology*, 29 (July, 1934): 28-35. Dix responded to this article in 'The Epiclesis: Some Considerations', *Theology*, 29 (1934): 287-294.

211 Atchley, *On the Epiclesis of the Eucharistic Liturgy*, pp. 3-13.

212 Ibid., pp. 199-200.

213 Ibid.

214 Ibid., pp. 176-180.

Atchley's methodology, however, is curious in that he simply presents the 'evidence' as he understood it but with the minimum of argument or discussion. For example, his *catena* of references by English divines is unrelated to current Anglican disputes about consecration and his only reference to Prayer Book revision comes in a footnote in his final chapter: 'it is greatly to be regretted that the last revision was rejected, in complete ignorance of the facts and the doctrine involved'.[215] This weakness was exploited in a critical review by E.C. Ratcliff.[216] Describing Atchley's book as 'misleading and inadequate', Ratcliff criticizes him for not researching the meaning of 'Spirit', 'Spirit of God', 'Holy Spirit' and 'the Holy Spirit' on the basis that he has interpreted all such references 'in terms of a fully developed Pneumatology'.[217] Ratcliff concluded: 'For the Epiclesis as a prayer for the change of the eucharistic elements into Christ's Body and Blood by the operation of the Holy Spirit there is no evidence earlier than the writings of Cyril of Jerusalem.'[218]

Walter Howard Frere

Frere's final contribution to eucharistic liturgical scholarship was made in 1938 with publication of the book *The Anaphora or Great Eucharistic Prayer*.[219] Something of Frere's seasoned reaction to the 1927-28 debacle is evidenced in his reference in the preface to the anglo-catholic opposition to the canon:

> ... a determined obscurantist and retrograde movement which poses noisily as catholic, but is really anarchist in method though medieval in outlook; for it aims at re-establishing, often in defiance of law, a position which is historically untenable, and a eucharistic theology which was not truly that of SS. Chrysostom, Ambrose, and Austin, but only that of their decadent successors.[220]

Frere argues his conviction that the primitive *anaphora* at an early date evolved the basic structure of (1) the recital of the accumulated mercies of God in creation and redemption; (2) an act of sacrifice with prayer for the acceptance of it; and (3) an act of communion, completing the sacrifice and sealing the union between the worshipper and God. This provides a basic ground-plan for any renewal of the Church's eucharistic thanksgiving today, namely, a preface, *anamnesis* of Christ's saving work with oblation and 'the commemoration of the Holy Spirit in some form', and finally the preparation for the act of communion by a series of petitions, concluded by the Lord's Prayer. Frere argued that there is a logical Trinitarian sequence inherent in the primitive pattern, and while he makes allowances for a degree of confusion between the role of the Spirit and the Word in the *ante*-Nicene period, clarification of the divinity of the Spirit and reflection on the Spirit's role as

215 Ibid., p. 200.

216 E.C. Ratcliff, Book Review of Atchley, *On the Epiclesis of the Eucharistic Liturgy*, *Theology*, 31 (1935): 173-178.

217 Ibid., p. 176.

218 Ibid., p. 178.

219 W.H. Frere, *The Anaphora or Great Eucharistic Prayer* (London, 1938).

220 Ibid., p. vi.

sanctifier naturally paved the way for a more developed realization and expression of the Spirit's work. Indeed, as Frere understands consecration as the divine response to and acceptance of the 'gift being offered by man to God', an *epiclesis* of the Spirit for the transformation of the elements following the *anamnesis*-oblation is 'the right thing' in 'the right place'.

In the light of this, Frere sought to account for the lack of references to a Spirit *epiclesis* in the Western rites, setting out the traditional arguments to explain the absence of a Spirit-*epiclesis* in the Roman canon and suggesting that what he calls a 'minimizing policy' probably under Roman influence led to a toning down of epicletic references in the Gallican tradition. He judged that it was unquestionably the fact that the Roman Church adopted the view that consecration was effected by the words of institution which led to the excising of an epicletic reference, and this view was reinforced by the Scholastic tradition. Cranmer's revision of the canon in 1552 had the unfortunate consequence of fastening upon the English Church 'an extreme and exaggerated acceptance of the Scholastic view in its most exclusive form'. In Frere's judgement, the canon of 1927-28 restored the form if not the wording of primitive catholic custom.[221]

Conclusion

1939 and the outbreak of the Second World War effectively brought the discussion on the *epiclesis* to a halt. The vigorous debate over the 1927-28 canon had reached stale-mate and there were no signs of any imminent attempts to re-open the question of liturgical revision. The growing strength of the anglo-catholic party, with the influence of Dix and Hebert, reinforced the western identity of this vibrant section of the Church. The publication in 1941 of G.W.O. Addleshaw's influential book *The High Church Tradition* represented a defence of the 1662 prayer of consecration over against that proposed in 1927-28. That concerns about the *epiclesis* were far from the minds of evangelicals, even of the liberal variety, is clear from the symposium edited by A.J. Macdonald, *The Evangelical Doctrine of Holy Communion*, in 1933; although questions of the nature of the eucharistic presence are discussed, there is no extended discussion of the role of the Spirit in relation to consecration. Moreover, attention was turning to the Jewish origins of Christian worship. Frank Gavin, in his study *The Jewish Antecedents of the Christian Sacraments* published in 1928, followed Armitage Robinson and Oesterley in arguing that the primitive form of consecration is found not in the invocation of the Spirit, but through the power of the holy Name recited in thanksgiving.[222] Similarly, in 1939, Felix L. Cirlot's book *The Early Eucharist* relates the origins of the eucharistic prayer to Jewish blessings over food, where *God* was blessed for food, rather than asking God to bless food.

221 Unsurprisingly, Frere's book was criticized both by A.G. Hebert, 'Anaphora and Epiclesis', *Theology*, 37 (1938): 89-94, and Gregory Dix, 'Primitive Consecration Prayers', *Theology*, 37 (1938): 261-283, and the debate was evaluated by E.G.P. Wyatt, 'Dr Frere and his Critics', *The Church Quarterly Review*, 128 (1939): 40-48.

222 Frank Gavin, *The Jewish Antecedents of the Christian Sacraments* (London, 1928).

His purpose was to demonstate that the developed *epiclesis*, as understood in later Orthodox teaching, was neither primitively nor universally the essential consecration of the eucharist.[223] In his stress on the role of thanksgiving, and his rejection of an early 'consecratory' *epiclesis*, his book in many ways is the harbinger of Dix's *The Shape of the Liturgy*.

The final word on the 1927-28 *epiclesis* in this period came from Lowther Clarke in *The Prayer Book of 1928 Reconsidered* published in 1943. In the preface, E.G. Selwyn characteristically called for the authorization of the canon of 1549. For Lowther Clarke, it was the turning around of centuries of tradition concerning the means of consecration that proved to be decisive.[224] He argues that while in English, the 1927 *epiclesis* could be interpreted as placing the emphasis on reception – 'that they may *so* be unto us ... that we ...', Frere's Latin translation of the canon,[225] including the phrase *ut nobis corpus et sanguis fiant*, drawn from the Roman rite, was the proof that the bishops regarded the *epiclesis* as consecratory. As a way out of the *impasse*, Lowther Clarke suggested that either a canon such as the first of the alternatives suggested by the House of Clergy in 1923 with a preliminary *epiclesis* should be adopted, or the *epiclesis* should be toned down to make it specifically a petition for fruitful reception, and he singled out the South African form as one that would be 'acceptable to many who opposed that of 1928'.[226]

223 Ibid., p. 213.

224 E.K. Lowther Clarke, *The Prayer Book of 1928 Reconsidered* (London, 1943), p. 46.

225 W.H. Frere, 'The 1928 Canon in Latin', *Theology*, 27 (1933): 332-333.

226 Lowther Clarke, *The Prayer Book of 1928 Reconsidered*, p. 84. This view was optimistic; the South African form included an *epiclesis* on the elements, begging the question of what is meant by it.

Chapter 7

Liturgical Renewal in England: 1945-2000

The Shape of the Liturgy

Gregory Dix published his magisterial book *The Shape of the Liturgy* in 1945. Its influence on subsequent liturgical revision in the Church of England cannot be overstated. Taking up the argument of his article 'Primitive Eucharistic Prayers', Dix criticizes what he termed as the traditionalist theory (most recently championed by Frere) that there was a universal primitive type or model for the eucharistic prayer. Rather, he argues what was primitive and universal was the now famous 'four-fold shape' of the liturgy: the taking of the bread and wine (which he equated with the offertory), the giving of thanks over them, the fraction and the distribution of the elements.[1]

Rather than a universal primitive *anaphora* Dix prefers to talk of a 'primitive nucleus' of the eucharistic prayer, out of which the various families of rites subsequently developed. He believed, by working backwards from the liturgical texts of the third and fourth centuries that fundamental to this nucleus, first of all was thanksgiving. Dix follows scholars such as Cirlot in finding the ultimate source of the Christian thanksgiving in the *birkat hamazon*. However, a comparison between this and the type of thanksgivings cited in, for example, Justin and Hippolytus, reveals that the connection is in relation to ideas and form only, a thorough Christianization having taken place. The primitive pattern, he argued, appears to have been a series of thanksgivings including the themes of creation, incarnation and redemption. The second part of the nucleus involves some kind of statement of what the Church 'does' at the eucharist in relation to what was done at the Last Supper, the action of the Church normally being expressed by the verb 'offer'. Dix is therefore able to conclude that behind the textual tradition, in the second and possibly the latter part of the first century, there were two *strata* in the eucharistic prayer:

(a) There are traces of an original stage when the prayer consisted simply of a 'Naming' of God, followed by a series of 'Thanksgivings' and ending with a 'hallowing' or 'glorifying of the Name'. This can be connected with the outline of the Jewish 'Thanksgiving'.

---

1 Dix, *The Shape of the Liturgy*, pp. 48, 214-215. However, Martin Stringer has argued that William Palmer's methodology of structure suggests that the principle of 'shape' or 'order' should be traced back to him, a century before Dix, 'Antiquities of an English Liturgist', p. 154. Bryan Spinks traces this further back to the writings of William Perkins (1558-1602) and William Attersoll (d. 1640), *Sacraments, Ceremonies and the Stuart Divines*, pp. 22, 44, 176-177.

(b) A second *stratum* appears to rise out of the reference to the Last Supper (which may or may not have formed the last member of the original series of Thanksgivings in the first *stratum*). This second *stratum* states the meaning of what is done in the celebration of the eucharist, and relates the present eucharistic action of the Church to what was done at the Last Supper.[2]

In relation to the *epiclesis*, Dix supports Connolly and Armitage Robinson in their suggestion that the term *epiclesis* was used before the later part of the third century in relation to the Jewish idea of the 'blessing of the Name'. But he also agrees with Dom Odo Casel's observation that this primitive definition cannot suffice for the use of the *epiclesis* in Cyril of Jerusalem where the word has a much wider meaning, 'another mark of the slow oblivion of jewish ideas in the increasingly hellenised churches of the period'.[3] Dix reiterates his arguments, already set out in his articles in *Theology*, that a theory of consecration by invocation of the Spirit is a later development, first appearing as a theological idea in the *Didascalia* (c. AD 250) and liturgically at Jerusalem in the fourth century.

In relation to Anglican revision, Dix's thesis had a number of consequences. First, in relation to the abortive 1927-28 revision, Dix argued that the canon was based on the mistaken premise that it reproduced the primitive pattern of the *anaphora*: 'it was the product of a particular technical theory about the early history of the liturgy which had been in debate among scholars for two centuries before 1928, and which at the least had been shewn to be open to serious historical criticism'.[4] Second, his emphasis on 'shape' gave a new direction to the eucharistic debate. The aim of liturgical revision became to restore the clarity of the shape. There was a further consequence. Dix's treatment of Cranmer was little short of revolutionary because rather than seeking to defend the catholicity of the 1552 rite, he asserted Cranmer's Protestantism, culminating in the famous words: 'As a piece of liturgical craftsmanship it is in the first rank – once its intention is understood. It is *not* a disordered attempt at a catholic rite, but the only effective attempt ever made to give liturgical expression to the doctrine of "justification by faith alone".'[5]

Notwithstanding the changes in the 1662 recension of Cranmer's rite, future liturgical reform in the Church of England must not be content with cosmetic changes in Cranmer's text, which simply destroy its integrity, but by a wholesale return to first principles. In relation to the eucharistic prayer this meant the restoration of the primitive nucleus: thanksgiving and statement of what the Church is 'doing', leading into prayer that the benefits of communion will be received. The scene was set for a prayer with the basic structure of preface, (*sanctus*) narrative, *anamnesis*-oblation, petition for fruitful reception, doxology. What was clear was that the *epiclesis* was off the agenda. Dix had demonstrated that the earliest understanding of what we call 'consecration' was that the bread and the wine were 'eucharistised' in the context of the *anamnesis* of Christ. The Christological focus was assured. The subsequent

2 Ibid., pp. 231-232.
3 Ibid., p. 275, fn. 1.
4 Ibid., p. 212.
5 Ibid., p. 672.

western development of focusing specifically on the eucharistic words can be regarded as a legitimate development of this Christological focus. The objection to the eastern development of consecration by invocation of the Spirit was that the role of Christ became increasingly passive, as Hebert also argues in his response to Atchley. So the *epiclesis* is viewed as late and doctrinally alien. Dix gave centre stage to an understanding of consecration as effected by thanksgiving, or thanksgiving related to the eucharistic words of Jesus.[6]

Other Significant Studies

G.A. Michell

Michell published his short book *Eucharistic Consecration in the Primitive Church* in 1948. Michell stresses that in Justin and Hippolytus, the dynamic of consecration is not the efficacy of the divine Name but the fact that thanks is given over the bread and the cup, and the dominant theological themes are sacrifice, thanksgiving, and memorial. He regards the 'Name theory' as a later development, found first in the gnostic *Acts of John* and *Acts of Thomas* and then in Clement of Alexandria, and signifying a new approach to eucharistic doctrine. Liturgical accommodation of the theory can be seen in Sarapion, with the absence of any reference to thanksgiving and memorial, and in the *anaphora* of Saints Addai and Mari. The invocation of the Name was then adapted to the invocation of the Spirit as witnessed in Cyril of Jerusalem. In all these cases the eucharistic prayer is no longer regarded as *eucharistia* but rather *epiclesis*, while the *anaphora* of St James is regarded a conflation of the Justin-Hippolytus model (thanksgivings, narrative, *anamnesis*–oblation) and the Jerusalem model (hymn of praise, *sanctus*, *epiclesis*, intercessions). However, the two types of prayer 'were the expressions of two mutually exclusive theories of consecration'.[7] The west also developed a new theory of consecration in its emphasis on the institution narrative; this was an understandable innovation in terms of the methodology of writers such as Tertullian, where argument about the reality of Christ's humanity is based on the eucharistic words. Once accepted, it was natural that a petition for consecration should precede the dominical words. However, the elements of sacrifice, memorial-oblation and thanksgiving are still to be found in the developing Roman canon, suggesting that the western eucharistic doctrine 'had remained unchanged, and her liturgical development had been of the nature of a gradual process of evolution'.[8] By contrast, the east had made a decisive break with primitive tradition, introducing first a 'Name' theory which in turn developed

6 Philip Pare, in 'The Doctrine of the Holy Spirit in the Western Church', *Theology*, 51 (1948): 293-300, argued that Dix had contributed to a marginalization of the role of the Spirit in the eucharist. While he judged that the consecratory *epiclesis* of 1928 was unwise, Dix suffered from a tendency 'always to end up at the Roman Canon of the Mass wherever he may begin from' (p. 299).

7 G.A. Mitchell, *Eucharistic Consecration in the Primitive Church* (London, 1948), p. 28.

8 Ibid., pp. 33-34.

into a theory of invocation of the Spirit. Michell's essay therefore strengthened the primitive/western approach argued by Dix.

J.E.L. Oulton

A new approach to the subject was undertaken by J.E.L. Oulton in 1951.[9] His book is essentially a New Testament study with the basic conviction that the New Testament understands the Holy Spirit as the 'immanent power indwelling not only in the whole body [of the Church] but also in each individual member of the body'.[10] The Spirit indwells the Christian through baptism; the eucharist is a renewal of fellowship with Christ and with fellow worshippers. Therefore any understanding of the presence of Christ in the sacrament must be understood within the broader context of the Spirit's indwelling. Oulton cites H.B. Swete with approval in his conviction that 'the attitude of the primitive Church towards the Spirit was rather one of joyful welcome than of invocation; the cry *Veni, Creator Spiritus* belongs to a later age, when the Spirit was sought and perhaps expected, but not regarded as a guest who had already come, and come to abide'.[11] Oulton takes up Atchley's argument that the *epiclesis* upon communicants was a late-fifth-century development. For Oulton, this innovation arose because of the loss of the conviction that the Spirit was a guest rather than a visitor. A Church which knew it possessed the Spirit could not pray for the sending of the Spirit upon it. He thus defends the *epiclesis* of the Spirit upon the elements (although he argues that the petition should also be brought into relation with the worshippers who already possess the Spirit), and rejects as unbiblical an *epiclesis* beseeching the *bestowal* of the Spirit upon the worshippers.[12] His book thus ran counter to the main thrust of Anglican scholarship; certainly by 1951, Dix was in the ascendancy over Atchley, and a major weakness of Oulton's book is that he does not engage with criticisms of Atchley's thesis. Moreover, he did not give sufficient attention to those New Testament passages which appear to suggest that those who possess the Spirit may also be filled with the Spirit.

E.L. Mascall

A position similar to that of Michell was adopted by E.L. Mascall in his influential study *Corpus Christi: Essays on the Church and the Eucharist*. Mascall argues that while the primordial essence of consecration was not narration but thanksgiving, the western stress on the narrative was a departure from the primordial rite but nevertheless a defensible development. He argues: 'It seems ... easier to associate the change in the elements with the words by which Christ himself declared their true

9 J.E.L. Oulton, *Holy Communion and Holy Spirit* (London, 1951).

10 Ibid., p. 53.

11 Ibid., p. 131.

12 Oulton defended the 1927-28 *epiclesis* on the basis that phrase 'may be unto us' related to persons; he disliked the Scottish *epiclesis* because the petition asked that the elements might become the Body and Blood of Christ in such a way as to be unrelated to persons (ibid., pp. 29-30).

significance than, as has come to be the practice of the Eastern Church, with words of purely ecclesiastical origin'.[13]

J.G. Davies

Oulton's line of argument was followed by J.G. Davies in *The Spirit, the Church and the Sacraments* published in 1954. Davies also argues that a petition to send the Spirit on the worshippers is incompatible with the New Testament emphasis on the abiding presence of the Spirit in the believer. Davies accepts Dix's criticism of the eastern liturgies that their emphasis on the Spirit relegates Christ to having a passive role in the eucharist. However, he also criticizes the use of the verb to 'send down' or 'descend' as used of the Spirit on the basis that the Spirit is immanent in the Christian worshipper. For Davies, Christ is transcendent in the eucharist as the one who pleads his sacrifice at the heavenly altar; the Spirit unites the worship of heaven with the worship on earth, and identifies the earthly and the heavenly sacrifices as the one who is both transcendent and immanent. Davies clearly desires a much more explicit liturgical reference to the work of the Spirit, but in this book did not suggest any texts.[14] A specimen text was included in a collaborative study by Davies, G. Cope and D.A. Tytler. In the *anamnesis*, the elements are presented 'through thy Holy Spirit', followed by the petition:

> And we beseech thee to accept this our sacrifice of praise and thanksgiving through the mediation of thy most dearly beloved Son, and so to renew us through thy Holy Spirit that he may bring forth in us the fruits of our redemption, and confirm us unto the end ...[15]

The Liturgical Commission

The way was paved for new procedures for liturgical reform by the Cecil Report of 1934, the report of the Canon Law Commission of 1947 and the work of the Moberley Commission in 1952. The eventual outcome was the Prayer Book (Alternative and Other Services) Measure of 1965, allowing the Convocations to authorize services alternative to the *BCP* and other services for which it makes no provision. In the expectation of new procedures, the Convocations requested the archbishops to appoint a Liturgical Commission and this duly began its work in 1955.[16] A memorandum by the new Commission was published in 1957 in preparation for the 1958 Lambeth Conference.[17] It made a survey of attempted liturgical reform in the twentieth century and focused particularly on the reasons for the defeat of the

13 E.L. Mascall, *Corpus Christi* (London, 1953), p. 75.

14 J.G. Davies, *The Spirit, the Church, and the Sacraments* (London, 1954), pp. 136-141.

15 G. Cope, J. G. Davies and D.A. Tytler, *An Experimental Liturgy* (London, 1958), pp. 42, 44.

16 C.O. Buchanan, *Recent Liturgical Revision in the Church of England* (Bramcote, 1973), pp. 6-7.

17 *Prayer Book Revision in the Church of England* (London, 1957).

1927-28 revision. The memorandum highlighted anglo-catholic opposition to the canon because of the position of contents of the *epiclesis*.[18] Sensitivities were still to the fore. This is underlined by a sub-committee of the Liturgical Commission which had met in Nottingham to discuss eucharistic revision. The archbishops asked the Commission to draw up a schedule of detailed amendments to the text or rubrics of the *BCP* of a kind 'not likely to arouse serious controversy' and the sub-committee was of the opinion that such terms of reference thereby ruled out a revision of the prayer of consecration. An amended prayer within the terms of reference would have to be 'sufficiently innocuous to escape censure' and would be 'unable to satisfy those who believe that a scientific revision of this part of the service is a serious need'.[19] The 1957 memorandum had hinted that the problem of conflicting theories of consecration might be side-stepped:

> We know now, in a way that was not realized in 1928, that the Eucharist has developed directly out of Jewish forms of thanksgiving, that the first Christians thought of consecration as effected by thanksgiving, and that controversies between Eastern and Western views of consecration (which played a great part in the debates on the Revised Prayer Book) belong to a later, not to the earliest period.[20]

In the end, progress came from those looking for a 'scientific' approach. The first principle was not the construction of a canon but the shape of the rite. Taking up Dix's thesis, Arthur Couratin and Douglas Harrison suggested that the ministry of the sacrament should be a four-fold movement of taking (the offertory), giving thanks, the fraction and the distribution of the elements.[21] A series of demonstration texts were produced for the offertory and the fraction. Couratin suggested, on the basis of early liturgical texts, that the offertory consisted of a twofold act: (i) the laying of the Table and the placing of the elements upon it normally by the deacon, and (ii) a formal acceptance of the gifts for 'consecration' by the president. This was probably done initially by a silent gesture, and later by a prayer. For example, he saw the origin of the *Oratio super oblata* in the Roman rite as such a prayer of acceptance.[22] He also cited the history of the offertory in the Church of England, drawing attention to the petition for the acceptance of the oblations in the prayer for the Church militant 'which has been interpreted in some quarters, at least since 1607, as meaning the elements' and so functioning as a kind of *Oratio super oblata*,[23]

18 Ibid., p. 11.

19 Liturgical Commission Memorandum 11, by D. Dunlop, G. Willis, R. Beddoes and R. Symonds.

20 Ibid., pp. 21-22. This was an over-statement, of course; the centrality of thanksgiving was argued for by W.C. Bishop as early as 1908, and his work influenced the South African texts of 1918 and 1919.

21 Liturgical Commission Memorandum 34, June, 1960. Although the question of what constitutes the 'taking' was discussed, it is clear that Dix's identification with the offertory was in view.

22 Liturgical Commission Memorandum 34A, January, 1961.

23 Although this interpretation is totally refuted by John Dowden in *Further Studies in the Prayer Book* (London, 1908), pp. 176-223, cited by Colin Buchanan, *The End of the Offertory* (Bramcote, 1978), p. 24, fn. 3.

and the prayer in the Coronation service, 'a reformed version of the words *Munera Domine quaesimus oblata sanctifica*'.[24] This led Couratin to propose a two-stage offertory sequence: a presentation of the alms with a prayer drawn from 1 Chronicles 29, 'Thine, O Lord, is the greatness ... All Things come of thee, O Lord, and of thine own do we give thee', followed by four prayers for use at the taking of the elements, the first of which, from the Coronation service, was highly invocatory:

> BLESS, O Lord, we beseech thee, these thy gifts and sanctify them unto this holy use, that by them we may be made partakers of the Body and Blood of thine only-begotten Son Jesus Christ, and fed unto everlasting life of soul and body; who liveth and reigneth ...[25]

General thinking about the eucharistic prayer was, however, still open-ended. The Commission proposed to publish a booklet on eucharistic revision and appointed Henry de Candole, Arthur Couratin and Cyril Naylor to do the drafting. The interim report of the 'booklet committee' reveals the scope of the issues in a series of questions on the nature of consecration.[26]

The booklet was eventually published in 1964 where de Candole and Couratin, after discussing thanksgiving, ask: 'In addition to thanksgiving, what else should the prayer contain? Should there be some express mention of the Holy Spirit? Should that take the form of petition for his being sent at some point? upon the worshippers? upon the bread and wine? upon both?'[27]

Series 2

However, the first draft of what would become Series 2 had already been presented to the Liturgical Commission in a Memorandum written by Ronald Jasper and Arthur Couratin in December 1963. The 'offertory' was now styled 'The Preparation of the Bread and Wine' with the single prayer, 'Thine, O Lord ...' while the eucharistic prayer, styled 'The Thanksgiving', did not have an *epiclesis* of the Spirit. The petition for consecration, following the *Sanctus,* was the simple form:

> HEAR us, O Father, through Christ thy Son our Lord; through him accept our sacrifice of praise; and according to his institution grant that these thy creatures of bread and wine may be unto us his body and his blood ...

24 Ibid.

25 Liturgical Commission Memorandum 34B, March, 1961. The other three prayers contained no petition for sanctification, being drawn from *Leonianum* VII and XXIII, and Irenaeus.

26 Liturgical Commission Memorandum 39, December, 1962.

27 H.H. de Candole and A.H. Couratin, *Reshaping the Liturgy* (London, 1964), p. 30.

This text is clearly influenced by Dix's view that the Eucharistic prayer is essentially a thanksgiving and that the notion of consecration by invocation of the Spirit was a later, unprimitive development.[28]

The Prayer Book (Alternative and Other Services) Measure came into force on 1 May 1966.[29] Whereas originally the bishops had hoped to introduce a schedule of permitted variation from 1662, the Measure only allowed the introduction of complete services. The bishops therefore issued under the title 'Series 1' light revisions of 1927-28.[30] The exception was holy communion where, because of the controversy over the canon, the Series 1 provision was the 1662 prayer of consecration or the 1662 prayer followed by a simple *anamnesis* with a longer or shorter version of the prayer of oblation. Apart from the 1662 petition for consecration, there was no invocation.[31]

The omission of a definite *epiclesis* in the draft Series 2 rite was cause of some comment. Liturgical Commission Memorandum 50H (March, 1965) includes specific responses, for example, contrasting the petition with the *epiclesis* in the Scottish rite and that the *epiclesis* had been the downfall of 1928 as it was 'in defiance of Anglican tradition' about the eucharistic words. The secretary concluded: 'Others feel "the epiclesis could have been inserted felicitously at many points" and "there is a great need to see that the Holy Spirit acts in his Church".'

However, the form of the prayer was defended by Ronald Jasper in that the Commission 'tried to compose a prayer which expresses the Eucharistic Memorial, and is centred on the Narrative of the Institution, upon which the Memorial is based'.[32] Clearly, the Commission did not judge the *epiclesis* question to be central.[33] Far more pressing was the question of eucharistic oblation, and the structure of the eucharistic prayer was unquestionably western, side-stepping the controversies surrounding 1928. There is some suggestion that an *epiclesis* on the people would

---

28 Dix, *The Shape of the Liturgy*, chapter 10. It is fair to say that the Commission was essentially western in its eucharistic theology. The one member with clear eastern interests was E.C. Ratcliff, but he was no lover of the *epiclesis*, Bryan D. Spinks, 'The Cleansed Leper's Thankoffering before the Lord: Edward Craddock Ratcliff and the Pattern of the Early Anaphora', in Bryan D. Spinks (ed.), *The Sacrifice of Praise* (Rome, 1981), pp. 168-171.

29 This was superseded by the Church of England (Worship & Doctrine) Measure of 1974. This retained Parliamentary rights concerning the Prayer Book, but empowered the General Synod to authorize alternative and new forms of worship independently of Parliament.

30 The bishops had requested the Liturgical Commission to undertake this, but the members declined.

31 *An Order for the Administration of the Lord's Supper or Holy Communion* (AS 120), pp. 17ff; C.O. Buchanan, *Recent Liturgical Revision in the Church of England*, pp. 16-17, 23-24. For the background see J.M.M. Dalby, 'Alternative Services: The Canon of Series 1', *The Church Quarterly Review*, 167 (1967): 446-447.

32 *Alternative Services: Second Series* (London, 1965), p. 147.

33 Jasper's essay, 'Gore on Liturgical Revision', *The Church Quarterly Review*, 166 (1965): 21-36, includes no discussion of the *epiclesis* in his practical suggestions for a contemporary liturgy written in the light of Gore's work.

not have been controversial.[34] Similarly, the Joint Liturgical Steering Committee proposed an amendment to Series 2 including a reference to the Spirit in the petition for fruitful reception:

> Accept, we pray thee, this our duty and service which we with all thy holy people offer unto thee, and grant that we who eat this bread and drink this cup may be united by the Spirit, and filled with thy grace and heavenly blessing.[35]

The final text of Series 2, however, limited its references to the Spirit to the preface and doxology.[36] Series 2 Holy Communion was authorized for experimental use for four years from July 1967. It was always intended that further revision of the service should take place. In the end, the desire for forms of service in contemporary English meant that a new series of services were planned and revision centred on the contemporary language service, Series 3.

Series 3 and the *Alternative Service Book 1980*

Between the authorization of Series 2 in 1967 and Series 3 in 1973, the reforms of Vatican II had borne fruit with the publication of the new *Saramentary*, in its normative Latin form in 1969 followed by the ICEL English language translation. The radical provision of four eucharistic prayers, the style of contemporary English adopted by the ICEL, and the provision of epicletic petitions in eucharistic prayers II, III and IV was bound to influence Church of England revision.[37] In 1971, the 'Windsor Statement' on the eucharist was published by ARCIC, also highlighting the role of the Spirit in the eucharistic action.

In August 1970, Ronald Jasper brought to the Commission a new draft revised text for the second part of the Series 2 canon, marking the change in language addressing God as 'you' rather than 'thou'. The text, including a notable reference to the Spirit, reads:

> Accept through him, we pray, this our sacrifice of praise and thanks-giving; and grant that by the outpouring of the Holy Spirit we may so eat and drink these holy gifts in the presence of your divine majesty that we may be filled with your grace and heavenly blessing, and united to the whole company of earth and heaven in the body of your Son, Jesus Christ our Lord; ...[38]

---

34 See, for example, a text written by the Revd Leo Stephens-Hodge, an evangelical, 'A Conservative Evangelical Liturgy', *Studia Liturgica*, 3 (1964): 175-177.

35 Liturgical Commission Memorandum 71(X), August, 1966.

36 The omission of an *epiclesis* in Series 2 was criticized by C.E. Pocknee in 'The Invocation of the Holy Spirit in the Eucharistic Prayer', *The Church Quarterly Review*, 169 (1968): 216-219.

37 We may also note the occasional epicletic reference appearing in hymns, e.g. *One Hundred Hymns for Today* (1969) included G.A. Tomlinson's hymn 'O Holy Father', the third stanza of which begins, 'O Holy Spirit, be thou nigh this bread and cup to sanctify'.

38 Liturgical Commission Memorandum 120, August, 1970. The background to this is given in Jasper, *The Development of the Anglican Liturgy*, p. 310.

This introduced a definite *epiclesis* on the worshippers, but it did make for a very long sentence. A more streamlined suggestion came to the Commission in the autumn:

> Accept through him this our sacrifice of praise and thanksgiving; and grant that in the power of the Holy Spirit we may so eat and drink these heavenly gifts that we may be filled with your grace and united in the body of your Son, Jesus Christ our Lord; ...[39]

This drew a response from Geoffrey Cuming. Responding to an article by W. Jardine Grisbrooke,[40] he suggested that the petition for consecration in Series 2 ('Hear us, O Father ... Body and Blood') represented too abrupt a transition from the *sanctus* to the narrative of institution. Following Grisbrooke, he made two suggestions for the text. The first was:

> Through him also, heavenly Father, accept this offering of praise, and fill it with your glory and the power of his coming, that these gifts of bread and wine may be for us his Body and Blood.

Although Cuming does not comment on the verb 'fill', it is drawn in the preliminary *epiclesis* of the *anaphora* of St Mark. The second suggestion was that the *epiclesis* should be inserted at this point rather than after the *anamnesis*:

> That by the overshadowing of the Holy Spirit these gifts of bread and wine ...

He commented:

> This would produce a Trinitarian structure which is otherwise absent from this part of the Thanksgiving ... It may be added that this position for the epiclesis is adopted in the three new Roman Canons and in the new Methodist service. (The word 'over-shadowing' is used because, if the previous proposal is accepted, 'power' will have already been used in the same sentence; it is the N.T. word for the work of the Spirit in the Incarnation.)[41]

'Overshadowing', however, would suggest far too strong an analogy between the eucharist and the Incarnation to be an acceptable suggestion across the Church of England. Ronald Jasper suggested the following text for the second half of the canon in December 1970:

> Accept through him this offering of praise and thanksgiving: and as we eat and drink these heavenly gifts in your presence, fill us with the Holy Spirit and unite us in the body of your Son, Jesus Christ our Lord.[42]

The Liturgical Commission minutes reveal that there was still concern over the transition from the *sanctus* to the institution narrative,[43] while Jasper's text for the post-*anamnesis* was recast:

---

39 Liturgical Commission Memorandum 133.

40 W. Jardine Grisbrooke, '"Series II": The New Communion Service of the Church of England Examined', *Studia Liturgica*, 7 (1970): 2-36.

41 Liturgical Commission Memorandum 133A, November, 1970.

42 Liturgical Commission Memorandum 133B.

43 While various texts were suggested, all of them amounted to a conservative re-casting of the Series 2 petition for consecration; there was no attempt to introduce a (new)

> ... and as we eat and drink these heavenly gifts in your presence, fire (or fill) us with the Holy Spirit, and unite us in the body of your Son, our Lord Jesus Christ.[44]

The minutes note that there was some desire to compress these references to the Spirit into a more compact form. The comment was made that the Spirit must not be depersonalized in the overuse of images such as 'outpouring'.[45] The Commission continued working over the rite, now styled 'Series 3', and it was published in a Report published in September 1971. The eucharistic prayer thus had a petition for consecration after the *sanctus*:

> Accept our praises, heavenly Father, through your Son our Saviour Jesus Christ; and as we follow his example and obey his command, grant that these gifts of bread and wine may be to us his body and his blood ...

and a petition for fruitful reception, naming the Spirit:

> Accept this our sacrifice of thanks and praise; and as we eat and drink these holy gifts in the presence of your divine majesty, renew us by your Spirit, inspire us with your love, and unite us in the body of your Son, Jesus Christ our Lord.[46]

Notwithstanding the fact that references to the Spirit had appeared in draft texts, a fully articulated *epiclesis* as such was not a central concern of the Commission. On 31 May 1972, the House of Bishops reported on Series 3 and made this statement on the work of the Spirit: 'As to the work of the Holy Spirit and the relating of the action to the Triune God, it is hoped that this might be made clearer by the insertion of a reference to the Holy Spirit in the first part of the prayer.'[47] This appears to be an allusion to the petition for consecration and in the light of what the 'Windsor Statement' said about the role of the Spirit in effecting the eucharistic gift. At General Synod, on 10 July, the Revd Douglas Carter moved as an amendment the insertion of 'by the power of your Spirit' so that the petition for consecration would read:

> Accept our praises, heavenly Father, through your Son our Saviour Jesus Christ; and as we follow his example and obey his command, grant that by the power of your Spirit these gifts of bread and wine may be to us his body and his blood.

His reasoning was essentially on ecumenical grounds, citing among others, the work of ARCIC, and developments in Roman Catholic, Lutheran and Reformed liturgical renewal. He also cited the statement of the House of Bishops, and the amendment was carried. Thus the first tangible application of the work of ARCIC to the worshipping life of the Church was realized, and the Church of England now had a Spirit *epiclesis*

Roman-style *epiclesis* of the Spirit.

44 Liturgical Commission Minutes, 1-3 December, 1970, p. 21.

45 Ibid.

46 *A Report of the Church of England Liturgical Commission to the Archbishops of Canterbury and York: Alternative Services Series 3: An Order for Holy Communion* (London, 1971).

47 *Holy Communion Series III: A Report by the House of Bishops* (GS83, London, 1972).

in a position corresponding to that in the new Roman Eucharistic prayers. In fact, the amendment was cleverly conceived; it falls short of an unambiguous invocation on the elements alone: the work of the Spirit could as easily be interpreted as relating to the 'may be to us' clause. Nichols and MacGregor categorize this as an 'open' *epiclesis*, giving 'a certain leeway of interpretation concerning the operation of the Holy Spirit on the bread and wine'.[48] The amendment has been durable. As well as being incorporated in the duly authorized Series 3,[49] it was incorporated in the revision of Series 1 and Series 2 Holy Communion issued as *Holy Communion: Alternative Services Series 1 & 2 Revised* (1976). The petition in eucharistic prayer A (Series 1) reads:

> Hear us, O merciful Father, we most humbly beseech thee; and grant that by the power of thy Holy Spirit we receiving these thy creatures of bread and wine, according to thy Son our Saviour Jesus Christ's holy institution in remembrance of his death and passion may be partakers of his most blessed body and blood.[50]

And prayer B (Series 2):

> Hear us, O Father, through Christ thy Son our Lord; through him accept our sacrifice of praise; and grant that by the power of thy Holy Spirit these gifts of bread and wine may be to us his body and his blood.[51]

This service became Rite B in the *Alternative Service Book 1980*. Modern English versions of the Series 1 & 2 Revised services were included in the report *Holy Communion Series 3 Revised* published in 1978, along with a revised Series 3 canon (Thanksgiving C) where the epicletic sections of the prayer are as Series 3.[52] These in turn became eucharistic prayers 1 (Series 3 revised), 2 (Series 2 revised) and 4 (Series 1 revised) in Rite A in the *ASB*. The second eucharistic prayer incorporated a revised prayer for fruitful reception:

> Accept through him this offering of our duty and service; and as we eat and drink these holy gifts, in the presence of your divine majesty, fill us with your grace and heavenly blessing; nourish us with the body and blood of your Son, that we may grow into his likeness and, made one by your Spirit, become a living temple to your glory.

Rite A included one entirely new eucharistic prayer (number 3) and a shortened form derived from prayers 1 and 2 which appears in the appendices styled 'A Eucharistic Prayer for Use with the Sick'.

---

48 Ibid., pp. xiii, 34. They designate the Series 3 text as 'open consecratory'.

49 *Alternative Services Series 3: An Order for Holy Communion* (AS 320, London, 1973). The form of supplementary consecration restored the words of institution, and was lightly revised for Rite A of the *ASB*.

50 *Holy Communion 1 & 2 Revised* (AS 127, London, 1976), p. 25.

51 Ibid.

52 *Alternative Services Holy Communion Series 3 Revised: A Report by the Liturgical Commission of General Synod of the Church of England* (GS364, London, 1978).

The third eucharistic prayer owed its origin to an agreement made between the Revd Brian Brindley, an anglo-catholic, and the Revd Roger Beckwith, a conservative evangelical. Brian Brindley wished to promote a recension of the eucharistic prayer from Hippolytus, the basis of eucharistic prayer II of the Roman missal; Roger Beckwith desired the Prayer Book communion service in modern English. They agreed a modern text of the Prayer Book rite and a recension of Hippolytus and both were incorporated in a document presented to the Revision Committee working on the revision of Series 3 in 1978.[53] The 1978 form of the prayer included a petition for consecration after the *Sanctus* invoking the 'word':

> Lord, you are holy indeed, the source of all holiness; by the power of your holy word, and according to your holy will, renew these your gifts of bread and wine and make them holy so that they may be to us the body and blood of our Lord Jesus Christ ...

and a Spirit *epiclesis* after the *anamnesis*:

> We pray you to accept this our duty and service, a spiritual sacrifice of praise and thanksgiving; send the Holy Spirit on all that your Church sets before you; may we who share in the body and blood of Christ be brought together in unity by that Spirit.

The invocation of the 'word' was intended to be a clear reference to the institution narrative on the basis that the recitation of the eucharistic words of Jesus are considered to be the main consecratory act. The Spirit *epiclesis* was revised by the Revision Committee; this was due to pressure from evangelicals who objected to an invocation of the Spirit upon material objects.[54] It became a invocation upon the worshippers:

> Send the Holy Spirit on your people
> and gather into one in your kingdom
> all who share this one bread and one cup.[55]

53 Brian Brindley and Roger Beckwith, *The Revision of Series Three: A Joint Catholic–Evangelical Approach* (printed paper, n.d.). Brindley was himself a member of the Revision Committee. Colin Buchanan points out that the deal was asymmetrical because the Revision Committee had already agreed to a modern language form of the *BCP* rite, *LAL*, p. 9. It was also contrary to the Commission's principle of 'agreed' texts rather than 'horse-trading' to suit specific constituencies.

54 Evangelical concerns were set out in a Memorandum by Colin Buchanan dated 6 Dec. 1978 [HCR (78) 177]. Responding to Beckwith's justification of the prayer, he states:

(a) He apparently restricts the term 'epiclesis' to forms of prayer mentioning the Spirit. (b) He apparently views texts of epicleses which *do* mention the Spirit before the institution as 'explicitly aimed at trans-substantiation'. (c) He apparently views the existing Brindley text as not so aimed at trans-substantiation, despite the wealth of other language involved. (d) He apparently views an invocation of the Spirit upon the elements ('all that your Church sets before you') as acceptable, provided that it comes after the narrative of institution. It is doubtful whether any, or certainly many, evangelicals would be able to follow him in these arguments.

55 Text from GS364A, p. 21.

The preliminary invocation of the word was also revised:

> ... grant that by the power of your holy word, and according to your holy will, these gifts of bread and wine may be to us ...[56]

The retention of the invocation of the 'holy word' was debated in General Synod in July 1979. The Bishop of Guildford, the Rt Revd D.A. Brown, moved an amendment to replace 'word' by 'Spirit' to bring this prayer into line with the other three and because it was ambiguous – which 'word' was being referred to? Brian Brindley informed the Synod that the suggestion came from Roger Beckwith for whom 'an explicit mention of the Holy Spirit at this point was obnoxious'.[57] In the end the amendment was carried by 97 votes to 96. Colin Buchanan (who was steering the debate in Synod) moved an amendment from the platform to insert 'and word', after Spirit for which there was precedent in 1549, but this was defeated by 106 votes to 98. The final text of the third eucharistic prayer thus has an *epiclesis* before the institution narrative:

> Lord, you are holy indeed, the source of all holiness; grant that by the power of your Holy Spirit, and according to your holy will, these your gifts of bread and wine may be to us the body and blood of our Lord Jesus Christ ...

while, after the *anamnesis*, there is a second invocation:

> Send the Holy Spirit on your people and gather into one in your kingdom all who share this one bread and one cup, so that we, in the company of all the saints, may praise and glorify you for ever, through him from whom all good things come, Jesus Christ our Lord.

Thus, by the slings and arrows of amendment on the floor of Synod, the prayer had a double reference to the Spirit, a preliminary *epiclesis* (but also carefully expressed as an 'open' petition) and a 'congregational' *epiclesis* on the worshipping community.

Evaluation: the *Epiclesis* in Series 3 and the *ASB 1980*.

The Church of England's eucharistic prayers during the period 1973-1980 share a basic structure, incorporating the so-called 'split-*epiclesis*'. The first *epiclesis* comes before the narrative of institution as the petition for consecration; the second comes after the *anamnesis* as part of the prayer for the fruitful reception of the sacrament. The second *epiclesis* is entirely uncontroversial. Geoffrey Cuming, commenting on the introduction of the phrase 'by the power of your Holy Spirit' into Series 3 in General Synod, wrote: 'This addition met with virtually no opposition, in marked contrast to the controversies over the epiclesis in the 1920s.'[58]

---

56 Text, ibid., p. 20. Revision Committee, Holy Communion Series 3 Revised, HCR (79) M1.

57 General Synod, *Report of Proceedings* 10 (July, 1979), p. 467.

58 Cuming, *A History of Anglican Liturgy*, p. 216.

The reasons are not difficult to discern. First, the major opposition in 1928 came from anglo-catholics anxious to defend 'western' views of consecration by the eucharistic words of Jesus. A preliminary *epiclesis* does not prejudice such an understanding as it is regarded as a lead-in to the consecratory words proper. Indeed, the adoption of a preliminary *epiclesis* in eucharistic prayers II, III and IV of the 1969 revised Roman *Sacramentary* scotched any views that an *epiclesis* at this point was un-western. This was further reinforced by the 1971 ARCIC statement on the eucharist asserting the role of the Spirit in the dynamic of consecration.

Second, evangelicals have traditionally been suspicious of an *epiclesis* related to the elements for three reasons: (i) there is no reference in Scripture to it; (ii) doubt is expressed as to whether the Holy Spirit can be invoked on inanimate objects; (iii) an *epiclesis* on the elements focuses too much attention on the elements themselves, which are rather understood as outward and visible signs of an encounter with Christ which is essentially inward and spiritual. The Series 3/*ASB* formula does not terminate on the elements or unambiguously invoke the Spirit on the elements.[59] Indeed, evangelicals will relate 'the power of the Spirit' to the clause 'may be to us' that is. it is in the receiving of the elements that there is a direct encounter and communion with the risen Christ by the power of the Spirit.[60]

Third, the broad consensus of scholarly opinion (including both evangelicals and anglo-catholics on the Commission) is that the whole eucharistic prayer is related to consecration (indeed, some would argue the whole eucharistic action including reception) so that there is no special consecratory formula within it.[61] There was some reference to this theory in its fledgling state in the lead-up to 1927-28 but in the main views of consecration were more mechanical and formula-based.

Fourth, the petition for consecration is now a Trinitarian formula, and Trinitarian formulae 'feel' theologically correct and orthodox.

Fifth, there is the apparent influence of the charismatic movement. It is impossible to know how many voting members of Synod were motivated by charismatic interests but the movement undoubtedly was an important factor in promoting the role of the Spirit in the Church and therefore in the sacraments.

Patterns for Worship and the 1996 Rejected Prayers

The *Patterns for Worship* report was published in 1989. It was produced on the request of the House of Bishops in the wake of General Synod debates on the reports *The Worship of the Church* (1985) and *Faith in the City* (1986). The former report requested a directory of supplementary material for use with the *ASB*, the latter

59 *The Alternative Service Book 1980: A Commentary by the Liturgical Commission*, p. 83, fn. 53.

60 It is equally true that the emphasis can be placed on 'these gifts' in a more catholic sense.

61 *The Alternative Service Book 1980: A Commentary by the Liturgical Commission*, pp. 78-79. The text goes on to assert: '"consecration" itself is not a word used in any biblical context in relation to eucharistic elements, and it is right that it has lost some prominence in the presentation of the text', p. 79.

forms of worship paying special attention to the needs of Urban Priority Area (UPA) parishes. The growth of 'family' or 'all-age' services with significant numbers of children present also informed the thinking. *Patterns for Worship* included four new eucharistic prayers. One of the most significant factors about them is the treatment of the *epiclesis*, for two reasons: first, structural, in that in all four prayers there is a single *epiclesis* in each case coming after the narrative of institution; and second, theological, insofar as in three of the prayers the *epiclesis* is specifically related to the eucharistic elements. In terms of the first, the Commission was much influenced by the research of Thomas Talley, the American Episcopalian, who argues that, for all the diversity and fluidity of Jewish and Christian prayer forms at the beginning of the Common Era, the discernible primitive structure of Christian eucharistic praying is that of thanksgiving followed by supplication. As the distinctive elements of the *anaphora* developed, components such as the preface, institution narrative and *anamnesis* belong to the former category and the *epiclesis* to the latter. He thus criticizes the Rite A preliminary *epiclesis*:

> While general rejoicing must greet the reintegration of the eucharistic prayer in the Alternative Service Book, it would be less than even-handed, in the light of what has been said above, to neglect to comment on the effect of such a consecratory epiclesis prior to the narrative, and especially in the Third Eucharistic Prayer, based as it is on Hippolytus. The supplicatory epiclesis interrupts the Thanksgiving within which Hippolytus situated the narrative and anamnesis in a way directly analogous to the Roman distortion of Coptic Basil.[62]

This basic structure of thanksgiving and supplication can be found in the all four eucharistic prayers: 'The Liturgical Commission has taken advantage of the diversity found in the early evidence, and the creativity of the Reformation, and has attempted to write some EPs with new patterns, but which *adhere to the basic structure of thanksgiving and supplication.*'[63] Hence, these 'deep structures' demand that the *epiclesis* which is a supplication should come in the second half of the prayer, after the narrative which is understood as part of the thanksgiving. The general structure of the four prayers is therefore *sursum corda*, preface, narrative, *anamnesis*, *epiclesis*, doxology. It was also recognized that the demand, arising from the needs of UPA parishes, for shorter eucharistic prayers might the more easily be met by a single, rather than a 'split', *epiclesis*.[64]

Equally significant is the treatment of the narrative of institution. There was some discussion of the possibility of issuing a eucharistic prayer without the narrative but this was deemed to be too radical. The prayers recognize the integrity of the various New Testament traditions about the eucharistic words, and eucharistic prayer A omits the 'This is' element traditionally so important for anglo-catholics. The introduction to *Patterns for Worship* states:

---

62 Thomas Talley, 'The Eucharistic Prayer: Tradition and Development', in Kenneth Stevenson (ed.), *Liturgy Reshaped* (London, 1982), p. 61.

63 Bryan Spinks, 'Introduction', *Patterns for Worship: Essays on Eucharistic Prayers* (GSMisc333, n.d.), pp. 8-9.

64 As argued by Kenneth Stevenson, 'The Epiclesis and the Eucharistic Prayer', in *News of Liturgy*, 161 (May, 1988), p. 6.

'Consecration' is by the whole prayer and action of the community, and cannot be identified with particular words or a particular stage in the prayer. This means we need not cling to particular forms of words, apart from those which are important for unity. So we would argue that the particular form of the narrative of institution is not so important as some have thought in the past. In the continuing debate on the development of the eucharistic prayer the narrative is regarded as a later insertion (which is not to question its legitimacy) in a sequence of thanksgiving and supplication.[65]

The phrase 'action of the community' is significant here and presumably includes reception. The approach of the Commission certainly turns well away from traditional Roman/western perceptions of consecration. However, there was no discussion of the new forms of *epiclesis* in *Patterns*, the very aspect that many regarded as the most radical innovation and departure from traditional Church of England forms. In terms of (ii), eucharistic prayers B and C contain a clear invocation upon the elements. The texts are:

(Prayer B) Father, as we plead with confidence his sacrifice made once for all,
we remember his dying and rising in glory,
and we rejoice that he prays for us at your right hand:
Pour out your Holy Spirit over us and these gifts
which we bring before you from your own creation;
Show them to be for us the body and blood of your dear Son.[66]

(Prayer C) God of all holiness, we are gathered in your name
to celebrate the sacrifice Jesus made for us all.
As we do this in remembrance of him,
May your Spirit show these gifts of bread and wine
to be for us his saving body and blood.
Holy Spirit, you are the power of God.[67]

The petition in Prayer D is rather more 'open'; the Spirit is invoked, but in somewhat general terms:

Pour out your Holy Spirit
as we bring before you these gifts
and remember his sacrifice
made once for all on the cross.
Feed us with his body and blood,
that we may live and grow in him.[68]

65 *Patterns for Worship: A Report by the Liturgical Commission of the General Synod of the Church of England* (GS898, London, 1989), p. 13.

66 Ibid., p. 244. Aspects of the language of the prayer are drawn from a text published by the ICEL. (*Eucharistic Prayer A*, Washington, DC, 1986).

67 *Patterns for Worship*, p. 248. Bryan Spinks states that this prayer takes its inspiration from Addai and Mari/*Sharar*, although the verb 'show' is from Basil, *Worship: Prayers from the East* (Washington, DC, 1993), p. 129.

68 *Patterns for Worship*, p. 250.

Eucharistic prayers B and C both employ the verb 'show', although the subject is different : in prayer B it is the Father, in C the Spirit. The verb had already appeared in Anglican usage in the North American ecumenical 'Common Eucharistic Prayer' adopted by the Episcopal Church and the Anglican Church of Canada. Kenneth Stevenson, commenting specifically on prayer B, writes:

> 'Show' (L.26) is a rhetorical word, taken from the early Greek EP's, antedating problematic words such as 'make' and 'become'.[69]

He amplifies the intention of the petition in another article:

> 'After the thanksgiving series, the narrative and anamnesis ("Therefore, Lord, we do this ..." in the corresponding ASB text), the Spirit is prayed for in order to ratify the eucharist, to accomplish the intentions of the community in celebrating the death of Christ with bread and wine.'[70]

William Crockett describes this as an 'epiphany' theology:

> The verb *anadeiknumi* (show forth) ... reflects a shift from the eschatological perspective toward an 'epiphany' theology, where the Spirit is invoked on the gifts in order that they may manifest the presence of Christ ... the Spirit is invoked on both the community and the gifts, and the theology of the epiclesis exhibits an intimate connection between the sanctification of the gifts and the sanctification of the community.[71]

The use of 'show' has not been without criticism. At the debate on *Patterns for Worship* in General Synod in February 1990 the Bishop of Birmingham (The Rt Revd Mark Santer) said:

> That word 'show' I find extremely slippery and difficult. To me, the natural interpretation is that it is suggesting some demonstration or revelation of something which is already the case, whether one has said the prayer or not, and therefore evades the question of what happens or what we ask God to do in offering the Eucharistic Prayer. This is not only a question about the Eucharist, it is about what happens whenever we pray.[72]

The word is also criticized by Colin Buchanan on the basis that it avoids a direct invocation of the Spirit upon the elements by 'artificially introducing an extraordinary verb from the eighth book of the *Apostolic Constitutions*' and that it would be unintelligible to those in UPA Parishes (for whom eucharistic prayer C was specially

---

69 Kenneth Stevenson, 'The Eucharistic Prayers in "Patterns for Worship"; A Commentary', in *Patterns for Worship: Essays on Eucharistic Prayers*, p. 18. In fact, two Greek verbs can be translated by the English verb 'show': *anadeiknumi*, 'show forth', 'exhibit', 'proclaim' (the two anaphoras bearing Basil's name) and *apophaino*, 'show forth', 'declare', or (of numbers) 'make' (*Apostolic Constitutions 8*). It is significant that R.C.D. Jasper and G.J. Cuming use the English verb 'make' in their translation of each *anaphora* in *Prayers of the Eucharist*, 3rd ed. (New York, 1987), pp. 71, 111, 119. They may well have been influenced by Atchley who gives examples of the former meaning to 'consecrate' or 'make', and the latter as 'transform', 'make-it-to-be', 'make', *On the Epiclesis*, pp. 137, fn. 4, 115.

70 'The Epiclesis and the Eucharistic Prayer', p. 5.

71 Crockett, *Eucharist: Symbol of Transformation*, p. 59.

72 General Synod: *Report of Proceedings* 21 (February, 1990), p. 277.

written).[73] He further asks: 'what kind of "showing" is appropriate (or possible, or desirable) in the outward and visible sign of an inward and spiritual grace which is received by faith? Even transubstantiation was never in any normal sense expected to be "shown".'[74] The Commission clearly hoped that a verb, falling short of notions of a 'change' in the elements, would carry the day.

Eucharistic prayer A is rather different:

> We are your new creation in Christ:
> Fill us with your Spirit,
> to bring good news to the poor,
> to heal the broken-hearted,
> to announce release to captives
> and freedom to prisoners.
> As we eat this bread and drink this wine:
> **Come, Holy Spirit, flow through us,**
> **fill our sacrifice of praise and thanksgiving**
> **with your power and love.**[75]

Here the role of the Spirit in reception is emphasized. 'Fill our sacrifice' recalls the preliminary invocation in the *anaphora* of St Mark. Colin Buchanan raises the question of in what sense the Spirit can be expected to 'fill' the sacrifice? There are other hints of fresh thinking in the essay by Bryan Spinks on the eucharistic prayers in *Patterns*. First, relating to the Holy Spirit generally: 'there are a number of theological issues which need addressing anew. One is the place of the Holy Spirit, and perhaps here the new EPs of *Patterns for Worship* have not explored this fully enough.'[76] Second, the intriguing statement: 'There are a number of us who would describe ourselves as High Calvinists. For such people the agreed formulas are rather feeble in expressing the importance of the Ascension and the eternal efficacy of the sacrifice of the obedient manhood which is now in heaven.'[77]

Spinks had written an important article on the *anamnesis* and *epiclesis* in the *Book of Common Order* (1940/79) of the Church of Scotland. It is clear that the 'high Calvinism' of the Scottish rite is one of the sources of inspiration for eucharistic prayer B. Spinks's article includes an exposition of Calvin's understanding of the role of the Spirit in the eucharist:

> Communion in the Lord's Supper is also due to the Spirit; we are by the Holy Spirit made partakers of him, and the Spirit effects this since he is the virtue of the living God proceeding from the Father and the Son. Appealing to Cyril of Alexandria, Calvin insists that the faithful communicate in the flesh and blood of Christ and at the same time enjoy participation of life; this comes about by the Spirit which 'truly unites things separated by

73 *News of Liturgy*, 165 (September, 1988), p. 5.
74 *News of Liturgy*, 183 (March, 1990), p. 2.
75 Ibid., p. 240.
76 Ibid., p. 6.
77 Ibid.

> space'. ... Indeed, Calvin's teaching on the place of the Holy Spirit in uniting us to Christ in the eucharist is the basis of the epiklesis of the Church of Scotland.[78]

Some, however, would relate Calvin's teaching as relating essentially to the *worshippers* and so argue that it does not demand an invocation on the elements as in the Scottish rite:

> ... send down Thy Holy Spirit to sanctify both us and these Thine own gifts of bread and wine which we set before Thee, that the bread which we break may be the Communion of the Body of Christ, and the cup of blessing which we bless the Communion of the blood of Christ.[79]

Church of Scotland liturgical renewal stemming from the 1867 *Euchologion* has acknowledged its debt to Patristic and eastern sources, reflecting Calvin's own grounding in the Fathers. The question is, however, whether the use of Syro-Byzantine sources behind the invocation above is the only means of giving liturgical expression of Calvin's insights.

The Liturgical Commission undertook to revise the *Patterns* prayers following the 1990 Synod debate. However, it was not until 1994 that alternative eucharistic prayers came back to General Synod and after a fairly tortuous synodical process, the six prayers eventually submitted for Final Approval in 1996 failed to secure a sufficient majority in the House of Laity and so fell.[80] Of the six prayers, three were revisions of the original *Patterns* prayers, one was inspired by ICEL texts for masses with children present, one was written with children in mind by representatives of the Liturgical Commission and Board of Education, and one was a responsive reworking of Eucharistic Prayer 1 from Rite A. Debate continued concerning the form of the *epiclesis*. For example, in prayer 1, the *epiclesis* ran:

> Pour your Holy Spirit on us now,
> as we feed on the body and blood of Christ,
> and live and grow in him.
> For your gift of the Spirit we thank you:
> **We praise your holy name.**[81]

The verb 'pour' was retained as an 'established biblical metaphor',[82] avoiding the unfortunate associations of 'pour out over'.[83] But the outpouring of the Spirit is

---

78 Bryan D. Spinks, 'The Ascension and the Victorious Humanity of Christ: The Christology and Soteriology Behind the Church of Scotland's Anamnesis and Epiklesis', in J. Neil Alexander (ed.), *Time and Community* (Washington, DC,1990), pp. 196-197.

79 Text from the *Book of Common Order* 1940/1979, cited by Spinks, ibid., p. 186.

80 See Colin Buchanan and Trevor Lloyd, *Six Eucharistic Prayers as Proposed in 1996* (Cambridge, 1996); also, David Hebblethwaite, *Liturgical Revision in the Church of England 1984-2004* (Cambridge, 2004), pp. 36-37.

81 *General Synod: Additional Eucharistic Prayers* (GS1138B), p. 4.

82 *Additional Eucharistic Prayers, Report of the Revision Committee* (GS1138Y), section 48.

83 Colin Buchanan had made his famous remark in the preceding November Synod that the petition 'Pour out your Holy Spirit over us and these gifts' reminded him of a jug of

clearly on the congregation. In Prayer 2, the original invocation on 'us and these your gifts' was softened to:

> Pour out your Holy Spirit
> as we bring before you these gifts from your own creation,
> that they may be for us the body and blood of your dear Son ...[84]

The contentious verb 'show' was deleted from this prayer, which, with the deletion of an explicit invocation on the gifts, makes it a more general, 'open' petition. 'Show' was also deleted from prayer 4, despite a plea that the verb is 'seen as expressing a view of sacramental presence which is strong and personal without being coldly objective'.[85] The new prayer 5 ran:

> Send your Holy Spirit,
> that the bread which we break
> and the cup which we bless
> may be the communion of the body and blood of Christ.
> Unite us with him
> and with all God's people in heaven and earth.[86]

This prayer similarly is an 'open' petition for the coming of the Spirit, combined with a form of words derived from 1 Corinthians 10:16, and found in, for example, the rites of the Church of Scotland and the Church of South India. By employing biblical language, it thus sidestepped contentious issues regarding the use of 'realist' sacramental language

Common Worship 2000

The Liturgical Commission returned to the question of eucharistic prayers in 1997, and began preparing drafts. At the July 1997 General Synod, it suggested that six texts might be appropriate, including revision of the present *ASB* Rite A set, and provision of one prayer with a Trinitarian structure, one prayer for use with substantial numbers of children present, and one employing vivid imagery.[87] A presentation on the eucharistic prayer in general was made to Synod, published subsequently with submitted responses. On the *epiclesis*, the presentation stated:

> ... the coming of the Holy Spirit is not something which finds its fulfilment in the bread and the wine; rather, the coming of the Holy Spirit in this way is entirely for the benefit of the church, so that the effect of the remembering and the effect of the presence of Christ is felt in the church in such a way that the church as a whole grows into the likeness of Christ ... the only real debate about the nature of the epiclesis is whether it is right to speak of the

custard.

84 GS1138B, p. 7.

85 GS1138Y, section 69.

86 Ibid., p. 83. One major source was the ecumenical 'Queen's Rite' of Queen's College, Birmingham (1990 edition, eucharistic prayer 4).

87 General Synod, *Report of Proceedings* 28 (July, 1997), pp. 180-181.

Holy Spirit coming simply on the bread and wine, without immediately linking that with the effect of the Holy Spirit on the whole church.[88]

The presentation also sought to tackle the issue around the structure of the prayer and so the *position* of the *epiclesis*.[89] After further work arising from comments from the House of Bishops, six prayers were issued for use in authorized parishes on an experimental basis in December 1997: prayer A was Rite A prayers 1 and 2 conflated; prayer B was prayer 3 revised; prayer C was prayer 4 revised. In all of these prayers, there were no significant changes to the epicletic texts. Prayer D, suitable for use with a substantial number of children present, was cast in narrative style with a 'Trinitarian' shape and so a single *epiclesis* on the communicants:

Send your Spirit upon us here
that by these gifts we may feed on Christ:
his body as broken bread, wine outpoured as his blood.

Prayer E, also suitable with children present, has a 'western' shape with a preliminary invocation:

We praise and bless you, loving Father
through Jesus Christ, our Lord;
and as we obey his command,
send your Holy Spirit on us and on these gifts
that broken bread and wine outpoured
may be for us the body and blood of your dear Son.

There was no reference to the Spirit in the supplicatory concluding section of the prayer. The direct invocation 'on these gifts' as well as the communicants was a further attempt to see, despite previous failures, whether such a petition would be acceptable across the whole Church. Prayer F is drawn from the eastern anaphoral tradition, with a single *epiclesis* after the institution narrative, drawing on imagery from the prayers associated with St Basil of Caesarea. The form of *epiclesis* is also reminiscent of the *ASB* texts:

As we recall the one, perfect sacrifice of our redemption,
Father, by your Holy Spirit let these gifts of your creation
be to us the body and blood of our Lord Jesus Christ;
form us in the likeness of Christ
and make us a perfect offering in your sight.
[Amen. Come, Holy Spirit.][90]

88 *Eucharistic Prayer in the Church of England: A Liturgical Commission Presentation, with Responses from the Synod*, GS Misc512, p. 16.

89 Ibid., pp. 19-20.

90 *Six Eucharistic Prayers in Contemporary Language*, 1997. The Bishops had first mooted the possibility of a Basiline text back in 1992.

The Bishops agreed that the six texts could begin Synodical process in July 1998. The *epiclesis* in prayers A, B, C, E and F[91] were unchanged from the 1997 drafts. D was recast to read:

> Send your Spirit on us now
> that by these gifts we may feed on Christ.
> Through blessed and broken bread
> may we know his presence here
> with opened eyes and hearts on fire.[92]

This retains the 'congregational' focus of the invocation; the story of the encounter with the risen Christ at Emmaus (Luke 24:30-32) lies behind the text, including the reference to 'blessed and broken bread' (v. 30). Issues around the *epiclesis* in the Synod debate can be illustrated by three contributions. One concerned what exactly we are asking when the Spirit is invoked – does the Spirit *change* the elements, or does he change *us* as they are consumed? A second wished for consistency in all the prayers, noting that prayer D the Spirit is invoked on the community *alone* with no reference to the elements. A third point related to unease with prayer E and its explicit invocation on the *gifts* rather than the eucharistic action more generally.[93] Having been given General Approval in 1998, the texts were remitted to a Revision Committee which reported for the July Synod of 1999.

In its Report, the Revision committee commented specifically on the question of the *epiclesis*, noting the historic absence of an *epiclesis* of the Spirit in the Prayer Book and Roman Rite until the twentieth century, and stating:

> The introduction of an *epiclesis* of the Spirit into recent liturgical drafting has not been so much a catholicizing move, as a means of drawing attention to a dormant strand in western prayer which has undergirded the eastern approach. In eastern understanding the Eucharist unites the Church in earth and heaven in common worship and the Spirit is invoked to nurture the fruits of Communion, not to identify a 'moment' of consecration. Viewed from that perspective the position of the *epiclesis* (whether before or after the words of institution) and its association with the elements and/or the worshippers, is of less significance than it sometimes appears when viewed from a 'western' perspective.[94]

The Report then goes on to state that 'transformation by the Spirit' is 'a complex concept not to be narrowly interpreted' and that 'such prayer is to transform the worshippers through the elements and to "catch them into God's future"'.[95] It then includes a section on 'blessing' in relation to the blessing of inanimate substances, in this context, the bread and the wine. The Report notes the biblical tradition of blessing lands, crops and houses, as well as people, and notes an 'ambiguity in

91 The text in F had one small change: 'form us in' rather than 'into' the likeness of Christ.

92 *Eucharistic Prayers: Report by the Liturgical Commission* (GS1299, June, 1998).

93 General Synod, *Report of Proceedings* 29 (July, 1998), pp. 640, 653, 656.

94 *Eucharistic Prayers: Report by the Revision Committee* (GS1299Y), p. 6. The texts themselves are in GS1299A.

95 Ibid.

the use of Greek words in the New Testament' which does not bear out any strict demarcation between different 'modes' of blessing. It concludes:

> Human beings, as spiritually aware and morally conscious beings able (uniquely in creation) to reflect the process of God at work in his world may legitimately claim that the Holy Spirit's work in and through created things is different from his work in and through other created things. Yet created things speak to human beings of God and convey something of his mystery to them. The essential place of matter and created things in incarnational religion, may never be disposed with.[96]

In the light of these convictions, the Revision Committee declined to amend any of the epicletic texts, save the restoration of the communion *epiclesis* of EP 1 of Rite A to prayer A.[97] It defended the invocation on 'us and these gifts' in prayer E as 'within the spectrum of acceptable Church of England doctrine'.[98] In an Annex, it also printed an adapted version of one of the 1996 rejected texts, the ICEL-inspired 'silent music' prayer.[99]

In the July 1999 Synod, there were a number of significant re-committals, including the text of the *epiclesis* in prayer E. The issues around prayer E were predictable: arguments in support of the text were that the reference to 'broken bread and wine outpoured' ensured that the *epiclesis* was on the eucharistic *action*, that invocation on 'us and on these gifts' is known in Anglican eucharistic teaching, as well as in liturgies of the Anglican Communion and of other (Protestant and Reformed) Churches, and that the spirituality of the texts was concerned with the Spirit's transformation of the whole creation and not with 'medieval views of consecration'. Evangelical concerns were predictably on the issue of invoking the Spirit on the gifts. In the light of this, Dr Christina Baxter, an evangelical, made a decisive intervention, that because of doctrinal sensitivities, a text such as 'Send your Holy Spirit that broken bread and wine outpoured …' might be acceptable. Her argument was based on God's sovereignty; that we do not have to tell him where to send the Spirit; that the Spirit 'can come where it will'.[100]

The Second Report of the Revision Committee again rehearsed the historical background to the *epiclesis*, but this time making explicit reference to Calvin, the Westminster Directory of 1644 and Baxter's Savoy Liturgy of 1661, noting that 'Reformed revisions of the rite have had little difficulty in retaining the *epiclesis*'.[101] It also notes:

---

96 Ibid., pp. 6-7.

97 Ibid., pp. 16, 177.

98 Ibid., p. 23. Charles Read, a member of the Revision Committee, speaks of a 'co-ordinated campaign' on the part of some evangelicals to get this petition removed, '"No way to run a railway": Revising the Eucharist for *Common Worship*', *Anvil*, 17 (2000): 263.

99 This was in an annex because the Revision Committee was careful not to exceed its mandate in bringing any new prayers, General Synod, *Report of Proceedings* 30 (July, 1999), p. 93.

100 An allusion to John 3:8; ibid., p. 405.

101 *Draft Eucharistic Prayers, Second Report of the Revision Committee* (GS1229X), p. 10.

> The Church of South India rite stresses the dynamic unity of the people, the elements and the action at this point. This is vital if a merely 'spatial' infusion of the Holy Spirit into the elements is to be avoided. As Charles Wesley's eucharistic hymns illustrate, the whole of the Eucharistic context is caught up into the life of God and infused with the life and power of the Holy Spirit.

It accepted Dr Baxter's proposal and the text was thus amended,[102] the Committee noting that in this revision, there was nothing 'to preclude a distinctly "catholic" interpretation'. Like other texts, it may be classified as 'open', relating the Spirit to the elements or worshippers or both. The amended text ran:

> … as we obey his command,
> send your Holy Spirit
> that broken bread and wine outpoured
> may be for us the body and blood of your dear Son.[103]

On the 'silent music' proposal, the Committee came to the judgement that the construction and ethos of the prayer would not commend itself as an alternative preface. It did, however, suggest that the entire prayer, set out in Annex 2 as eucharistic prayer G, might be added to the range of eucharistic prayers.[104] The *epiclesis* ran:

> Pour out your Holy Spirit as we bring before you
> these gifts of your creation;
> may they be for us the body and blood of your dear Son.[105]

Annex 2 also included a second prayer, prayer H, drafted in response to a re-committal concerning congregational participation. This is a highly responsive, short prayer, with a single *epiclesis* on the worshippers, followed by a petition for consecration:

> Father, send you Holy Spirit on us now;
> may this bread and this wine,
> be to us the body and blood of your dear Son.[106]

The re-committed texts thus came back to the November General Synod. The amendment to prayer E was accepted;[107] however, arguments in favour of invoking

---

102 As the prayers would be voted on as a package, fears that conservative evangelical opposition might bring down the whole project prompted the Revision Committee so to act, despite its own reluctance, Read, '"No way to run a railway": Revising the Eucharist for *Common Worship*', p. 264.

103 *Draft Eucharistic Prayers* (GS1299B), p. 1.

104 GS1299X, p. 11.

105 GS1299X, Annex 2.

106 Ibid.

107 In introducing the debate, Bishop Christopher Herbert stated that he regarded the debate on the *epiclesis* as 'curiously Newtonian' – all about cause and effect; Heisenberg's Uncertainty Principle 'should blow our Newtonian theology out of the water', General Synod, *Report of Proceedings* 30 (November, 1999), p. 263. An attempt to insert 'on us' after 'Spirit' was resisted, ibid., pp. 306-308.

the Spirit on inanimate objects were made by Bishop Kenneth Stevenson and Professor Anthony Thistleton; the former cited James 5:14 and John 9:11 to illustrate material objects as vehicles of divine grace; the latter stated:

> It is profoundly evangelical not to restrict the work of the Holy Spirit simply to persons but to persons and things. I believe that the first reference, in terms of biblical canon, to the Holy Spirit, is 'the creativity of the Spirit bringing order out of chaos through material creation being ordered and differentiated'. Second, God's willingness through his Holy Spirit to re-shape the material world seems to be to be a profoundly evangelical conviction … It is very evangelical to use the Grace, 'Bless this food to our use and us to thy service', and it is a very positive thing to be asking the Spirit to be active both in us, the recipients, and in material things.[108]

Prayer G was voted for by a substantial majority; prayer H after torturous synodical procedures, was referred back to the Revision Committee.[109] The Committee met in December 1999, the text was confirmed by the House of Bishops in February 2000, and it came to Synod for Final Approval. The final text, as well an including an anamnetic reference, retained the strong verb 'send' but deleted the words 'on us', preferring an 'open' petition in the *ASB* tradition:

> As we proclaim his death and celebrate his rising in glory,
> send your Holy Spirit that this bread and this wine
> may be to us the body and blood of your dear Son.[110]

The eucharistic prayers therefore came to General Synod for Final Approval in 1 March 2000.[111] An second attempt (by another Member) to insert 'on us' after 'Holy Sprit' in prayer E lapsed,[112] and the material was duly carried with large majorities and so incorporated into *Common Worship*.

Conclusion

The period 1989-2000 is significant for a number of developments in thinking about the *epiclesis*.

---

108 Ibid., p. 301. Thistleton also regarded the role of the Spirit in relation to the elements to be the big divide between Calvin and Zwingli on the one hand and the Roman tradition and Luther on the other, ibid.

109 Ibid., pp. 313-320, 349-361, 407-410, 419-420. For an account of the genesis of this prayer, see Colin Buchanan, '"Common Worship" Eucharistic Prayer H', *Ushaw Library Bulletin and Liturgical Review*, 13 (2000): 23-36.

110 The insertion of a succinct *anamnesis* was important for the acceptance of the prayer by more catholic-minded Anglicans.

111 See GS1211C, GS1299 C and (prayer H) GS1299W. While this study has concentrated on Order 1, Order 1 in Traditional Language includes eucharistic prayers A and C only. Order 2 is based on the Prayer Book Communion service, in traditional and contemporary language.

112 General Synod, *Report of Proceedings* 31 (February, 2000), pp. 31-32.

Different Structures to the Eucharistic Prayer

Back in 1989, the Synod Report version of *Patterns for Worship* stressed that, given the diversity of the earliest traditions of the Church's eucharistic praying, the Church ought to recognize the legitimacy of different structures. The light revision of three *ASB* prayers, all with a 'western' structure, with the addition of five prayers, one of which has a 'western' shape and four of which have an 'eastern' shape, is a happy and balanced outcome, from which there has been little dissent. The only outstanding issue, perhaps, has been questions about how the 'eastern'-shaped prayers are ritualized, particularly among those who would instinctively look to the entirely 'western' *Missale Romanum* and *General Instruction on the Roman Missal* for guidance on ceremonial matters. The 'eastern-shaped' model has also led to broader supplicatory expression in prayer F and prayer G (optional, but with provision for petitionary insertion) and eloquent expressions of eschatological hope. Prayer D has a distinctive sequential 'narrative' style, the petition for the Spirit following articulation of Jesus's death and resurrection. The economy of prayer H is aided by the structure narrative–*anamnesis*–*epiclesis*.

Invocation on the Elements

Assisted by the findings of the 1995 IALC, there has been a strong consensus in the Liturgical Commission that the *epiclesis* is best understood as an invocation on the eucharistic action, that is, the whole process embracing consecration and reception of the elements. The eucharistic prayer is a single prayer; there is no precise 'moment of consecration'; the institution narrative and *epiclesis* have an important role in articulating aspects of the spiritual dynamics of the rite. This has led to a broad measure of agreement across tradition churchmanship divides. There is, however, clearly still considerable evangelical unease about a clear invocation upon the elements, although it would be inaccurate to state that this embraces the whole evangelical wing of the Church, especially as evangelical members of the Liturgical Commission have been content to 'road-test' prayers with such an invocation and have been involved in their creation. Charismatic evangelicals may also be more open to the *epiclesis* per se. But dissent from an *epiclesis* on the elements is long-standing,[113] and has surfaced in successive Synodical debates. Concern is at its strongest where epicletic petitions appear to terminate on the elements without any relation to the benefits of communion in the worshipper, but, as the debate over Prayer E illustrates, even carefully nuanced petitions are still regarded with suspicion, on an *a priori* assumption that it is unscriptural to invoke the Spirit on inanimate objects. The scriptural examples cited by Kenneth Stevenson and Anthony Thistleton in November 1999 may indicate that this issue has not been accorded the theological the exegetical rigour it requires. Moreover, it raises the issue of whether the phrase 'eucharistic action' needs further unpacking, for the action does indeed embrace the elements, and there is still a recognized concept of 'consecration' in the Anglican

113 See, for example, N.A.D. Scotland, *Eucharistic Consecration in the First Four Centuries and Its Implications for Liturgical Reform* (Oxford, 1989), p. 43.

tradition, and this must in some sense relate to the work of the Spirit. There are also, clearly, some catholic Anglicans who will only countenance prayers with a 'western shape' so as not to prejudice the central role of the institution narrative. Here, the issue is not the *epiclesis per se* or a so-called consecratory *epiclesis*, but a matter of logic, that the petition leads into the consecratory heart of the prayer, the narrative of institution, the *verba Christi*.

Attempts at Different Verbal Expressions

The attempt to find new modes of expression for the *epiclesis*, avoiding heavily conversionalist language, is illustrated by the verbs 'pour out over', 'pour out', 'show', 'send'. 'Pour out' has survived in prayer G, and 'send' has been employed in prayers E and H. Both verbs have enabled the continuance of a certain studied ambiguity all contemporary Church of England prayers, apart from prayer D with its *epiclesis* on the community. The careful and imprecise epicletic formulae enable liberty of interpretation, and as no liturgical gestures are stipulated by rubric, a liberty of presidential style. The fact that this has been done across such a range of prayers and with a variety of structures, can be regarded as a notable fulfilment of the primary aim, that all prayers should be acceptable and useable across the breadth of traditions in the Church.

A Note on the Coronation Eucharist

This survey of the epicletic petitions in Church of England eucharistic worship ends on a Constitutional note, namely the rite for the coronation of the Sovereign. The coronation is set in the context of the eucharist, celebrated, to date, according to the *Book of Common Prayer* but with the addition of an offertory prayer said by the Archbishop after the offering of bread and wine by the Sovereign. The prayer first appeared at the coronation of James I, was revised slightly for the coronation of William and Mary, and has been used at all coronations since.[114] The text, from the coronation of the present Queen is as follows:

> Bless, O Lord, we beseech thee, these thy gifts, and sanctify them unto this holy use, that by them we may be partakers of the Body and Blood of thine only-begotten Son Jesus Christ: And that thy servant Queen ELIZABETH may be enabled to the discharge of her weighty office, whereunto of thy great goodness thou hast called and appointed her. Grant this, O Lord, for Jesus Christ's sake, our only Mediator and Advocate.[115]

The prayer is a translation of one of the two secret offertory prayers from the medieval *Liber Regalis*.[116] Ratcliff comments that it is a matter of surprise that Henry Compton, in revising the rite for the coronation of William and Mary, retained this

---

114 Buxton, *Eucharist and Institution Narrative*, pp. 106-109.

115 Text from E.C. Ratcliff, *The Coronation of Queen Elizabeth II* (London and Cambridge, 1953), p. 55.

116 Ibid.

prayer with little alteration,[117] and Buxton draws attention to the fact that the phrase 'by them' appears to suggest a view of consecration higher than that of the Prayer Book.[118] It illustrates the strength of tradition in such circumstances. The prayer does not invoke the Spirit and, as with many offertory prayers relating to the elements, trespasses on the ground of the prayer of consecration. But it provides a grand, if anomalous, place to finish![119]

117 Ibid., p. 16.

118 Ibid., p. 108.

119 For a wider discussion of the Coronation Rite, see Henry Everett, Paul Bradshaw and Colin Buchanan, *Coronations Past, Present and Future* (Cambridge, 1997).

Chapter 8

The Anglican Communion: Case Study 1: The Episcopal Church in the USA and the Anglican Church of Canada

The Episcopal Church in the USA

The 1928 Prayer Book

Twentieth-century revision of the liturgy of the Episcopal Church was inaugurated by the appointment of a commission in 1913 to consider revision and enrichment of the Prayer Book. This led to the authorization of a new Prayer Book at the General Convention of 1928. The prayer of consecration remained unchanged from 1790. The 1928 General Convention reconstituted the 1913 commission as a Standing Liturgical Commission (SLC).

Towards the 1979 Prayer Book

The year 1969 was significant both ecumenically with the publication of the new Roman Missal with four eucharistic prayers and the consequent rendering of the Roman texts in contemporary English, and the empowerment of the SLC at a special meeting of the General Convention to undertake a full revision of the eucharistic rite and to prepare a report for the 1970 General Convention.[1] There had been previous suggestions for revision, both in 1953 and 1967. In 1953, a specimen rite was published in *Prayer Book Studies IV*. The *epiclesis* follows the oblation and reads:

> AND we most humbly beseech thee to accept upon thine altar on high this our sacrifice of praise and thanksgiving, our bounden duty and service; and vouchsafe to bless and sanctify with thy Holy Spirit these thy gifts and creatures of bread and wine, that they may be unto us the most blessed Body and Blood of thy dearly beloved Son Jesus Christ.[2]

An accompanying commentary was critical of the 1928 canon, including the reference in the *epiclesis* to 'Word', and the phrase 'in remembrance of his death and passion' which duplicated a phrase in the *anamnesis*. The new text, however, with its reference to the heavenly altar and adoption of the *ut nobis Corpus et Sanguis*

1 Peter R. Rodgers, 'The Protestant Episcopal Church of the U.S.A', in *FAL*, p. 123.
2 *Prayer Book Studies IV: The Eucharistic Liturgy* (New York, 1953) p. 333.

fiat of the Roman Rite was hardly likely to command a consensus.[3] Consequently, a fresh start on eucharistic revision was made in 1960 under the chairmanship of Bishop Goodrich Fenner, and including Massey Shepherd whose influence was all-pervasive. Work on a revised rite was completed in 1966, published as *Prayer Book Studies XVII*, and duly authorized for trial use by the General Convention in 1967.[4] The commentary, as well as reviewing responses to *Prayer Book Studies IV*, drew out the profound changes in the liturgical scene in the previous 15 years. The effects of Lambeth 1958, the Second Vatican Council, the progress of ecumenical liturgical initiatives and revisions undertaken in the Anglican Communion and within other Churches, had influenced Episcopal Church thinking.

However, with the exception of statements about unity and eschatology in the *epiclesis* inspired by Harry Boone Porter, the prayer of consecration still reads as a revision of a Cranmerian text rather than as a text arising from a return to first principles. The text of the *epiclesis* of the new rite ran:

> WE PRAY THEE, GRACIOUS FATHER, of thine almighty power, to bless and sanctify us and these holy Mysteries with thy Life-giving Word and Holy Spirit. Fill with thy grace all who partake of the Body and Blood of our Lord Jesus Christ. Make us one Body, that he may dwell in us and we in him. And grant that with boldness we may confess thy Name in constancy of faith, and at the last Day enter with all thy saints into the joy of thine eternal kingdom ...[5]

The text is of note because the invocation of the Spirit is not directly related to the elements 'becoming' the Body and Blood of Christ. The full-stop between 'Spirit' and 'Fill' makes an implicit rather than an explicit link.[6] The Study set out the rationale for the new rite. On the *epiclesis*, it said:

> The Invocation paragraph has been very much rewritten. The double blessing of the Word and the Holy Spirit is maintained from our present rite. For the Word no less than the Spirit is re-creative in his function. Sanctification is sought for ourselves as well as 'these holy Mysteries', so that the totality of what is here present, what is here done, and what is here offered, may be caught up in the new creation of the Word and Spirit. We have attempted to avoid any notion of a 'moment of consecration' or any definition of how consecration is effected. We affirm only the reality and the effectual fruits of this sanctification, and the final end to which it points. The eschatological note that rounds off the prayer returns us to the opening 'Lift up your hearts' – indeed to the very opening of the liturgy itself: 'Blessed be his Kingdom, now and forever.'[7]

---

3 See Bernard Wigan, 'Transatlantic Liturgy', *Theology*, 57 (1954): 424-425.

4 The 1961 General Convention had accepted an amendment to the Constitution to permit trial use of new forms of worship.

5 *Prayer Book Studies XVII: The Liturgy of the Lord's Supper* (New York, 1966), pp. 15-16.

6 Harry Boone Porter desribed it as 'vague, probably to allow theological elbow room to those who saw as consecratory the Words of Institution', 'Meaning and Theology in Eucharistic Prayers A and B', *The Anglican*, 24 (1995): 7.

7 *Prayer Book Studies XVII*, pp. 47-48.

The form of supplementary consecration was entirely new, and in post-1662 Anglican terms, radical by not including the words of institution:

> HEAR US, O heavenly Father, and with thy Word and Holy Spirit bless and sanctify this Bread (*or*, Wine) that it may be the Sacrament of the precious Body (*or*, Blood) of thy Son Jesus Christ our Lord. *Amen.*

The SLC was keen to set the form of supplementary consecration in the context of a prayer for the sanctification of the elements in a fully Trinitarian framework. It regarded the petition as a 'synopsis of the entire Consecration Prayer'.[8]

In response to the special meeting of the General Convention, the SLC. agreed the following motion in June 1969:

> That in a revised Book of Common Prayer there be three eucharistic rites: a traditional rite (being the 1928 rite re-arranged to conform to the order of parts in the Liturgy of the Lord's Supper), a version of the Liturgy of the Lord's Supper in contemporary language, and an outline for an informal celebration with a simple but adequate canon.

Prayer Book Studies 21

The report was duly published as *Prayer Book Studies 21* for the 1970 General Convention. The Convention accepted the eucharistic rites therein and authorized them without amendment for three years. The texts were published in *Services for Trial Use* (the 'Green Book') in 1971. They came back to the 1973 General Convention with a schedule of minor amendments, and were duly approved and published the same year as *Authorized Services 1973* (the so-called 'Zebra Book' owing to its striped cover). As the text of the *epiclesis* was not affected, it will be convenient to consider them as a single unit. In the First Service, the text was based on the 1928 form:

> And we most humbly beseech thee, O merciful Father, to hear us; and, of thy almighty goodness, vouchsafe to bless and sanctify, with thy Word and Holy Spirit, these Gifts of bread and wine; that we, receiving them according to thy Son our Savior Jesus Christ's holy institution, may be partakers of his most blessed Body and Blood.[9]

The changes are the capitalization of the first letter of 'gifts'; the omission of the archaism 'creatures'; and the omission of the phrase 'in remembrance ... passion', to avoid the 'double commemoration' of 1928. Two other forms of the Great Thanksgiving were appended. The first was the 1967 *Prayer Book Studies XVII* text; the second, a shortened version of the adapted 1928 text, with an identical *epiclesis* to the main canon above.

In the Second Service, the main text of the Great Thanksgiving has the following *epiclesis* after the *anamnesis*:

8 Ibid., p. 51.

9 *Prayer Book Studies 21: The Holy Eucharist* (New York, 1970), p. 65.

We celebrate the memorial of our redemption, O Father,
in this sacrifice of praise and thanksgiving,
and we offer you these Gifts.
Sanctify them by your Holy Spirit
to be for your people the Body and Blood of your Son,
the holy food and drink of new and unending life in him.
Sanctify us also
that we may faithfully receive this holy Sacrament,
and serve you in unity, constancy, and peace;
and at the last day bring us with all your saints
into the joy of your eternal kingdom.[10]

This text was drafted by Porter at Evanston, Illinois, in 1969.[11] An appended alternative form was based on the 1967 prayer but cast in contemporary idiom.[12]

The third rite, entitled 'An Order for Celebrating the Holy Eucharist', provided four eucharistic prayers. Prayer A was modelled on *Apostolic Tradition*:

Remembering his death and resurrection,
we offer in thanksgiving this Bread and this Cup.
And we pray you to send your Holy Spirit
upon this Offering and upon your people,
to change us, and to make us one in your kingdom.[13]

Prayer B ran:
Remembering now his suffering and death,
and celebrating his resurrection,
and looking for his coming again
to fulfil all things according to your will,
we ask you, Father,
through the power of the Holy Spirit,
to accept and bless these Gifts.
Make us one with your Son in his sacrifice,
that his life may be renewed in us.[14]

This prayer was drafted by the Revd Frank T. Griswold.[15] Prayers C and D are distinctive because they have a single *epiclesis* in the preliminary position. They were doubtless influenced by Roman Catholic eucharistic revision and represent, in this sense, a departure from historic Episcopal Church usage. Prayer C, dubbed the 'Star Trek' *anaphora* because of its cosmological references, was included at a later

10 1970, p. 91; 1971, p. 73; 1973, p. 65.

11 H. Boone Porter, 'Episcopal Anaphoral Prayers', in Frank C. Senn (ed.), *New Eucharistic Prayers* (New York, 1987), p. 67. This is a revised and enlarged version of his essay 'An American Assembly of Anaphoral Prayers', in Spinks, *The Sacrifice of Praise*, pp. 181-196. See also Marion J. Hatchett, *Commentary on the American Prayer Book* (San Francisco, 1980), p. 374.

12 1970, p. 96; 1971, p. 78; 1973, p. 70.

13 1970, p. 101; 1971, p. 83; 1973, p. 75.

14 1970, p. 102; 1971, p. 84; 1973, p. 76.

15 Hatchett, *Commentary on the American Prayer Book*, p. 375.

stage and drafted by Captain Howard Galley of the Church Army.[16] It included this preliminary invocation:

And so, Father, we who have been redeemed by him,
and made a new people by water and the Spirit,
now bring before you these gifts.
Sanctify them by your Holy Spirit
to be for us the Body and Blood
of Jesus Christ our Lord.[17]

It links the two Gospel sacraments of baptism and the eucharist. Prayer D is very similar:

And so, Father, we bring you these gifts.
Sanctify them by your Holy Spirit
to be for your People the Body and Blood
of Jesus Christ our Lord.[18]

In both prayers there is a deliberate ordering of ideas. The gifts are 'brought before' the Father, not in the *anamnesis*, but before the *epiclesis* and narrative, which preserves the dynamic of oblation–invocation.[19] The form of supplementary consecration retained the 1967 petition but with the addition of the relevant section of the institution narrative. The rubric also permitted recitation of the prayer of consecration from the post-*sanctus* to the *epiclesis* as an alternative.[20]

The 1973 General Convention requested the S.C to prepare a draft of a proposed revised Prayer Book for the 1976 Convention. The Convention declined to support a motion calling for the incorporation of the 1928 rites in the new prayer book.[21] The final stages of work on the eucharist was undertaken by committees working on different aspects of revision, and in particular the 'First Services' committee and the 'Second Services' committee.[22]

The First Service

The First Services committee met under the chairmanship of the Revd Donald L. Garfield. The committee had been advised by 'higher authorities' (presumably the bishops) that the 1928 canon should be retained at least as an alternative with minimal adjustment. In addition, a second prayer, firmly within the Cranmerian tradition, should be included with an enlarged preface and a more joyful tone. At

16 Ibid., p. 377.

17 1970, p. 104; 1971, p. 86; 1973, p. 78.

18 1970, p. 106; 1971, p. 88; 1973, p. 80.

19 Porter, 'Episcopal Anaphoral Prayers', p. 69. There is no oblation of the elements in the *anamnesis*; the oblation is of 'this sacrifice of praise and thanksgiving'.

20 1970, p. 146; 1971, p. 128, 129; 1973, p. 119, 120.

21 Rodgers, 'The Protestant Episcopal Church of the U.S.A', p. 129.

22 It was at this time that as well as Massey Shepherd, Boone Porter and Charles Guilbert became highly influential voices in the development of the eucharistic rites.

the meeting in May 1974, the committee suggested three canons: (i) 1928 virtually intact; (ii) a revision of 1928; (iii) a considerably shorter canon in traditional language, following the short form version being considered by the Second Services committee. The committee drafted three texts: (i) the 1928 *epiclesis* with the deletion of 'in remembrance of his death and passion'; (ii) the revised 1928 text with the following *epiclesis*:

> And we most humbly beseech thee, O merciful Father, to hear us; and of thy almighty goodness, to bless and sanctify, with thy Word and Holy Spirit, these gifts of bread and wine, that they may be unto us the Body and Blood of thy dearly-beloved Son Jesus Christ.

(iii) the Great Thanksgiving of 1970/73 Holy Eucharist Second Service cast in traditional language. Text (ii) was prepared by the Very Revd Dr Robert Greenfield, becoming known as the 'Greenfield canon'; 'Word and Spirit' are invoked on the elements only. After further refinements, the First Services Committee completed its work on the texts in November, 1974. The 1928 canon was retained virtually unchanged,[23] and the *epiclesis* of the 'Greenfield canon' was slightly revised :

> And we most humbly beseech thee, O merciful Father, to hear us, and with thy Word and Holy Spirit, to bless and sanctify these gifts of bread and wine, that they may be unto us the Body and Blood of thy dearly-beloved Son Jesus Christ.

The texts were presented to the SLC Drafting Committee on the Holy Eucharist, which agreed that Holy Eucharist Rite I (as it would be designated in the proposed Prayer Book) should include the 1928 canon and the Greenfield alternative only.

The Second Service

The Drafting Committee on the Holy Eucharist met in November 1974. The committee considered the range of canons in 1970/73, and instructed the Second Services committee to undertake revision, including the possibility of conflating prayers A and B from 'An Order for Celebrating the Holy Eucharist' and to write an alternative to prayer D that drew on material from B. The Second Services committee duly engaged with its task, and produced draft texts for the for Second Service and 'An Order'. In the Second Service, the Great Thanksgiving in the main text was left unaltered save for the addition of a clause in the *anamnesis*. The 'Star Trek' *anaphora* was moved from 'An Order' to become prayer A; its *epiclesis* was left unchanged. A new prayer B was the result of the conflation of prayers A and B from 'An Order':

(Old A) And we pray you to send your Holy Spirit
upon this Offering and upon your People,
to change us, and make us one in your kingdom.

23 A substantial number of proper prefaces were added, the *benedictus* was added to the *sanctus*, and a rubric concerning manual acts, Porter, 'Episcopal Anaphoral Prayers', p. 65.

(Old B) ... we ask you, Father,
through the power of the Holy Spirit,
to accept and bless these Gifts.
Make us one with your Son in his sacrifice,
that his life may be renewed in us.

(New B) And we pray you to send your Holy Spirit
upon this offering and upon your people.
Unite us to your Son in his sacrifice
that his life may be renewed in us.
Gather us, and make us one in your eternal kingdom.

Prayer B was followed by a rubric stating that prayer 'C' would be a new ecumenical text now in preparation.

The Second Services committee also worked on 'An Order for Celebrating the Holy Eucharist'. The draft for 'An Order' (sometimes referred to unofficially as 'Rite III') included two appended eucharistic prayers. Prayer 1 was prayer D from 1970/73 and prayer 2 a new composition, drawing principally on the conflated text above. The text read:

Send your Holy Spirit upon these gifts,
and grant that we who eat this Bread
and drink this Cup
may be filled with your life and goodness.
Renew us by your Holy Spirit
that we may be united in the Body of your Son
and be brought with all your people
into the joy of your eternal kingdom.[24]

The conflated prayer B from the Second Service (now designated Rite II) was further revised at the meeting of the SLC in March 1975, so that the *epiclesis* became:

We pray you to send your Holy Spirit
upon your people and upon these gifts.
Grant that they may be the Sacrament of the
Body of Christ
and his Blood of the New Covenant.
Unite us to your Son in his sacrifice, that we may
be acceptable through him,
being sanctified by the Holy Spirit.

The revised text thus relates the *epiclesis* directly to a petition that the elements may be the *sacrament* of Christ's Body and Blood, a creative use of a term that is central to Anglican formularies. The final line is drawn from Romans 15:16.[25]

24 The petition for the fruits of communion drew on the Australian 1973 rite, Hatchett, *Commentary on the American Prayer Book*, p. 416.

25 Porter, 'Episcopal Anaphoral Prayers', p. 68. Hatchett's comment is that the 'epiclesis upon the gifts is explicit, that upon the people more subtle', *Commentary on the American Prayer Book*, p. 375.

A booklet, *Alternative texts for Trial Use 1975-76*, included the alternative eucharistic prayer for Rite I; the new ecumenical text (see below), and 'A Revised Conflation of Eucharistic Prayers A & B (pp. 74-76) of *Authorized Services 1973*'. The text of the *epiclesis* of the conflated prayer was unchanged, save that the final clause became:

> Unite us to your Son in his sacrifice,
> that his life may be renewed in us.
> Gather us, and make us one in your eternal kingdom.

A further draft revision suggested by Porter greatly strengthened the eschatological dimension of the prayer:

> And we offer our sacrifice of praise and thanksgiving to you, O Lord of all; presenting to you, from your creation, this bread and this wine.
>
> We pray you, gracious God, to send your Holy Spirit upon these gifts that they may be the Sacrament of the Body of Christ and his Blood of the new Covenant. Unite us to your Son in his sacrifice, that we may be acceptable through him, being sanctified by the Holy Spirit. In the fulness of time, put all things in subjection under your Christ, and bring us to that heavenly country where, with [... and] all your saints, we may enter the everlasting heritage of your sons and daughters; through Jesus Christ our Lord, the firstborn of all creation, the head of the Church, and the author of our salvation.

Thus the prayers for Rite II received a final editing in preparation for presentation to the 1976 General Convention. The *epiclesis* of eucharistic prayer A, the main text from the Second Service of 1970/73, remained unchanged. The amended *epiclesis* of eucharistic prayer B, the conflated text, was as above. Eucharistic prayer C was the 'Star Trek' *anaphora*, retaining its preliminary petition:

> And so, Father, we who have been redeemed by him, and made a new people by water and the Spirit, now bring before you these gifts. Sanctify them by your Holy Spirit to be the Body and Blood of Jesus Christ our Lord.

Eucharistic prayer D was the final text of the 'Common Eucharistic Prayer', which itself had an interesting process of development. The Drafting Committee at its meeting in November 1974 sanctioned Episcopal Church involvement in the formation of an ecumenical committee to consider the ecumenical potential of eucharistic prayer IV of the Roman Rite. The Episcopal Church was represented by Howard Galley and Marion Hatchett. They were joined by Eugene Brand, a Lutheran; Hoyt Hickman and Don Saliers, Methodists; Ross Mackenzie, a Presbyterian; and Aidan Kavanagh and Ralph Keifer, Roman Catholics.[26] The Roman prayer is an adaptation of the Alexandrian version of the *anaphora* of St Basil, a text which was thus deemed to have considerable ecumenical potential as an 'eastern' text lying behind a modern western recension. Howard Galley reported to the SLC in January 1975 that several Roman Catholic scholars had expressed dissatisfaction with the prayer as it stood in the Roman Missal, and the official English translation of the

26 Marion J. Hatchett, *A Common Eucharistic Prayer* (1975), p. 1.

normative Latin text, not least because it imposed a 'western' shape on an eastern prayer by including a preliminary invocation.

The ecumenical committee, under Dr Hatchett's chairmanship, decided to re-examine the sources of the prayer. The first draft was prepared by Eugene Brand; the text of the *epiclesis* drew on Alexandrian Basil, and it restored the West Syrian shape. Further drafts followed, some including an *optional* preliminary *epiclesis*, until in April 1975, the preliminary *epiclesis* was abandoned, leaving a single invocation after the *anamnesis* and thus restoring the original West Syrian shape. The text was worked over again at a final meeting, and so that the published form of the *epiclesis* reads:

> Lord, we pray that in your goodness and mercy
> your Holy Spirit may descend upon us,
> and upon these gifts,
> sanctifying them and showing them to be
> holy gifts for your holy people,
> the bread of life and the cup of salvation,
> the Body and Blood of your Son Jesus Christ.

The *epiclesis* owes most to the Alexandrian version of St Basil with its less developed idea of consecration. Leonel Mitchell commends the Alexandrian form of the *epiclesis* because: 'the development is not of the epiclesis upon the gifts but upon the congregation. The brief petition to send the Holy Spirit upon us and upon the gifts leads to a prayer that we who communicate may be numbered with the saints, and then into intercessions for the Church'.[27] The implication is that the 'Common Eucharistic Prayer' is similarly weighted, although the insertion of 'the Body and Blood of your Son Jesus Christ' and the start of a new paragraph thereafter rather firms up and isolates the invocation from its context.

As a further note to the 'Common Eucharistic Prayer', it is significant that one of its Roman Catholic drafters, Ralph A. Keifer, reported on a meeting of the North American Academy of Liturgy in January 1976:

> How the role of the Spirit is expressed in the eucharistic prayer was also a matter of concern. It was agreed that the eucharistic prayer should evoke a sense of the Spirit's presence, and there was doubt whether current prayers do this in an effective way. This matter was seen as needing further investigation, not only in terms of the epiclesis, but also in broader theological terms: How should the relation of Christology and Pneumatology be expressed in the eucharistic prayer? The perennial question of the epiclesis made its expected appearance, but with certain new dimensions. Some protested the affront to the Churches of the East in Roman Eucharistic Prayer IV's 'corrective' insertion of an epiclesis before the institution narrative. At the same time, there was a general unwillingness to see the epiclesis as primarily a prayer for the consecration of the gifts. Rather, it was agreed that the proper thrust of the epiclesis is prayer for the sanctification of the Church – a gentle dissent from the 'split' epiclesis pattern of most of the new Roman prayers.'[28]

---

27 Leonel L. Mitchell, 'The Alexandrian Anaphora of St. Basil of Caesarea: Ancient Source of "A Common Eucharistic Prayer"', *Anglican Theological Review*, 58 (1976): 203.

28 Ralph A. Keifer, 'The Eucharistic Prayer', *Worship*, 50 (1976): 317-318.

'An Order for Celebrating the Holy Eucharist', designed for informal and occasional services, contains two eucharistic prayers. The *epiclesis* of Form 1 remained unchanged (as above), namely the preliminary invocation of prayer D from 1970/73. Form 2, with an *epiclesis* following the *anamnesis*, also retained the text as quoted above, but with two important additions. An extra sentence was added, again relating the *epiclesis* to the desired reception of Christ's Body and Blood:

> Send your Holy Spirit upon these gifts. Let them be for us the Body and Blood of your Son. And grant that we who eat this bread and drink this cup may be filled with your life and goodness ...
>
> *The Celebrant then prays that all may receive the benefits of Christ's work, and the renewal of the Holy Spirit.*

The rubrics also make provision for the use of any of the Rite II eucharistic prayers.

The draft of the proposed Prayer Book was published in February 1976. It was accepted by the General Convention in September 1976, and authorized as an alternative to 1928 from Advent Sunday, 1976. It was published as the 'Proposed' Book of Common Prayer in February 1977. It was duly declared to be *The Book of Common Prayer* at the General Convention of September 1979. Charles R. Price wrote in *Prayer Book Studies 29* of the significance of the position of the *epiclesis* in the new Prayer Book for the concept of consecration:

> The English Book of 1549 placed its epiklesis before the Words of Institution, as in certain ancient liturgies. American Books, following the Scottish Book of 1637, have placed the epiklesis after the anamnesis, as in Orthodox liturgies. Arguments for one position or another might be significant if one believed in a 'moment of consecration'. DPB services express no such moment, consistent with Anglican tradition. The whole service consecrates. Consequently, it is as appropriate that the work of the Spirit should be expressed near the end of the prayer (in A, B, D) as near the beginning (in C).[29]

Similarly, Porter insists that the *epiclesis* has to be interpreted broadly. The *epiclesis* is on the elements and worshippers but in the context of the eucharistic thanksgiving. The thanksgiving embraces creation, salvation history, the whole Christ event, the communion of saints. The sanctification of the elements is thus related to the whole of the thanksgiving; 'this whole story has been invoked upon them'.[30]

Supplemental Liturgical Texts

In the decade following the publication of the new *BCP*, the question of inclusive language, later designated as 'balanced language' and then 'expansive language', became more and more pressing. Consequently, following a decision by the 1985

29 Charles R. Price, *Introducing the Draft Proposed Book: Prayer Book Studies 29* (New York, 1976), p. 84. Leonel Mitchell also stresses the fact that there is no 'moment' of consecration, *Prayer Shapes Believing* (Minneapolis, 1985), p. 171.

30 Porter, 'Episcopal Anaphoral Prayers', pp. 72-73.

General Convention, the SLC in 1986 appointed a committee on Supplemental Liturgical Texts. The committee included two eucharistic 'writing teams', one to adapt Rite II and another to create 'Alternative Eucharists'. The former presented adapted texts during 1986-87 which then went through a process of evaluation. In the end, because of the difficulties experienced in adapting familiar texts successfully, the drafts were not submitted to the General Convention. The 'Alternative Rites' team, chaired by the Revd Robert J. Brooks, used the principle of 'root metaphor' to develop a dozen new eucharistic prayers. Four of them were presented to the full committee, which in turn submitted two texts to the SLC.[31] The texts came to the 1988 General Convention, and were published in 1989 as *Supplemental Liturgical Texts: Prayer Book Studies 30*. The study included the newly composed eucharistic rite, regarded as a supplement to Rite II in the *BCP*,[32] as well as a revised form of the Daily Office. The eucharistic rite included two eucharistic prayers, both of which have an *epiclesis* in the 'Antiochene' position. The first prayer, whose theme is 'the creation of all people in the image of God as the source of Christian inclusiveness',[33] expresses the *epiclesis* thus:

> And we present to you from your creation,
> this bread and this wine.
> By your Holy Spirit may they become for us
> the bread of life and the cup of salvation,
> the Body and Blood of our Saviour Jesus Christ,
> that we may be Christ's Body in the world.[34]

The second prayer, where the central metaphor is 'God bringing to birth and nourishing the whole creation', incorporates the sense of the Hebrew word *ruah*, and draws on Genesis 1:2:

> Pour out your love and blessing on all we offer here. Breathe your Spirit into these gifts of bread and wine, to make of them the Body and Blood of Christ. Let your Spirit who broods over the whole creation dwell within us. Gather us to be your holy people, the Body of Christ given for the world you have made. Draw us, O God, to your heart at the heart of the world.[35]

The publication of *Prayer Book Studies 30* initiated a wide-ranging debate and evaluation of the texts. In the light of responses received, the committee on Supplemental Liturgical Texts undertook a wide-ranging revision, submitted for the 1991 General Convention. Rather than an entire eucharistic rite, supplementary materials for use with Rite II from the *BCP* were provided. The revision included three complete eucharistic prayers, and two further forms modelled on those from

---

31 *The Blue Book: Supplement to the Report of the Standing Liturgical Commission* (1988), pp. 189-194.

32 *Supplemental Liturgical Texts: Prayer Book Studies 30* (New York, 1989), p. 58.

33 Ibid.

34 Ibid., p. 68.

35 Ibid., p. 73. The form of supplementary consecration was essentially that of the *BCP*, ibid., p. 82.

'An Order for Celebrating the Holy Eucharist' from the Prayer Book. Eucharistic prayer 1 is a revised form of the first prayer in 1989:

> Remembering his death and resurrection,
> we now present to you from your creation
> this bread and wine.
> By your Holy Spirit may they be for us
> the Body and Blood of our Savior Jesus Christ.
> Grant that we who share these gifts
> may be filled with the Holy Spirit
> and live as Christ's Body in the world.[36]

The revised text thus replaces 'become' by 'be', and includes a fuller statement of the gift of the Spirit in the worshippers. Similarly, eucharistic prayer 2 is a remodelling of the second 1989 prayer:

> Pour out your Spirit upon these gifts
> that they may be the Body and Blood of Christ.
> Breathe your Spirit over the whole earth
> and make us your new creation,
> the Body of Christ given for the world you have made.[37]

This is a more compact petition than 1989, the verb 'be' replaces 'make of them', and the language generally is more conventional. The notes on the text cite Joel 2:28 as the source of 'Pour out your Spirit',[38] and Genesis 2:7 for 'Breathe your Spirit'.[39] Eucharistic prayer 3 is a new text developed from the theme of 'Wisdom'. It also has a single *epiclesis* following the *anamnesis*:

> Look with favor on your people's sacrifice,
> and send your Holy Spirit to sanctify these gifts,
> that this bread may be the Body of Christ,
> and this wine the Blood of Christ,
> that all who receive them may be made one in Christ,
> and be filled with the grace of your life-giving Spirit.[40]

The prayer was not approved for liturgical use by the General Convention, but referred for refinement by the SLC in consultation with the Theology Committee of the House of Bishops. It has not resurfaced![41] Of the forms for use with 'An Order',

---

36 *The Blue Book: Supplement to the Report of the Standing Liturgical Commission* (1991), p. 264.

37 Ibid., p. 267.

38 Although the passage in Joel concerns the outpouring of the Spirit on people!

39 Ibid., p. 268.

40 Ibid., p. 269.

41 The issues here were theological, especially the relationship between 'Wisdom' and 'Word', see Ruth A. Meyers with Jean Campbell, 'Expanding Liturgical Language in the Episcopal Church USA', *Studia Liturgica*, 26 (1996): 119-127. For a broader discussion of 'expansive language', see Ruth A. Meyers, 'Treasures New and Old: Imagery for Liturgical

the first (Form A) reproduced the *epiclesis* of Form 1 in the *BCP* with the deletion of 'Father'. Form B recasts the 1979 text thus:

> ... we bring before you these gifts.
> Sanctify them by your Holy Spirit
> to be for your people the Body and Blood of Christ.
> *The Celebrant then prays that all may receive the benefits of Christ's work, and the renewal of the Holy Spirit.*[42]

The revised text makes explicit that the invocation sanctifies the gifts to be the Body and Blood by embracing the petition in a single sentence; it also allows the desired work of the Spirit in the communicants to be entirely extemporaneously expressed. Eucharistic prayers 1 and 2 and the two forms for use with 'An Order' were duly published in *Supplemental Liturgical Materials* (*SLM*) in 1991, superseding *Prayer Book Studies 30*.[43]

The 1994 General Convention authorized continued development of supplemental expansive language texts as well as continued use of *SLM*. It also requested 'a rationale and a pastorally sensitive plan' for the next revision of the Prayer Book. A schedule of changes and additions to *SLM* was duly presented to the 1997 General Convention. Changes to the two main eucharistic prayers and the eucharistic prayers for use with 'A Form' were minimal and the epicletic texts were unchanged. A newly-composed third eucharistic prayer was added, incorporating the Christological titles 'Word' and 'Wisdom'. The structure of the prayer followed the 'thanksgiving–supplication' model commended by Thomas Talley at the 1993 Untermarchtal Anglican liturgical conference, and also set out in an essay in *A Prayer Book for the 21st Century*.[44] The prayer therefore has a single *epiclesis*, following the memorial acclamations:

> Send your Holy Spirit upon us
> and upon these gifts of bread and wine
> that they may be to us
> the body and blood of your Christ.
> Grant that we, burning with your Spirit's power,
> may be a people of hope, justice and love.[45]

Prayer', in Ruth A. Meyers and Phoebe Pettingell (eds), *Gleanings: Essays on Expansive Language with Prayers for Various Occasions* (New York, 2001), pp. 24-42.

42 *The Blue Book: Supplement to the Report of the Standing Liturgical Commission*, p. 275.

43 *Supplemental Liturgical Materials* (New York, 1991): pp. 37, 41, 44, 46.

44 Thomas Talley, 'Eucharistic Prayers, Past, Present and Future', in Holeton, *Revising the Eucharist*, pp. 6-19; and 'The Structure of the Eucharistic Prayer', in Ruth A. Meyers (ed.), *A Prayer Book for the 21st Century* (New York, 1996), pp. 76-101. Marion Hatchett has also argued that existing prayers in the *BCP* should be revised to conform to this pattern, 'Unfinished Business in Prayer Book Revision', in Paul V. Marshall and Lesley A. Northup (eds), *Leaps and Bounds: The Prayer Book in the 21st Century* (Harrisburg, 1997) pp. 27-8.

45 *The Blue Book: Supplement to the Report of the Standing Liturgical Commission* (1997), p. 277.

This form of *epiclesis* is careful to embrace both the elements and worshippers; indeed, it incorporates *three* references to the people: 'upon us … may be to us … that we …'. The prayer was accepted by the General Convention, with one amendment in the post-*sanctus* section and the capitalization of 'Body' and 'Blood' in the *epiclesis*, and published with the other material in *Enriching our Worship* in 1998.[46] The texts have been subsequently further authorized by the General Conventions of 2000, 2003 and 2006, the last empowering the SLC to create additional liturgical materials drawing on the Church's liturgical, racial, generational, gender and ethnic diversity, for inclusion in *Enriching our Worship 1*.[47]

The Anglican Church of Canada

The background to Canadian revisions of the Book of Common Prayer in 1918/21 and 1959/62 is fully set out in studies by W.J. Armitage and William R. Blott.[48] For the record, the Prayer of Consecration in the 1918 Prayer Book was identical to 1662, and the 1962 prayer retained the 1662 petition for consecration before the institution narrative but added a reference to the Holy Spirit after the *anamnesis*:

> … and all other benefits of his passion; And we pray that by the power of thy Holy Spirit, all we who are partakers of this holy Communion may be fulfilled with thy grace and heavenly benediction … [49]

Experiment and Liturgy

Although the adoption of the new *BCP* might have been expected to herald a period of liturgical calm, the mid-1960s saw the first signs of the major period of liturgical reappraisal and renewal that has lasted to the present. The 1965 General Synod sanctioned limited experimentation at the discretion of diocesan bishops, and looked towards the production of a version of the *BCP* in contemporary English.[50] The first contribution to this process came in 1966, in the form of a book, *Say What You Mean ... And Do What You Say*, by the Revd Paul Gibson. The eucharistic prayer retained a split invocation, the first a simple petition for consecration, and the second, following a post-*anamnesis* petition for acceptance of the sacrifice of praise and thanksgiving:

46 *Enriching our Worship* (New York, 1998); later designated *Enriching our Worship 1*, to distinguish it from subsequent volumes covering other rites.

47 Resolution A069, General Convention, 2006.

48 W.J. Armitage, *The Story of the Canadian Revision of the Prayer Book* (Cambridge, 1922); William R. Blott, *Blessing and Glory and Thanksgiving* (Toronto, 1998).

49 *The Book of Common Prayer* (Toronto, 1962), p. 85.

50 The issue was referred to the Committee on Revision of the Prayer Book. In the end the Canadian Church opted for the production of official alternatives to the *BCP*.

Send your Holy Spirit upon us and our eucharist;
when we eat this bread and drink this cup
may we be filled with your life and blessing.[51]

The invocation of the Spirit upon 'us and our eucharist' was far-sighted. Local experimental forms of eucharistic liturgy were forthcoming and three of the most note-worthy were included in an official booklet issued by the Church in 1971, entitled *Experiment and Liturgy*. For example, 'The Qu'appelle Liturgy' (Diocese of Qu'appelle) was the most widely used of all the experimental rites. The post-*sanctus* section of the prayer has a kind of invocation:

Give us then, Father, through this Eucharist,
The true life and presence of our Lord …

The *anamnesis* commemorates the sending of the Spirit, followed by an *epiclesis*:

And so, Father,
We remember Christ's death, his resurrection, his ascension,
His sending of the Holy Spirit,
And rejoicing in his presence in the world,
We look for his coming again in glory.
Accept Lord, our sacrifice,
And send on us here
And on this Eucharist
The Holy Spirit of love and peace and strength.[52]

The *epiclesis* was clearly on the agenda.

The Holy Eucharist: An Alternative Canadian Use

The newly constituted Doctrine and Worship Committee was charged with the production of official modern language liturgies as alternatives to those in the *BCP*. A draft revision of the eucharistic rite was eventually authorized in 1975. The rite went through various stages of redrafting during the period 1973-1974. The first draft, dated 24 January 1973, included a 'Thanksgiving and Consecration' prayer with a preliminary *epiclesis* based on the *BCP*:

Father, accept our praise through Jesus and grant that these gifts of bread and wine may be for us his Body and Blood; who at the meal ...

The post-narrative section continued:

HE LIVES AND SO WE LIVE.
HE IS IN THE FATHER AS WE ARE IN HIM,
AND HE IN US.

---

51 Paul Gibson, *Say What You Mean … And Do What You Say* (Department of Religious Education of the Anglican Church in Canada, 1966), p. 48.

52 *Experiment and Liturgy* (Anglican Church of Canada, n.d.), p. 47.

So, Father, we present with this bread and cup his holy life, his saving death, his rising and exaltation to heaven. Transform us and these gifts by your life-giving Word and
Holy Spirit, that we may partake of the holy Bread of eternal life and the Cup of everlasting salvation of our Lord Jesus Christ.
So we proclaim the death of the Lord until he comes.
AMEN.
Lord Jesus
COME.[53]

The verb 'transform' was a bold verb to use as it was without precedent; the Episcopal Church-type invocation of Spirit and Word was also adopted. This text was submitted to the General Synod in May 1973, but returned to the Committee for further work. A new draft prepared by Gordon Baker and William Crockett was presented to the Doctrine and Worship Committee in November 1973. The structure of the eucharistic prayer was significant for the abandonment of a split invocation. The new *epiclesis* text involved a double invocation first on the elements and then on the people:

Sanctify these gifts by your Holy Spirit to be for your people the Body and Blood of your Son.

Sanctify us also that receiving them we may serve you faithfully, be made one Body in your Son, and share in your eternal kingdom.[54]

The form of the *epiclesis* draws heavily on the main eucharistic prayer of the Second Service of *Services for Trial Use/Authorized Services* (1970/73) of the Episcopal Church. The text was further modified in January 1974 when the Very Revd Brian Whitlow's name was added to the two above:

By your Holy Spirit sanctify these gifts that they may be
for your people the Body and Blood of your Son.
Sanctify us also that receiving them we may serve you faithfully,
be made one Body in your Son,
and share the life of your eternal kingdom.[55]

The final form was published in *The Holy Eucharist: An Alternative Canadian Use*, number 4 in the series of booklets, *Canadian Anglican Liturgical Series* (CALS4). From the *anamnesis* the text reads:

Wherefore, O Father, recalling his death, proclaiming his resurrection and ascension, and looking to his coming in glory, we celebrate the memorial of our redemption as we offer this bread and this cup of new and unending life in him. Sanctify these gifts by your Holy Spirit, that they may be for your people the body and blood of your Son. Receiving them, may we serve you faithfully, be made one body in your Son, and share in your eternal kingdom.[56]

53 *Working Draft*, 24 January, 1973.

54 *Holy Eucharist in Contemporary Form: A Working Draft*, November 1973.

55 *A Working Draft,* January 1974.

56 *The Holy Eucharist: An Alternative Canadian Use* (1974), pp. 6-7.

The final text thus avoided the repetition of the verb 'sanctify'. The text was authorized for experimental use by the 1975 General Synod. In a short commentary on the rite, one of its drafters, A. Gordon Baker, comments on the above text as follows:

> There follows the *anamnesis* in which our Lord's command is truly followed: 'We celebrate the memorial of our redemption, and we offer this bread and this cup of new and unending life in him.' In the invocation God is asked to send his Holy Spirit to enable the material gifts of bread and wine to be what Jesus intended them to be – 'a means of participation in and union with his very life.' This phrase by Massey Shepherd in his *Oxford American Prayer Book Commentary* beautifully expresses the purpose of eucharistic worship.[57]

1976-1985: Third Canadian Order *and* The Book of Alternative Services

The next two rounds of eucharistic revision cover the period 1976-81, culminating in the publication of *The Holy Eucharist: Third Canadian Order* (*TCO*), and 1982-85, with the publication of *The Book of Alternative Services* (*BAS*). The process of revision was complicated with many drafts and renumbering of eucharistic prayers; for that reason, it will be convenient to consider both periods together. The Doctrine and Worship Committee began work on the first stage of revision in March 1976. Following the Roman Rite and The Episcopal Church, the Committee decided that various eucharistic prayers should be considered; indeed, they outstripped other Churches and Anglican Provinces by suggesting seven texts:

1. A translation of the eucharistic prayer in the *Apostolic Tradition* attributed to Hippolytus.
2. The 'Ecumenical Canon' being prepared by an ecumenical group of liturgists in the USA.
3. A eucharistic prayer for family celebrations with young children present.
4. The so-called 'Star Trek' eucharistic prayer the Episcopal Church.
5. A 'salvation history' *anaphora*.
6. An 'immanentist' prayer, 'leading from our experience to our knowledge of God'.
7. A text from the 'Eastern Church', probably the *Anaphora* of SS Addai and Mari.[58]

In the end, with the publication of *BAS* in 1985, six prayers were adopted. All of them have an 'Antiochene' shape, with the *epiclesis* following the *anamnesis*.

Prayer 1 (prayer II, *TCO*) draws on *Apostolic Constitutions 8*, and fulfils the desire for a 'salvation history' prayer. The *epiclesis* has the following text:

---

57 A. Gordon Baker, *Do This: An Analysis of the Basic Structure of the Eucharist and How it Relates to Our Culture* (Toronto, 1978), p. 87.

58 *Third Canadian Eucharistic Order: Proposed Shape of the Liturgy*, March 1976.

Send your Holy Spirit upon us
and upon these gifts,
that all who eat and drink at this table
may be one body and one holy people,
a living sacrifice in Jesus Christ, our Lord.[59]

The earlier *TCO* version was nearer to *Apostolic Constitutions* in form:

Send your holy spirit upon us your servants,
and upon the sacrifice of your church,
that we may be a holy people,
united in the body of your Son,
Jesus Christ our Lord.

This revision was probably in response to a change in the text drawing on *Apostolic Tradition* which also includes reference to the 'sacrifice of your church'. *Apostolic Constitutions 8* prays for the sending of the Spirit upon the sacrifice of the Church accompanied by a 'theophany-type' petition that the gifts will be 'shown to be' the body and blood of Christ. It was probably in order to avoid having two texts saying essentially the same thing that Eucharistic prayer 1 adopted the more familiar invocation of the Spirit on the gifts and worshippers.

Prayer 2 (prayer I, *TCO*), is the Canadian recension of the model eucharistic prayer in *Apostolic Tradition*:

We ask you to send your Holy Spirit
upon the offering of your holy Church.
Gather into one
all who share in these sacred mysteries,
filling them with the Holy Spirit
and confirming their faith in the truth,
that together we may praise you
and give you glory
through your Servant, Jesus Christ.[60]

This draws on the ICEL translation and is more faithful to the Latin Verona text of *Apostolic Tradition*. It thus preserves a much more primitive form of the *epiclesis*, not so much as an invocation of the Spirit upon the elements alone as upon the whole eucharistic action. It can be compared with the version in *TCO*:

---

59 *The Book of Alternative Services of the Anglican Church of Canada* (Toronto, 1985), p. 203.

60 Ibid., p. 197. William Crockett commented on prayer 2: 'In the *epiclesis*, the phrase "the offering of your holy Church" does not refer exclusively to the elements but to the eucharistic action as a whole culminating in the act of communion ("all who share in these sacred mysteries") on the analogy of a communion-sacrifice', 'The Theology of the Eucharistic Prayers in *The Book of Alternative Services of the Anglican Church of Canada*', *Toronto Journal of Theology*, 3 (1987): 104.

Send your Holy Spirit on these gifts
that they may be for your people
the body and blood of your Son.
Receiving them, may we be one body in him,
serve you faithfully,
and at the last day come, with all your saints,
into the joy of your eternal kingdom.

This text was significant, because for the first time the strong verb 'send ... on' replaces 'sanctify' in relation to the elements.

Prayer 3 draws on prayer B of Rite II of the 1979 *BCP* of the Episcopal Church:

We pray you, gracious God,
to send your Holy Spirit upon these gifts,
that they may be the sacrament
of the Body of Christ
and his Blood of the new Covenant.
Unite us to your Son in his sacrifice,
that we, made acceptable in him,
may be sanctified by the Holy Spirit.[61]

The adoption of this Episcopal Church prayer provided the solution to a problematic aspect of the revision process. The original prayer 3 was intended to provide a prayer 'in contemporary idiom'. An early draft of the *epiclesis* ran:

Send your Holy Spirit on us and these gifts,
and renew the face of all creation;
Then your Name will be made holy,
O God, our Father,
through Jesus Christ our Lord,
in the fellowship of the Holy Spirit.

A more radical revision was undertaken for the draft of March 1979. The *epiclesis* read:

Send your Holy Spirit on us and these gifts,
that we who eat this bread
and drink this cup
may be one with him in his self-giving,
that through us he may comfort the broken-hearted
and console the mourners,
open the eyes of the blind
and proclaim liberty to the captives;
until justice flows like water
and righteousness like an unfailing stream,
and the city of God is among us.[62]

61 *The Book of Alternative Services of the Anglican Church of Canada*, p. 199.
62 *Third Canadian Eucharistic Order: Fourth Draft*, 5 March 1979.

In May, 1979, however, the National Executive Council of the Church passed a resolution approving the printing of *TCO* with the exception of prayer III. The prayer was referred to the House of Bishops, which upheld the reservations about a number of aspects, including a statement about expectations concerning the nature of the *epiclesis*.[63] The bishops would expect 'An adequate epiclesis for the calling down of the Holy Spirit on ourselves and the gifts that we may be nourished by the body and blood of the Lord and made one body and one spirit with Him'. The issue appears to be the lack of an explicit linking of the invocation to a reference to the body and blood of Christ. The bishops appear to be drawing on liturgical consensus, possibly influenced by the fact that the new forms of the Episcopal Church were being used in Canada following the experimentation allowed by the 1965 General Synod. The prayer of consecration in the *BCP*, of course, did not fulfil this guideline for the *epiclesis*!

Prayer 4 (prayer III, *TCO*) draws on prayer C ('Star Trek') of Rite II of the Episcopal Church. Between 1981 and 1984, the Canadian revisers abandoned the preliminary *epiclesis* of both the Episcopal Church and the *TCO* versions and so brought this text into structural conformity with the other *BAS* texts. By deciding for a single *epiclesis* they were able to bring together the invocation on the elements and the people with the petition for the whole earth:

> We who have been redeemed by him,
> and made a new people by water and the Spirit,
> now bring you these gifts.
> Send your Holy Spirit upon us
> and upon the offering of your Church,
> that we who eat and drink at this holy table
> may share the divine life of Christ our Lord.
> **Glory to you for ever and ever.**
>
> Pour out your Spirit upon the whole earth
> and make it your new creation.
> Gather your Church together
> from the ends of the earth into your kingdom ... [64]

Prayer 5 (prayer IV, *TCO*) is designed 'for families':

> Send your Holy Spirit on us and on these gifts,
> that we may know the presence of Jesus
> in the breaking of the bread,
> and share in the life of the family of your children.
> **Glory to you for ever and ever.**[65]

This can be compared with the *TCO* version:

---

63 This real issue was not so much the *epiclesis*, as the Christology: 'we cannot accept it as an adequate Eucharistic Prayer because we believe that such a prayer should clearly proclaim the saving acts of Our Lord, His resurrection, ascension, and coming again, and our atonement'. House of Bishops Minutes, Oct. 29-Nov. 1, 1979, p. 46.

64 *The Book of Alternative Services of the Anglican Church of Canada*, p. 203.

65 Ibid., p. 206.

Father, you raised Jesus from death to life for us.
Send now your Holy Spirit on us,
and on these gifts which we offer to you.
Give us a share in your life,
that we may live as friends in the joy of your family forever.
We praise you, we bless you, we thank you.

Prayer 6 (prayer V, *TCO*) reproduces the 'Common Eucharistic Prayer' *verbatim*.

The Book of Alternative Services also includes 'The Holy Eucharist – A Form in the Language of the Book of Common Prayer'. The rite includes two eucharistic prayers: prayer A is the 1962 prayer of consecration and prayer B a light revision of the 'Alternative Form of the Great Thanksgiving' from Holy Eucharist I of the *BCP* of the Episcopal Church. The form of supplementary consecration for both rites is:

> We thank you, heavenly Father, for your saving love, and we pray you to bless and sanctify this bread (wine) with your Word and Holy Spirit, that it also may be the sacrament of the precious body (blood) of your Son, our Lord Jesus Christ. **Amen.**[66]

This text is drawn from the Episcopal Church and it is noteworthy for its retention of a double invocation of Word and Spirit. The Canadian form looks back to *Prayer Book Studies XVII* in its omission of any repetition of the eucharistic words of Jesus. While there is no invocation of 'Word and Spirit' in the Canadian main texts of the *epiclesis*, the form enables supplementary consecration to be accomplished by invocation of the Trinity. The text certainly underlines the fact that the institution narrative cannot be considered as a consecratory formula.

The new eucharistic prayers in *The Book of Alternative Services* have provoked a vigorous debate within the Anglican Church of Canada, with particular misgivings from the evangelical section of the Church. During the period of revision, the issues clustered around the theology of the atonement and the question of eucharistic sacrifice. The vast majority of dissenting letters stored in Church archives relate to this question. The criticism of Cranmer's sacrificial theology in the introduction to the eucharistic section of *BAS* is another pointer to the debate, as is the section devoted to sacrifice in *Rites for a New Age: Understanding the Book of Alternative Services* by Michael Ingham.[67] The question of eucharistic sacrifice is also the dominant theme of the essay by William Crockett, one of the drafters of the eucharistic rite, in an essay in the *Toronto Journal of Theology*.[68]

By contrast, criticism of the *epiclesis* seems to have arisen *since* the publication of *BAS*. Again, this is primarily the concern of the evangelical constituency. The *epiclesis* as such is only mentioned in passing in Michael Ingham's book, but the debate can be discerned from a paper, 'The Prayer for the Spirit' by Paul Gibson,

66 Ibid., p. 184.

67 Michael Ingham, *Rites for a New Age* (Toronto, 1986), pp. 57-135.

68 Crockett, 'The Theology of the Eucharistic Prayers in *The Book of Alternative Services of the Anglican Church of Canada*', pp. 100-109.

and by the fact that consecration and the role of the *epiclesis* featured in the first two editions of the publication *Liturgy Canada*.[69]

The major issues appear to cluster around the question of whether the Spirit can be invoked upon material objects. Stephen Reynolds in his article 'Upon us and upon these Gifts' in *Liturgy Canada* casts the objections to a double invocation upon the elements and the worshippers in the following form, before dismantling the argument:

> Such a petition is impossible ... because it is impossible for the Holy Spirit to bless and sanctify mere things. Bread and wine are inanimate creatures, they have no spiritual principle of life. Moreover, they serve only our bodies; they cannot nourish our souls. So asking God to send the Spirit and bless these elements is not only false; it is also useless.[70]

Both he and Paul Gibson defend a double invocation on the eucharistic gifts and the worshippers on the basis that 'there can be no polarization of spirit and matter'.[71] Human beings are fundamentally material entities, intrinsically part of creation. A similar point is make by William Crockett:

> The danger today is that people will fail to connect the acts of sacramental eating and drinking with their bodies and with the earth. We must eat and drink the elements with our bodies as a sign that the goal of the eucharist is the transformation of our entire bodily existence in the world.[72]

Moreover, Stephen Reynolds makes the point that the forms of the *epiclesis* have been worded very carefully; the invocation on the gifts is to a specific end, that the worshippers may be blessed through the material objects.[73] This is certainly true for prayers 1-5.[74] Moreover, prayers 1, 2, 4 and 5 contain no explicit statement that the invocation of the Spirit in any sense 'changes' the bread and wine into Christ's body and blood, and prayer 3 has the restrained Episcopal Church formula that the gifts may be the 'sacrament' of the body and blood. Eucharistic prayers 2 and 4 invoke the Spirit on the 'offering of your (holy) church'. Here the force of the petition appears to be a general invocation of the Spirit upon the *entire* eucharistic action including reception. All of this underlines the fact that the Canadian invocations are strongly related to the communicants and that consecration itself is set in a broad theological context in which there is no question of consecration by formula.

---

69 Stephen Reynolds, 'Consecration of the Eucharist: 1. Prayer and Narrative', *Liturgy Canada* (Epiphany, 1991): 2-7 and '2. Upon Us and Upon These Gifts', *Liturgy Canada* (Easter, 1991): 1, 6-9.

70 Reynolds, 'Upon Us and Upon These Gifts', p. 1.

71 Paul Gibson, 'The Prayer for the Spirit', *Resources for Liturgy* 11 (November, 1987).

72 Crockett, *Eucharist: Symbol of Transformation*, p. 261.

73 Reynolds, 'Upon Us and Upon These Gifts', p. 6.

74 Prayer 6 has a different structure for the *epiclesis*, and is the only completely 'imported' prayer without revision by the Canadian drafters because of its ecumenical pedigree.

The General Synod of 1995 requested eucharistic rites to embrace inclusive language, inculturation and, in the light of evangelical concerns, a 'Reformed theological conscience'. A sub-group of the Faith Worship and Ministry Committee met from 1995 to 1998, and presented three draft eucharistic prayers, rather than complete rites, to the 1998 General Synod, which, after revision in Synod, were authorized for trial use. After further revision, the prayers were approved for use by the House of Bishops and the Council of General Synod, and published in 2001. All three prayers follow the same structure as *BAS* with a single post-narrative *epiclesis*. The first two prayers reflect inclusivity concerns. Supplementary Eucharistic Prayer 1 (S1) responds to questions of inclusive language and imagery and so, echoing the language used in the Episcopal Church, seeks 'to incorporate images of God and God's work in a balanced way', using resources of the Christian tradition 'to expand the language of prayer'.[75] The *epiclesis* employs a new main verb in Canadian usage:

> Breathe your Holy Spirit,
> the wisdom of the universe,
> upon these gifts that we bring to you:
> this bread, this cup,
> ourselves, our souls and bodies,
> that we may be signs of your love for all the world
> and ministers of your transforming purpose.[76]

The verb 'breathe' had appeared in supplemental prayers of the Episcopal Church (Second Supplemental Eucharistic Prayer, 1989; Eucharistic Prayer 2, 1991), where Genesis 2:7 is cited as the biblical background (the Hebrew *ruach* means both 'breath' and 'spirit'), although no reference is made to John 20:22 and so a link between creation and the new creation. The phrase 'the wisdom of the universe' is expounded by Kevin Flynn thus:

> The Spirit as 'wisdom of the universe' is an evocation of those texts, especially in the deuterocanonical books of Wisdom and Sirach, in which *Hokmah* (Hebrew), or *Sophia* (Greek), appears to have characteristics and qualities associated with the Spirit. This appealing feminine figure creates and vivifies the natural world (Genesis 1:2; Judith 16:14; Proverbs 8:22-31) and is at work, as well, in human history. She is at work in salvation, leading slaves to freedom (Wisdom 10:15), establishing justice and teaching life-giving ways to receptive mortals (Wisdom 7:27-29; 8:7; Proverbs 8:1-21).[77]

This *epiclesis*, like those in prayers 1, 2, 4 and 5 of *BAS*, does not explicitly mention the body and blood of Christ, but employs the language of transformation, where new creation is implied.

---

75 General Synod, 1998: *Supplementary Liturgical Material*, p. 1.

76 *Eucharistic Prayers, Services of the Word, and Night Prayer: Supplementary to The Book of Alternative Services* (Toronto, 2001), p. 16.

77 Kevin Flynn, 'The Work of the Spirit and the Work of the People (Part III)', *Liturgy Canada* (Lent 2002), cited from a transcript.

Supplementary Eucharistic Prayer 2 (S2) is based on the tradition of lament in Scripture; the 1998 Synod report states that it seeks to respond to times 'when praise is difficult: times of anger, frustration, disappointment, and loss', and then needs of groups 'who feel alienated from God or the Church'.[78] Such concerns are reflected in the *epiclesis*:

> Pour out your Spirit on these gifts
> that through them you may sustain us
> in our hunger for your peace.
> We hold before you
> all those whose lives are marked by suffering,
> our sisters and brothers.
> When we are broken and cast aside,
> embrace us in your love.
> **Restore us, O God, let your face shine!**[79]

Like S1, the text includes no reference to Christ's body and blood, and so is not in that sense directly 'consecratory', and the image of 'hunger' naturally relates to *physical* eating and drinking.

Supplementary Eucharistic Prayer 3 (S3) is the text written from a 'Reformed' perspective. It has an explicit invocation on the worshippers, employing the more 'receptionist' language of the Prayer Book tradition:

> Send your Holy Spirit on us
> that as we receive this bread and this cup
> we may partake of the body and blood
> of our Lord Jesus Christ,
> and feed on him in our hearts
> by faith with thanksgiving.[80]

An earlier draft sought to broaden the scope of the invocation:

> Send your Holy Spirit on this meal we share,
> granting that we who receive this bread and this cup,
> may partake of the body and blood of our Lord Jesus Christ
> and feed on him in our hearts …

This was rejected by the 1998 Synod on the basis that the 'meal' by definition includes the eucharistic elements, although the text itself seeks to relates the gift of the Spirit to the whole *action*. Evangelical unease about an invocation of the Spirit on material objects was not therefore entirely met by the draft text.[81] The 1998 Synod report

78 General Synod, 1998: *Supplementary Liturgical Material*, p. 1.

79 Ibid., p. 19.

80 Ibid., p. 22.

81 The point was made in Synod by Archbishop David Crawley that such a 'Reformed' prayer had been asked for and so the text should be one that could in good conscience be prayed, 'Whither the Canon?: Reflections on the Development of Canadian Eucharistic Prayers', *Liturgy Canada*, 6/3 (1998): 7.

sets out an understanding of the term 'Reformed', relating it historically to Calvin, and to the Thirty-Nine Articles 'generally regarded as consonant with, and perhaps historically inspired by, Reformed doctrine'. Five criteria were set out reflecting Reformed Eucharistic theology, the last of which states: '(5) claims should not be made for the physical elements of bread of wine which obscure the truth that God is at work in all creation'.

This somewhat opaque statement seems to relate to evangelical concerns about an explicit invocation on the elements. The two issues are whether the Spirit *can*, as a matter of theological principle, be invoked on inanimate objects, and the understanding of the mode of Christ's presence in the eucharist. The divisions over eucharistic sacrifice in the formation of *BAS* revealed a concern to defend the Reformed theology of the Prayer Book. If the locus of the presence of Christ is deemed to be in the heart of the believer then there will be a natural distrust of anything that is interpreted as drawing too much attention to the elements. By contrast, there is no such problem when the Spirit is invoked on the worshippers or indeed with a petition that the worshippers will enjoy a fruitful communion.

There can be no doubt, however, that throughout the whole process of liturgical renewal in Canada since the 1970s, in the minds of the Canadian drafters, the eucharistic prayer is a single prayer, that there is no specific 'moment' of consecration and that the epicletic texts need to be interpreted in the context of the whole eucharistic action. Canada, perhaps more than any other Province of the Anglican Communion, has genuinely sought to be creative and innovative here with a rich epicletic theology as expounded by William Crockett in *Eucharist: Symbol of Transformation*.

Conclusion

A perusal of the American and Canadian canons in Bernard Wigan's *The Liturgy in English*, reveals, in the early 1960s, both common roots in the English Prayer Book tradition, but also significant divergences. The American prayer has a consecratory *epiclesis*, the Canadian form a communion *epiclesis*. By the turn of the twenty-first century, and not withstanding some further, particularly structural, divergences since, there are signs of a growing *convergence* in North America. A number of factors have been influential. The impact of the 'Lima Text', and ecumenical dialogue through ARCIC, between Anglicans and Lutherans, and the remarkably common approach to liturgical renewal as witnessed in the published prayer books of the historic denominations, including Methodists and Presbyterians, has been immense. *BEM* in particular has encouraged a consciously Trinitarian approach to the eucharistic prayer through its exposition of the eucharist as thanksgiving to the Father, *anamnesis* of Christ and invocation of the Spirit. The applied exposition of eucharist as the communion of the faithful and the meal of the kingdom has enabled development of diverse epicletic formulae freed of the narrow constraints of a petition for consecration, still less as encapsulating a 'moment' of consecration, as the Canadian texts in particular reveal. This breadth of expression has also been enabled through the acceptance of multiple eucharistic prayers. Thomas Talley's seminal work on the model of 'thanksgiving–supplication', so closely related to

Trinitarian shape, and the IALC 'Dublin Statement' have commended a liturgical spirituality which embraces the preface, post-*sanctus*, institution narrative and *anamnesis* under the 'deep structure' of 'thanksgiving', and *epiclesis*, intercession and petition for fruitful reception under 'deep structure' of 'supplication'. This has brought a welcome clarity and logic to the shape of the eucharistic prayer. While the two Churches do not as yet have uniformity of structure, the principles are well enunciated and inform ongoing revision. More recently, explorations in expansive language with some experimentation in new forms of epicletic text are evident, even if such supplemental forms of prayer are still at an interim stage.

Chapter 9

The Anglican Communion: Case Study 2: The Churches of the Indian Subcontinent

Historical Background

A Liturgy for India

The first Anglican bishopric in India was established at Calcutta in 1814. For the first century of their life, Anglican Churches used the *Book of Common Prayer*, 1662. The first suggestions for the revision of the eucharistic liturgy came in 1920. The liturgy was published in order for it to be considered at the 1920 Lambeth Conference in a book entitled *The Eucharist in India: A Plea for a Distinctive Liturgy for the Indian Church with a Suggested Form.*[1] The rite was unashamedly eastern in character, mainly because of the presence of the Syrian Church of Malabar in India whose liturgy, while not indigenous to India, nevertheless 'had been acclimatised to the soil of India for several centuries'.[2] The basic model for the *anaphora* was the Syriac version of the *anaphora* of St James. It thus conformed to the classical West Syrian shape. A table of sources at the end of the book confirms that the *epiclesis* is a considerably abridged version of Syriac St James.[3] The text of the *epiclesis* is as follows:

> *Then the Deacon shall give warning to the people, saying*:
> How fearful is this hour, O my brethren, how aweful is this time, wherein the holy and quickening Spirit descends and moves upon our Eucharist to the hallowing thereof. Let us fall and prostrate ourselves with fear and trembling.
> *And therewith they shall all fall prostrate with their faces to the ground, and shall so continue at least until the prayer following be ended. And the people being thus prostrate, the Priest shall say secretly or in a low tone the Invocation of the Holy Spirit:*
> SHEW thou thy mercy upon us, O Lord, and upon these thy gifts of bread and wine send down thy Holy Spirit, that by his power they may become unto us the Body and Blood of thy Son, our Saviour Jesus Christ, and may hallow the spirits, the souls, and the bodies of all who partake of them, to the bringing forth of the fruit of good works and to the strengthening of thy Church upon the rock of faith; (*and in a loud voice*) through the same Jesus Christ, thy Son, our Lord, to whom with thee and the Holy Spirit be all honour and glory, world without end. Amen.
> *Then shall silence be kept for a space, the people worshipping.*

---

1 J.C. Winslow, J.E.G. Festing, Dr Athavale and E.C. Ratcliff, *The Eucharist in India* (London, 1920).

2 CIPBC, *Principles of Prayer Book Revision*, p. 82.

3 Ibid., p. 113.

J.C. Winslow underlined the importance of the *epiclesis* as the 'culminating moment of the Consecration', followed by the prostration of the people in adoration. He criticized the association of the consecration with the dominical words on the grounds that it 'almost inevitably conveys the suggestion of a magic formula, whereas the prayer to the Holy Spirit to sanctify the Gifts to our use is free from this suggestion'.[4] The prostration 'in adoring contemplation of the Mystery in which the Holy Spirit moves upon our Sacrament to make it the means of our participation in the Divine Life' was also deemed to give expression to the mystical and contemplative strand in Indian spirituality.[5]

The 1920 Lambeth Conference accepted the principle that liturgical uniformity was not to be regarded as a necessity for churches in the 'Mission Field'.[6] The Lambeth committee of liturgical experts judged that the rite conformed to the essentials for a service in use in the Anglican Communion. After revision, the Episcopal Synod of India authorized the new liturgy with minor emendations for experimental use in the Diocese of Bombay in 1922 and published it in 1923.[7] As well as revising the English generally, the 1922 recension modified the deacon's bidding before the *epiclesis*,[8] omitted the direction that it should be said 'secretly or in a low tone', and emended the text of the *epiclesis* itself to include an explicit invocation on the worshippers as well as the elements:

> SHEW us thy mercy, we pray thee, O Lord, and upon us and upon these gifts here set before thee send down thy Holy Spirit, that by his power this bread and wine may become unto us the Bo+dy and the Bl+ood of thy Son, our Saviour Jesus Christ, and may hallow the spirits ...[9]

In March 1930, the Churches under the Metropolitical See of Calcutta gained their autonomy from the Church of England as the Church of India, Burma and Ceylon (CIBC). The English 1928 services were authorized for use and in 1933 the 'Bombay Liturgy' was authorized for use in other dioceses within the newly autonomous Church subject to the permission of the individual bishop. The liturgy went through a minor revision in 1942 and a more extensive revision in 1947. It was published in 1948 as *An Order for the Administration of the Holy Communion Commonly Known as the Indian Liturgy*.[10] In his foreword, Bishop Noel Chota Nagpur commented that

---

4 Winslow *et al.*, *The Eucharist in India*, p. 11.

5 Ibid., pp. 11-12.

6 *Conference of Bishops of the Anglican Communion* (London, 1920), resolution 35, pp. 36, 88.

7 *An Order for the Administration of the Holy Communion Sanctioned by the Episcopal Synod of India For Experimental Use in the Diocese of Bombay in Places Selected by the Bishop of Bombay* (London, 1923). Because of this use in Bombay, Bernard Wigan dubbed the rite 'The Bombay Liturgy', ibid., p. 94.

8 'How solemn, O my brethren, is this time, wherein we implore the holy and quickening Spirit to descend and hallow this our Eucharist. Let us fall and worship in holy fear', ibid., p. 27.

9 Ibid., p. 28.

10 *An Order for the Administration of the Holy Communion Known as the Indian Liturgy* (London and Bombay, 1948). During the course this revision, the Church of India lost

experience confirmed that the rite was 'too eclectic'. The present revision sought to adhere more closely to St James 'so as to bring it into line with the worship of the Churches of Malabar which reject the papal allegiance'.[11] This was deemed to be important as a concordat with the Mar Thoma Church had established eucharistic hospitality between the Churches. However, the bishop acknowledged that the rite was marginal in its use. The text of the *epiclesis* was very similar in substance to 1922; the rubric requiring the prostration of the people was abandoned; the rubric requiring silence for worship after the invocation was retained.[12]

The later report of a Select Committee of the CIPBC, entitled *Principles of Prayer Book Revision*, comments on the 'Indian Liturgy': 'But it has to be acknowledged that the hopes entertained by the compilers of the Liturgy have remained largely unfulfilled; it is regularly used only in a very few parishes, all within the Diocese of Bombay, and is in no sense generally used even in that Diocese.'[13] A main reason for this, the report continued, was the suggestion that the rite implied

> a doctrine of the eucharistic Presence which is not held by a large number of Anglicans. For instance, the Indian Liturgy reproduces those expressions of awe and fear in the presence of the eucharistic sacrifice which have been characteristic of the Liturgy of St James since the days of St Cyril of Jerusalem and specially associates such language with the moment when the Holy Spirit is invoked.[14]

The Ceylon Liturgy

The Ceylon Liturgy was first authorized for experimental use by the Episcopal Synod in 1933, having been approved by the Colombo Diocesan Synod in September 1932. It was approved for general use in 1938. W.K. Lowther Clarke commented on the 1932 draft rite that it would be condemned by extreme 'Westernizers' as a hybrid of east and west. He continued, 'But if ever conflation is justifiable it is in India where the Anglican Communion and the Syrian Church of Malabar work side by side as two non-Roman Episcopal Communions.'[15] The rite was well received in Ceylon. The *epiclesis* was clearly dependent on the Scottish Liturgy and rather less on the 1928 English form:

> And we beseech thee, most merciful Father, to hear us, and to send thy Holy Spirit upon us and upon these thy gifts, that they, being blessed and hallowed by his life-giving power, may be unto us the Body and Blood of thy most dearly beloved Son, to the end that we, receiving the same, may be sanctified both in body and soul, and preserved unto life everlasting. **Amen.**[16]

---

its southern dioceses to the newly formed Church of South India.

11 Ibid., p. vi.

12 Ibid., p. 22.

13 CIPBC, *Principles of Prayer Book Revision*, p. 84.

14 Ibid.

15 W.K. Lowther Clarke, 'The Ceylon Liturgy', *Theology*, 26 (1933): 101.

16 *The Ceylon Liturgy: An Order for the Administration of the Holy Communion* (Madras, 1938), pp. 15-16.

Dr N. Francis Wickremesinghe comments on a matter of ceremonial:

> In this liturgy, in ceremonially inclined parishes, during the epiclesis the President waves his hands up and down over the elements like the fluttering wings of a dove, and soon after the second 'Amen' the people prostrate and adore. This was a ceremonial act introduced by the late Metropolitan of the C.I.P.B.C. (the late Dr. Lakdasa De Mel) when he was a priest in the thirties and the action continues to date.[17]

The 'Order for a Second Consecration' required the repletion of the narrative and the *epiclesis*.[18]

The 1960 Prayer Book of the Church of India, Pakistan, Burma, and Ceylon.[19]

In 1945, the Episcopal Synod instructed its Liturgical Committee to prepare a new Prayer Book. A *Proposed Book* was presented to Synod in 1951. It included three communion services: 1662, the 'Indian Liturgy' as revised in 1948 and a revision of 1928. *A Proposed Prayer Book* was duly published in 1952.[20] Geoffrey Cuming commented on the 1928-type rite as follows:

> ... the order is the same as that in 1928, except that the Prayer of Humble Access immediately precedes the Communion. The Prayer of Consecration follows that of Ceylon in beginning 'Holy in truth art thou ...' as suggested by Frere, but resembles the South African Prayer in retaining what Frere called the 'intruded clause' ('Hear us, O merciful Father ...').[21]

The result was that the new 1951 canon had a double invocation, the first as in 1662 before the narrative of institution and the second after the *anamnesis* and petition for the acceptance on high of the sacrifice of praise and thanksgiving:

> And we most humbly beseech thee, most merciful Father, to send down thy holy and life-giving Spirit upon us and these thy gifts, that they may be unto us the Body and Blood of thy most dearly beloved Son; entirely desiring thy fatherly goodness to accept upon thy heavenly altar this our sacrifice of praise and thanksgiving, that by the merits and death of the same thy Son ...[22]

This canon was further revised in 1954, omitting the first invocation and substituting for the second a form adapted from the 1950 liturgy of the Church of South India:

> And we humbly beseech thee, most merciful Father, to send down thy holy and life-giving Spirit upon us and upon these thy gifts, that the Bread which we break may be the communion of the Body of Christ and the Cup which we bless may be the communion of his Blood; and grant that all who are partakers of this Holy Communion may be fulfilled

---

17 From personal correspondence.

18 *The Ceylon Liturgy*, p. 21.

19 'Pakistan' was added to the title in 1947.

20 *A Proposed Prayer Book* (Madras, Delhi and Lahore, 1952).

21 Geoffrey Cuming, Review of *A Proposed Book for the Church of India, Pakistan, Burma and Ceylon*, *Theology*, 56 (1953): 428.

22 *A Proposed Prayer Book*, p. 341.

> with thy grace and heavenly benediction, and made one body in thy Son, our Saviour Jesus Christ. *Amen.*

This was in response to evangelical objections that the earlier text taught an objective change in the substance of the elements. On the revision, Kenneth Sansbury commented, 'the Epiclesis is thus clearly a petition for the fruits of a right communion and not a form of consecration'.[23] The Episcopal Synod then met at Deolali in June 1955, and in the light of criticisms received by diocesan liturgical committees, the Synod agreed to include controversial items in a supplementary book. Thus, the 'Indian Liturgy' was relegated to the supplement;[24] 1662 and the new order were included in the 'standard' book.

Because of the process of Prayer Book revision being undertaken by the Church, the Archbishop of Canterbury invited the Church to write a report for the 1958 Lambeth Conference. This was duly published as *Principles of Prayer Book Revision.* The report did not include the lack of *epiclesis* of the Spirit in the list of deficiencies in 1662.[25] It also surveyed subsequent Anglican revisions but without evaluation.[26] However, it did face the question of whether the inclusion of an *epiclesis* involved a deviation from Anglican standards. The report required the liturgical expression of a definite consecration of the elements and was worried by a view 'that the whole action is a consecratory process in which Priest and people are dependent throughout on the Almighty Power of God'.[27] On the other hand it acknowledged that the 1928 English canon was regarded by many as 'a departure from the tradition of the Church of England since the days of Augustine' and that an *epiclesis* of this type ought 'to be recognized frankly as involving doctrinal change'.[28] It also asserted that many anglo-catholics and evangelicals regarded a view of the Holy Spirit as transforming inanimate objects to be unscriptural so that an 'Epiclesis which attributes to His agency the uniting of the faithful with Christ through the sacramental means is consequently much more easily defensible than one which invokes His power on the elements for the purpose of effecting a mysterious change in them'.[29] It also acknowledged that conversionist language was more readily associated with the *epiclesis* than the older theory of sanctification through thanksgiving. To balance this, the report cited John Dowden's exposition of eighteenth-century Scottish Episcopalian divines who held a virtualist view of the eucharist so that 'there is no necessary connection between Conversionist notions and the adoption of an Oriental type of Epiclesis'.[30]

---

23 C. Sansbury, 'Recent Anglican Revisions of the Eucharistic Prayer', *Theology*, 59 (1956): 285.

24 *The Supplement to the Book of Common Prayer* (Madras, Delhi and Lahore, 1961). The rite includes forms for the blessing of all kinds of inanimate objects.

25 *Principles of Prayer Book Revision*, p. 37.

26 Ibid., pp. 44-45.

27 Ibid., p. 52.

28 Ibid.

29 Ibid.

30 Ibid., p. 53.

Not surprisingly, therefore, the report came to no firm conclusion on the *epiclesis* although it interpreted the CIPBC text as essentially a petition for the Spirit to confer the benefits of communion.[31] Its conclusion was as follows:

> There is a considerable cleavage of opinion in this Province as to whether the Liturgy should include an Epiclesis or not, and if it does what should be its nature. One group, particularly those accustomed to the Ceylon or Indian Liturgies, sees it not only as a valuable link with the Eastern Church but also as a practice which conforms to the presuppositions of the relation of the divine presence to the physical world implicit in the invocation to the Holy Spirit to consecrate the eucharistic gifts by His illapse upon them. Another group who regard the essential act of consecrating as the Thanksgiving and the recitation of the Dominical Words of Institution believe that the Holy Spirit can only rightly be invoked on people. They would prefer either to have an Epiclesis on the people, or no Epiclesis at all. A third group would allow an Epiclesis on the people and the gifts outside the Canon, preferably at the Offertory, so that the people and the gifts are set apart in the power of the Holy Spirit to offer the sacrifice of Praise and Thanksgiving.
>
> These diverse views have very deep psychological roots in the apprehension of God and His indwelling in His creation. They are characteristic of the Eastern Church and the Western Church respectively. But it is evident that these differences are not exclusively to be attributed to theological or liturgical traditions only: they are seated in men's deepest self-consciousness as human beings in relation to God.[32]

The new *BCP* was thus finally published in January 1960.[33] While the eucharistic prayer of the 1960 order included differences from 1954 (notably in the *anamnesis*), the *epiclesis* was the form accepted in 1954 (as above).[34]

Ecumenical Churches in Communion

The fruits of the ecumenical movement led to the formation of new ecumenical Churches involving Anglicans from the Indian subcontinent.

The Church of South India

The Church of South India was formed in 1947 upon the union of Anglicans, Methodists and the South India United Church (Presbyterians and Congregationalists). The 1948 General Synod set up a Liturgical Committee which presented a draft eucharistic liturgy in 1950. The Synod authorized it and a slight revision was made in 1954. The 1950/54 rite was revolutionary in its day, as the first service to incorporate Gregory Dix's thesis on the fourfold shape of the ministry of the sacrament, and its advocacy of the westward position, the kiss of peace and congregational acclamations in the

31 Ibid., p. 52.

32 Ibid., p. 72.

33 *The Book of Common Prayer and Administration of the Sacraments According to the Use of the Church of India, Pakistan, Burma and Ceylon* (Madras, Delhi and Lahore, 1963). The text of the *epiclesis* is on p. 368.

34 According to Church law, the Book was confirmed at the 1963 Synod.

eucharistic prayer. The eucharistic prayer had a West Syrian structure, as a point of identity with the Indian Syrian Churches. The text of the *epiclesis* ran:

> And we most humbly beseech thee, O merciful Father, to sanctify with thy Holy Spirit us and these thine own gifts of bread and wine, that the bread which we break may be the communion of the body of Christ, and the cup which we bless the communion of the blood of Christ. Grant that being joined together in him, we may all attain to the unity of the faith, and may grow up in all things unto him who is the Head, even Christ, our Lord ... [35]

The *epiclesis* alludes to 1 Corinthians 10:16 and Ephesians 4:13, 15 (although neither text is about the Holy Spirit), and T.S. Garrett suggested the liturgies of the Church of Scotland and the United Church of Canada were sources.[36] The position also conformed to the rites of the Orthodox Churches in India and the *Ceylon Liturgy*. The Presbyterian tradition is clearly the primary influence here. Garrett rejects any notion of the *epiclesis* as constituting a 'moment of consecration'; the root idea of consecration is 'setting apart for holy use and consists in the whole movement of the liturgy from Offertory to Communion, made by a congregation which has been prepared for this movement by confession of sins and the hearing of God's Word'.[37] The *epiclesis* remained unchanged in successive booklets published from 1950 to 1962 and in a further edition incorporated in *The Book of Common Worship* published in 1963.[38]

One further significant feature of the editions of the C.S.I. eucharistic rite from 1950 to 1963 was the prayer of invocation said by the presbyter and people immediately before the eucharistic prayer:

> Be present, be present, O Jesus, thou good High Priest, as thou wast in the midst of thy disciples, and make thyself known to us in the breaking of the bread, who livest and reignest with the Father and the Holy Spirit, one God, world without end.[39]

H. Boone Porter has researched the background to this prayer. The immediate source for the South Indian rendering is William Bright's *Ancient Collects* (8th edition, 1908) where Bright's text reads:

> Be present, be present, Jesus, Good High Priest, in the midst of us, as Thou wast in the midst of Thy disciples. Sanctify this oblation.[40]

---

35 *The Service of the Lord's Supper or the Holy Eucharist* (London, 1950), p. 13.

36 T.S. Garrett, *The Liturgy of the Church of South India*, 2nd ed. (London, 1954), p. 64. See the *Book of Common Order of the Church of Scotland* (London, 1940), p. 119. The United Church of Canada was formed by the union of Methodists and Presbyterians; see the *Book of Common Order of the United Church of Canada* (Toronto, 1932), p. 80. The second edition, published in 1950, contained an identical invocation.

37 Garrett, *The Liturgy of the Church of South India*, p. 64. The rite made optional provision for supplementary consecration which did not include an *epiclesis*, ibid., p. viii.

38 *The Book of Common Worship* (London, 1963), pp. 16-17. For the historical background, see Robert Gribben, 'The Formation of the Liturgy of the Church of South India', *Studia Liturgica*, 30 (2000): 129-142.

39 1950 edition, p. 11.

40 H. Boone Porter, 'Be Present, Be Present', *Studia Liturgica*, 21 (1991): 158-159.

Porter further argues that the ultimate source of the prayer was Mozarabic as a petition for consecration before the narrative of institution at a time when 'increasing emphasis was given to the words of Christ at the Last Supper'.[41] The South Indian form omits any reference to 'sanctify this oblation' and Porter does not discuss the relationship of this invocation of Christ to the South Indian *epiclesis*.

A revised version of *The Lord's Supper* was authorized in 1972. The eucharistic prayer follows the same structure as 1950/60, but the text of the *epiclesis* is recast thus:

> And we humbly ask you, Father, to take us and this bread and wine that we offer to you, and make them your own by your Holy Spirit, so that our breaking of the bread will be a sharing in Christ's body and the cup we bless a sharing in his blood. Join us all together in him. Make us one in faith. Help us to grow up as one body, with Jesus as our head. And let us all together, in the Holy Spirit, bring glory to you ...[42]

A new inculturated liturgy was authorized for experimental use by the CSI Synod Executive Committee in 1985. It was written by the Revd Dr Eric J. Lott and the Revd Dr Christopher Duraisingh, and lightly revised by the Executive Committee. The rite is radical both as an example of an inculturated liturgy and in its treatment of the eucharistic action. For example, there is no eucharistic prayer as such, but rather a series of units:

- *Saranam* in the Triune God (a Trinitarian invocation) or the *sanctus*.
- *Nama-Smarana* or *Nama-Jeba* (or recital of the names of God that serve to recall the dramatic acts of divine redemption).
- The 'Redemption Prayer' (including narrative of institution).
- The 'Bread Prayer' (*anamnesis* and supplication).[43]

There are two main epicletic references. The first comes before the above sequence, in a section of the rite concerned with the presentation of offerings:

> Let us now bring our offerings to God as signs of our self-giving praying for God's Spirit to transform us and our gifts.[44]

The role of the Spirit as transformer is reiterated in the third petition of the '*Saranam* in the Triune God':

> L: The transforming Spirit is with us to bless us.
> P: **Saranam, Saranam, Saranam.**[45]

41 Ibid., p. 161.

42 *The Lord's Supper or the Holy Eucharist* (1972), p. 36. For comments on this and the 1985 rite, see Thomas Samuel, Jr, 'Some Reflections on the Church of South India Liturgy since 1961', *Studia Liturgica*, 30 (2000): 143-150.

43 *Church of South India Liturgy: The Holy Eucharist (An Alternative Version)* (Madras, 1985), pp. 14-16.

44 Ibid., p. 12.

45 Ibid., p. 14.

The second reference comes at the end of 'The bread prayer' and is said (or sung) by the whole congregation:

L: And grant to all the faithful departed a share in your bliss that with them we too at the end may be welcomed into your eternal kingdom through your inexhaustible grace, through the guidance of your indwelling Spirit.
P: **Sanctify us, sanctify this bread, sanctify this wine, so that together we may be the body of Christ.**
Or
Spirit of the living God, fall afresh upon us (*chorus-sung*)[46]

This congregational element was not in the original form of the rite, as drafted by Dr Lott and Dr Duraisingh, but was added by the Synod Committee.[47] The inclusion was clearly to heighten the epicletic aspect of the rite, perhaps not surprisingly in view of the liturgical tradition of the CSI. The alternative forms show, however, differing understandings of *epiclesis*: the first is an invocation on the worshippers and the elements, the second on the worshippers alone. However, it would be a mistake to isolate the epicletic texts, for the rite was intended to reflect aspects of Indian spirituality, including an understanding of the whole rite as a meditation on divine grace and as an act of invocation. While the original drafters were not opposed to the addition to the 'bread prayer' they would resist any emphasis on specific 'moments'; invocation is intrinsic to the whole. Thus the rite begins with a rite of *Pravesa* or 'entry into the presence of God' followed by *Prabodha* or 'awakening to the presence of God'. The prayers are intended to make explicit the link between God's presence in worship and his presence in the world, and in this part of the rite, the symbol of that presence is a lighted oil lamp. In the main eucharistic action, as well as the texts invoking the Spirit, the epicletic nature of the rite is expressed immediately before reception, the new position for an adapted form of the 'Be present' prayer, styled 'Prayer for *Darsana*' or 'inner vision':

L: Risen Lord, be present.
P: **Be present, even though we are unworthy for you to come to us. Only your peaceful presence can nourish us in faith, bind us together in love, and fill us with hope, so that we might share in your service. Amen.**[48]

---

46 Ibid., p. 16. The full text of the chorus is not given, but the most common version is:

Spirit of the living God, fall afresh on us.
Spirit of the living God, fall afresh on us.
Break us, melt us, mould us, fill us.
Spirit of the living God, fall afresh on us

47 The original version is given in Eric J. Lott (ed.), *Worship in an Indian Context* (Bangalore, 1986) pp. 68-77, with a short introduction. Dr Lott expounds the rite in greater depth in an essay, 'Faith and Culture in Interaction: The Alternative C.S.I. Liturgy', in S. Clarke (ed.), *Reflections* (Madras, 1989), pp. 120-140. I am grateful to Dr Lott for supplying background information to this rite.

48 *Church of South India Liturgy: The Holy Eucharist (An Alternative Version)*, p. 17. The rite makes no provision for supplementary consecration.

The most recent round of liturgical revision was inaugurated in 1994, culminating in the authorization of a new edition of *The Book of Common Worship* in 2004. 'An Order for the Lord's Supper' includes three eucharistic prayers (the Great Thanksgiving). The first is a recasting of the 1950/60 prayer in contemporary idiom. The *epiclesis* runs:

> And we most humbly ask you, O merciful God, to sanctify with your Holy Spirit us and these your own gifts of bread and wine, that the bread which we break may be the communion of the body of Christ, and the cup which we bless the communion of the blood of Christ. Grant that, being joined together in him, we may all attain to the unity of faith, and may grow up [in, *sic*] all things, unto him who is the Head, even Christ our Lord...[49]

The second draws on the 1985 experimental rite, but adapted as a single eucharistic prayer with the structure:

Saranam in the Triune God (responsory equivalent to *sursum corda*)
Institution narrative (formerly 'The Redemption Prayer', with congregational responses)
Anamnesis (formerly 'The Bread Prayer', part 1, remembering the poor and oppressed and praying for liberation)
Memorial acclamations
Further supplication and prayer for the departed (formerly 'The Bread Prayer', part 2)
Congregational *epiclesis* and Amen.

The congregational *epiclesis* is identical to 1985, although the alternative chorus 'Spirit of the living God' is omitted and 'Amen' added.[50] The third prayer is based on creation themes. It has a single *epiclesis*, following the institution narrative and congregational memorial acclamations (but no other anamnetic material), and continues:

> Eternal God, let your Holy Spirit move in power over us and over these earthly gifts of bread and wine, that they may be the communion of the body and blood of Christ, and that we may become one in him. May his coming in glory find us ever watchful in prayer, strong in truth and love, and faithful in the breaking of the bread. Then, at last, all peoples will be free, all divisions healed, and with your whole creation, we will sing your praise, through your Son, Jesus Christ.[51]

This part of the prayer is taken in its entirety from Great Thanksgiving E from the Service for the Lord's Day from the *Book of Common Worship* of the Presbyterian Church (USA) and the Cumberland Presbyterian Church.[52] The rite retains the 'Be present' prayer, immediately preceding the Great Thanksgiving.

---

49 *The Book of Common Worship* (2004), pp. 16-17.

50 Ibid., pp. 17-18.

51 Ibid., p. 18; this prayer alone also appears in 'A Short Order for the Lord's Supper', ibid., pp. 24-32.

52 *Book of Common Worship* (Louisville and London, 1993), p. 145. The rest of Prayer E is adapted from the 1984 ICEL Eucharistic Prayer, text 1.

The Church of North India

The Church of North India (CNI) was formed in November 1970, incorporating dioceses from the CIPBC as well as Baptists, Brethren, Disciples of Christ, Methodists and the United Church of North India (mainly Congregationalists and Presbyterians). The new Church appointed a Liturgical Commission and the first edition of *An Order for the Lord's Supper or Holy Communion* appeared in 1973.[53] Series 3 of the Church of England was very influential although such Reformed emphases as the reading of the narrative of institution as a warrant were incorporated. The 1973 CNI liturgy follows Series 3 almost verbatim for both the preliminary and second *epiclesis*:

> Accept our praises, heavenly Father, through your Son, our Saviour Jesus Christ; and as we follow his example and obey his command, grant that by the power of your Spirit these gifts of bread and wine may be to us the body and blood of him who died for us and rose again;
>
> ... and as we eat and drink these holy gifts in the presence of your divine majesty, renew us by your Spirit, inspire us with your love, and unite us in the body of your Son, Jesus Christ our Lord.[54]

The rite has been through successive editions between 1974 and 1987, without change to the epicletic sections.

In 1983 *An Alternative Order for the Lord's Supper or Holy Communion* was authorized by the Synod Executive Committee. This rite had first been drawn up in 1979, and a second edition appeared in 1988. The sub-title of the 1988 edition reads 'A Recommended Outline for a celebration of the Lord's Supper in which a set text is not used'. As the subtitle suggests, the rite is a series of rubrics giving structure and coaching about content but no actual text. The section on the eucharistic prayer reads:

> He [the Presbyter] offers a **Prayer of Thanksgiving and Invocation** in traditional or modern language. The prayer should include joyful commemoration of all God's mighty acts, in creation, in the incarnation, death and resurrection of Christ, and in the gift of the Spirit, and a prayer that the Holy Spirit may bless us and our gifts of Bread and Wine so that they may be to us the Body and the Blood of Christ, who died for us and rose again.
>
> Where the Scripture Warrant has not already been read, the Lord's words instituting the Sacrament should also be included in this prayer.[55]

---

53 The background to the formation of the Church and its liturgy are given by Colin Buchanan in *MAL*, pp. 264-265.

54 *An Order for the Lord's Supper or The Holy Eucharist* (Delhi, 1990), pp. 21-22.

55 *An Alternative Order for the Lord's Supper or Holy Communion* (Delhi, 1988), p. 5.

The Book of Worship was finally published in 1995, incorporating both the above orders, the rubric in the Alternative Order being amended to 'He/she offers **a Prayer of Thanksgiving and Invocation'**.[56]

The Church of Pakistan

The Church of Pakistan was also inaugurated in 1970 with the union of Anglicans, United Methodists, United Presbyterians and the Pakistan Lutheran Church. The Liturgical Commission produced an experimental rite in 1974,[57] incorporating the 1950 CSI eucharistic prayer and the 'Be present' prayer, styled in the instructions as 'for the Real Presence'.[58] The most recent English revision, entitled *Order for the Lord's Supper also Called the Eucharist (Thanksgiving)* was authorized in March 1986 by the Bishop of Karachi. The eucharistic prayer does not include an *epiclesis*; rather, at the presentation of the gifts, the prayer of the veil (characteristic of the Presbyterian tradition) is followed by a re-working of 'Be present':

> Be present, be present, O Jesus, great High Priest, as you were with your disciples, and make yourself known to us in the breaking of the bread. By your Holy Spirit sanctify us, and this bread and wine that they may become for us your body and blood. For through you we all have access to the Father in the one Spirit.[59]

The prayer is significant as a rare example of an epicletic prayer addressed to the Son. The last sentence relates back to the prayer of the veil. The Church had also authorized a rite in Urdu in 1985. The eucharistic prayer includes no invocatory petitions.[60]

The Church of Bangladesh

The Church of Bangladesh, formed in 1970, and also a united Church embracing Anglicans, and various Protestant traditions including Methodists and Reformed, issued a new liturgy in 1989. The definitive version is in Bengali, but an English translation has been made for the benefit of the three English-speaking congregations in the Church. The rite has four eucharistic prayers. They share a common *sursum corda*, preface (with provision for proper prefaces) and *sanctus/benedictus*. Eucharistic prayer 1 is a slight modification of the CNI prayer which, of course, is

56 *The Book of Worship of the Church of North India* (Delhi, 1995), p. 144.

57 *The Church of Pakistan, Experimental Services* (Church of Pakistan Liturgical Commission, 1974).

58 Ibid., p. 8. One difference to CSI 1950 was the rubric ordering the use of the words of institution for supplementary consecration (p. 34).

59 Ibid., p. 9. The eucharistic prayer is modelled basically on the 1662 prayer of consecration. The 'Hear us' clause is replaced by 'Remember His sacrifice and have mercy on us … and your whole church, through him, who in the same night ...' (p. 10).

60 *Common Prayer: Approved Document of the Church of Pakistan* (Diocese of Karachi, n.d.). Introductory remarks at the beginning of the book are dated 1985. I am indebted to the Revd David Cooper for translation of the relevant sections of this text.

derived from the first eucharistic prayer of *ASB* Rite A (England, 1980); it has a 'split *epiclesis*', the first before the narrative:

> And as we follow the example of your Son, our Saviour, Jesus Christ, and obey his command, grant that, by the power of your Spirit, these gifts of bread and wine may be to us the body and blood of him who died for us and rose again.[61]

The second comes after the *anamnesis*, including a petition for the Father's blessing on the worshippers:

> Send your blessing upon us, O Lord, that as we eat these gifts in the presence of your divine majesty, we may be renewed by your Spirit, strengthened in your love, and united in the body of your Son.[62]

Eucharistic Prayer 2 has a single *epiclesis*, after the *anamnesis*:

> We come to him, that living stone, rejected by men, but in your sight chosen and precious, and on him are built into a living temple, a holy priesthood, to offer spiritual sacrifices and to declare the wonderful deeds of him who called us out of darkness into his marvellous light. In him, alone, we ask you to accept these praises, and, with your Holy Spirit, to bless these gifts of bread and wine, that they may be to us his body and his blood.
>
> Bless us, as here we offer ourselves as a holy and living sacrifice, restore establish and strengthen us, and grant that we, and all who share in this bread and this cup, may receive the benefits of his passion.
>
> Be mindful of your church, deliver it from evil, make it perfect in your love, and, as grain once scattered on the hillsides was in this bread made one, we pray that you will gather your children from every place into the Kingdom of Christ Jesus, your Son, our Lord.[63]

The prayer is a new composition. It draws richly on biblical imagery and language in which Bangladeshi Christians are steeped, and so was written as 'an authentic expression of the Bangladeshi Christian experience'.[64] The *epiclesis* embraces a petition relating to the elements, a petition relating to the worshippers and a supplication for the Church. Eucharistic prayer 3 is based on the eucharistic prayer from the *Apostolic Tradition* of Hippolytus. It retains the *epiclesis* in the Hippolytan position, after the *anamnesis*:

> And we pray you, send your Spirit upon these, the gifts of your Church, that they may be to us his body and his blood.

61 *The Lord's Supper* (Dhaka, 1989), p. 8.

62 Ibid., p. 10.

63 Ibid., pp. 10, 12.

64 From personal correspondence with the Revd John Webber, to whom I am indebted for background information to this rite.

> Gather into one all who share this bread and wine. Fill us with your Holy Spirit, that we may be established firmly in your faith and truth, and may praise you through your Son, Jesus Christ.[65]

Eucharistic prayer 4 is a lightly revised form of the so-called 'Lima Liturgy'.

The Revd John Webber, former convenor of the Liturgical Committee of the Church of Bangladesh comments that the Church has no single theology of the *epiclesis*. Rather, both Anglican and Reformed strands agree that the entire eucharistic prayer and action of the eucharist effects consecration. Two prayers adopt the West Syrian structure, ruling out an over-emphasis on the narrative of institution (which can in any case be read as a warrant before the *anaphora*). A fuller expression of the role of the Spirit reflects ecumenical consensus but is also related to the presence of Syrian Orthodox Churches in the Indian subcontinent; a number of features in the rite reflect the Syrian heritage.

The Mar Thoma Syrian Church

The Mar Thoma Syrian Church is a reformed section of the Syrian Orthodox Church in India and is in communion with the See of Canterbury. Reform was initiated in 1836 by a group led by a priest, the Revd Abraham Malpan, through the influence of the Church Missionary Society (CMS).[66] CMS missionaries had published the Scriptures in the vernacular Malayalam tongue, and the call for reform was in the light of conformity to Scripture. While the movement for reform was initially within the Syrian Orthodox Church, it led in time to the establishment of the Mar Thoma Church as a separate reformed Orthodox Church. Abraham Malpan began using a reformed version of the Syrian rite in the vernacular from 1836. The present eucharistic liturgy of the Church may be classified as part of the West Syrian pattern of rites and is in Malayalam with an authorized English translation.

The present Mar Thoma eucharistic liturgy, the *Holy Qurbana*, dates from 1954. It was the work of the Liturgy Revision Committee appointed in 1945. The committee issued its report in 1954 and the revised liturgy was published by Metropolitan Juhanon Mar Thoma in the same year. It is known as 'The Liturgy of the Synod'. The *epiclesis*, in the official English translation, is as follows:

Priest	Answer unto us, O Lord; answer unto us, O Lord; answer unto us, O Lord; and by your grace have mercy upon us.[67]
People	Kyrie eleison *(3 times)*

65 Church of Bangladesh, *The Lord's Supper*, pp. 11, 13.

66 George Mathew, 'Example 5: Syrian Versus Hindu Conflict over Inculturation in India: Two Reports', in David R. Holeton (ed.), *Liturgical Inculturation in the Anglican Communion* (Bramcote, 1990), p. 48.

67 The Syrian Orthodox text has 'Hear me' repeated three times. It recalls the cry of Elijah in 1 Kings 18:37, calling down fire upon the sacrifice; this was interpreted as a type of the eucharistic *epiclesis*. Phillip Tovey cites the view of K.K. Kuruvilla that the Mar Thoma revision is in reaction to the priestly overtones of the Orthodox petition; however, K.N. Daniel has argued that the Syrian tradition knows variations in this petition, possibly calling into

	or
	Lord, have mercy.
THE EPICLESIS	
Priest, blessing the bread:	MAY THE HOLY SPIRIT SANCTIFY THE BREAD THAT IT MAY BE THE BODY OF OUR LORD JESUS CHRIST.
People	Amen.
Priest, blessing the chalice:	MAY THE HOLY SPIRIT SANCTIFY THE WINE IN THIS CHALICE THAT IT MAY BE THE BLOOD OF OUR LORD JESUS CHRIST.
People	Amen.
Priest	Sanctify, O Lord, the bodies and souls of those who receive these gifts that they may bear fruit for the stability of your holy Church. Establish ever more firmly your Church founded on the rock of faith, against which the gates of hell shall not prevail, and preserve her to the end from strife and error.[68]

The petitions in capitals are identical with an earlier liturgy published in 1942 known as 'The Liturgy of Titus II',[69] itself a slight modification of the rite produced by the Third Liturgy Committee and presented to the General Assembly of the Church in 1927. The Mar Thoma version can be compared with the Syrian Orthodox petition; the form is that given by James Hough as being in use at the time of the Malpan's reform:

> ... send down upon us and upon these oblations thy Holy Spirit ... [70]
> Answer me, O Lord etc. and congregational *kyries*..
> That by overshadowing He may make this bread the life-giving body +, the saving body +, the body of Christ our God +. **Amen**.
> And may perfectly make this cup the Blood of the New Testament +, the saving Blood +, the blood of Christ our God +. **Amen**.
> That so they may sanctify the souls and spirits and bodies of those that communicate in them, to the yielding of the fruit of good works, to the confirmation of the Holy Church

---

question Kuruvilla's assertion. Phillip Tovey, 'Receptionism and the Mar Thoma Epiclesis', *Christian Orient*, 16 (1995): 89.

68 *Holy Qurbana* (Tirvalla, 1972), pp. 51-52. A new edition of the English translation was published in 1988; the *epiclesis* is identical to the 1972 version. For a comparison with other currently used versions of St James, see Phillip Tovey, *The Liturgy of St James as presently used* (Cambridge, 1998). For the *epiclesis*, see pp.16-18.

69 *An English Translation of the Order of the Holy Qurbana of the Mar Thoma Syrian Church of Malabar* (Madras, 1947); for the *epiclesis*, see pp. 10-11.

70 The preceding silent prayer, invoking the Spirit, is found in the Malayalam Mar Thoma Service, but not in the English translation; there have been some calls for its restoration, G. Mathew, 'Development and Revision of Liturgies: A Historical Evaluation', in M.V. Abraham *et al.* (eds), *A Study On The Malankara Mar Thoma Church Liturgy* (Kottayam, 1993) p. 17. He argues for a public prayer by the congregation. See also Tovey, *The Liturgy of St James as presently used*, p. 16.

> which is founded upon the rock of faith, and against which the gates of hell shall not prevail ... [71]

The substitution of 'sanctify ... that it may be' for 'Send ... overshadowing ... may make' allows for a broader theological framework. The verb 'sanctify' is indeed present in the diaconal interjection in the Syrian Orthodox order.[72] Sanctify, however, does not demand the conversionist associations of 'make'. The 1954 rite also includes an alternative form:

> May the Holy Spirit bless and sanctify this bread that it may be to us the communion of the Body of your beloved Son, our Lord and our God Jesus Christ.
> May the Holy Spirit bless and sanctify this cup that it may be the to us the communion of the Blood of your beloved Son, our Lord and Saviour Jesus Christ.[73]

The phrase 'the communion of' is reminiscent of the *epiclesis* of the 1950 rite of the CSI, while 'be to us' makes room for a more subjective view of Christ's presence. The prayer of inclination, said by the priest while the people say the *kyries*, is omitted in the English translation. It is, however, present in the Malayalam order:

> Father, have mercy upon us ...
> Send out your Holy Spirit to sanctify this Holy Qurbana and us.[74]

This prayer is important because it makes explicit that the work of the Spirit is related to both the sanctification of the elements and also the communicants. The question of the meaning of consecration was discussed in the report of the Liturgy Revision Committee published in 1927. The report states: 'It is admitted by the whole Church that the Christians receive Jesus Christ in and through Holy Qurbana'. The means of that reception, however, was expressed in different ways by members of the Church:

> 1. There is a view that the Holy Spirit sanctifies the bread and wine to be the symbols of the body and blood of Christ, and only in a symbolic sense can the bread and wine be called the Body and Blood.
> 2. There is another view that when the priest consecrated the bread and wine there comes into existence a relation between Christ and these elements, which is incomprehensible by human intelligence but is nevertheless most real. Thus Christ is present in a particular manner in the midst of his worshippers and it is not merely in a symbolic sense that the

71 James Hough, *The History of Christianity in India, Vol. IV* (London, 1845), p. 635. The text is cited, not altogether accurately, by Lucas Vithuvattical, 'The Reformed Missal of Abraham Malpan', in J. Vellian (ed.), *The Malabar Church* (Rome, 1970), p. 36.

72 '*Deacon*: How terrible is this hour, how dreadful this time, my beloved, when the living and Holy Spirit comes from the heights of heaven, descends and lights on this Eucharist, and sanctifies it. Stand we with awe and dread'. Hough, *The History of Christianity in India, Vol. IV*, p. 635.

73 Ibid., p. 29.

74 *Order of the Holy Qurbana of the Mar Thoma Syrian Church* (Tirvalla, 1977), p. 36. Translated by the Revd George Mathew.

> bread and wine become the Body and Blood of Jesus Christ. The Church should permit its members freedom to hold either of these views.[75]

This liberty of interpretation was indeed permitted by the Church. The liturgies of 1942 and 1954 were drawn up in conformity with the 1927 report.[76]

Common Liturgy for the Eucharist

The Communion of Churches in India (CCI), embracing the Church of South India, the Church of North India and the Mar Thoma Church, marks a new development in ecumenical endeavour between the three Churches. It held its first General Assembly in 2004. At that meeting, the Commission on Worship and Mission of the CCI presented a 'Common Liturgy', prepared for the annual Festival of Unity and for other occasions of combined worship. 'The Liturgy of the Sacrament (Anaphora)' has the structure:

The Great Thanksgiving:	*Sursum corda*
Preface	
Sanctus	
Words of Institution:	Institution narrative (with congregational response, 'Bless, O Lord' and 'Amen'
Anamnesis:	*Anamnesis* and Memorial Acclamations
Epiclesis:	(based on Mar Thoma) Our heavenly Father, have mercy upon us. Send your Holy Spirit to sanctify us, and this offering of bread and wine. Lord, have mercy (thrice). May the Holy Spirit sanctify this bread that it may be the body of our Lord Jesus Christ. **Amen**. May the Holy Spirit sanctify this wine in the chalice that it may be the blood of our Lord Jesus Christ. **Amen**. **Accept this offering of praise and thanksgiving; make us one body Jesus Christ our Lord** … [doxology].

This order is incorporated in the CSI *Book of Common Worship*, 2004.[77]

---

75 Juhanon Mar Thoma, *Christianity in India and a Brief History of the Mar Thoma Syrian Church* (Madras, 1968), p. 42.

76 It is apparent that the *epiclesis* has been a sensitive theological issue. The story of the development of the Mar Thoma revisions of St James has been set out fully in a dissertation by Zecharia John, 'The Liturgy of the Mar Thoma Syrian Church of Malabar in the Light of its History' (MA dissertation, University of Durham, 1994). I am indebted to the Revd Phillip Tovey for drawing my attention to this work. John collates the relevant texts. See also K.K. Kuruvilla, *A History of the Mar Thoma Church and Its Doctrines* (Madras, 1951), pp. 32-33.

77 Ibid., pp. 155-168.

The Church of the Province of Myanmar

Of the dioceses formerly constituting the Church of India, Pakistan, Burma and Ceylon, Burma alone is now an autonomous Church of the Anglican Communion. It adopted the name Myanmar in 1990 (*Myanmanainggan Karityan Athindaw*). Two Eucharistic rites are in use, the form from the CIPBC Prayer Book,[78]and a new order, approved by the General Meeting of the Provincial Council in 1999. The rite includes some notable aspects of inculturation in a predominantly Buddhist context, and was written in Burmese with a parallel English translation.[79] The eucharistic prayer follows a similar structure to 1960, while developing a broader range of theological themes. After the institution narrative, the prayer continues:

> Father, we celebrate this sacrifice by the remembrance of the death of Jesus Christ, the proclamation of his resurrection, and looking for his coming again with power and great glory. And we humbly pray to you Lord, to send down the Holy Spirit to us and to these gifts; and that all we who are partakers of this Holy Communion may be one with Jesus Christ and become living sacrifices.[80]

The Church of Ceylon

When the Church of North India and the Church of Pakistan were formed in 1970, it was expected that the Church of Ceylon would also become the United Church of Lanka. However due to litigation, no united Church was formed. The Church of Ceylon comprises of two extra-provincial dioceses, the Diocese of Colombo and the Diocese of Kurunagala, both of which are under the jurisdiction of the Archbishop of Canterbury. The following rites are in use in Anglican Churches in Sri Lanka: *The Ceylon Liturgy* of 1938; the 1960 CIPCB rite; 1662 in a few places; the 1982 Ceylon rite, a conservative revision of 1938; and a new eucharistic rite, authorized in 1988.[81]

The 1988 rite is entitled *The Holy Eucharist or the Lord's Supper (1988) – A Liturgy for Sri Lanka*.[82] Dr N. Francis Wickremesinghe comments that the Church has no General Council and that the Canons, Constitution and Rules have remained unchanged with a legal embargo on introducing change. Therefore the 1988 rite has been issued on the *ius liturgicum* of the diocesan bishops and the Metropolitan.[83] The rite represents a turning point from adaptation of 1938 to the evolution of a

78 *Order for the Administration of the Lord's Supper* (1960).

79 Katharine E. Babson, 'The Province of Myanmar (Burma)', in Charles Hefling and Cynthia Shattuck (eds), *The Oxford Guide to The Book of Common Prayer: A Worldwide Survey* (Oxford, 2006), pp. 409-410. She cites a 2001 edition of the rite.

80 *The Church of the Province of Myanmar, The Holy Communion* (Yangoon, 1999), pp. 19-20.

81 I am grateful to the Revd Sydney L.C. Knight for this information.

82 *The Holy Eucharist or the Lord's Supper (1988) – A Liturgy for Sri Lanka* (Ratmalana, 1988).

83 From personal correspondence.

genuinely inculturated liturgy. The eucharistic prayer has a single *epiclesis* following the *anamnesis*:

> And we entreat you most merciful Father that your all holy Spirit may + bless and hallow us (and these your gifts by his life-giving power that they may be for us the Body and Blood of your most dearly loved Son.)[84]

The rite is distinctive in the placing of brackets around the invocation on the elements. In an unpublished paper on the rite, Dr Wickremesinghe comments:

> The epikletic character of the 1938 Ceylon Liturgy ... is retained. It is to be noted that the W.C.C.'s Ecumenical Lima Liturgy (1983), now used at all ecumenical gatherings, has two Epicleses ... A characteristic peculiarity of the 1938 Ceylon Liturgy amongst Anglican Liturgies was the use of the original Marcan and Hebrew and Eastern form of 'bless' in the Institution Narrative – but this has now been revised to the more Anglican 'thanks' to accommodate strong Evangelical Party reservations, and for the same reason the epiclesis could, optionally omit the hallowing of inanimate gifts.[85]

The *epiclesis* leads into the doxology making it the virtual climax of the prayer. This was to enable the people to prostrate themselves during the doxology and to emphasise that the entire prayer is consecratory. The rite includes a form of additional consecration:

> We entreat you Father that your all-holy Spirit may hallow + this bread (wine) that it too may become for us the Body (Blood) of your Son Jesus, who took bread (the cup) gave thanks, and gave it to the disciples saying 'This is my Body (Blood)'. **Amen.**[86]

Here there is no concession to evangelical scruples. However, the commentary (though not the rubrics) asserts that any blessing may be used or none at all as supplementary consecration is 'a medieval practice without precedent in the primitive Eucharist'![87] The rite also includes in an appendix instructions for a 'Liturgy of the Spirit' which could be used for communion services using the reserved sacrament or non-sacramental worship. Two thanksgiving prayers are included, both of which invoke the Holy Spirit on the worshippers. The first includes the petition:

> And we entreat you most merciful Father to send down your holy and life-giving Spirit to renew us in the likeness of your Son, Christ Jesus
> (*Brief silence for recollection*)
> and to stir us into action for him.

The second has the congregational text:

---

84 *The Holy Eucharist or the Lord's Supper (1988)*, p. 11.

85 N.F. Wickremesinghe, 'A Commentary on the Holy Eucharist or Lord's Supper – A Liturgy for Sri Lanka' (unpublished paper, 1988), p. 6.

86 Ibid., p. 13.

87 Ibid., p. 7.

Grant us the gift of your Spirit, that we may know him and make him known.[88]

The prayers are set within a fourfold action, but without any institution narrative. They clearly understand reception of the sacrament as a means of the bestowal of the Spirit.

Apart from the 1988 rite, official Anglican liturgy has remained conservative and inculturation has been carried out in relation to musical settings rather than the words, and in ecumenical liturgies such as the 'New World' liturgy of Devasarana, and 'Workers' Mass' of the Christian Workers' Fellowship.[89]

Conclusion

The Churches of the Indian subcontinent provide a fascinating snapshot of various unresolved issues related to the eucharist in general and the *epiclesis* in particular.

1. The presence of the ancient Thomas Churches with their use of the Liturgy of St James has influenced the shape of the eucharistic prayer; as would be expected, the West Syrian pattern dominates, although early attempts to model eucharistic prayers directly on St James failed to win widespread support, partly because of doctrinal and churchmanship issues surrounding consecration. The presence and influence of a *reformed* Orthodox Church with its own story of liturgical revision and toned down epicletic texts adds further interest to the question of how doctrine and liturgical form influence each other.
2. The influence of the Presbyterian tradition provided a Reformed model for the *epiclesis* in the united Church of South India. This reflected the High Calvinism, informed by study of Patristic theology and Orthodox liturgy, that was so influential in Scotland and in other places through the *Euchologion* of 1867 and the 1940 *Book of Common Order*. That such an approach to the *epiclesis* arose from an unambiguously Protestant tradition may have helped side-step contentious doctrinal disputes in other parts of the Anglican world dominated by reference to the Roman and Orthodox liturgical and dogmatic concerns. The liturgical traditions and freedoms cherished by some of the uniting Churches in North India are evident in the permissive rubrics of the CNI's *Alternative Order.*
3. The first steps towards genuine inculturation, evident in the revised CSI rite of 1985, in the encouragement to use indigenous symbols in the CNI *Alternative Order* and more recently in Myanmar, illustrate the distinct possibility of

88 I am indebted to the Revd Phillip Tovey for drawing my attention to these texts. They are set out in his dissertation *'Extended Communion, a thesis submitted for the Archbishop's Examination in Theology'*, Lambeth Diploma, 1994, p. 47.

89 *Thanksgiving and Communion: A Liturgy Authorised for use at Devasaranaramaya* (ibbagamuwa, n.d.); N. Francis Wichremesinghe, 'The Workers' May Day Mass in Sri Lanka', in Holeton, *Liturgical Inculturation in the Anglican Communion*, pp. 51-54. Both examples have included creative epicletic petitions.

increasing liturgical *divergence*. It suggests that rites formed out of indigenous contexts, with distinctive forms of language, symbol and ceremonial, may abandon the kind of ecumenical convergence that has so characterized liturgical renewal in the historic denominations in the post-war period, dominated as they are by Europe and North America, and so result in very different forms of theology, spirituality and language. The pervading theology of 'Presence' in the CSI 1985 rite sets narrower concerns of what effects consecration and what consecration effects in a much broader context.

Chapter 10

The *Epiclesis*: The Spiritual Dynamics of Sacramentalism

The *Epiclesis* in Retrospect: The Eastern and Western Divide Reconsidered

The fact that the overwhelming majority of twentieth-century Anglican eucharistic prayers include some form of *epiclesis* is a witness both to the place accorded to the Spirit in contemporary eucharistic theology and to the desire for a more consciously Trinitarian approach to the eucharistic prayer. This has been underlined by ecumenical consensus on the eucharist, built on the comparative study of prayer texts, and theological writings, from the first five centuries. Of course, the Scottish–American tradition had already reincorporated the *epiclesis* in an attempt to restore supposed primitive and apostolic norms. However, even here the motivation appears to have arisen more from a characteristically Anglican respect for tradition rather than theological first principles. And even a post-anamnetic *epiclesis* did not prejudice the devotional and theological weight given to the institution narrative. This underlines the fact that Anglicanism, arising as it did from within the Latin Church, has an essentially western identity. Even the Scottish and American canons could not be interpreted entirely without reference to 1662, and of course, the prayer of consecration was the only major deviation from the 1662 Prayer Book. The catholic revival in the Church of England and through it to other Churches of the Anglican Communion only served to underline the western inheritance and, indeed, initiated a fresh enquiry into the nature of Anglican eucharistic formularies and theology against the background of Scholastic thought. This western background is important because of the ambivalence of the work of the Spirit in the western tradition. This is certainly true of western eucharistic theology, where as far back as Ambrose's *De Sacramentis*, the words of institution are regarded as effecting consecration and the fact that the Roman canon, fixed from the end of the sixth century, includes no reference to the Spirit apart from the final doxology. It is not that there is no theological enquiry or expression of the work of the Spirit in the eucharistic action,[1] but that such enquiry is subsumed under the weight given to Christology[2] Bryan

1 Yves Congar sets out an impressive list of citations in *I Believe in the Holy Spirit, Vol. III* (New York and London, 1983), pp. 250-257.

2 Edward J. Kilmartin argues that Roman Catholic eucharistic theology has tended to understand the sanctification of the elements in terms of the actualization of the personal mission of Christ through his word spoken by his minister. As the Spirit is not generally awarded a personal mission of sanctification, sanctifying activity can only attributed to the Spirit by appropriation. 'The Active Role of Christ and the Holy Spirit in the Sanctification of the Eucharistic Elements', *Theological Studies*, 45 (1984): 233-234. See also Patrick Regan, 'Quenching the Spirit: The Epiclesis in Recent Roman Documents', *Worship*, 79 (2005): 386-404.

Spinks has shown that the western tradition, dominated as it was by Augustine's stress on the One God as the starting point for his Trinitarian theology, failed to give to give liturgical expression to the *homoousios* of Father, Son and Spirit. By contrast, the east, influenced by Athanasius and the Cappadocians, did adapt their liturgies to reflect a fully Trinitarian theology.[3]

Eastern theologians have thus often argued that western theology has a tendency towards Christomonism. Part of this tendency historically may lie with the nature of New Testament material, in Paul and certainly in John where there does appear to be a functional subordination of the Spirit to the Son as well as the Son to the Father. This presents the difficulty of how to express such functional subordination in a way that still leaves room for the Spirit's distinctive work and affirms the Spirit's personhood. This is where the heart of eastern unease lies. In their terms, western theology historically has expounded the work of the Spirit in an overly Christological framework, especially in the realm of ecclesiology. This has had two main consequences. The first is a too literalistic interpretation of the Pauline model of the Church as the Body of Christ. The extreme application of this model came in the ultra-Augustinian representation of the Church as the 'whole Christ' and in this sense the real and actual extension of the Incarnation, the very presence of Christ in the world. Such a doctrine does not leave very much room for the Spirit in the life of the Church. The second, and most famous expression of this tendency is, of course, following Augustine, the addition of the Filioque clause to the Niceno-Constantinopolitan Creed.[4] So Vladimir Lossky could write: 'The Greeks saw in the formula of the procession of the Holy Spirit from the Father and the Son a tendency to stress the unity of nature at the expense of the real distinction between the persons.'[5]

Put more strongly, this presented the danger that the Spirit is deemed to have a merely relational status to the Second Person of the Trinity, and so is not accorded a full hypostatic status in his own right but rather undertakes a function that is seen as merely cognitive in regard to Christ. The combination of these two strands led in time to the virtual exclusion of the Spirit in western ecclesiology, so that no distinctive work was ascribed to the Spirit. Christ was seen in relation to the Father and Christians in relation to Christ. Any expression of pneumatology, therefore, was incidental, and could only be in terms of a kind of spiritual power demanded of

3 Spinks, 'Trinitarian Theology and the Eucharistic Prayer', pp. 209-224.

4 Discussion of the *Filioque* has been a major element in Anglican–Orthodox Dialogue; see 'The Dublin Agreed Statement' (1984), section 95 (c). 'The Cyprus Agreed Statement' (2006) states that Anglicans and Orthodox are agreed about the inadequacies of the *Filioque*, and the need to develop Christology and pneumatology in the closest possible connection, ibid., pp. 16-17, 37.

5 V. Lossky, *The Mystical Theology of the Eastern Church* (Cambridge, 1957), p. 57. Lossky's view that the *Filioque* is *the* problem between east and west in terms of Trinitarian theology is now widely regarded as an overstatement, see J.D. Zizioulas, 'The Doctrine of God the Trinity Today: Suggestions for an Ecumenical Study', in Alasdair I.C. Heron (ed.), *The Forgotten Trinity* (London, 1991), p. 20; cf. Jürgen Moltmann, *History and the Triune God* (London, 1991), p. 58.

Christology. So the work of the Spirit is essentially a subjective revelation of Christ, an agent of Christ in humanity, and consequently lacking in objectivity.

Of course, western theologians have not been slow to react to such criticisms;[6] nevertheless, it is a historic fact that the failure of the west to produce a rich theology of the Spirit with the marginalization of the Spirit in ecclesiology had natural consequences for sacramental theology. Indeed, rather than seeing the work of the Spirit as the dynamic and re-creating presence of God, in Nikos Nissiotis's expression, working in the Church in the here and now, the salvation wrought by Christ,[7] the Spirit was rather, as it were, 'controlled' and dispensed by the Church in certain strictly defined sacramental rites such as confirmation and ordination. Rather than the Spirit in his freedom responding to the prayer of the Church, western consecration proceeded according to an authoritative juridical 'formula'. The emphasis on the institution narrative in conjunction with the developed Latin doctrine of the priesthood, meant that the eucharistic prayer was not deemed to be an expression of the life of the Trinity, and even the prayer context became secondary. Paul Evdokimov expressed the contrast succinctly:

> For the Latins, the *verba substantialia* of the consecration, the institutional words of Christ, are pronounced by the priest *in persona Christi*, which bestows on them a value that is immediately consecratory. For the Greeks, however, a similar definition of the priestly action – *in persona Christi*– which identifies the priest with Christ is absolutely unknown. Indeed, it is quite unthinkable. For them, the priest invokes the Holy Spirit precisely in order that the words of Christ, *reproduced and cited* by the priest, acquire all the effectiveness of the speech-act of God.[8]

Rather than a notion of the Spirit as merely the validator of Christ's words, the eastern pattern pictures a dynamic partnership of the Second and Third Persons of the Trinity in the eucharistic action as well as anchoring the role of the Church in petition.[9] For the Orthodox, the eucharistic words were spoken once in time; instituting the eucharist for all time. It is the work of the Spirit to take those words, uttered once, and to make them effective in all their power, in response to the petition of the priest. It could perhaps be added that even this discussion assumes that the eucharistic words are absolutely necessary for every eucharistic celebration, a

---

6 For example, Congar, *I Believe in the Holy Spirit, Vol. III*, pp. 208-212; Joseph H. Crehan, 'The Theology of Eucharistic Consecration', *Theological Studies*, 40 (1979): 334-343; 'Eucharist and Epiklesis: New Evidence and a New Theory', *Theological Studies*, 41 (1980): 698-712. The importance of Crehan's work is his demonstration that discussion of the 'moment' of consecration needs to be pushed back much earlier than for example the twelfth-century starting point advocated by Edmund Bishop.

7 See, for example, Nikos Nissiotis, 'Pneumatological Christology as a Presupposition of Ecclesiology' in *Oecumenica 1967* (Minneapolis, 1967), pp. 240-241.

8 Cited by Congar, *I Believe in the Holy Spirit, Vol. III*, p. 236.

9 Geoffrey Wainwright rightly criticizes any notion of trying to 'play off' one Person of the Trinity against another in relation to the agent of consecration, *Eucharist and Eschatology* (London, 1971), p. 96.

position challenged by some liturgical scholars,[10] as well as the issue of how the role of the priest is understood in relation to the assembly.[11]

The Church of England was heir to the medieval eucharistic inheritance of the Latin Church. The view that Cranmer's incorporation of an invocation of word and Spirit in 1549 was a conscious *via media* between east and west cannot be proven. In any case it was too short-lived to enable any sustained theological reflection. The Reformation, however, has to be interpreted according to its own lights as well as the background to it. We have already seen how Cranmer's second Prayer Book illustrates his own biblicism. Rites were reformed not according to scientific enquiry into the patterns of worship of the undivided Church, but according to perceived biblical principles. While 1549 can be compared with Sarum, indeed in many ways is a revision of Sarum, no such comparison can be made between 1549 and 1552, because 1552 is clearly a biblically inspired devotion, incorporating some elements from tradition and some of the 1548/49 prayers but in a radically new *schema*. The fact is that the Scriptures include no direct references to the work of the Spirit in relation to holy communion,[12] in contra-distinction to baptism where there are direct references. Cranmer's essential source for 1552 is 1 Corinthians 11; the eucharist is a solemn proclamation of the death of the Lord, demanding the testing of self so that reception may be made worthily. Immediately before reception, the communicant hears the words of institution, cast in the context of prayer that we, receiving, may be partakers of Christ's body and blood. Apart from the Collect for Purity, culled from the private preparatory prayers of the priest in the Sarum Rite (and clearly still a prayer of preparation; to see it as an *epiclesis* on the whole rite is fanciful in the extreme), there is no other significant reference to the Holy Spirit in the rite. The other references are passing or occasional: the exhortations, the proper prefaces of Christmas, Whitsunday and Trinity Sunday, the doxological conclusions to collects, the post-communion prayers of oblation and thanksgiving, the *Gloria in excelsis*, and the pneumatological references in the Nicene Creed. The superimposing on Cranmer's text of a definite theology of consecration in the 1662 book, and especially the five indented rubrics specifying manual acts in the newly styled 'prayer of consecration' and the rubric requiring the repetition of the narrative for supplementary consecration underlined the place of the words of institution. Even in the Scottish rites of 1637 (preliminary *epiclesis*) and 1764 (single post-narrative *epiclesis*) and the American 1790 rite (single post-narrative *epiclesis*), manual acts at the narrative were retained

10 Bryan Spinks, 'The Institution Narrative in the Eucharistic Prayer', *News of Liturgy*, 157 (January, 1988): 2-4. He argues on the basis of Isaiah 55 that once the divine word is spoken it is effective for all time. On the role of the institution narrative see also Terrance W. Klein, 'Institution Narratives at the Crossroads', *Worship*, 67 (1993): 407-418.

11 Kilmartin draws attention to the writings of Orthodox theologians Paul Evdokimov and Cyprian Kern that the priest acts *in nomine Christi* or *in persona ecclesia*, 'The Active Role of Christ and the Holy Spirit in the Sanctification of the Eucharistic Elements', p. 236.

12 The two possible references are 1 Cor. 10:3-4 and 1 Cor. 12:13. The possibility of a eucharistic reference is entertained by Wainwright, *Eucharist and Eschatology*, pp. 99-100, cf. pp. 115-116.

with none specified for the *epiclesis*,[13] suggesting that the narrative constituted the consecratory heart of the rite.

The western and Reformed heritage of Anglicanism, therefore, reflected a 'double absence' in relation to the role of the Spirit: the relative absence of an explicit pneumatology in western eucharistic theology, and the implicit absence of a eucharistic pneumatology in the New Testament. Both of these absences are reflected in the rites of 1552/1662. Moreover, despite retaining a clear understanding that consecration is effected in the context of prayer, the 1662 rite left itself open to the charge of merely according with the 'irreducible minimum' concerns of the Schoolmen. While it is clear that Anglican theologians in the post-Reformation period were united in their rejection of the doctrine of transubstantiation and the philosophical presuppositions demanded by that doctrine, successive attempts to supplement the Prayer Book consecration prayer betray a basic feeling that the prayer context was not nearly explicit enough, that the Spirit was marginalized, that the text was 'Roman' rather than primitive. The legacy was reflected in the highly Christological concerns of the catholic revival in Anglicanism, and in the high degree of suspicion concerning the *epiclesis* in Anglican evangelicalism. Thus, mainline catholic thought demanded that if an *epiclesis* be restored, it must not prejudice the central role of the institution narrative; evangelicals were concerned whether an *epiclesis* on the elements was unscriptural and a kind of 'Trojan Horse', smuggling a doctrine of the real presence of Christ in the elements into the rite under the guise of pneumatology. The Anglican Communion is still grappling with this heritage.[14] What the 1764 Scottish and 1790 American rites did achieve was an alternative structure. If the 1552/1662 model is seen as 'equivalent western', that is, an Anglican recension of *Quam Oblationem* and the institution narrative, the 1764/1790 tradition is 'equivalent eastern' with the sequence: narrative, (*anamnesis*), invocation. The Scottish–American tradition can, of course, be criticized as betraying a preoccupation with consecration; they do not follow the eastern anaphoras in linking the invocation of the Spirit to both elements and communicants. Nevertheless they did achieve their own theological benefits. For example, Thomas Talley has observed that where the sequence: narrative, *anamnesis*-oblation and *epiclesis* occurs (rather than *epiclesis*, narrative, *anamnesis*-oblation), the oblation of the bread and wine is not nearly so controversial because it is clear that there is not a simplistic notion that bread and wine are consecrated (transubstantiated) and then offered to the Father. The later *epiclesis* itself sets consecration in a much broader framework.[15]

---

13 Rattray's *An Office for the Sacrifice of the Holy Eucharist* included manual acts at the narrative and *epiclesis*. The 1764 Scottish rite included them at the narrative only and capitalised the eucharistic words.

14 A potentially unitive aspect of contemporary Anglicanism is charismatic renewal, which has influenced both catholic and evangelical spirituality. John Gunstone sees a parallel movement in the spread of a charismatic renewal and the greater stress on the role of the Spirit in Anglican liturgy, *Sacraments and Spiritual Gifts* (London, 1994), p. 115; cf. 'The Spirit and the Lord's Supper', *Theological Renewal*, 10 (1978): 29-32.

15 Talley, 'Eucharistic Prayers, Past, Present and Future' in Holeton, *Revising the Eucharist*, p. 15. He makes a similar point in discussing the 'Windsor Statement' of ARCIC and the forms of *anamnesis* in *ASB* Rite A, 'The Windsor Statement and the Eucharistic

The twentieth century has, however, seen an immense amount of work into the origins of the eucharistic prayer and of the implications of structure to which we will turn below. Fundamentally, however, these concerns about the form and structure of the historic Anglican rites raise the issue of what is the scope of the *epiclesis*. Is consecration of the elements the central issue, or does this need to be seen in the context of a much wider and richer understanding of the work of the Spirit in the eucharist, the Church and the world? It is to these concerns that we must now pass.

The Structure of the Eucharistic Prayer

If the dominant academic voice on the structure of the eucharistic prayer during the period 1945 to c.1975 in Anglican circles was Gregory Dix with his tripartite *schema* of thanksgiving, *anamnesis* and prayer for reception of the benefits of communion, the most influential Anglican writer over the last 20 years has been the American Episcopalian Thomas Talley. Talley's major contribution to eucharistic liturgical scholarship has concerned enquiry into the origins and development of the eucharistic prayer. He belongs to the illustrious group of twentieth-century liturgists who have traced the origins of the Christian eucharistic prayer to Jewish table prayers. Following Louis Bouyer and Louis Ligier, Talley looked to the grace after meals, the *birkat ha-mazon*, with its tripartite structure of blessing–thanksgiving–supplication, a structure clearly discernible in the prayer described in *The Book of Jubilees* chapter 22, a document of the second century BCE. However, rather than seeking to relate the Christian eucharistic prayer to the *berakah* formula, Talley drew attention to the second element, the prayer of thanksgiving, *nodeh lekah*, as the form most likely to have influenced Christian usage. He compared the *birkat* with the thanksgiving after food in *Didache* 10, which has the structure thanksgiving–thanksgiving–supplication, suggesting that this was a conscious adaptation of the Jewish prayer to express the primacy of thanksgiving over blessing. In other words, in Christian usage, the distinction between blessing and thanksgiving became subsumed under thanksgiving. Initially, Talley followed an argument posited by Henri Cazelles, that the verb *eucharistein* was linked to the Old Testament concept of the sacrifice of praise, *zebah todah*[16] and so provided a sacrificial allusion congenial to the early Christian understanding of the eucharist as the 'pure sacrifice' referred to, and in their terms prophesied by, Malachi 1:11. In more recent writing, he draws attention to the research of Cesare Giraudo, who analyses Old Testament prayer formulae to find a bipartite literary structure he calls *toda*, consisting of a proclamation of God's actions on behalf of Israel and a supplication for God's further action on behalf of his people. It was this proclamation which in Christian usage was rendered

---

Prayer', from Thomas J. Talley, *Worship: Reforming Tradition* (Washington, DC, 1990), pp. 44-45. There are, however, other theological issues surrounding the oblation.

16 Thomas J. Talley, 'From *Berakah* to *Eucharistia*: A Reopening Question', *Worship*, 50 (1976): 115-137, reprinted in R. Kevin Seasoltz (ed.), *Living Bread, Saving Cup* (Collegeville, 1982), pp. 80-101; cf. Thomas J. Talley, 'The Eucharistic Prayer of the Ancient Church According to Recent Research: Results and Reflections', *Studia Liturgica*, 11 (1976): 136-158.

eucharistein.[17] This bipartite structure could be discerned in *Apostolic Tradition*, Epiphanius, the 'Strasbourg Papyrus' and the Roman canon.

Talley related his work directly to questions of Anglican liturgical reform in a paper 'Eucharistic Prayers, Past, Present and Future' given at a conference held at Untermachtal, Germany, in August 1993, to prepare for the International Anglican Liturgical Consultation to be held in Dublin in the summer of 1995.[18] Talley's basic concern was the structure of the eucharistic prayer, as issues of structure had clear consequences for theology. He reiterated his thesis that the eucharistic prayer had two primitive movements, thanksgiving and supplication. The supplication in the *birkat* and the *Didache* is related to the community. In subsequent Christian use, however, this supplication attracted to itself a reference to the work of the Spirit, an *epiclesis*. In developed prayers, the thanksgiving embraced those parts normally designated preface, *sanctus*, post-*sanctus*, narrative of institution and *anamnesis*; the supplication embraced the *epiclesis* and further petition.[19] The result is that the *epiclesis* thus marks the transition from thanksgiving to supplication, and this pattern is faithfully followed in the 'Antiochene' family of prayers.[20] It also gives a clearly Trinitarian structure of praise to the Creator in the preface, a Christological salvation history in the post-*sanctus*, narrative and *anamnesis*, and pneumatological supplication in the *epiclesis*. The understanding of the role of the narrative of institution is central. In this context, it constitutes part of the agenda of thanksgiving for the work of Christ and so is intimately linked with the post-*sanctus* and the *anamnesis*. A bipartite pattern can even be traced in the west, fragmentary evidence suggesting that in fourth-century Italy, a variable thanksgiving, composed by the bishop, was followed by a fixed formula, including the narrative of institution and *anamnesis* but setting them in an entirely supplicatory context. While the equivalent of the *Quam oblationem* in Ambrose's *De Sacramentis* falls short of an explicit petition to consecrate the elements, nevertheless, the tendency in western theology, as evidenced by Ambrose's catechesis, was to make the narrative itself the focus of eucharistic consecration so that by the twelfth century, the locus of consecration was the recitation of the narrative and the rest of the canon was 'hardly more than literary decoration'.[21] It was a sense of the inviolability of the narrative that led the Roman

17 Thomas J. Talley, 'Sources and Structures of the Eucharistic Prayer', in *Worship: Reforming Tradition*, pp.18ff. This is a revised version of his article 'The Literary Structure of the Eucharistic Prayer', *Worship*, 55 (1984): 404-420.

18 Subsequently published in Holeton, *Revising the Eucharist: Groundwork for the Anglican Communion*, pp. 6-19.

19 On this point, see Anthony Gelston, 'The Origin of Intercession in the Eucharistic Prayer', *Studia Patristica*, 40 (2006): 37-41.

20 Talley draws attention to different structures in early Oriental rites, such as the suggested form of the *anaphora* derived from Cyril of Jerusalem's Mystagogical Catechesis 5, the 'Strasbourg Papyrus' and the developed form of St Mark; he notes, however, that the *anaphora* of James, succeeding Cyril, is classically 'Antiochene' in structure and that in the Coptic tradition, St Basil came to replace St Mark in normal usage, 'Eucharistic Prayers, Past, Present and Future', p. 9.

21 Ibid., p. 11. He cites the research of Pierre-Marie Gy to illustrate the medieval belief that only the words of institution are necessary to effect consecration.

Catholic revisers after Vatican 2, to distinguish between a consecratory *epiclesis* before the narrative and sanctificatory *epiclesis* after the *anamnesis* in prayers II, III and IV of the Missal of Paul VI, thus marking the shift to supplication after the *sanctus* and setting the narrative in a supplicatory context, while returning to thanksgiving in the *anamnesis*. Even in prayer IV, which in its salvation history approach looks to the 'Antiochene' tradition, the preliminary and consecratory *epiclesis* isolates the narrative from the Christological *kerygma*. While the rationale was to preserve the Roman character of the eucharistic prayers, for Talley, the result is 'institutionalized vacillation'.[22] Talley defends the logic of the 1662 arrangement, where because thanksgiving is marginal and distribution follows the narrative, the petition for consecration comes before the narrative. However, he sees no rationale for Anglicans to follow the Roman pattern where the desire is to restore a much fuller form of thanksgiving.[23] The narrative ought to be part of that thanksgiving rather than separated from it, along with a rejection of any specific 'moment' of consecration. He also argues that the structural fulcrum from thanksgiving to supplication would be clearer if congregational acclamations followed the *anamnesis*, citing the Byzantine text: 'We praise thee, we bless thee, we give thanks unto thee, O Lord, *and we pray unto thee*, O our God' as an example of the transition from thanks and praise to prayer.[24]

Talley is therefore commending to Anglicans a common structure, according to the 'Antiochene' pattern, on the basis of historical enquiry into eucharistic origins. It is, however, at this point, where aspects of his work have been challenged by what Bryan Spinks calls the 'English' view of anaphoral development.[25] Spinks, in an article published in 1985, replied to Talley's thesis, questioning in particular the assumption that Jesus used the *birkat ha-mazon*. Spinks draws attention to Joseph Heinemann's seminal study *Prayer in the Talmud: Forms and Patterns* where he suggests that the Lord's Prayer and the prayer recorded in Matthew 11:25-26 belong to the tradition of Jewish private and non-statutory prayer. This raises the possibility that Jesus repudiated the statutory *berakoth*, and so throws wide open what he might have said at the Last Supper[26] Spinks conjectures that Heinemann's observation that formulae such as 'We give you thanks' were characteristic of private thanksgivings gives an alternative suggestion for the Church's preference for *eucharistein*.[27] The diversity of practice in early Christianity and the freedom accorded to the eucharistic president to extemporize adds further weight to Spinks's argument and this has also

22 Ibid., p. 14. For a fuller discussion of the oblation in Roman eucharistic prayer IV, see Talley's essay 'The Windsor Statement and the Eucharistic Prayer', in *Worship, Reforming Tradition*, pp. 40ff.

23 Talley made explicit his criticism of the structure of the *ASB* eucharistic prayers in this respect in his essay 'The Eucharistic Prayer: Tradition and Development', in Stevenson, *Liturgy Reshaped*, p. 61.

24 Talley, 'Eucharistic Prayers, Past, Present and Future', p. 16, emphasis mine.

25 Bryan D. Spinks, *The Sanctus in the Eucharistic Prayer* (Cambridge, 1991), p. 111.

26 Bryan D. Spinks, 'Beware the Liturgical Horses! An English Interjection on Anaphoral Evolution', *Worship*, 59 (1985): 213-214.

27 Spinks, *The Sanctus in the Eucharistic Prayer*, p. 111.

been stressed by Paul Bradshaw[28] and Anthony Gelston.[29] Nevertheless, Talley's structural *schema* has much to commend it, not least in the realm of eucharistic spirituality. It would seem beyond doubt that many Christian worshippers and indeed liturgical presidents have little idea as to why particular eucharistic prayers are structured as they are. An understanding that the traditional elements found in the Christian *anaphora* can be understood under two essential movements of thanks and petition will enable a much clearer grasp of what the Church is doing in the central action of its worship.

While the dynamic of thanksgiving and supplication is thus helpful, we must be clear that thanksgiving is the primary movement. It would be wrong to see thanksgiving and supplication as somehow equal constituents. The supplication is made on the basis of the thanksgiving and is dependent upon it. The thanksgiving proclaims the love and goodness of God and so of our total dependence on the divine initiative in both creation and redemption. Indeed, we dare to ask because of what we know of the character of God through his revelation in history and principally through the sending of his Son. The work of the Spirit is to glorify Christ, to point to Christ.

A further caveat to the Talley thesis must be made in relation to salvation history. The clear Trinitarian progression of the Antiochene *anaphora*, namely the preface related to creation with God the Father chiefly in view; the post-*sanctus*, narrative and *anamnesis* related to the redemption wrought by Christ; and an *epiclesis* related to the Spirit is a perfectly legitimate approach. But it also has its dangers. For example, Christian theology relates all three Persons of the Trinity to creation and redemption. More seriously, the place of the Spirit in the *anaphora* can become limited to his role as the agent of sanctification thus marginalizing any sense of thanksgiving for the gift of the Spirit or the work of the Spirit within the Church. It is of note that the *anaphora* of St James, which seeks to give a chronological account of salvation history throughout the prayer (in the Christological section it maintains the order of incarnation and institution narrative in the post-*sanctus* and passion, resurrection, and ascension in the *anamnesis*) includes within the *epiclesis* a salvation history of the Spirit, embracing the inspiration of the Law and Prophets, the baptism of Jesus, and the Day of Pentecost. But this is somewhat exceptional.

The attempt to achieve an Anglican consensus, however, is likely to founder on the close association of a significant section of the Communion with the tradition Roman and western stress on the role of the narrative of institution, necessitating a preliminary *epiclesis*. All of the contemporary Roman eucharistic prayers have a preliminary *epiclesis* leading into the narrative. Annibale Bugnini, in his magisterial work *The Reform of the Liturgy 1948-1975* reveals how the suggestion to include a recension of the Alexandrian anaphora of St Basil narrowly failed to secure a majority in the *Consilium*, and in the light of such a close vote was referred to the Pope who did

28 Paul F. Bradshaw, *The Search for the Origins of Christian Worship*, 2nd ed. (London, 2002), pp. 139-143. In the same volume, he also points to the probable variations and fluidity in forms of grace at meals in the first century, pp. 44-46.

29 A. Gelston, *The Eucharistic Prayer of Addai and Mari* (Oxford, 1992), pp. 2-21.

not reverse the decision.[30] The inclusion of the *anaphora* was desired for ecumenical reasons and not least for the fact that it was used by Uniate Ukrainians, Melkites and Copts. Bugnini's account outlines two main objections, namely the position of the *epiclesis* and the elevation. The position of the *epiclesis* was deemed to present no theological difficulty especially in the light of papal pronouncements affirming the orthodoxy of eastern texts and the complementarity of eastern and western eucharistic traditions. In relation to the position of the elevation, the suggestion was that this should be made at the conclusion of the eucharistic prayer 'because in the anaphoras of this Eastern tradition the full expression of the Church's intention in using the words of Christ is not complete until that point'.[31] Despite the failure of the attempt to authorize Alexandrian Basil, Roman Catholic liturgists such as Aidan Kavanagh,[32] John McKenna[33] and Richard Albertine[34] have continued to press for a single *epiclesis* in the 'Antiochene' position.

The Scope of the *Epiclesis*

Understanding the *epiclesis*, therefore, as marking the transition from thanksgiving to supplication, we shall consider the scope of the *epiclesis*. The first issue is a preliminary, namely, a discussion of the question of invoking the Spirit on material elements of bread and wine. This has been a major area of difficulty for some Anglicans, notably those of the evangelical tradition. This leads on to what the *epiclesis* both affirms and implies about the doctrine of creation and salvation in its re-creating and eschatological manifestations. Closely allied to this is the unity of the Church and the eucharist as the sacrament of unity. Only then, and in the light

30 Annibale Bugnini, *The Reform of the Liturgy 1948-75* (Collegeville, 1990), pp. 458-462.

31 Ibid., p. 460.

32 Aidan Kavanagh, 'Thoughts on the New Eucharistic Prayers', *Worship*, 43 (1969): 2-12, reprinted in Seasoltz, *Living Bread, Saving Cup*, pp. 102-113. Kavanagh regrets that the 'split-*epiclesis*' divides the hallowing and unifying functions of the Spirit, makes the preliminary invocations more strongly consecratory than the *Quam oblationem*, and isolates the institution narrative from the narrative of divine mercies articulated. He criticizes Vagaggini's defence of the double invocation as not properly based on historical enquiry into early Roman, Gallic and Mozarabic sources, outlines significant differences between the Egyptian/Alexandrian forms and the new Roman forms, and points to the united *epiclesis* in Hippolytus and the Byzantine tradition.

33 McKenna, *Eucharist and Holy Spirit*, pp. 206-207. He essentially follows Kavanagh's reasoning here.

34 Richard Albertine, 'Problem of the (Double) Epiclesis in the New Roman Eucharistic Prayers', *Ephemerides Liturgicae*, 91 (1977): 192-202; 'The Epiclesis Problem – The Roman Canon (Canon 1) in the Post-Vatican Liturgical Reform', *Ephemerides Liturgicae*, 99 (1985): 337-348; 'The Post-Vatican Consilium's (*Coetus X*) Treatment of the Epiclesis Question in the New Eucharistic Prayers', *Ephemerides Liturgicae*, 100 (1986): 489-507; 'The Post-Vatican Consilium's (*Coetus X*) Treatment of the Epiclesis Question in the Context of Select Historical Data (Alexandrian Family of Anaphoras) and the Fragment of "Der Balyzeh"', *Ephemerides Liturgicae*, 102 (1988): 385-405.

of the whole discussion do we consider the *epiclesis* in the light of the theology of consecration and the realization of the presence of Christ in the eucharist.

Invoking the Holy Spirit on the Elements

The objection to invoking the Spirit upon the eucharistic elements, normally associated with evangelical and 'low Church' Anglicans reflects two concerns. One is the apparent lack of biblical citations to demonstrate that the Spirit relates to material things and a second is whether the invocation of the Spirit on the elements suggests a theology of consecration in which the Spirit is deemed objectively to change the eucharistic elements themselves. Such concerns are reflected, for example, in the response of the Church of Ireland to *BEM* where an *epiclesis* on the elements is deemed to go beyond Anglican tradition.

References to matter as the vehicle of spiritual blessing are not numerous in the New Testament. However, there are examples, in addition to the water of baptism and the bread and wine of the eucharist, to the application of oil (James 5:14), clay (John 9:11) and spittle (Mark 7:33, 8:23) in the context of healing and examples such as the woman touching the hem of Jesus's garment (Mark 5:27ff.) and the use of handkerchiefs and aprons for healing after contact with the body of Paul (Acts 19:12). But none of these has any suggestion of a formula of blessing or consecration. The reference in 1 Timothy 4:5 is perhaps more fruitful: 'For everything created by God is good, and nothing is to be rejected if it is received by thanksgiving; for then it is consecrated by the word of God and prayer.' J.N.D. Kelly comments on this verse:

> The sentence does not claim that an additional sanctification, over and above its intrinsic goodness as God's creature, is imparted to food by saying grace. What it states is that the grace sets the food in its true perspective and in that way enables us to regard it as sacred.[35]

Kelly is doubtless correct but it is significant that what appears to us to be a strong verb (*hagiazetai*) is used unself-consciously. The issue to be explored is whether there is a strand in certain aspects of western Protestant theology which seeks to make too stark a distinction between the 'spiritual' and the 'material', in a way that is not fully biblical. As an illustration, we shall examine two Old Testament categories, namely 'blessing' and 'consecration', both of which in verbal form are often employed in epicletic petitions.

The Blessing of Objects

In an Anglican discussion of the concept of blessing prepared by the Diocese of Melbourne there is the stark statement: 'Objects are not blessed in the Scriptures, since one does not have a living relationship with an object.'[36] This may be true if we are looking for formulas of blessing. There are, however, references in the Old Testament to God bestowing blessing on objects, and in the eucharistic prayer in

35 J.N.D. Kelly, *A Commentary on the Pastoral Epistles* (London, 1963), pp. 96-97.

36 Charles Sherlock (ed.), *An Anglican Pastoral Handbook* (Canberra, 1988), p. 70.

the Anglican tradition, God (the Father) is invariably the One invoked in epicletic petitions. While it is admitted that the references are not numerous and are generally late in the Old Testament period,[37] they are nevertheless not without significance, and are set out thus:[38]

> *Exodus 23:25* (Book of the Covenant): You shall serve the LORD your God, and I will bless your bread and your water; and I will take sickness away from the midst of you.
> *Genesis 27:27* (J): See, the smell of my son is as the smell of a field which the LORD has blessed!
> *Deuteronomy 7:13-14*: ... he will love you, bless you, and multiply you; he will also bless the fruit of your body and the fruit of your ground, your grain and your wine and your oil, the increase of your cattle and the young of your flock, in the land which he swore to your fathers to give you. You shall be blessed above all peoples ...
> *Deuteronomy 26:15*: Look down from thy holy habitation, from heaven, and bless thy people Israel and the ground which thou hast given us, as thou didst swear to our fathers, a land flowing with milk and honey.
> *Deuteronomy 28:2*: And all these blessings shall come upon you and overtake you, if you obey the voice of the LORD your God. Blessed shall you be in the city, and blessed shall you be in the field. Blessed shall be the fruit of your body and the fruit of your ground, and the fruit of your beasts, the increase of your cattle, and the young of your flock. Blessed shall be your basket and your kneading trough. Blessed shall you be when you come in, and blessed shall you be when you go out.
> *Deuteronomy 33:11*: Bless, O LORD, his substance, and accept the work of his hands ...
> *1 Samuel 9:13*: As soon as you enter the city, you will find him, before he goes up to the high place to eat; for the people will not eat till he comes, since he must bless the sacrifice ...
> *Jeremiah 31:23*: The LORD bless you, O habitation of righteousness, O holy hill!
> *Genesis 1:22* (P, creation of great sea monsters, all sea creatures, birds): And God blessed them, saying, ‘Be fruitful and multiply and fill the waters in the seas, and let birds multiply on the earth.’
> *Genesis 2:3* (P): So God blessed the seventh day and hallowed it, because on it God rested from all his work which he had done in creation.
> *Psalm 65:10*: Thou waterest its furrows abundantly, settling its ridges, softening it with showers, and blessing its growth.
> *Psalm 132:15*: I will abundantly bless her provisions ...
> *Proverbs 3:33*: The LORD’s curse is on the house of the wicked, but he blesses the abode of the righteous.

J.B. Taylor, in a doctoral dissertation, draws attention to Mowinckel’s observation that ancient Israel understood blessing in an objective sense – that it ‘can be enclosed

---

37 J. Scharbert, ‘ רב ך, brk’, in G. Johnannes Botterweck and Helmer Ringgren (eds), *Theological Dictionary of the Old Testament, Vol. 2* (Grands Rapids, 1977), p. 295. He states that with the exception of Ex. 23:25 and Gen. 27:27, virtually no reference is earlier than the time of Deuteronomy.

38 While it is notoriously difficult, if not impossible, to log individual verses according to date, the following order follows the general conventions of the dating of particular traditions in Old Testament scholarship.

or embodied in physical objects'.[39] Material things such as bread, wine, water, oil can be understood as containing blessing and dispensing blessing through their use. In this sense, '"Blessing the ground" is a prayer asking God to make actual the potential within it', the possibility such gifts have to enrich life.[40] He concludes that in cases like this: 'it is appropriate to speak of blessing, where blessing is the potential that these things possess for good. It is not inappropriate either to ask God to bless such things in terms of releasing that potential for the benefit of his children'[41] as, indeed, Deuteronomy 33:11 does. The crucial point is that in the Old Testament, God's blessing is related to the gifts he has bestowed for his covenant people. As well as being a blessing in themselves, they bestow blessing when the people partake of the fruits of the fields, the wine, bread and oil. This point is also stressed by Jean-Marie Tillard. Commenting on the Deuteronomy 26 text he writes: 'God's blessing ... is an assurance and a guarantee that the goods on which fullness of life depends are possessed and enjoyed'.[42] They are, therefore, the sign and the experience of divine favour which accompanies obedience. For Tillard, the important point is the link here between salvation and creation; the reality of salvation is experienced through receiving gifts of creation: 'It is, after all, not so much the vine, the harvest or the livestock that is blessed by God or his priests as the believer (and his family), by giving him a splendid crop or magnificent livestock.'[43] Westermann makes the same point:

> The connection between blessing and creation remains basic to all further uses of the word. When God blesses, it is the creator who blesses, and the blessing itself works itself out effectively in the life of what is blessed or the one asking the blessing. Blessing implies creation and is effective as the work of the creator.[44]

The point is that blessing is not an end in itself; it is intimately connected to the reception of the blessing. When the Old Testament speaks of God blessing material things, it is in the context of God's relationship to his people. Such blessing therefore is not to be regarded as a quasi-magical incantation, or as a kind of power bringing about a change in the material things, but rather a figure of speech, a way of expressing a truth that these material things are given by God to be the vehicle of divine grace and favour within a covenantal relationship.[45] Sirach 11:22 is an apt summary: 'The blessing of the Lord is the reward of the godly, and quickly God

---

39 John Brian Taylor, *The Theology of Blessing in the Hebrew Scriptures* (PhD dissertation, The Open University, 1992), p. 289.

40 Ibid., p. 290.

41 Ibid., p. 291. Taylor also criticizes uncritical use of the adjective 'inanimate' in that to speak of *anima* is to introduce a Latin concept into a Hebrew context. However, he suggests that in Hebrew terms, the word 'inanimate' can be applied to something if it does not possess the seeds of its own continuance, ibid.

42 Tillard, 'Blessing, Sacramentality and Epiclesis', p. 98.

43 Ibid., p. 99.

44 C. Westermann, *Genesis 1-11: A Commentary* (London, 1984), p. 140.

45 This interpretation is confirmed by Christopher Wright Mitchell's exhaustive study *The Meaning of BRK 'To Bless' in the Old Testament* (Atlanta, 1987). Commenting on the Deuteronomic terms he says:

causes his blessing to flourish.' Although the characteristic liturgical form of blessing became in Jewish statutory prayer in the pre-Rabbinic period the *berakah*, where God is blessed for his goodness and providential care,[46] the biblical strand of God blessing 'inanimate' entities did not entirely disappear. It is present, for example, in the following benediction, an ancient Palestinian rendering of benediction 9 of the Eighteen Benedictions:

> Bless, O Lord our God, this year for us,
> and let it be good in all the varieties of its produce.
> Hasten the year of our redemptive End.
> Grant dew and rain upon the face of the earth,
> and satiate the world out of the treasuries of Your goodness;
> and grant a blessing to the work of our hands.
> You are praised, O Lord, who blesses the years.[47]

While it is possible that New Testament references to Jesus blessing food (Matthew 14:19; 26:26; Mark 6:41; 8:7; 14:22; Luke 9:16; 24:30) refer to the *berakah* form of thanksgiving,[48] it is also possible that he used other forms of expression; beyond that we can say no more.[49] The Pauline reference in 1 Corinthians 10:16, 'The cup of blessing which we bless' is a firmer reference.

> the statement that 'the fruit of your womb/land/animals will be blessed' means 'you will be blessed with numerous and healthy offspring, and abundant good produce'. The emphasis is on the reception of good benefits by the Israelites rather than on the reception of blessing by the offspring or produce. Similarly, 'Your basket and kneading trough will be blessed' (v 5) could be paraphrased as 'You will be blessed with a full basket and full kneading trough.' (p. 41)

He concludes: 'The factor that makes a blessing a blessing is the relationship between God and the person blessed' (p. 165).

46 We may note the theory advanced by Lawrence A. Hoffman, that in terms of spirituality, the *berakah* was not so much a prayer for God to 'consecrate' material entities such as food, but rather, because all things come from God, it was to release that which is by its very nature sacred into the profane so that ordinary people could consume it. So the blessing releases food from its natural sacred state into common use. Lawrence A. Hoffman, 'Rabinic *Berakah* and Jewish Spirituality', in *Concilium*, 3, pp. 18-30. The question is whether this interpretation was universal throughout the Rabbinic period; certainly, if 1 Timothy 3:4-5 is to be interpreted against the background of Jewish *berakoth*, thanksgiving is deemed to sanctify.

47 Text from 'Jewish Prayer Texts of the Rabbinic Period', in J.J. Petuchowski and M. Brocke (eds), *The Lord's Prayer and Jewish Liturgy* (London, 1978), pp. 28-29. This version is termed 'An Ancient Palestinian Version' (p. 27).

48 As prescribed in *Mishnah berakoth* 6:1; while the *Mishnah* in its present form was compiled at the end of the second century CE, many of the precepts were observed in the Rabbinic period.

49 Joseph Heinemann stresses the variety of expression in private and non-statutory prayer at the time of Christ; he also understands Jesus's prayers as standing against the prayer of the synagogue and fixed statutory prayer in general, *Prayer in the Talmud* (Berlin and New York, 1977), ch. 7. The issue is also raised by B.D. Spinks in relation to the Passover *birkat hamazon*, 'Beware the Liturgical Horses!', pp. 213-214.

The Consecration of Objects

The Hebrew root *q-d-s*, translated normally by *hagios* and its cognates in the LXX, is a wide-ranging concept, principally related in the Old Testament to people, places and objects in the context of the worship of God. The origin of *q-d-s* is unclear, possibly related to the base root *q-d* 'to divide' and so marking the separation of people and things for use in the worship and service of God.[50] The Old Testament use of the concept is illustrated by Leviticus 10:10: 'You are to distinguish between the holy and the common, and between the unclean and the clean ...'. Holy people, objects, and places are those which are distinguished or separated from what is common, ordinary, secular. There are many examples of the holiness of objects in the Old Testament. The following quotations illustrate the scope of the concept:

> *Exodus 29:34*: And if any of the flesh for the ordination, or of the bread, remain until the morning, then you shall burn the remainder with fire; it shall not be eaten, because it is holy.
> *Exodus 29:43-44*: There I will meet with the people of Israel, and it shall be sanctified by my glory; I will consecrate the tent of meeting and the altar; Aaron also and his sons I will consecrate, to serve me as priests.
> *Joshua 6:19*: But all silver and gold, and vessels of bronze and iron, are sacred to the Lord ...
> *2 Chronicles 29:33*: And the consecrated offerings were six hundred bulls and three thousand sheep.

Jacob Milgrom makes the helpful observation that what 'sets apart' entities described as 'holy'is not human volition but divine decree. Commenting in the light of Semitic polytheism he writes:

> 'Holy' is thus aptly defined, in any context, as 'that which is unapproachable except through divinely imposed restrictions', or 'that which is withdrawn from common use' ... In opposition to this widespread animism we notice its marked absence from the Bible. Holiness there is not innate. The source of holiness is assigned to God alone. Holiness is the extension of his nature; it is the agency of his will. If certain things are termed holy – such as the land (Canaan), person (priest), place (sanctuary) or time (holy day) – they are so by virtue of divine dispensation.[51]

---

50 O. Procksch, 'αγιος', in Gerhard Kittel (ed.), *Theological Dictionary of the New Testament Vol. 1* (Grand Rapids, 1964), p. 89.

51 Jacob Milgrom, *Leviticus 1-16* (New York, 1991), p. 730. A distinction is made between what is holy (*qodes*) and what is most holy (*qodaism*), the latter relating to portions of sacrifices which are eaten (Lev. 2:3, 10; 7:1, 6; 10:12, 17); the irredeem-ability of the 'devoted things' (Lev. 27:28); the tabernacle, altar and utensils (Ex. 40:10; Num. 4:4, 19); and incense (Ex. 30:36), as well as the 'Most Holy Place', the adytum of the Tabernacle/Temple. Milgrom comments that in P the designation 'most holy' is reserved, apart from sacrifices, to the Tabernacle *sancta*, but there is a 'plasticity' in its use. Sometimes, objects designed 'most holy' are at other times simply described as 'holy' (e.g. incense in Ex. 30:37, the altar in Ex. 40:9). He further demonstrates that this distinction was not invented by Israel, ibid., pp. 183, 320-321; 'The Compass of Biblical Sancta', *The Jewish Quarterly Review*, 65 (1975):

Westermann draws out the same emphasis in his discussion of the hallowing of the seventh day: 'In Gen. 2:3 God sanctifies the seventh day and this means that it is God's sanctifying action alone that sets it apart. Human action, human observance or non-observance, can make no difference.'[52] The holiness of material things is thus related intimately to divine institution. What sets them apart is not the priest or any human agency, but divine decree.[53] The holiness accruing to them is essentially contextual, that is, is determined by their use on the basis of divine decree. Once, however, something is set apart for sacred use it is not to be returned to common use, hence the regulations to burn the remains of the sacrifice in Exodus 29.

Therefore, as with blessing, this concept seemed more bound up with how certain things are viewed and regarded than by notions of metaphysical change. A standard objection by some Christians is that the Old Testament usage of the idea of the holy, particularly in its cultic context, presupposes a dualism between what is 'holy' and what is 'common', a cultic distinction rendered null and void by the Gospel. This is underlined by the Old Testament connection between the concepts of holiness and ritual purity with its cultic distinction between what is clean and unclean, a distinction abrogated by the teaching of Jesus. Although Leviticus 10:10 may suggest the concepts of holy/common and clean/unclean are in apposition, Milgrom comments:

> Persons and objects are subject to four possible states: holy, common, pure and impure. Two of them can exist simultaneously, either holy or common and either pure or impure. Still, one combination is excluded in the Priestly system: whereas the common may be either pure or impure, the sacred may never be impure.[54]

De Vaux also distinguishes the two concepts thus: 'purification meant removing the obstacle which hindered a man from coming near to God, whereas sanctification either prepared a man to meet God or resulted from close contact with God. Purification expressed the negative, sanctification the positive, aspect.'[55] What is 'common' is 'made holy' through divine dispensation but what is not holy simply remains common, but not necessarily unclean. Therefore, concepts of holiness need not imply a dualistic view of reality; there is no need to introduce the related but distinguishable idea of ritual purity. The language of holiness appears once again to be figurative and designatory, according to the institution of God in the context of the worship of his people, rather in the same way that Christians designate the sacraments as 'holy baptism' or 'holy communion'.

205-216. This distinction also appears to be about the esteem in which certain objects were held because of the nature of their use in worship.

52 Ibid., p. 172.

53 Although Roland de Vaux comments that late in Israel's history rites were instituted to bring about consecration. The use of oil is significant here (Ex. 30:26ff.; 40:9ff.; Lev. 8:10), *Ancient Israel* (London, 1961), p. 465. However, anointing in the Scriptures usually carries with it the idea of God's choice, and so these ceremonies are still related essentially to divine institution.

54 Milgrom, *Leviticus 1-16*, p. 732; cf. p. 616.

55 de Vaux, *Ancient Israel*, p. 464.

There is also an important strand in the Gospel tradition and other New Testament passages that is happy to employ conventional designations, e.g. 'holy city' (Matthew 4:5; 27:53; Revelation 11:2, cf. 21:2), 'holy mountain' (2 Peter 1:18), and the sanctifying 'power' of the Temple and altar (Matthew 23:16ff.)

Whereas the Hebrew root *q-d-s* is invariably translated by *hagios* and its cognates in the LXX, the Vulgate employs a range of verbs: *sanctificare* (the main use), *consecrare* and *vovere*. Variety is also apparent in English translations: 'sanctify', 'consecrate', 'hallow', 'make holy', as illustrated by the verses above.

The variety of expression in Latin and English relating to the description of divine activity with regard to objects in the Old Testament is further confirmed by the observation of J.-M. Tillard. Commenting on the blessings found in Pope Pius XI's *Rituale Romanum* with the appendix added in 1935, he says this of the verbs:

> These include, for example, *sanctificare* and even *consecrare*, and sometimes even, without any clear difference in meaning within the space of a few lines and both referring to the same action, either *benedicere* or *consecrare*. Despite this, however, with the exception of the altar, where the rite is explicitly called a *consecratio*, all these cases are classified under the heading of 'blessings'. It would seem that the idea of blessing is not at all precise and even borders on the equivocal.[56]

This observation underlines the fact that whatever space there is between the concepts of blessing and sanctification in the Bible, the liturgical tradition is more imprecise and fluid.

This survey of biblical material serves to underline the fact that the utter distinction between the 'material' and the 'spiritual' is alien to the Jewish background out of which Christianity sprung. All is created by God and there is an inter-dependence of all created things.[57]

Blessing, Consecration and the Epiclesis

Our consideration of the concepts of the blessing of objects and the consecration of objects in the Old Testament reveals a similar unselfconsciousness about the use of language that we observed in the New Testament citation from 1 Timothy 3. God is described as 'blessing' objects but the context is related to the promise of or the enjoyment of the good things that God has given in creation to his people in a covenantal relationship. Objects in worship are declared to be 'consecrated' because God has instituted them for use in worship so that, in de Vaux's phrase, they are 'automatically consecrated',[58] separated for an exclusive cultic use. Therefore, on a biblical understanding, neither concept carries with it any sense of material change and both concepts find their meaning in the context of the life of the community. It would appear that the Old Testament concept of consecration is not dissimilar to that of Cranmer's *Defence*:

56 Tillard, 'Blessing, Sacramentality and Epiclesis', p. 97.

57 Alasdair Heron, *Table and Tradition* (Edinburgh, 1983), p. 27.

58 de Vaux, *Ancient Israel*, p. 464.

> Consecration is the separation of any thing from a profane and worldly use unto a spiritual and godly use ... Even so when common bread and wine be taken and severed from other bread and wine to the use of the holy communion, that portion of bread and wine, although it be of the same substance that the other is from the which it is severed, yet it is now called consecrated, or holy bread and holy wine.[59]

The significant distinction is that whereas there is a tendency to regard the 'separation' in Anglican terms as a human action, something the Church does, the biblical material stresses divine institution, an insight which the Anglican tradition would absorb well:

> ... that we receiving these thy creatures of bread and wine, *according to thy son our Saviour Jesus Christ's holy institution* ... (Holy Communion 1552/1662)

That is, we set aside bread and wine for communion in response to Christ's institution.

Sensitivities about the concept of blessing can be illustrated by the commentary by the English Liturgical Commission on two prayers in the *ASB* (1980) where petition for blessing occurs. The first is in the baptismal rite:

> Bless this water, that your *servants* who *are* washed in it may be made one with Christ in his death and resurrection, to be cleansed and delivered from all sin.[60]

The commentary affirms:

> ... it has been taught and believed that the water acquires through the act of blessing a potency which it does not normally possess, a potency which is there for as long as the water exists, and which is independent of the use to which it is put. It is therefore necessary to explain that in this prayer God is asked to bless the water for a particular and limited purpose. The prayer is a request that God will make use of the water and through it perform his own work on the candidates present. The petition terminates therefore with the candidates, not with the water.[61]

The second is the prayer before the exchange of rings in the marriage service:

> Heavenly Father, by your blessing, let *this ring* be to *N* and *N* a symbol of unending love and faithfulness, to remind them of the vow and covenant which they have made this day.[62]

The commentary here is more explicit about the debate:

> Some people desire to have the ring blessed while to others the blessing of an inanimate object is anathema. The form of words at section 13 is a prayer that by God's blessing the

59 *Defence*, p. 181.

60 *ASB*, p. 231.

61 *The Alternative Service Book 1980: A Commentary by the Liturgical Commission*, p. 111.

62 *ASB*, p. 292.

ring may be set apart as a symbol of unending love, reminding the couple of the covenant between them. The words seek to unite in prayer those of differing points of view.[63]

While both of these explanatory comments have the ring of political wheeling and dealing about them, the end result (in which the blessing is related to the benefits bestowed in baptism in the lives of the candidates and the on-going relationship of the married couple) is in fact utterly biblical, where, as we have suggested, blessing is not an end itself but is related to the life experience of the covenant people of God. The formula 'bless ... that ...' can be defended to the uttermost on biblical principles.[64]

The basic issue is that whether Christian theological reflection on the role of the Spirit in the sacraments and the Christian understanding of intercessory prayer can be applied to these spheres of blessing and consecration, so that we can ask the Father to 'bless' the elements by the power and presence of the Spirit so that the eucharistic blessing will be bestowed through receiving them. Similarly, whether verbs such as 'sanctify' or 'make holy' can rightly be used where the intention is that through the power of the Spirit and in obedience to Christ's institution, they should be the vehicles of sacramental grace. Whereas Anglicans are used to the notion of 'The Prayer of Consecration' or a description of the elements as 'consecrated', there appears to be a certain unease in parts of the Communion about petitions that the elements might be 'sanctified' or 'made holy', although biblically and doctrinally there is no distinction in meaning to be made. Interestingly, both concepts find expression side by side in the *epiclesis* of the 1549 rite:

> Heare us (o merciful father) we beseche thee; and with thy holy spirite and worde, vouchsafe to bl+esse and sanc+tifie these thy gyftes, and creatures of bread and wyne, that they maie be unto us the bodye and bloude of thy moste derely beloued sonne Jesus Christe.[65]

We have already observed Bryan Spinks's argument that the 1549 *epiclesis* is inspired by reformed rather than eastern sources. Spinks suggests that Peter Martyr's understanding of consecration, namely,

> ... bread and wine are translated from the natural order, and profane degree in which they were, to a sacramental state and order, both by the work of the Holy Spirit and by the institution of the Lord ...[66]

may have influenced Cranmer's formula. The problem was that western catholic orthodoxy could also be read into it. Part of the difficulty was the preliminary position

63 *The Alternative Service Book 1980: A Commentary by the Liturgical Commission*, p. 128.

64 The same principle is set out in the introduction in the *Book of Blessings* of the Roman Ritual (as approved for use in the USA): 'such blessings are invoked always with a view to the people who use the objects to be blessed and frequent the places to be blessed', *Book of Blessings* (New York, 1989), p. 24.

65 *The First and Second Prayer Books of Edward VI* (London and New York, 1910), p. 222.

66 Spinks, "'And with thy Holy Spirit and Word'", p. 99.

of Cranmer's 1549 *epiclesis* where the formula seems only to relate to the elements and not the elements and communicants. The 'blessings' to the communicants are not articulated until later on in the prayer, far removed from the *epiclesis*:

> ... humbly besechyng thee, that whosoeuer shalbee partakers of thys holy Communion, maye worthely receiue the most precious body and bloude of thy sonne Jesus Christe: and bee fulfilled with thy grace and heauenly benediccion, and made one bodye with thy sonne Jesu Christe, that he maye dwell in them, and they in hym.[67]

Moreover, the post-communion prayer emphasises the communion as a pledge of divine favour towards the people of God:

> ... and haste assured us (duely receiuing the same) of thy fauour and goodnes toward us, an that we be very membres incorporate in thy Misticall bodye, whiche is the blessed companye of all faythfull people, and heyres through hope of thy euerlasting kingdome ...

in a way similar in intent to the biblical concept of blessing.

This examination of the blessing and consecration of objects suggests that the biblical material is more nuanced and contoured than is sometimes allowed. The unselfconscious use of active verbs in a contextual framework ought to enable Anglicans to adopt forms of the *epiclesis* which relate the work of the Spirit to the elements in ways that do prejudice fidelity to the Scriptures or suggest a theology of consecration contradictory to 'Anglican tradition' as expressed in such historic formularies as the 1662 *Book of Common Prayer*.

Creation, Re-Creation and Eschatology

Reference has been made to evangelical concerns that to include an *epiclesis* on the elements is to adopt uncritically a dualistic cultic distinction rendered obsolete by the teaching of Jesus and the achievement of the Cross. However, those defending an *epiclesis* on the elements also raise the charge of dualism against those who wish to distinguish between how the Spirit operates in relation to people and matter. This debate has been strong in Canada and is outlined above with reference to the views of Paul Gibson, Stephen Reynolds and William Crockett. A central issue in this discussion is the question of creation and re-creation. Whatever meaning was intended by the author of the Priestly account of creation, traditional Christian interpretation has normally applied the Hebrew *ruach* in Genesis 1:2-3 to the Holy Spirit: 'The earth was without form and void, and darkness was upon the face of the deep; and the Spirit of God was moving over the face of the waters. And God said, "Let there be light."' The Spirit as creator-Spirit is a central pillar of pneumatology (Genesis 2:7; Psalm 104:30; Ecclesiastes 12:7). Moreover, the Genesis creation accounts present a picture of the fundamental unity of creation. The creation of human beings is set in the context of the goodness of the whole created order. All creation reflects the love, beauty and craftsmanship of God. It is this insight which enables the psalmist to say 'The heavens are telling the glory of God; and the

67 *The First and Second Prayer Books of Edward VI*, p. 223.

firmament proclaims his handiwork' (Psalm 19:1). In this sense, creation reflects the divine glory, and is itself the vehicle of the praise of God. So, in the spirituality of the *Benedicite*, human beings give voice to the created order to return the praise of the One whose glory they manifest. But creation is not a static concept; it is a dynamic movement of time, a theatre of the continuing activity of the Spirit. Psalm 104 speaks of God withdrawing his *ruach*, and so created things die, but 'When thou sendest forth thy Spirit (*ruach*), they are created; and thou renewest the face of the ground' (Psalm 104:30). Through the Spirit life is created, sustained and renewed. But just as all creation in its goodness is of a piece, so all creation in its brokenness, pain and incompleteness, is also of a piece. In Genesis 1-11, human rebellion against God has consequences not only for humanity, but humanity's context (for example, Genesis 2:17-end). The dislocation between God and humanity is cosmic in scope. So the salvation proclaimed in and through Christ in the New Testament embraces not only human subjection to sin and death but the hope of 'new heavens and a new earth in which righteousness dwells' (2 Peter 3:13). The New Testament offers the hope of eschatological re-creation through the Christ-event. Nowhere is this more eloquently stated than in Romans 8:19-23:

> For the creation waits with eager longing for the revealing of the sons of God; for the creation was subjected to futility, not of its own will but by the will of the him who subjected it in hope; because the creation itself will be set free from its bondage to decay and obtain the glorious liberty of the children of God. We know that the whole creation has been groaning in travail together until now; and not only the creation, but we ourselves, who have the first fruits of the Spirit, groan inwardly as we wait for adoption as sons, the redemption of our bodies.

Here Paul envisages the setting free of the entire cosmos.[68] The question is in what sense is the creation to be set free and by whom? Earlier in verse 11, he expounds his conviction that the breaking in of the age to come has been through the resurrection of Christ and that for Christ and for all redeemed by him, the agent of the transformation into the life of the new age is the Spirit: 'If the Spirit of him who raised Jesus from the dead dwells in you, he who raised Christ Jesus from the dead will give life to your mortal bodies also through his Spirit which dwells in you.'

The connection between the resurrection and the Spirit is illustrated by a strand in the biblical material expounded by Jürgen Moltmann and Tom Smail, that the Spirit transfigured Jesus's humanity at the resurrection. Drawing on Acts 2:33, Romans 1:4, and 1 Corinthians 15:45, Smail argues that the resurrection and glorification of Christ constitute a new imparting of the Spirit, in addition to the regenerative imparting at his conception, and the messianic anointing at his baptism. By these outpourings the Spirit perfects 'all his work in Christ's humanity'. So it is 'the eschatological Spirit of resurrection and glorification' which Christ pours out upon the Church at Pentecost,

---

68 Although the definition of 'the creation' (*he ktisis*) has been disputed, most commentators agree that Paul envisages the whole of the created order in distinction to humankind; C.E.B. Cranfield, *A Critical and Exegetical Commentary on the Epistle to the Romans, Vol. I* (Edinburgh, 1975), pp. 411-12; J.D.G. Dunn, *Romans 1-8* (Dallas, 1988), pp. 469-470, 487.

inaugurating the last days and guaranteeing their consummation.[69] So Moltmann, also employing the language of transfiguration, speaks of Christ's resurrection as 'the Spirit's first eschatological "work"'. Christ who before the resurrection is an *object* of the Spirit's activity now becomes the *subject* of the sending of the Spirit on the Church, the beginning of the 'messianic era' in which the Spirit is poured out on all flesh, and through the Spirit, 'God always comes to be at home in his own world'.[70]

In Romans 8:11, the future tense of 'will give life' strongly suggests that Paul is referring to the final resurrection of Christians. 'Mortal' in this sense includes the dead, but Paul sees a fundamental link between this present earthly body and the body of the resurrection (1 Corinthians 15:42ff.) Certainly, here Paul wishes to make no distinction between 'spirit' and 'matter', or in this sense between what is living and what is dead. It is the work of the Spirit to give life even to our mortal bodies.[71] The resurrection of Christ and the eschatological resurrection of Christians is, in Barrett's phrase, 'connected by the presence and activity of the Holy Spirit ..., who brought the life-giving activity of God to bear upon every stage of the intervening period ..., so that even our *mortal* bodies ... are transformed and quickened'.[72]

Although Paul tantalizingly leaves us to speculate about what the liberating of creation means, it seems reasonable to expect that, by analogy with what he has said about the transformation of humanity, this sovereign eschatological act of liberating creation or, in the language of Revelation 21:1, realizing re-creation, will also be by the power of the Spirit who once brooded upon the waters of chaos.

The gift of the Spirit and the present experience of salvation in the Christian is rightly seen as the sign of the in-breaking of the life of the age to come, a foretaste and pledge of the full and final salvation which Christ has prepared, in Paul's language, a deposit guaranteeing what is to come (2 Corinthians 5:5). The possession of the Spirit by the Christian is the firstfruits of the new creation (Romans 8:23). While Paul primarily relates his teaching to Christians and certainly does not relate his teaching to the sacraments, there is an important strand in liturgical scholarship that seeks to understand the origins of *epiclesis* in an eschatological framework.[73] Cranfield

---

69 Tom Smail, *The Giving Gift: The Holy Spirit in Person*, 2nd ed. (London, 1994), pp. 104-107.

70 Jürgen Moltmann, *The Trinity and the Kingdom of God* (London, 1981), pp. 122-125.

71 Moltmann underlines the 'physical nature' of the Pauline doctrine of resurrection: 'The Old Testament idea of the resurrection of the dead already resists every form of spiritualizing reinterpretation. The eschatological "work" of the Holy Spirit is physical resurrection, physical transfiguration, and transformation of the physical form of existence. It is from the transfigured humanity of the risen Christ that the Holy Spirit proceeds. It is through this that the Spirit is mediated. The One who is physically transfigured, transfigures physically, as the first-born, his brothers and sisters, who are made in the same form as himself'. Ibid., pp. 123-124.

72 C.K. Barrett, *The Epistle to the Romans* (London, 1957), pp. 159-160.

73 See Crockett, *Eucharist: Symbol of Transformation*, pp. 54-57. But note Richard McCall's argument that the development of epicletic formulae actually shifted the focus *away* from eschatology to petition for God's purposes in the world, 'The Shape of the Eucharistic

understands the liberating of creation to mean 'the freedom fully and perfectly to fulfil its Creator's purpose for it'.[74] If the eucharist celebrates and proclaims the salvation wrought by Christ on the Cross, and offers communion with a risen Lord, and is itself the pledge and foretaste of the eternal life of the kingdom, is it illegitimate to see in the invocation of the Spirit upon the eucharistic action, including both the worshippers and in this context the elements, a pledge of the transformation of all creation, as these created things indeed fulfil God's purpose as the medium of the spiritual blessings bestowed upon the communicants?[75] Once again we are using the language of symbol and metaphor to convey a spirituality, and witness to a pledge, a promise of future glory. While there is no biblical proof-text to confirm this line of argument, the basic question is whether it is theologically responsible. Colin Gunton urges that rather than being dominated by questions of how and in what sense bread and wine become something *else*, attention should be given to the *materialism* of the elements. So that their *representative* function

> … the Church offers not only itself as a 'living sacrifice, holy and acceptable to God' (Rom. 12:1-2) but also the whole created order, in anticipation of its final perfecting … It is the eschatological office of the Spirit that he is the one by whom the Father brings particular created things to perfection through the ascended Christ, beginning with the first fruits, his body incarnate, crucified and raised from the tomb.[76]

Certainly, the Christ we encounter in the eucharist is not simply the Christ of two thousand years ago; it is rather the cosmic, glorified Christ whose presence fills all things (Ephesians 4:10); the eschatological Christ who calls us into his future. The Spirit is both the 'remembrancer divine' (to use Charles Wesley's phrase) and the one who unites us to Christ in his eschatological fullness. The elements take us back to the Cross, Christ's body given and blood shed for our salvation, but also forward to the consummation of what the cross achieved, the promise of ultimate perfection of all things in Christ.

One further point needs to be made. The adoption of the 'Antiochene' shape for the eucharistic prayer makes clear a fundamental link between *anamnesis* and *epiclesis*. St Paul in 1 Corinthians 11:26 follows his account of the institution with application that the eucharistic eating and drinking is a proclamation of the death of the Lord until he comes. Cranmer included this eschatological reference in 1549 and it has remained as an important element in Anglican eucharistic theology ever since. More

---

Prayer: An Essay on the Unfolding of an Action, *Worship*, 74 (2001): 321-333. The issues raised in (his) footnote 27 need further investigation.

74 Cranfield, *A Critical and Exegetical Commentary on the Epistle to the Romans, Vol. I*, p. 416.

75 Wainwright rules out any quasi-gnostic division of material and spiritual; God's purposes are for creation; the eucharistic elements confirm the picture from the beginning of Genesis of a material creation destined to be the scene and vehicle of God's intended communion between himself and humankind. He writes: 'Any eschatology which reduces the cosmic reference to anthropology, and the anthropology to "spiritualism", is guilty simply of ignoring the bread and wine of the eucharist', *Eucharist and Eschatology*, p. 149.

76 Colin E. Gunton, *Father, Son and Holy Spirit* (London, 2003), pp. 119-120.

recent eucharistic revisions, in incorporating a verbal *anamnesis*, include within the scope of the remembrance an anticipation of the *parousia*. Joachim Jeremias, in his seminal work *The Eucharistic Words of Jesus*, interpreted the phrase 'until he come' in an active sense, i.e. we proclaim the Lord's death in order that he might come; that God might hear the prayer of his people and hasten the *parousia*.[77] While we need not follow his reasoning that in 1 Corinthians 11, the eucharistic proclamation is made to God, he is probably correct in interpreting the 'until he comes' as the longing plea of the Church. If the *anamnesis* thus articulates the eschatological hope of the coming of the kingdom, the *epiclesis*, following it, becomes the natural prayer for its fulfilment. The point is well made by David Power; the *anamnesis*, he argues:

> ... has an eschatological character, not only because it may include an anticipation of the second coming, but more importantly because it points to the eucharist itself as the fulfillment and presence of the divine blessings given to humanity in Jesus Christ who is remembered and who is the ever present Lord of the church and humanity. It is therefore the proper foundation for the invocation of the eschatological Spirit, who holds the church in the unity of the one Body of Christ and of the one hope of mercy and immortality.[78]

The Unity of the Church

We have already noted the important strand in Nissiotis's theology, that the Spirit is the continual presence in the Church of the uncreated energies of the grace of the Trinity, and hence full communion between God and his Church is established by the Spirit and this is what gives the Church its unity. Sacramentally, such a union is constituted by baptism, and we may note the central role ascribed to the Spirit in Pauline thought; so, in 1 Corinthians 12:13: 'For by one Spirit we were all baptized into one body – Jews or Greeks, slaves or free – and all were made to drink of one Spirit.'[79] We note also, however, a similar use of the phrase 'one body' in a eucharistic context:

> The cup of blessing which we bless, is it not a participation in the blood of Christ? The bread which we break, is it not a participation in the body of Christ? Because there is one bread, we who are many are one body, for we all partake of the one bread. (1 Corinthians 10:16-17)

While, here, there is no explicit citation of the Spirit, we see both sacraments establishing the unity of the body. But this is no mere human construct; baptism into the body is an action of the Spirit, eucharistic union is through participation in the body and blood of Christ. Nor should the references to Christ and the Spirit be

---

77 Joachim Jeremias, *The Eucharistic Words of Jesus*, 3rd ed. (London, 1966), pp. 253-254.

78 David N. Power, 'The Anamnesis: Remembering, We Offer' in Senn, *New Eucharistic Prayers*, p. 165.

79 Some commentators see a reference to the eucharist in Paul's use of the verb 'drink'; the passage is, however, entirely understandable in the context of baptism alone in which 'drinking' is used as a metaphor.

interpreted in an exclusive sense; in his teaching on baptism Paul uses Christological imagery as well as pneumatological; we can surely assume an equivalence in relation to the eucharist. In this sense, the eucharist can be understood as a renewal of the Church's unity; an intense symbol and means of not only understanding the action of God in creating a united, reconciled humanity, but through the divine action in the sacrament being drawn into a deeper experience of that unity. And the sense of unity works on different levels; a personal and corporate unity with the Godhead, a corporate unity within the local congregation, a greater corporate unity with all who share Christ's bread in each and every place, and the expectation of an ultimate unity, to which the eucharist points, at the end when sacraments shall cease. Professor James Torrance argues that worship is not a merely human activity but a participation in the life of the Trinity; 'the Triune God is not only the *object* of our worship, but that our worship is seen as the gift of participating through the Spirit in Christ's communion with the Father'.[80] While this is true of all worship, it is especially true of the eucharist, as through the presence and power of the Spirit we are united to Christ and so share in the communion of the Father and the Son, and through the Spirit are united to each other within the body of Christ. The *epiclesis* is a most appropriate liturgical expression of these truths as the articulation of the prayer, having set out the great panorama of God's redemptive work in Christ, that we may participate in the divine life, and be drawn together through the Spirit into that unity which is God's will and gift.[81]

The Consecration of the Elements

On a number of occasions, reference has been made to the conviction, present in much contemporary debate about the eucharist, that the entire eucharistic prayer effects consecration; the elements of bread and wine become for the communicant the body and blood of Christ because thanks have been given over them. This is the understanding of the dynamic of the eucharist gift found in Justin Martyr and *Apostolic Tradition*. It builds on the place of thanksgiving, or more strictly, blessing and thanksgiving found in Jewish domestic prayer and liturgy. We have seen how this strand has appeared in Anglican thinking, for example, in Thorndike and in the twentieth century in Dix. It is this understanding which has encouraged Christians to understand the institution narrative as part of the agenda for thanksgiving rather than as an independent consecratory unit or formula, and the *epiclesis* as part of the supplication rather than as a consecratory formula or complement to the narrative as together effecting consecration. Such an understanding therefore ought to take the heat out of epicletic formulae. The challenge is how to express the *epiclesis* so that it doesn't *look* like a 'formula'. This is most clearly achieved if epicletic petitions include an explicit reference to the dynamic of thanksgiving. Interestingly, the prayer in *Apostolic Tradition* achieves this:

80 James B. Torrance, 'The Doctrine of the Trinity in our Contemporary Situation,' in Heron, *The Forgotten Trinity*, p. 7.

81 See Louis Weil, 'The Holy Spirit: Source of Unity in the Liturgy', *Anglican Theological Review*, 83 (2001): 409-415.

> ... we offer to you the bread and the cup, giving thanks because you have held us worthy to stand before you and minister unto you. And we ask that you would send your Holy Spirit upon the offering of your holy Church; that, gathering her into one, you would grant to all who receive the holy things ... [82]

The offering of the bread and cup is in this sense a thank-offering, related intimately to the preceding Christological narrative; moreover, the invocation is upon the oblation, which in context must mean far more than the material elements; we might say that it is upon the whole action, embracing elements and communicants in a single sweep and spirituality.

The point underlines the structural issue about thanksgiving and supplication; the supplication arises out of and depends upon the thanksgiving. But the petition is still necessary; indeed, John Zizioulas goes as far as to say that to 'make Trinitarian doctrine decisive for Ecclesiology, we must give to the Holy Spirit a *constitutive* role in the structure of the Church' – the Spirit *'con-stitutes'* the Church while Christ *'in-stitutes'* it: 'This is the *epicletical* character of Ecclesiology, evident in the first place in the Eucharist itself which, although based on the given assurance of the words of institution, stands constantly in need of the invocation of the Spirit in order to be that which it is.'[83]

If consecration by thanksgiving has created a broader room, the same is true in the related issue of the presence of Christ in the eucharist. It has perhaps been characteristic of Anglican methodology not to speculate unduly on the 'how' but rather the 'who'. Henry McAdoo has sought to re-establish a theologically defensible notion of 'mystery'.[84] However, Catholic as well as Protestant theologians prefer to speak of the presence of Christ in wider terms than simply in association with the eucharistic elements. The presence of Christ is recognized in the assembly – 'where two or three are gathered together in my name there am I in the midst of them' – as eucharistic worship is seen rightly as the common celebration of the people of God. The concept of presidency recognizes that the president is part of the assembly, undertaking a particular role by virtue of the authority bestowed by the Church. Christ is present in the proclamation of the Word, through Scripture reading and preaching; Christ the Word of God addressing the Church through the power of the Spirit. Christ is present in the eucharistic action, in the taking and thanking, the breaking of the bread and the distribution of the bread and cup.[85] The eucharistic action is a movement, embracing consecration and culminating in the reception of the elements. John McKenna emphasizes the fact that an *epiclesis* on *both* the elements and communicants (an *epiclesis* proper as he calls it) naturally underlines the reception of the gifts by the assembly and so affirms the 'unity of "consecration"

---

82 Text from Jasper and Cuming, *Prayers of the Eucharist*, p. 35.

83 Zizioulas, 'The Doctrine of God the Trinity Today: Suggestions for an Ecumenical Study', p. 28.

84 H.R. McAdoo and Kenneth Stevenson, *The Mystery of the Eucharist in the Anglican Tradition* (Norwich, 1995), pp. 1-104.

85 *The General Instruction on the Roman Missal* (2005) expresses Christ's presence as being in the liturgical assembly, in the person of the minister, in Christ's word, and 'substantially and continuously under the Eucharistic species', ibid., p. 11.

in the narrower sense, and Communion'.[86] This would seem an obvious enough point, although written against a background in the Roman tradition where non-communicating attendance had been the norm for centuries and the popularity of *extra*-eucharistic devotions. Anglican sensitivities come from a different route, the fear, even the abhorrence of 'receptionism', the term applied to followers of the Cranmerian tradition of eucharistic theology and, for that reason, many contemporary evangelicals. Receptionism has been criticized not only because of an implied individualism – the individual 'worthy communicant', but because of a suspicion, born chiefly out of misrepresentation, that faith creates the sacrament, rather than what the formularies say, that the sacramental gift is received by faith. For this reason, much Anglican discussion of consecration has tended to underplay the dynamic of reception.[87] McAdoo reminds us of its centrality, as he defines the Anglican tradition as teaching: 'Through the Holy Spirit's action, by the instrumentality of the effectual symbols, the eucharist embodies uniquely the living activity of the risen and glorified Christ imparting to his faithful people "who have duly received these holy mysteries" (*BCP*) all the benefits of his paschal sacrifice.'[88]

The point is that this broad understanding of *epiclesis*, set in the context of the entire eucharistic prayer and action, enables a much more creative and varied form of expression. So modern Anglican texts from Canada, Australia and New Zealand can follow Hippolytus, invoking the Spirit on the 'offering' or 'celebration' of the Church. The Canadian prayers, with this broad understanding, do not even always include a reference to Christ's body and blood; prayer 1 says:

> Send the Holy Spirit upon us
> and upon these gifts,
> that all who eat and drink at this table
> may be one body and one holy people,
> a living sacrifice in Jesus Christ, our Lord.

Prayer 4 is bolder, invoking the Spirit on the earth, but also including no explicit reference to the *epiclesis* effecting a change in the elements:

> Send your Holy Spirit upon us
> and upon the offering of your Church,
> that we who eat and drink at this holy table
> may share the divine life of Christ our Lord.
> **Glory to you for ever and ever.**
>
> Pour out your Spirit upon the whole earth
> and make it your new creation.
> Gather your Church together ...

---

86 McKenna, *Eucharist and Holy Spirit*, pp. 190-191.

87 Geoffrey Cuming, following McKenna, defends Anglicanism's historic concern for the individual while recognizing that the corporate understanding of the Church's response is crucial. Geoffrey Cuming, *He Gave Thanks: An Introduction to the Eucharistic Prayer* (Bramcote, 1981), pp. 32-33.

88 Ibid., p. 82.

Similarly, prayer 6 emphasizes the presence of Christ in the action:

> Send your Holy Spirit on us and on these gifts,
> that we may know the presence of Jesus
> in the breaking of the bread,
> and share in the life
> of the family of your children.[89]

The Limits of the *Epiclesis*

Notwithstanding the role of the *epiclesis* in helping to articulate a rich expression of the work of the Spirit, the *epiclesis* cannot bear the whole weight of this. A ground-plan of thanksgiving and supplication does not necessarily mean that the thanksgiving is dominated by praise to the Father for salvation wrought through the Son to the exclusion of mention of the Spirit. Creation and redemption are rightly seen in the Christian tradition as the work of the Triune God. One of the strengths of the preface of Eucharistic Prayer A of *Common Worship* Order 1 is the succinct Trinitarian movement, which itself resonates with the thrice repeated 'holy' of the *sanctus*. If Anglican Churches are likely to provide a range of eucharistic prayers for use (as the trend seems to be), genuine variety of theme and expression is to be both desired and welcomed. The same is true for other aspects of the rite; David Power expresses it like this: 'The action of the Spirit is pervasive of the entire eucharistic celebration. Christ is present to the baptized people through the power of the Spirit, moves them to memorial through the Spirit, and gives himself in the gift of bread and wine in the power of this same Spirit.'[90] He incorporates a strong pneumatology in the *anamnesis* of a published eucharistic prayer:

> Remembering, compassionate and loving God, we proclaim the presence of your Word in our human flesh.
> We proclaim the Spirit who settled upon him, drove him into the wilderness to wrestle with profane hopes, and led him into the company of the blind, the lame, the diseased, the imprisoned, and the very dead.
> We remember your Word bursting asunder the bonds of death, and rising to your right hand, so that through the Spirit he might continue to live amid the struggles of a torn world.[91]

While the eucharistic prayer provides many opportunities for expression of the Spirit's work, collects (of the day, 'over the gifts', post-communion), intercessions, Scripture sentences and acclamations, and, of course, the retention of the Collect for Purity at least as an option, are also part of the equation.

---

89 Quotations from the *Book of Alternative Services*, pp. 195, 203, 206.

90 David Power, 'The Eucharistic Prayer: Another Look', in Senn, *New Eucharistic Prayers*, p. 244. For a discussion of the Edward Kilmartin's understanding of the relationship of pneumatology and the eucharistic memorial, see John H. McKenna, 'Eucharist and Memorial', *Worship*, 79 (2005): 516-520.

91 Power, 'The Eucharistic Prayer: Another Look', pp. 253-254.

Conclusion

The plea of this study is that the eucharistic *epiclesis* is not simply a relic of tradition, incorporated into contemporary rites because of its antiquity, or under ecumenical pressure of convergence, or because we have to say something about the Spirit to prove our Trinitarian credentials. Rather it is because of its significance theologically and devotionally in articulating a eucharistic spirituality for the twenty-first century, a spirituality which witnesses to the eternal and transforming presence of God in his world, in which humanity and all creation is being restored. This is a spirituality of hope which enables Christians to bring hope as they engage in the mission of the Triune God, which keeps before them the pledge of a 'new heaven and a new earth in which righteousness dwells' and so inspires them to witness to a gospel of reconciliation and to work for justice and peace; a spirituality which understands the Spirit as the one who brings to the Church all the grace and life of Christ, all the love and power of God, and so enables the return of worship and costly self-giving, glorifying the Father and the Son.

It is appropriate to conclude with some specimen texts; all presuppose an 'Antiochene' shape to the eucharistic prayer, the *epiclesis* following the *anamnesis*. The first is an adaptation of the 'Lima prayer':

Lord God, send upon this eucharist the life-giving Spirit,
who spoke by Moses and the Prophets,
who overshadowed the Virgin Mary with grace,
who descended upon Jesus in the river Jordan
and upon the Church on the Day of Pentecost.
Come, Holy Spirit!

May the outpouring of this Spirit of fire accomplish the words of your Son,
that, sharing in his body and blood, we may be united to him and each other, and be filled with grace to serve you in the world.
Come, Holy Spirit!

Pour out your Spirit on all flesh,
renew the face of the earth,
and hasten the day of Christ's coming.
Maranatha, Come, Lord Jesus!
[Doxology]

The second reflects themes of unity and eschatology:

Gracious Father,
as we bring these gifts of your creation before you in thanksgiving,
sanctify them by your transforming Spirit,
that they may be holy gifts for your holy people,
the bread of life and the cup of salvation,
the body and blood of your Son Jesus Christ.
As your new creation in the Spirit,
fill us with your grace
and unite us in the body of Christ,

while we wait with joyful expectation for that day
when all things in heaven and on earth
shall be made perfect in your Son;
[Doxology]

And the third, based partly on Canada's *BAS* prayer 4, draws directly on imagery from Romans 8:

We who have been redeemed by him,
and made a new people by the water of baptism,
stand before you with these gifts.
Send your Holy Spirit upon our celebration
that as we eat and drink at this holy table
we may share the divine life of Christ our Lord.
Glory to you for ever and ever.

Pour out your Spirit upon the whole earth.
Liberate a groaning creation
and hasten the day of our redemption,
that all that you have made
may share the freedom of the glory of the children of God,
when the new creation is brought to perfection
Glory to you for ever and ever.

Give us grace to work for peace and justice,
to proclaim the wonders of your salvation,
and, by the power of the Spirit, to overflow with hope;
through Jesus Christ our Lord;
[Doxology]
Glory to you for ever and ever. Amen.

Even so, come, Holy Spirit, and renew the face of the earth.

Select Bibliography

The full Bibliography can be accessed via the page for this book on Ashgate's website, www.ashgate.com

Albertine, Richard, 'Problem of the (Double) Epiclesis in the New Roman Eucharistic Prayers', *Ephemerides Liturgicae*, 91 (1977): 192-202.

—— 'The Epiclesis Problem – The Roman Canon (Canon 1) in the Post-Vatican Liturgical Reform', *Ephemerides Liturgicae*, 99 (1985): 337-348.

—— 'The Post-Vatican Consilium's (*Coetus X*) Treatment of the Epiclesis Question in the New Eucharistic Prayers', *Ephemerides Liturgicae*, 100 (1986): 489-507.

—— 'The Post-Vatican Consilium's (*Coetus X*) Treatment of the Epiclesis Question in the Context of Select Historical Data (Alexandrian Family of Anaphoras) and the Fragment of "Der Balyzeh"', *Ephemerides Liturgicae*, 102 (1988): 385-405.

Atchley, E.G. Cuthbert F., 'The Epiclesis', *Theology*, 3 (1921): 90-98.

—— 'The Epiclesis: A Criticism', *Theology*, 29 (1934): 28-35.

—— *On the Epiclesis of the Eucharistic Liturgy and in the Consecration of the Font* (Alcuin Club Collections 31, Oxford: Oxford University Press, 1935).

Bishop, W.C., 'The Primitive Form of Consecration of the Holy Eucharist', *The Church Quarterly Review*, 66 (1908): 385-404.

Brightman, F.E., *The English Rite* (2 vols, London: Rivingtons, 1915).

—— 'Invocation in the Holy Eucharist', *Theology*, 9 (1924): 33-40.

—— 'The New Prayer Book Examined', *The Church Quarterly Review*, 104 (1927): 219-252.

Buchanan, Colin O. (ed.), *Modern Anglican Liturgies 1958-1968* (London: Oxford University Press, 1968). [= *MAL*]

—— *Further Anglican Liturgies 1968-1975* (Bramcote: Grove Books, 1975). [= *FAL*]

—— *Eucharistic Liturgies of Edward VI: A Text for Students* (Grove Liturgical Study 34 (Bramcote: Grove Books, 1983).

—— *Latest Anglican Liturgies 1976-1984* (London: SPCK / Bramcote: Grove Books, 1985). [= *LAL*]

Burn, A.E., 'Invocation in the Holy Eucharist', *Theology*, 8 (1924): 317-321.

Buxton, Richard F., *Eucharist and Institution Narrative* (Alcuin Club Collections 58, Great Wakering: Mayhew-McCrimmon, 1976).

Clarke, W.K. Lowther, 'The Epiclesis in the 1549 and 1928 Rites', *Theology*, 26 (1933): 93-97.

—— *The Prayer Book of 1928 Reconsidered* (London: SPCK, 1943).

Connolly, R. Hugh, 'On the Meaning of ἐπίκλησις', *Downside Review*, 41 (1923): 28-43.

—— '"The Meaning of ἐπίκλησις": A Reply', *The Journal of Theological Studies*, 25 (1924): 337-364.

Crehan, Joseph H., 'The Theology of Eucharistic Consecration', *Theological Studies*, 40 (1979): 334-343.

—— 'Eucharist and Epiclesis: New Evidence and a New Theory', *Theological Studies*, 41 (1980): 698-712.

Crockett, William R., 'The Theology of the Eucharistic Prayers in *The Book of Alternative Services of the Anglican Church of Canada*', *Toronto Journal of Theology*, 3 (1987): 100-109.

—— *Eucharist: Symbol of Transformation* (New York: Pueblo, 1989).

Dinesen, Palle, 'Die Epiklese im Rahmen altkirchlicher Liturgien: Ein Studie über die eucharistische Epiklese', *Studia Theologica*, 16 (1962): 42-107.

Dix, Gregory, 'The Origins of the Epiclesis', Parts I & II, *Theology*, 27 (1934): 125-137; 28 (1934): 187-202.

—— 'The Epiclesis: Some Considerations', *Theology*, 29 (1934): 287-294.

—— 'Primitive Consecration Prayers', *Theology*, 37 (1938): 261-283.

—— *The Shape of the Liturgy*, 2nd ed. (1945, London: Black, 1986).

—— 'Dixit Cranmer et non Timuit – I: A Supplement to Mr. Timms', *The Church Quarterly Review*, 145 (1948): 145-176; 146 (1948): 44-60.

Drury, T.W., 'The *Epiclesis* in the Service of Holy Communion', *The Church Quarterly Review*, 97 (1923): 1-13.

Flynn, Kevin, 'The work of the Spirit and the work of the people', *Liturgy Canada*, 8 (2001); part II, 8 (2001); part III, 9 (2002).

Frere, W.H., *The Primitive Consecration Prayer* (Alcuin Club Prayer Book Revision Pamphlets 8, London: Mowbray, 1922).

—— 'The 1928 Canon in Latin', *Theology*, 27 (1933): 332-333.

—— *The Anaphora or Great Eucharistic Prayer: An Eirenical Study in Liturgical History* (London: SPCK, 1938).

Gelston, A., *The Eucharistic Prayer of Addai and Mari* (Oxford: Clarendon Press, 1992).

Gummey, Henry Riley, *The Consecration of the Eucharist* (Philadelphia: Henry Anners, 1908).

Hebert, A.G., 'The Meaning of the Epiclesis', *Theology*, 27 (1933): 198-210.

—— 'Anaphora and Epiclesis', *Theology*, 37 (1938): 89-94.

Holeton, David R. (ed.), *Revising the Eucharist: Groundwork for the Anglican Communion* (Alcuin/GROW Joint Liturgical Study 27, Bramcote: Grove Books, 1994.

—— *Our Thanks and Praise: The Eucharist in Anglicanism Today* (Toronto: Anglican Book Centre, 1998).

Hunkin, J.W., *The Invocation of the Holy Spirit in the Prayer of Consecration* (Cambridge: Heffer, 1927).

Jasper, R.C.D. (ed.), *Walter Howard Frere: A Collection of His Papers on Liturgical and Historical Subjects* (Alcuin Club Collections 35, London: Oxford University Press, 1940).

—— *Walter Howard Frere: His Correspondence on Liturgical Revision and Construction* (Alcuin Club Collections 39, London: SPCK, 1954).

Kennedy, David J., *The Epiclesis in the Eucharistic Rites of the Church of England and the Churches of the Anglican Communion with Special Reference to the Period 1900-1994* (PhD dissertation, University of Birmingham, 1996).

—— 'Walter Howard Frere and Liturgical Reform', *In Illo Tempore*, 17 (2001): 3-18.

Kilmartin, Edward J., 'The Active Role of Christ and the Holy Spirit in the Sanctification of the Eucharistic Elements', *Theological Studies*, 45 (1984): 225-253.

Lockton, W., 'The Eucharistic Prayer', *The Church Quarterly Review*, 86 (1918): 305-332.

—— 'The Proposed South African Liturgy', *The Church Quarterly Review*, 86 (1918): 345-348.

McKenna, John H., *Eucharist and Holy Spirit: The Eucharistic Epiclesis in 20th Century Theology* (Alcuin Club Collections 57, Great Wakering: Mayhew-McCrimmon, 1975).

—— 'Eucharistic Epiclesis: Myopia or Microcosm?', *Theological Studies*, 36 (1975): 265-284.

—— 'The Eucharistic Epiclesis in 20th Century Theology (1900-1966)', *Ephemerides Liturgicae*, 90 (1976): 289-328, 446-482.

—— 'The Epiclesis Revisited', in Frank C. Senn (ed.), *New Eucharistic Prayers: An Ecumenical Study of their Development and Structure* (New York: Paulist Press, 1987), pp. 169-194.

—— 'Eucharistic Presence: An Invitation to Dialogue', *Theological Studies*, 60 (1999): 294-317.

—— 'Eucharist and Memorial', *Worship*, 79 (2005): 504-522.

Michell, G.A., *Eucharistic Consecration in the Primitive Church* (London: SPCK, 1948).

Nichols, Bridget and MacGregor, Alistair, *The Eucharistic Epiclesis* (Ushaw Library Publications No. 4, Durham: Ushaw College Library, 2001).

Oulton, J.E.L., *Holy Communion and Holy Spirit: A Study in Doctrinal Relationship* (London: SPCK, 1951).

Ratcliff, E.C., 'The English Usage of Eucharistic Consecration 1548-1662 – I & II', *Theology*, 60 (1957): 229-236, 273-280.

Regan, Patrick, 'Quenching the Spirit: The Epiclesis in Recent Roman Documents', *Worship*, 79 (2005): 386-404.

Reynolds, Stephen, 'Consecration of the Eucharist: 1. Prayer and Narrative', *Liturgy Canada* (Epiphany, 1991): 2-7.

—— 'The Consecration of the Eucharist: 2. Upon Us and Upon These Gifts', *Liturgy Canada* (Easter, 1991): 1, 6-9.

Robinson, J. Armitage, 'The "Apostolic Anaphora" and the Prayer of St. Polycarp', *The Journal of Theological Studies*, 21 (1920): 97-105.'Invocation in the Holy Eucharist', *Theology*, 8 (1924): 89-100; 9 (1924): 175-177.

Simpson, W.J. Sparrow, *Revision of the Prayer of Consecration* (London: SPCK, 1918).

—— 'The Eucharistic Canon: Why the Invocation Should Come First', in Darwell Stone (ed.), *The Deposited Prayer Book: By a Group of Priests* (London: Philip Allan, 1927), pp. 57-77.

Spinks, Bryan D., 'The Consecratory Epiklesis in the Anaphora of St. James', *Studia Liturgica*, 11(1976): 19-38.

—— *From the Lord and 'The Best Reformed Churches': A Study of the Eucharistic Liturgy in the English Puritan and Separatist Traditions* (EL Subsidia 33, Rome: Edizioni Liturgiche, 1984).

—— 'Beware the Liturgical Horses! An English Interjection on Anaphoral Evolution', *Worship*, 59 (1985): 211-219.

—— '"And with Thy Holy Spirite and Worde": Further Thoughts on the Source of Cranmer's Petition for Sanctification in the 1549 Communion Service' in Margot Johnson (ed.), *Thomas Cranmer: A Living Influence for 500 Years* (Durham: Turnstone Ventures, 1990), pp. 94-102.

—— 'The Ascension and the Vicarious Humanity of Christ: The Christology and Soteriology Behind the Church of Scotland's Anamnesis and Epiklesis', in J. Neil Alexander (ed.), *Time and Community* (Washington, DC: The Pastoral Press, 1990), pp. 185-201.

—— 'Two Seventeenth-Century Examples of *Lex Credendi, Lex Orandi*: The Baptismal and Eucharistic Theologies and Liturgies of Jeremy Taylor and Richard Baxter', *Studia Liturgica*, 21 (1991): 165-189.

—— 'Trinitarian Theology and the Eucharistic Prayer', *Studia Liturgica*, 26 (1996): 210-224.

—— *Sacraments, Ceremonies and the Stuart Divines: Sacramental Theology and Liturgy in England and Scotland 1603-1662* (Aldershot: Ashgate, 2002).

Srawley, J.H., *The English Consecration Prayer* (London: SPCK, 1923).

Stevenson, Kenneth W., *Eucharist and Offering* (New York: Pueblo, 1986).

—— *Covenant of Grace Renewed: A Vision of the Eucharist in the Seventeenth Century* (London: Darton, Longman & Todd, 1994).

Taft, Robert, 'From Logos to Spirit: On the Early History of the Epiclesis' (printed paper, 1991).

Talley, Thomas, 'From *Berakah* to *Eucharistia*: A Reopening Question', *Worship*, 50 (1976): 115-137, reprinted in R. Kevin Seasoltz (ed.), *Living Bread, Saving Cup* (Collegeville: Liturgical Press, 1982), pp. 80-101.

—— 'The Eucharistic Prayer: Directions for Development', *Worship*, 51 (1977): 316-325.

—— 'The Eucharistic Prayer: Tradition and Development', in Kenneth Stevenson (ed.), *Liturgy Reshaped* (London: SPCK, 1982), pp. 48-64.

—— 'The Literary Structure of the Eucharistic Prayer', *Worship*, 55 (1984): 404-420.

—— *Worship: Reforming Tradition* (Washington, DC: The Pastoral Press, 1990).

—— 'The Structure of the Eucharistic Prayer', in Ruth A. Meyers (ed.), *A Prayer Book for the 21st Century* (Liturgical Studies 3, New York: The Church Hymnal Corporation, 1996), pp. 76-101.

Tillard, Jean-Marie R., 'Blessing, Sacramentality and Epiclesis', in David Power and Mary Collins (eds), *Blessing and Power* (*Concilium*, 178, 1985): 96-110.

Tyrer, J.W., *The Eucharistic Epiclesis* (London: Longmans, 1917).

—— 'The English Canon of 1549 and Its Invocation', *Theology*, 9 (1924): 259-265.

—— 'The Meaning of ἐπίκλησις', *The Journal of Theological Studies*, 25 (1924): 139-150.

Vischer, Lucas, 'The Epiclesis: Sign of Unity and Renewal', *Studia Liturgica,* 6 (1969): 30-39.

Index